TEACHER'S EDITION

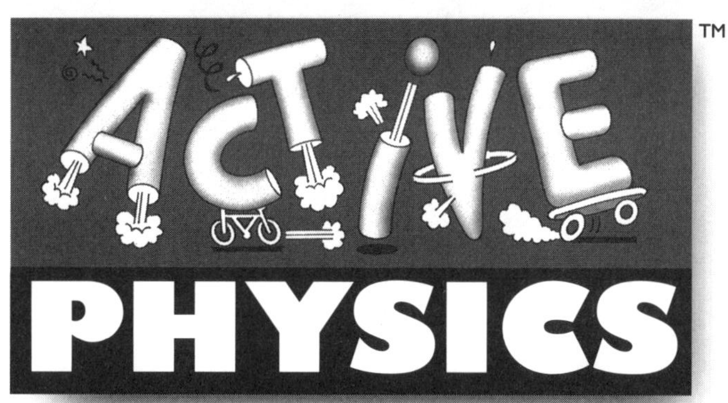

Arthur Eisenkraft, Ph.D.

Active Physics has been developed in association with the American Association of Physics Teachers (AAPT) and the American Institute of Physics (AIP)

HOME

IT's ABOUT TIME®

Published by
IT'S ABOUT TIME, Inc.
Armonk, NY

Published in 1999 by

It's About Time, Inc.

84 Business Park Drive, Armonk, NY 10504
Phone (914) 273-2233 Fax (914) 273-2227
Toll Free (888) 698-TIME
http://www.Its-About-Time.com

Publisher
Laurie Kreindler

Project Director
Dr. Arthur Eisenkraft

Project Manager
Ruta Demery

Design
John Nordland

Production Manager
Barbara Zahm

Studio Manager
Leslie Jander

Cover Illustration
Steven Belcher

Student's Edition Illustrations and Photos

Chapter 1: Tomas Bunk pages 8, 19, 24, 29, 33, 37; PhotoDisc Inc. pages 1-4, 7, 9, 11, 13, 17-18, 21, 23, 26, 28, 30, 32, 34, 36, 40, 42; Amla Sanghvi page 4 (lower right): Michael Simpson/FPG International LLC page 5; The Home Depot page 27; **Chapter 2:** Tomas Bunk pages 46, 50, 55, 60, 64, 74, 79; PhotoDisc Inc. pages 43-45, 47, 49, 53-54, 56, 62, 66, 71, 78, 80, 82, 84; KRUPS, Inc. page 58; **Chapter 3**: Tomas Bunk pages 88, 93, 109, 113; PhotoDisc Inc. pages 85-87, 91-92, 94, 96, 99, 102, 108, 110, 112, 117.

Teacher's Edition Illustrations

Kathleen Bowman, Robert Hansmann, Cathy Vidal

Printed and bound in the United States of America

ISBN 1-891629-07-7

2 3 4 5 D 02 01 00 99

This project was supported, in part, by the

National Science Foundation

Opinions expressed are those of the authors and not necessarily those of the Foundation

TABLE OF CONTENTS

Acknowledgments

Project Director

Arthur Eisenkraft teaches physics and serves as science coordinator in the Bedford Public Schools in N.Y. Dr. Eisenkraft is the author of numerous science and educational publications. He holds a US Patent for a laser vision testing system and was featured in *Scientific American.*

Dr. Eisenkraft is chair of the Duracell Science Scholarship Competition; chair of the Toyota TAPESTRY program giving grants to science teachers; and chair of the Toshiba/NSTA ExploraVisions Awards competition for grades K-12. He is co-author of a contest column and serves on the advisory board of *Quantum* magazine, a collaborative effort of the US and Russia. In 1993, he served as Executive Director for the XXIV International Physics Olympiad after being Academic Director for the United States Team for six years. He served on the content committee and helped write the National Science Education Standards of the NRC (National Research Council).

Dr. Eisenkraft received the Presidential Award for Excellence in Science Teaching at the White House in 1986, and the AAPT Distinguished Service Citation for "excellent contributions to the teaching of physics" in 1989. In 1991 he was recognized by the Disney Corporation as Science Teacher of the Year in their American Teacher Awards program. In 1993 he received an Honorary Doctor of Science degree from Rensselaer Polytechnic Institute.

Primary and Contributing Authors

Home

Jon L. Harkness
Active Physics Regional Coordinator
Wausau, WI

Douglas A. Johnson
Madison West High School
Madison, WI

John J. Rusch
University of Wisconsin, Superior
Superior, WI

Ruta Demery
Blue Ink Editing
Stayner, ON

Hugh Brown
Atlas Communications
St. Albert, AB

Communication

Richard Berg
University of Maryland
College Park, MD

Ron DeFronzo
Eastbay Ed. Collaborative
Attleboro, MA

Harry Rheam
Eastern Senior High School
Atco, NJ

John Roeder
The Calhoun School
New York, NY

Patty Rourke
Potomac School
McLean, VA

Larry Weathers
The Bromfield School
Harvard, MA

Medicine

Russell Hobbie
University of Minnesota
St. Paul, MN

Terry Goerke
Hill-Murray High School
St. Paul, MN

John Koser
Wayzata High School
Plymouth, MN

Ed Lee
WonderScience, Associate Editor
Silver Spring, MD

Predictions

Ruth Howes
Ball State University
Muncie, IN

Chris Chiaverina
New Trier Township High School
Crystal Lake, IL

Charles Payne
Ball State University
Muncie, IN

Ceanne Tzimopoulos
Omega Publishing
Medford, MA

Sports

Howard Brody
University of Pennsylvania
Philadelphia, PA

Mary Quinlan
Radnor High School
Radnor, PA

Carl Duzen
Lower Merion High School
Havertown, PA

Jon L. Harkness
Active Physics Regional Coordinator
Wausau, WI

David Wright
Tidewater Comm. College
Virginia Beach, VA

Transportation

Ernest Kuehl
Lawrence High School
Cedarhurst, NY

Robert L. Lehrman
Bayside, NY

Salvatore Levy
Roslyn High School
Roslyn, NY

Tom Liao
SUNY Stony Brook
Stony Brook, NY

Bob Ritter
University of Alberta
Edmonton, AB, CA

Principal Investigators

Bernard V. Khoury
American Association of Physics Teachers

Dwight Edward Neuenschwander
American Institute of Physics

Consultants

Peter Brancazio
Brooklyn College of CUNY
Brooklyn, NY

Robert Capen
Canyon del Oro High School
Tucson, AZ

Carole Escobar

Earl Graf
SUNY Stony Brook
Stony Brook, NY

Jack Hehn
American Association of Physics Teachers
College Park, MD

Donald F. Kirwan
Louisiana State University
Baton Rouge, LA

Gayle Kirwan
Louisiana State University
Baton Rouge, LA

James La Porte
Virginia Tech
Blacksburg, VA

Charles Misner
University of Maryland
College Park, MD

Robert F. Neff
Suffern, NY

Ingrid Novodvorsky
Mountain View High School
Tucson, AZ

John Robson
University of Arizona
Tucson, AZ

Mark Sanders
Virginia Tech
Blacksburg, VA

Brian Schwartz
Brooklyn College of CUNY
New York, NY

Bruce Seiger
Wellesley High School
Newburyport, MA

Clifford Swartz
SUNY Stony Brook
Setauket, NY

Barbara Tinker
The Concord Consortium
Concord, MA

Robert E. Tinker
The Concord Consortium
Concord, MA

Joyce Weiskopf
Herndon, VA

Donna Willis
American Association of Physics Teachers
College Park, MD

Safety Reviewer

Gregory Puskar
University of West Virginia
Morgantown, WV

Equity Reviewer

Leo Edwards
Fayetteville State University
Fayetteville, NC

Spreadsheet and MBL

Ken Appel
Yorktown High School
Peekskill, NY

Physics at Work

Barbara Zahm
Zahm Productions
New York, NY

Physics InfoMall

Brian Adrian
Bethany College
Lindsborg, KS

Unit Reviewers

George A. Amann
F.D. Roosevelt High School
Rhinebeck, NY

Patrick Callahan
Catasaugua High School
Center Valley, PA

Beverly Cannon
Science and Engineering Magnet High School
Dallas, TX

Barbara Chauvin

Elizabeth Chesick
The Baldwin School
Haverford, PA 19041

Chris Chiaverina
New Trier Township High School
Crystal Lake, IL

Andria Erzberger
Palo Alto Senior High School
Los Altos Hills, CA

Elizabeth Farrell Ramseyer
Niles West High School
Skokie, IL

Mary Gromko
President of Council of State Science Supervisors
Denver, CO

Thomas Guetzloff

Jon L. Harkness
Active Physics Regional Coordinator
Wausau, WI

Dawn Harman
Moon Valley High School
Phoenix, AZ

James Hill
Piner High School
Sonoma, CA

Bob Kearney

Claudia Khourey-Bowers
McKinley Senior High School

Steve Kliewer
Bullard High School
Fresno, CA

Ernest Kuehl
Roslyn High School
Cedarhurst, NY

Jane Nelson
University High School
Orlando, FL

John Roeder
The Calhoun School
New York, NY

Patty Rourke
Potomac School
McLean, VA

Gerhard Salinger
Fairfax, VA

Irene Slater
La Pietra School for Girls

Pilot Test Teachers

John Agosta

Donald Campbell
Portage Central High School
Portage, MI

John Carlson
Norwalk Community
Technical College
Norwalk, CT

Veanna Crawford
Alamo Heights High School
New Braunfels

Janie Edmonds
West Milford High School
Randolph, NJ

Eddie Edwards
Amarillo Area Center for
Advanced Learning
Amarillo, TX

Arthur Eisenkraft
Fox Lane High School
Bedford, NY

Tom Ford

Bill Franklin

Roger Goerke
St. Paul, MN

Tom Gordon
Greenwich High School
Greenwich, CT

Ariel Hepp

John Herrman
College of Steubenville
Steubenville, OH

Linda Hodges

Ernest Kuehl
Lawrence High School
Cedarhurst, NY

Fran Leary
Troy High School
Schenectady, NY

Harold Lefcourt

Cherie Lehman
West Lafayette High School
West Lafayette, IN

Kathy Malone
Shady Side Academy
Pittsburgh, PA

Bill Metzler
Westlake High School
Thornwood, NY

Elizabeth Farrell Ramseyer
Niles West High School
Skokie, IL

Daniel Repogle
Central Noble High School
Albion, IN

Evelyn Restivo
Maypearl High School
Maypearl, TX

Doug Rich
Fox Lane High School
Bedford, NY

John Roeder
The Calhoun School
New York, NY

Tom Senior
New Trier Township High School
Highland Park, IL

John Thayer
District of Columbia Public Schools
Silver Spring, MD

Carol-Ann Tripp
Providence Country Day
East Providence, RI

Yvette Van Hise
High Tech High School
Freehold, NJ

Jan Waarvick

Sandra Walton
Dubuque Senior High School
Dubuque, IA

Larry Wood
Fox Lane High School
Bedford, NY

Field Test Coordinator

Marilyn Decker
Northeastern University
Acton, MA

Field Test Workshop Staff

John Carlson

Marilyn Decker

Arthur Eisenkraft

Douglas Johnson

John Koser

Ernest Kuehl

Mary Quinlan

Elizabeth Farrell Ramseyer

John Roeder

Field Test Evaluators

Susan Baker-Cohen

Susan Cloutier

George Hein

Judith Kelley

all from Lesley College,
Cambridge, MA

Field Test Teachers and Schools

Rob Adams
Polytech High School
Woodside, DE

Benjamin Allen
Falls Church High School
Falls Church, VA

Robert Applebaum
New Trier High School
Winnetka, IL

Joe Arnett
Plano Sr. High School
Plano, TX

Bix Baker
GFW High School
Winthrop, MN

Debra Beightol
Fremont High School
Fremont, NE

Patrick Callahan
Catasaugua High School
Catasaugua, PA

George Coker
Bowling Green High School
Bowling Green, KY

Janice Costabile
South Brunswick High School
Monmouth Junction, NJ

Stanley Crum
Homestead High School
Fort Wayne, IN

Russel Davison
Brandon High School
Brandon, FL

Christine K. Deyo
Rochester Adams High School
Rochester Hills, MI

Jim Doller
Fox Lane High School
Bedford, NY

Jessica Downing
Esparto High School
Esparto, CA

Douglas Fackelman
Brighton High School
Brighton, CO

Rick Forrest
Rochester High School
Rochester Hills, MI

Mark Freeman
Blacksburg High School
Blacksburg, VA

Jonathan Gillis
Enloe High School
Raleigh, NC

Karen Gruner
Holton Arms School
Bethesda, MD

Larry Harrison
DuPont Manual High School
Louisville, KY

Alan Haught
Weaver High School
Hartford, CT

Steven Iona
Horizon High School
Thornton, CO

Phil Jowell
Oak Ridge High School
Conroe, TX

Deborah Knight
Windsor Forest High School
Savannah, GA

Thomas Kobilarcik
Marist High School
Chicago, IL

Sheila Kolb
Plano Senior High School
Plano, TX

Todd Lindsay
Park Hill High School
Kansas City, MO

Malinda Mann
South Putnam High School
Greencastle, IN

Steve Martin
Maricopa High School
Maricopa, AZ

Nancy McGrory
North Quincy High School
N. Quincy, MA

David Morton
Mountain Valley High School
Rumford, ME

Charles Muller
Highland Park High School
Highland Park, NJ

Fred Muller
Mercy High School
Burlingame, CA

Vivian O'Brien
Plymouth Regional High School
Plymouth, NH

Robin Parkinson
Northridge High School
Layton, UT

Donald Perry
Newport High School
Bellevue, WA

Francis Poodry
Lincoln High School
Philadelphia, PA

John Potts
Custer County District High School
Miles City, MT

Doug Rich
Fox Lane High School
Bedford, NY

John Roeder
The Calhoun School
New York, NY

Consuelo Rogers
Maryknoll Schools
Honolulu, HI

Lee Rossmaessler, Ph.D
Mott Middle College High School
Flint, MI

John Rowe
Hughes Alternative Center
Cincinnati, OH

Rebecca Bonner Sanders
South Brunswick High School
Monmouth Junction, NJ

David Schlipp
Narbonne High School
Harbor City, CA

Eric Shackelford
Notre Dame High School
Sherman Oaks, CA

Robert Sorensen
Springville-Griffith Institute and
Central School
Springville, NY

Teresa Stalions
Crittenden County High School
Marion, KY

Roberta Tanner
Loveland High School
Loveland, CO

Anthony Umelo
Anacostia Sr. High School
Washington, D.C.

Judy Vondruska
Mitchell High School
Mitchell, SD

Deborah Waldron
Yorktown High School
Arlington, VA

Ken Wester
The Mississippi School for
Mathematics and Science
Columbus, MS

Susan Willis
Conroe High School
Conroe, TX

Meeting Active Physics for the First Time

Welcome! A Five-Minute Introduction

Active Physics is a different species of physics course. It has the mechanics, optics, and electricity you anticipate, but not where you expect to find them. In a traditional physics course, we teach forces in the fall, waves in the winter, and solenoids in the spring. In *Active Physics*, students are introduced to physics concepts on a need-to-know basis as they explore issues in Communication, Home, Medicine, Predictions, Sports, and Transportation.

Every chapter is independent of any other chapter. You can begin the year with any one of three chapters in any one of the six thematic units. As an example, let's start the year with Chapter 3 of the Sports unit.

On Day One, students are introduced to the chapter challenge. NASA, recognizing that residents of a future moon colony will need physical exercise, has commissioned our physics class to develop, adapt, or create a sport for the moon.

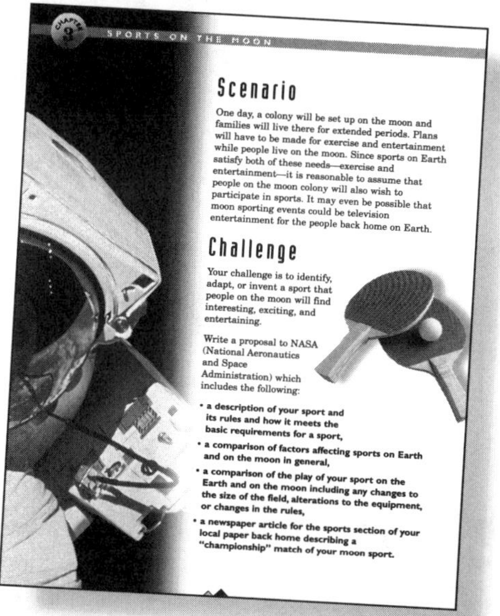
SPORTS ON THE MOON

Scenario

One day, a colony will be set up on the moon and families will live there for extended periods. Plans will have to be made for exercise and entertainment while people live on the moon. Since sports on Earth satisfy both of these needs—exercise and entertainment—it is reasonable to assume that people on the moon colony will also wish to participate in sports. It may even be possible that moon sporting events could be television entertainment for the people back home on Earth.

Challenge

Your challenge is to identify, adapt, or invent a sport that people on the moon will find interesting, exciting, and entertaining.

Write a proposal to NASA (National Aeronautics and Space Administration) which includes the following:

- **a description of your sport and its rules and how it meets the basic requirements for a sport,**
- **a comparison of factors affecting sports on Earth and on the moon in general,**
- **a comparison of the play of your sport on the Earth and on the moon including any changes to the size of the field, alterations to the equipment, or changes in the rules,**
- **a newspaper article for the sports section of your local paper back home describing a "championship" match of your moon sport.**

Our proposal to NASA will have to include the following:

a) a description of a sport and its rules;

b) a comparison of factors affecting sports on Earth and the moon in general;

c) a comparison of play of the sport on Earth and the moon including any changes to field, rules, or equipment;

d) a newspaper article for the people back 'home' describing a championship match of the moon sport.

How can students get started? How can students complete such a challenge without the requisite physics knowledge? Before the chapter activities begin, a discussion takes place about the criteria for success. The class discusses what is expected in an excellent proposal. How will this proposal be graded? For instance, the rubric for grading will describe whether "a comparison of factors affecting sports on Earth

SPORTS

Criteria

The NASA proposal will be graded on the quality, creativity, and scientific accuracy of your invented sport as well as the description of your sport, the factors affecting sports on the Earth and on the moon, the comparison of play of your sport on the Earth and on the moon, and the newspaper article. NASA proposals which include a mathematical analysis of the sport will be considered superior to those that describe the sport qualitatively (without numbers). In your pursuit of finding the "best" sport for the moon, you may investigate sports that would not be suitable for the moon. Descriptions of these rejected sports and the reasons that they were rejected would raise the quality of your proposal.

For each subject of the final proposal, your class should decide on what should be included and what point value each part should have. How many points should be allocated for creativity and how many should be allocated for mathematical analysis? How many points should be allocated for the comparison of the play on the Earth and on the moon, and how many points should be allocated for the newspaper article? When writing the newspaper article, should points be provided for the quality of the writing, for sketches or drawings which illustrate the article, and for reader interest? What are the attributes that make a superior newspaper article?

If a group is going to hand in one proposal, how will the individuals in the group get graded? How will the grading ensure that all members of the group complete their responsibilities as well as help the other members of the group? The grading criteria should satisfy every person's need for fairness and reward.

In February, 1970, Alan Shepard was the first person to hit a golf ball on the moon.

S 113

and the moon" implies two factors or four factors and whether an equation or graph or description should be a part of the comparison. Similarly, do the factors and newspaper article carry equal weight, or does one have a greater impact on the final grade? Students will have a sense of what is required for an excellent proposal before they begin. This will be revisited before work on the project begins.

Day Two begins with the first of nine activities. Each successive day begins with another activity. *Active Physics* is an activity-based curriculum. Let's look at Activity Seven: **Friction on the Moon**.

The activity begins by mentioning, "The Lunar Rover proved that there is enough frictional force on the moon to operate a passenger-carrying wheeled vehicle." The students are then asked, "How do frictional forces on Earth and the moon compare?"

ACTIVITY SEVEN: Friction on the Moon

Activity Seven

Friction on the Moon

WHAT DO YOU THINK?

The Lunar Rover proved that there is enough frictional force on the moon to operate a passenger-carrying wheeled vehicle.

- **How do frictional forces on Earth and the moon compare?**

Record your ideas about this question in your Active Physics log. Be prepared to discuss your responses with your small group and the class.

This **What Do You Think?** question is intended to find out what students know about friction—to get into the 'friction part' of their brains. Formally, we say that this question is to elicit the student's prior understanding and is part of the constructivist approach. Students write a response for one minute and discuss for another two minutes. But we don't reach closure. The question opens the conversation.

Students then begin the **For You To Do** activity.

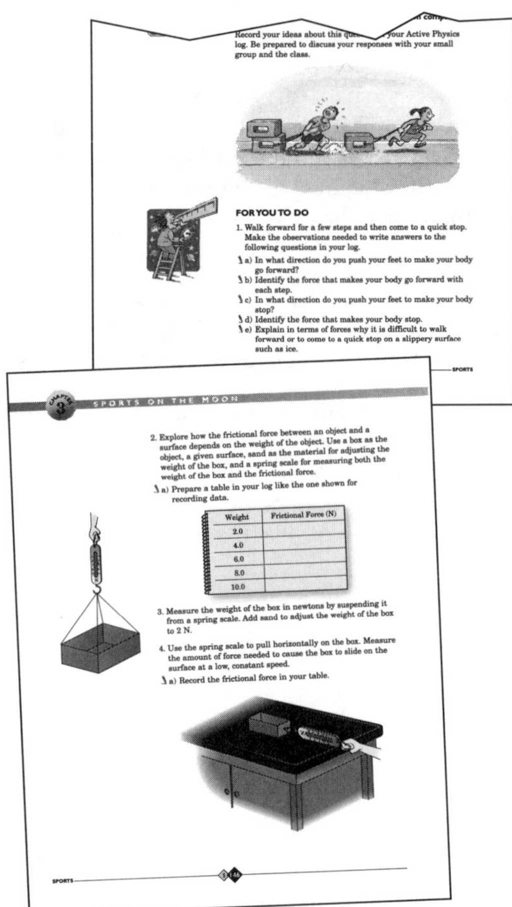

Record your ideas about this question in your Active Physics log. Be prepared to discuss your responses with your small group and the class.

FOR YOU TO DO

1. Walk forward for a few steps and then come to a quick stop. Make the observations needed to write answers to the following questions in your log.
   a) In what direction do you push your feet to make your body go forward?
   b) Identify the force that makes your body go forward with each step.
   c) In what direction do you push your feet to make your body stop?
   d) Identify the force that makes your body stop.
   e) Explain in terms of forces why it is difficult to walk forward or to come to a quick stop on a slippery surface such as ice.

SPORTS

SPORTS ON THE MOON

2. Explore how the frictional force between an object and a surface depends on the weight of the object. Use a box as the object, a given surface, sand as the material for adjusting the weight of the box, and a spring scale for measuring both the weight of the box and the frictional force.
   a) Prepare a table in your log like the one shown for recording data.

Weight	Frictional Force (N)
2.0	
4.0	
6.0	
8.0	
10.0	

3. Measure the weight of the box in newtons by suspending it from a spring scale. Add sand to adjust the weight of the box to 2 N.
4. Use the spring scale to pull horizontally on the box. Measure the amount of force needed to cause the box to slide on the surface at a low, constant speed.
   a) Record the frictional force in your table.

SPORTS 148

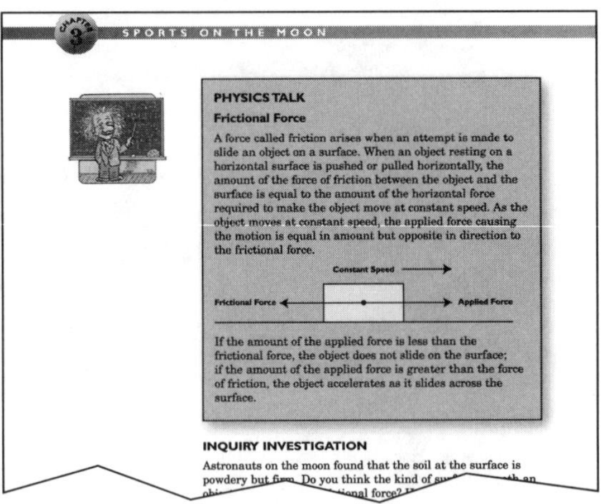

SPORTS ON THE MOON

PHYSICS TALK

Frictional Force

A force called friction arises when an attempt is made to slide an object on a surface. When an object resting on a horizontal surface is pushed or pulled horizontally, the amount of the force of friction between the object and the surface is equal to the amount of the horizontal force required to make the object move at constant speed. As the object moves at constant speed, the applied force causing the motion is equal in amount but opposite in direction to the frictional force.

If the amount of the applied force is less than the frictional force, the object does not slide on the surface; if the amount of the applied force is greater than the force of friction, the object accelerates as it slides across the surface.

INQUIRY INVESTIGATION

Astronauts on the moon found that the soil at the surface is powdery but firm. Do you think the kind of surface beneath an object also affects the frictional force? ...

An **Inquiry Investigation** is presented for specific students or classes who wish to go further independently. In this case, they can investigate the effect of friction of different surfaces.

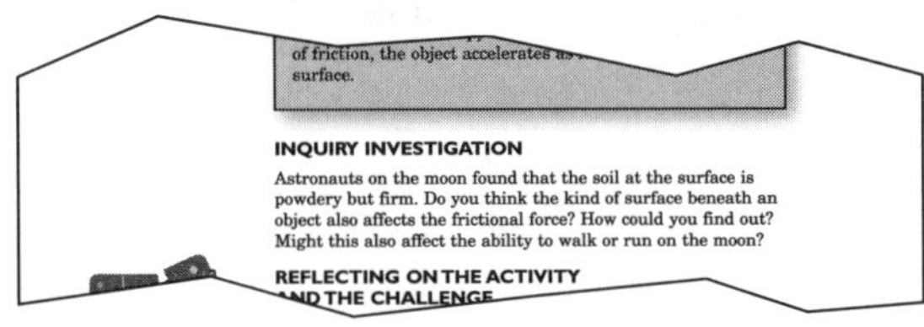

of friction, the object accelerates as it slides across the surface.

INQUIRY INVESTIGATION

Astronauts on the moon found that the soil at the surface is powdery but firm. Do you think the kind of surface beneath an object also affects the frictional force? How could you find out? Might this also affect the ability to walk or run on the moon?

REFLECTING ON THE ACTIVITY AND THE CHALLENGE

A **Reflecting On The Activity And The Challenge** relates the activity to the larger challenge of developing the moon sport.

In this activity, students weigh a box with a spring scale and measure the force required to pull it across a table at constant speed. By adding sand to the box, they take repeated measurements of weight and frictional force. A graph then shows them that the frictional force is directly proportional to the weight—more weight, more friction. An earlier activity convinced students that all objects weigh less on the moon. And so they can now conclude that friction must be less on the moon.

A **Physics Talk** summarizes the physics principle and includes equations where appropriate.

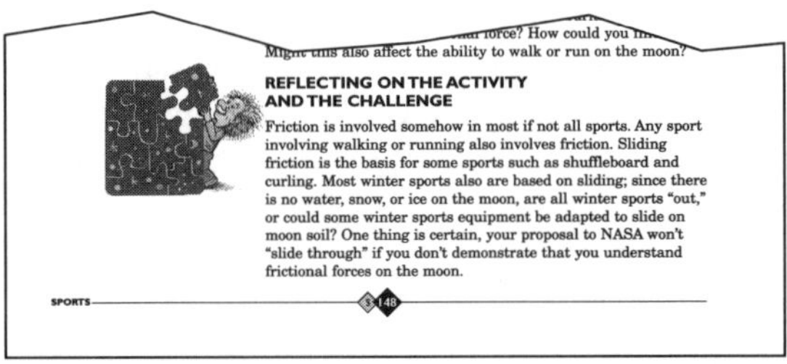

... force? How could you find out? Might this also affect the ability to walk or run on the moon?

REFLECTING ON THE ACTIVITY AND THE CHALLENGE

Friction is involved somehow in most if not all sports. Any sport involving walking or running also involves friction. Sliding friction is the basis for some sports such as shuffleboard and curling. Most winter sports also are based on sliding; since there is no water, snow, or ice on the moon, are all winter sports "out," or could some winter sports equipment be adapted to slide on moon soil? One thing is certain, your proposal to NASA won't "slide through" if you don't demonstrate that you understand frictional forces on the moon.

SPORTS 148

"Friction is involved somehow in most if not all sports. . . One thing is certain, your proposal to NASA won't 'slide through' if you don't demonstrate that you understand frictional forces on the moon." Students have been given another piece of the jigsaw puzzle. How is the sport that they are developing going to be modified because of the decreased friction on the moon?

The activity concludes with a **Physics To Go** homework assignment.

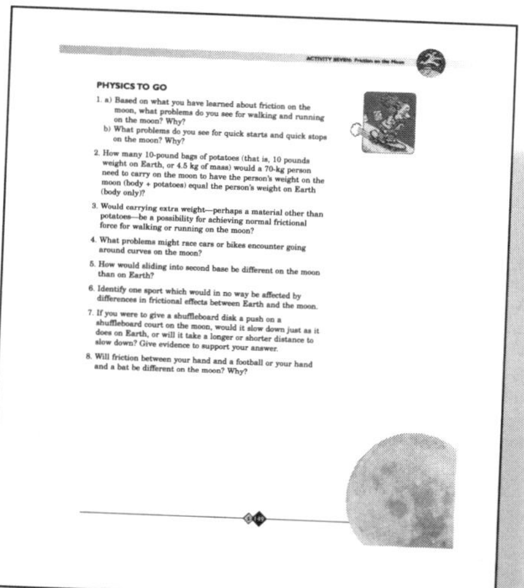

ACTIVITY SEVEN: Friction on the Moon

PHYSICS TO GO

1. a) Based on what you have learned about friction on the moon, what problems do you see for walking and running on the moon? Why?
   b) What problems do you see for quick starts and quick stops on the moon? Why?
2. How many 10-pound bags of potatoes (that is, 10 pounds weight on Earth, or 4.5 kg of mass) would a 70-kg person need to carry on the moon to have the person's weight on the moon (body + potatoes) equal the person's weight on Earth (body only)?
3. Would carrying extra weight—perhaps a material other than potatoes—be a possibility for achieving normal frictional force for walking or running on the moon?
4. What problems might race cars or bikes encounter going around curves on the moon?
5. How would sliding into second base be different on the moon than on Earth?
6. Identify one sport which would in no way be affected by differences in frictional effects between Earth and the moon.
7. If you were to give a shuffleboard disk a push on a shuffleboard court on the moon, would it slow down just as it does on Earth, or will it take a longer or shorter distance to slow down? Give evidence to support your answer.
8. Will friction between your hand and a football or your hand and a bat be different on the moon? Why?

The chapter concludes with a **Physics At Work** profile where students are introduced to someone whose job is related to the chapter challenge. In this chapter, astronaut Linda Godwin describes adapting to zero gravity during flight and space walks.

SPORTS ON THE MOON

PHYSICS AT WORK

Linda M. Godwin, Ph.D.

NASA ASTRONAUT

It was while working on her Doctorate in physics at the University of Missouri in the late 1970s that Linda first thought about becoming a NASA Astronaut. Prior to that time, there had been only male Astronauts. When NASA began putting the word out that they were interested in breaking down the gender barriers for their scientific mission specialists, Linda responded.

Now she is a veteran of three space flights and has logged over 633 hours in space, including a six-hour space walk. Her six-hour space walk has been one of her greatest and most thrilling challenges. During a space walk she leaves the shuttle attached only by a tether, and goes out into space wearing and depending solely on the pressurized life-support space suit. Dr. Godwin went up on Atlantis with the third docking mission to the Russian space station Mir. She performed the space walk in order to mount experiment packages on the Mir docking module to detect and assess debris and contamination in a space station environment. Setting up equipment under the micro gravity environment, while wearing the life support apparatus, was very difficult. "The suit is over 500 pounds, and even though you really don't weigh anything, you still have all the properties of mass. So, in terms of starting or stopping it's like you're moving 500 pounds—all the inertia is still there. You just have to learn to move a little differently. For example, it's harder to stay in one place, because you can get this motion build up."

"Seeing the earth go by while up in space is just an incredible experience," says Linda. "Earth is so beautiful and peaceful. In the space craft we are orbiting her every 90 minutes, so we see a sunrise and a sunset every 45 minutes. At nighttime you see all the city lights and during daylight you see the oceans, clouds, land masses and weather like storms and lighting flashes. You get a sense of how we're all tied together. You can look down and see that little surface of air that we have shining through the horizon during a sunrise or sunset and you realize there isn't much of that either. It really makes you think about how fragile and vulnerable our planet is."

SPORTS 162

Here students are asked about the specifics of the activity and required to explain how sliding into second base would be different on the moon; how shuffleboard play would be different on the moon; and whether the friction between your hand and a football would be different on the moon.

The chapter also has activities which help students discover that projectiles travel differently on the moon, how mass and weight relationships change sports, how running and jumping are different and how collisions could be changed to limit the range of a golf ball.

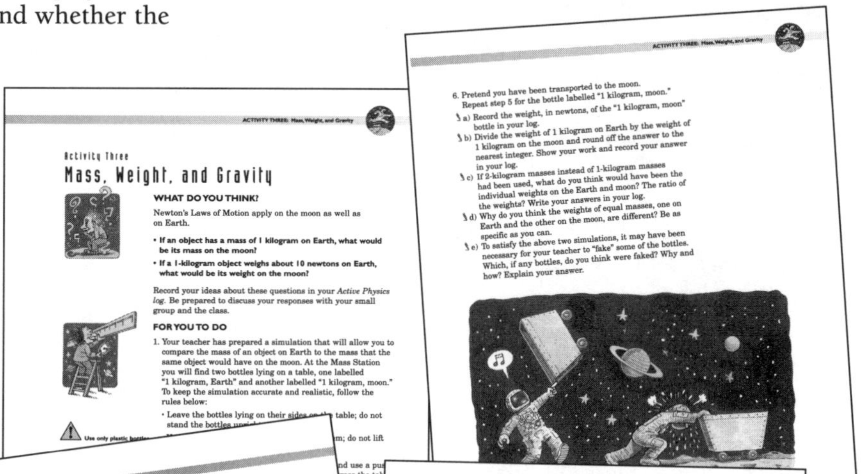

ACTIVITY THREE: Mass, Weight, and Gravity

Activity Three

Mass, Weight, and Gravity

WHAT DO YOU THINK?

Newton's Laws of Motion apply on the moon as well as on Earth.

- If an object has a mass of 1 kilogram on Earth, what would be its mass on the moon?
- If a 1-kilogram object weighs about 10 newtons on Earth, what would be its weight on the moon?

Record your ideas about these questions in your *Active Physics log*. Be prepared to discuss your responses with your small group and the class.

FOR YOU TO DO

1. Your teacher has prepared a simulation that will allow you to compare the mass of an object on Earth to the mass that the same object would have on the moon. At the Mass Station you will find two bottles lying on a table, one labelled "1 kilogram, Earth" and another labelled "1 kilogram, moon." To keep the simulation accurate and realistic, follow the rules below:

6. Pretend you have been transported to the moon. Repeat step 5 for the bottle labelled "1 kilogram, moon."
   a) Record the weight, in newtons, of the "1 kilogram, moon" bottle in your log.
   b) Divide the weight of 1 kilogram on Earth by the weight of 1 kilogram on the moon and round off the answer to the nearest integer. Show your work and record your answer in your log.
   c) If 2-kilogram masses instead of 1-kilogram masses had been used, what do you think would have been the individual weights on the Earth and moon? The ratio of the weights? Write your answers in your log.
   d) Why do you think the weights of equal masses, one on Earth and the other on the moon, are different? Be as specific as you can.
   e) To satisfy the above two simulations, it may have been necessary for your teacher to "fake" some of the bottles. Which, if any bottles, do you think were faked? Why and how? Explain your answer.

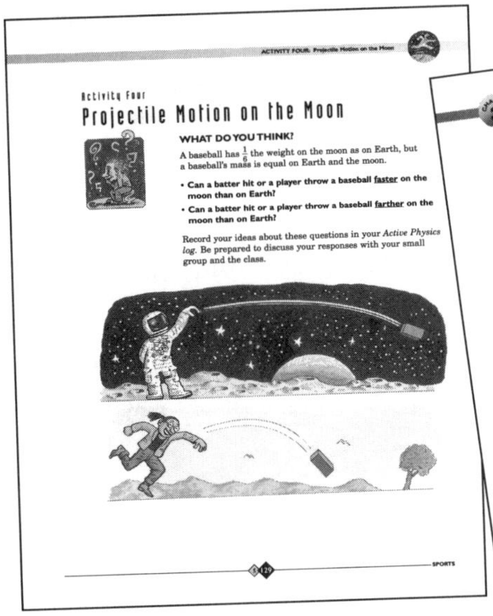

ACTIVITY FOUR: Projectile Motion on the Moon

Activity Four

Projectile Motion on the Moon

WHAT DO YOU THINK?

A baseball has $\frac{1}{6}$ the weight on the moon as on Earth, but a baseball's mass is equal on Earth and the moon.

- Can a batter hit or a player throw a baseball faster on the moon than on Earth?
- Can a batter hit or a player throw a baseball farther on the moon than on Earth?

Record your ideas about these questions in your *Active Physics log*. Be prepared to discuss your responses with your small group and the class.

129 SPORTS

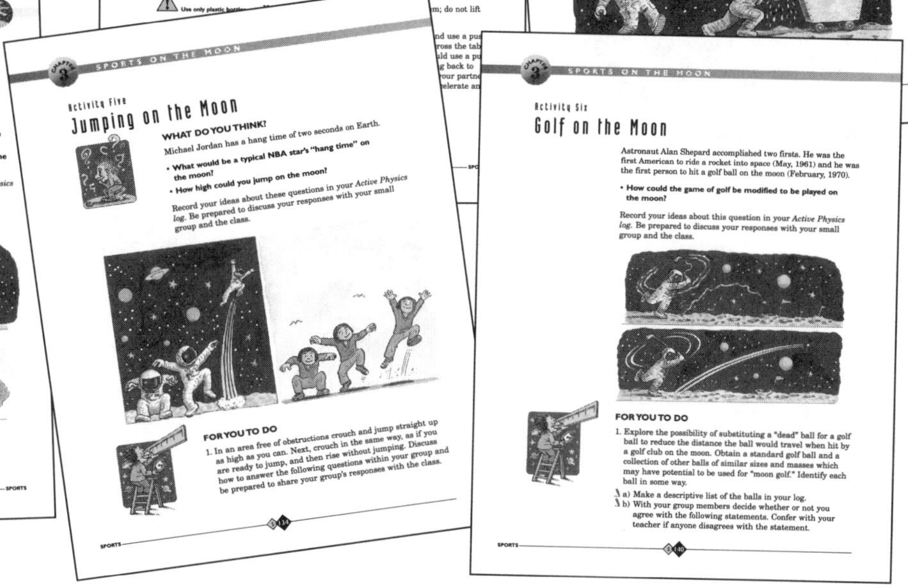

SPORTS ON THE MOON

Activity Five

Jumping on the Moon

WHAT DO YOU THINK?

Michael Jordan has a hang time of two seconds on Earth.

- What would be a typical NBA star's "hang time" on the moon?
- How high could you jump on the moon?

Record your ideas about these questions in your *Active Physics log*. Be prepared to discuss your responses with your small group and the class.

FOR YOU TO DO

1. In an area free of obstructions crouch and jump straight up as high as you can. Next, crouch in the same way, as if you are ready to jump, and then rise without jumping. Discuss how to answer the following questions within your group and be prepared to share your group's responses with the class.

SPORTS 134

SPORTS ON THE MOON

Activity Six

Golf on the Moon

Astronaut Alan Shepard accomplished two firsts. He was the first American to ride a rocket into space (May, 1961) and he was the first person to hit a golf ball on the moon (February, 1970).

- How could the game of golf be modified to be played on the moon?

Record your ideas about this question in your *Active Physics log*. Be prepared to discuss your responses with your small group and the class.

FOR YOU TO DO

1. Explore the possibility of substituting a "dead" ball for a golf ball to reduce the distance the ball would travel when hit by a golf club on the moon. Obtain a standard golf ball and a collection of other balls of similar sizes and masses which may have potential to be used for "moon golf." Identify each ball in some way.
   a) Make a descriptive list of the balls in your log.
   b) With your group members decide whether or not you agree with the following statements. Confer with your teacher if anyone disagrees with the statement.

SPORTS 140

With the results of all of the activities before them, student teams now complete the challenge. They put the jigsaw pieces of friction, trajectories, collisions, running and jumping all together to construct their sport. Each team creates their own sport, reflecting the interests and creativity of the team members. The teams share their work with the rest of the class and the *Sports* chapter concludes.

CHAPTER 1 HEARING

Scenario

A 23-year-old rock musician has difficulty understanding speech. The musician goes to an audiologist, a medical person who helps people with hearing loss. A hearing test shows that the musician has a loss of hearing at high frequencies. The audiologist says that loud noise can cause a hearing loss, but the loss may be only temporary. Hoping the problem will go away, the musician stops playing music for a month. Unfortunately, the hearing loss remains. The audiologist suggests a hearing aid. Another musician, who plays in a symphony orchestra, has no hearing loss. What is the difference between the two situations?

Challenge

Your committee has been put in charge of the school dance. You enjoyed the local band that played last year, but the principal of your school objects to inviting them back. He explains that, after leaving the last dance, his ears were "ringing" for the rest of the evening. You try to calm him down by explaining that this is normal at rock concerts and the famous bands are actually much louder than the local band. The principal decides that there will be no school dances where hearing loss or damage could occur.

M 2

One strength of *Active Physics* is the independence of the chapters. After finishing *Sports*, we begin anew. Let's choose Chapter 1 of *Medicine* as the next adventure. In this chapter, students are challenged to write a position paper to the school principal convincing him that a school dance can be held and guaranteeing that nobody's hearing will be damaged. It is for this purpose that students will learn about sound travel, decibels and frequency response, or human hearing. Or perhaps Chapter 2 of *Transportation* should be initiated. In this chapter, students are required to design and build an improved safety device for cars or bicycles. And it is in this context that students will learn about impulse, momentum, forces, and acceleration.

The beginning of a new chapter has two distinct advantages. For the students who did not do well on the *Sports* unit, they have a fresh start. Maybe they didn't do well because *Sports* didn't interest them and rock concerts or car collisions will. Or maybe they didn't do well because they missed school due to illness or a suspension. It's time to start over. The horizon for success is only four weeks. *Active Physics* does not ask students to worry about a final exam that will be given eight months from now, but rather to focus on one challenge that will be completed within a month.

A second advantage is apparent when one considers the transient nature of our school populations. In most courses, when that new student arrives in November, we do our best as teachers to greet the student and help them make the transition to the class. But we are also keenly aware of how much the student has missed and how difficult the learning situation really is. In an *Active Physics* course, that new student in November is asked to hang in for a week, get used to the class, work with the group over there and is reassured that we will soon be beginning a brand new chapter where they will be full participants irrespective of their late arrival. This removes one of the large hurdles which some students must face as they transfer programs, schools or communities.

Active Physics offers 18 chapters: six units with three chapters each. In a one-year physics or physical science course, students can be expected to complete 12 of the chapters at the most. This provides the teacher and students with a wide selection of content that meets local interests and course objectives.

Students in *Active Physics* never ask, "Why am I learning this?" Teachers of *Active Physics* never have to respond, "Because one day it will be useful to you." *Active Physics* is relevant physics. Students know that they have a challenge and they know that the activities will help them to be successful.

Please take a more careful, leisurely look at *Active Physics*. It's probably just what you and your students have been looking for.

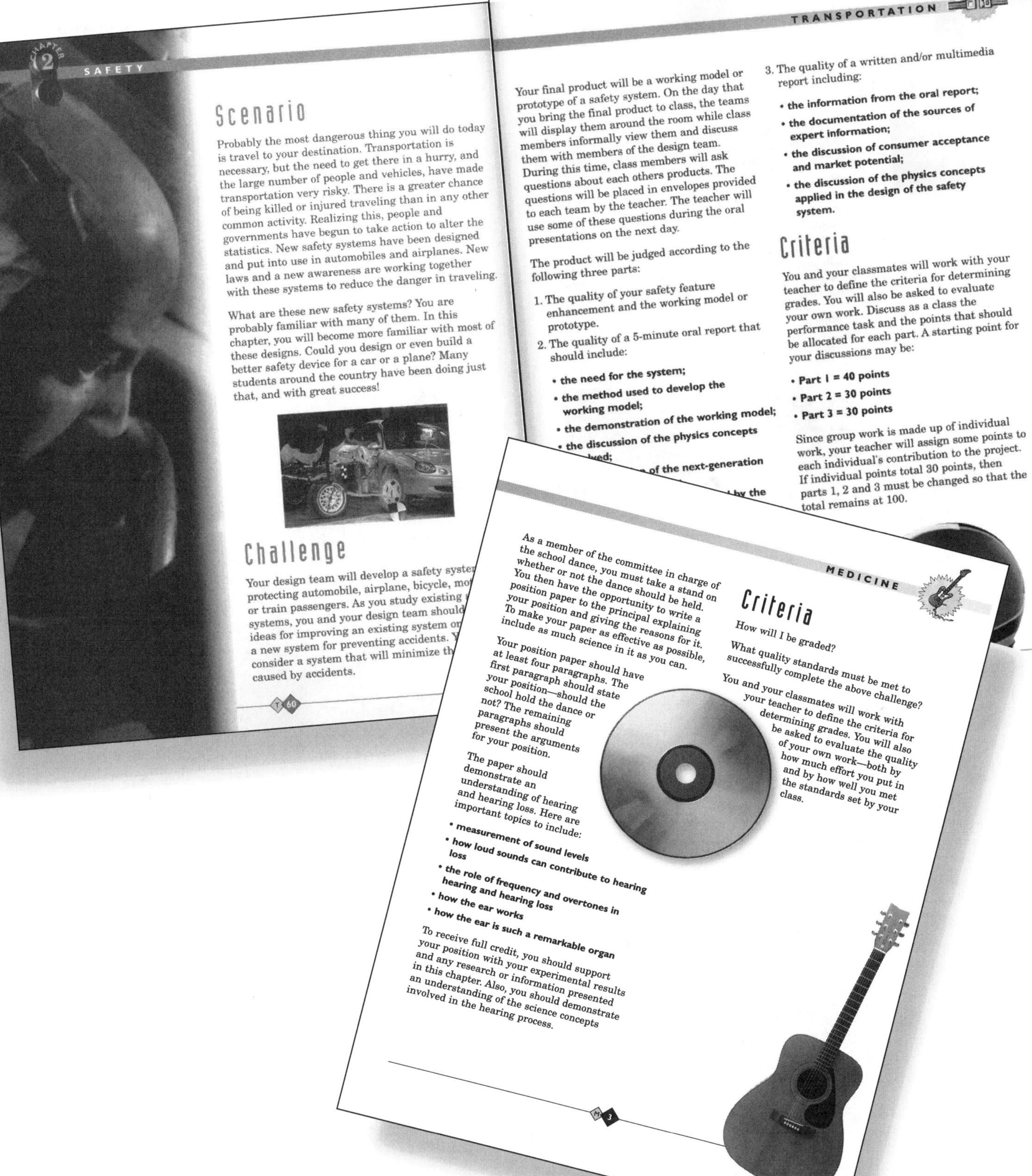

CHAPTER 2 SAFETY

Scenario

Probably the most dangerous thing you will do today is travel to your destination. Transportation is necessary, but the need to get there in a hurry, and the large number of people and vehicles, have made transportation very risky. There is a greater chance of being killed or injured traveling than in any other common activity. Realizing this, people and governments have begun to take action to alter the statistics. New safety systems have been designed and put into use in automobiles and airplanes. New laws and a new awareness are working together with these systems to reduce the danger in traveling.

What are these new safety systems? You are probably familiar with many of them. In this chapter, you will become more familiar with most of these designs. Could you design or even build a better safety device for a car or a plane? Many students around the country have been doing just that, and with great success!

Challenge

Your design team will develop a safety syster protecting automobile, airplane, bicycle, mo or train passengers. As you study existing systems, you and your design team should ideas for improving an existing system or a new system for preventing accidents. consider a system that will minimize th caused by accidents.

T 60

TRANSPORTATION

Your final product will be a working model or prototype of a safety system. On the day that you bring the final product to class, the teams will display them around the room while class members informally view them and discuss them with members of the design team. During this time, class members will ask questions about each others products. The questions will be placed in envelopes provided to each team by the teacher. The teacher will use some of these questions during the oral presentations on the next day.

The product will be judged according to the following three parts:

1. The quality of your safety feature enhancement and the working model or prototype.
2. The quality of a 5-minute oral report that should include:
   - **the need for the system;**
   - **the method used to develop the working model;**
   - **the demonstration of the working model;**
   - **the discussion of the physics concepts ...lved;**
   - **... of the next-generation**
   - **... by the**
3. The quality of a written and/or multimedia report including:
   - **the information from the oral report;**
   - **the documentation of the sources of expert information;**
   - **the discussion of consumer acceptance and market potential;**
   - **the discussion of the physics concepts applied in the design of the safety system.**

Criteria

You and your classmates will work with your teacher to define the criteria for determining grades. You will also be asked to evaluate your own work. Discuss as a class the performance task and the points that should be allocated for each part. A starting point for your discussions may be:

- **Part 1 = 40 points**
- **Part 2 = 30 points**
- **Part 3 = 30 points**

Since group work is made up of individual work, your teacher will assign some points to each individual's contribution to the project. If individual points total 30 points, then parts 1, 2 and 3 must be changed so that the total remains at 100.

MEDICINE

As a member of the committee in charge of the school dance, you must take a stand on whether or not the dance should be held. You then have the opportunity to write a position paper to the principal explaining your position and giving the reasons for it. To make your paper as effective as possible, include as much science in it as you can.

Your position paper should have at least four paragraphs. The first paragraph should state your position—should the school hold the dance or not? The remaining paragraphs should present the arguments for your position.

The paper should demonstrate an understanding of hearing and hearing loss. Here are important topics to include:

- **measurement of sound levels**
- **how loud sounds can contribute to hearing loss**
- **the role of frequency and overtones in hearing and hearing loss**
- **how the ear works**
- **how the ear is such a remarkable organ**

To receive full credit, you should support your position with your experimental results and any research or information presented in this chapter. Also, you should demonstrate an understanding of the science concepts involved in the hearing process.

Criteria

How will I be graded?

What quality standards must be met to successfully complete the above challenge?

You and your classmates will work with your teacher to define the criteria for determining grades. You will also be asked to evaluate the quality of your own work—both by how much effort you put in and by how well you met the standards set by your class.

M 3

Features of Active Physics

1. Scenario

SPORTS ON THE MOON

Scenario

One day, a colony will be set up on the moon and families will live there for extended periods. Plans will have to be made for exercise and entertainment while people live on the moon. Since sports on Earth satisfy both of these needs—exercise and entertainment—it is reasonable to assume that people on the moon colony will also wish to participate in sports. It may even be possible that moon sporting events could be television entertainment for the people back home on Earth.

Challenge

Your challenge is to identify, adapt, or invent a sport that people on the moon will find interesting, exciting, and entertaining.

Write a proposal to NASA (National Aeronautics and Space Administration) which includes the following:

- a description of your sport and its rules and how it meets the basic requirements for a sport,
- a comparison of factors affecting sports on Earth and on the moon in general,
- a comparison of the play of your sport on the Earth and on the moon including any changes to the size of the field, alterations to the equipment, or changes in the rules,
- a newspaper article for the sports section of your local paper back home describing a "championship" match of your moon sport.

S 112

Each *Active Physics* chapter opens with an engaging scenario. Students from diverse backgrounds and localities have been interviewed in order to find situations which are not only realistic but meaningful to the high school population. The scenarios (only a paragraph or two in length) set the stage for the chapter challenge which immediately follows. Many teachers choose to read the scenario aloud to the class as a way of introducing the new chapter.

2. Challenge

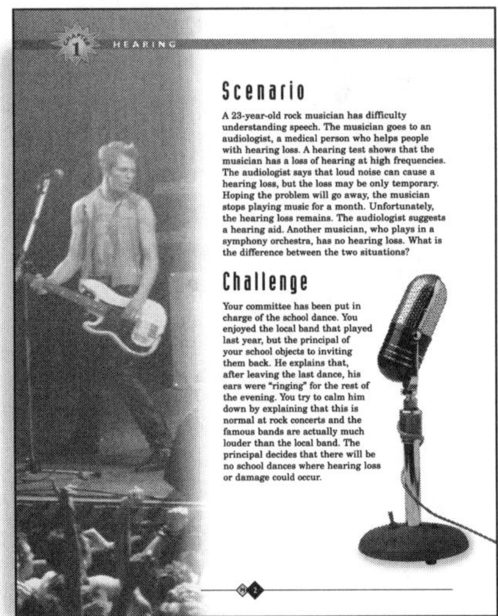
1 HEARING

Scenario

A 23-year-old rock musician has difficulty understanding speech. The musician goes to an audiologist, a medical person who helps people with hearing loss. A hearing test shows that the musician has a loss of hearing at high frequencies. The audiologist says that loud noise can cause a hearing loss, but the loss may be only temporary. Hoping the problem will go away, the musician stops playing music for a month. Unfortunately, the hearing loss remains. The audiologist suggests a hearing aid. Another musician, who plays in a symphony orchestra, has no hearing loss. What is the difference between the two situations?

Challenge

Your committee has been put in charge of the school dance. You enjoyed the local band that played last year, but the principal of your school objects to inviting them back. He explains that, after leaving the last dance, his ears were "ringing" for the rest of the evening. You try to calm him down by explaining that this is normal at rock concerts and the famous bands are actually much louder than the local band. The principal decides that there will be no school dances where hearing loss or damage could occur.

M 2

The chapter challenge is the heart and soul of *Active Physics*. It provides a purpose for all of the work that will follow. The challenges provide the rationale for learning. One of the common complaints teachers hear from students is, "Why am I learning this?" In *Active Physics*, no students raise this criticism. Similarly, no teacher has to answer, "Because one day it will be useful to you." The complaint is avoided because on Day One of the chapter students are presented with a challenge that, in essence, becomes their job for the next few weeks.

In *Medicine*, Chapter 1, students are challenged with a situation where the school principal is not going to permit a school dance because his ears were ringing after the last band performed. Students must write a position paper either agreeing with the principal or convincing him that nobody's hearing will be damaged if another dance is held. This is why the students then learn about decibels, frequencies and human response to sound.

In *Transportation*, Chapter 2, students are challenged to design and build an improved safety device for an automobile. The study of momentum, forces and Newton's Laws will be integral to their understanding of the required features in a safety device.

In *Home*, Chapter 2, students must create an appliance package that can be used in developing nations. The appliance package is limited by the wind generator available to the households. Students must also supply a rationale for how each suggested appliance will enhance the well-being of the family using it. This requires students to be able to differentiate between power and energy. It also provides a basis for students to reflect on quality of life issues in parts of the globe that they learn about in their social studies classes.

The beauty of the challenges lies in the variety of tasks and opportunities for students of different talents and skills to excel. Students who express themselves artistically will have an opportunity to shine in some challenges, while the student who can design and build may be the group leader in another challenge. Some challenges have a major component devoted to writing while others require oral or visual presentations. All challenges require the demonstration of solid physics understanding.

The challenges are not contrived situations for high school students. Professional engineers also design and build improved safety devices. Medical writers and illustrators design posters and pamphlets. The challenge in Chapter 3 of *Sports* requires students to create, invent, or adapt a sport that can be played on the moon. This challenge has been successfully completed by 9th grade high school students, 12th grade *Active Physics* students, and by NASA engineers. The expectation may be different for each of these audiences, but the challenge is consistent.

3. Criteria

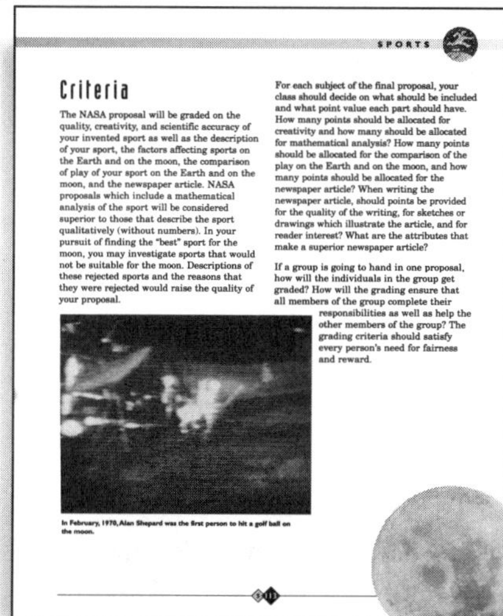

SPORTS

Criteria

The NASA proposal will be graded on the quality, creativity, and scientific accuracy of your invented sport as well as the description of your sport, the factors affecting sports on the Earth and on the moon, the comparison of play of your sport on the Earth and on the moon, and the newspaper article. NASA proposals which include a mathematical analysis of the sport will be considered superior to those that describe the sport qualitatively (without numbers). In your pursuit of finding the "best" sport for the moon, you may investigate sports that would not be suitable for the moon. Descriptions of these rejected sports and the reasons that they were rejected would raise the quality of your proposal.

For each subject of the final proposal, your class should decide on what should be included and what point value each part should have. How many points should be allocated for creativity and how many should be allocated for mathematical analysis? How many points should be allocated for the comparison of the play on the Earth and on the moon, and how many points should be allocated for the newspaper article? When writing the newspaper article, should points be provided for the quality of the writing, for sketches or drawings which illustrate the article, and for reader interest? What are the attributes that make a superior newspaper article?

If a group is going to hand in one proposal, how will the individuals in the group get graded? How will the grading ensure that all members of the group complete their responsibilities as well as help the other members of the group? The grading criteria should satisfy every person's need for fairness and reward.

In February, 1970, Alan Shepard was the first person to hit a golf ball on the moon.

In creating *Active Physics*, we had thought that the generation of the challenge was good enough. Upon reflection, we soon realized that criteria for success must also be included. When students agree to the matrix by which they will be measured, the research has shown that the students will perform better and achieve more. It makes sense. In the simplest situation of cleaning a lab room, the teacher may simply state, "Please clean up the lab." The results are often a minimal cleanup. If the teacher begins by asking, "What does a clean lab room look like?" and students and teacher jointly list the attributes of a clean lab room (i.e., no paper on the floor, all beakers put away, all materials on the back of the lab tables, all power supplies unplugged and all water removed), the students respond differently and the cleanup is better. When students are asked to include physics principles in an explanation, the students should know whether the expectation is for three physics principles or five.

The discussion of grading criteria and the creation of a grading rubric is a crucial ingredient for student success. *Active Physics* requires a class discussion, after the introduction of the challenge, about the grading criteria. How much is required? What does an "A" presentation look like? Should creativity be weighed more than delivery? The criteria can be visited again at the end of the chapter, but at this point it provides a clarity to the challenge and the expectation level that the students should set for themselves.

4. What Do You Think?

ACTIVITY FOUR: How Images Are Made: Converging Lenses

Activity Four

How Images Are Made: Converging Lenses

WHAT DO YOU THINK?

A successful movie can bring in over 100 million dollars.

- **How is the image of a movie projected onto a large screen from a small piece of film?**

Record your ideas about this question in your *Active Physics log*. Be prepared to discuss your responses with your small group and your class.

During the past few years much has been written about a constructivist approach to learning. Videos of Harvard graduates, in caps and gowns, show that the students are not able to explain correctly why it is colder in the winter than it is in the summer. These students have previously answered these questions correctly in 4th grade, in Middle School, and then again in High School. How else would they have gotten into Harvard? We believe that they never internalized the logic and understanding of the seasons. One reason for this problem is that they were never confronted by what they did believe, and were never adequately shown why they should give up that belief system. Certainly, it is worth writing down a "book's perfect answer" on a test to secure a good grade, but to actually believe requires a more thorough examination of competing explanations.

The best way to ascertain a student's prior understanding is through extensive interviewing. Much of the research literature in this area includes the results of these interviews. In a classroom, this one-on-one dialogue is rarely possible. The **What Do You Think?** question introduces each activity in a way in which to elicit prior understandings. It gives students an opportunity to verbalize what they think about friction, or energy, or light, before they embark on an activity. The brief discussion of the range of answers brings the student a little closer in touch with that part of his/her brain which understands friction, energy, or light. The **What Do You Think?** question is not intended to produce a correct answer or a discussion of the features of the questions. It is not intended to bring closure. The activity which follows will provide that discussion as experimental results are analyzed. The **What Do You Think?** question should take no more than a few minutes of class time. It is the lead into the physics investigation. Students should be strongly encouraged to write their responses to the questions in their logs, to ensure that they have in fact addressed their prior conceptions. After students have discussed their responses in their small groups, activate a class discussion. Ask students to volunteer other students' answers which they found interesting. This may encourage students to exchange ideas without the fear of personally giving a "wrong" answer.

5. For You To Do

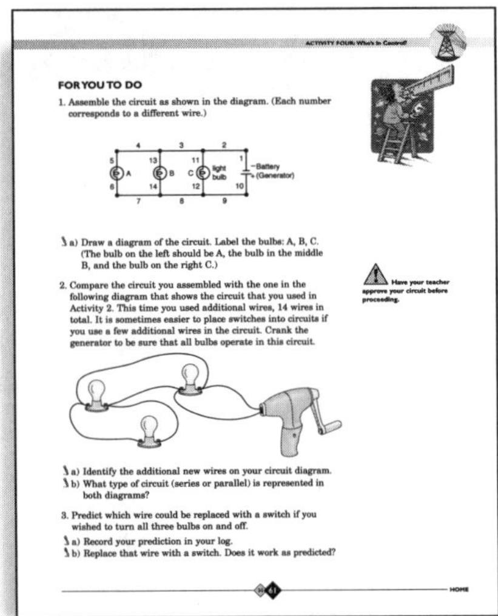
ACTIVITY FOUR: Who's in Control?

FOR YOU TO DO

1. Assemble the circuit as shown in the diagram. (Each number corresponds to a different wire.)

a) Draw a diagram of the circuit. Label the bulbs: A, B, C. (The bulb on the left should be A, the bulb in the middle B, and the bulb on the right C.)

Have your teacher approve your circuit before proceeding.

2. Compare the circuit you assembled with the one in the following diagram that shows the circuit that you used in Activity 2. This time you used additional wires, 14 wires in total. It is sometimes easier to place switches into circuits if you use a few additional wires in the circuit. Crank the generator to be sure that all bulbs operate in this circuit.

a) Identify the additional new wires on your circuit diagram.
b) What type of circuit (series or parallel) is represented in both diagrams?

3. Predict which wire could be replaced with a switch if you wished to turn all three bulbs on and off.

a) Record your prediction in your log.
b) Replace that wire with a switch. Does it work as predicted?

H 61 HOME

Active Physics is a hands-on, minds-on curriculum. Students *do* physics; they do not *read* about doing physics. Each activity has instructions for each part of the investigation. The pencil icons are provided to remind students that data, hypotheses, or conclusions should be recorded in their log or laboratory manual.

Activities are the opportunity for students to garner the knowledge that they will need to complete the chapter challenge. Students will understand the physics principle involved because they have investigated it. In *Active Physics*, if a student is asked, "How do you know?" the response is, "Because I did an experiment!"

Recognizing that many students know how to read, but do not like reading, background information is provided within the context of the activity. Students have demonstrated that they will read when the information is required for them to continue with their exploration.

Occasionally, the activity will require the entire class to participate in a large, single demonstration simultaneously. The teacher, on other occasions, may decide that a specific activity is best done as a demonstration. This would be appropriate if there is limited equipment for that one activity, or the facilities are not available. Viewing demonstrations on an ongoing basis, though, is not what *Active Physics* is about.

There are specific **For You To Do** activities where computer spreadsheets, force transducers, or specific electronic equipment is required. Most of these activities have 'low-tech' alternatives provided in the Teacher's Edition. In the initial teaching of *Active Physics*, the low-tech alternative may be the only reasonable approach. As the course becomes a staple of the school offerings, it is hoped that funds can be set aside to improve the students' access to equipment.

Most of the **For You To Do** activities require between one and two class periods. With the present trend toward block scheduling, there are so many time structures that it is difficult to predict how *Active Physics* will best fit with your schedule. The other impact on time is the achievement and preparation level of the students. In a given activity, students may be required to complete a graph of their data. This is considered one small part of the activity. If the students have never been exposed to graphing, this could require a two-period lesson to teach the rudiments of graphing with suitable practice in interpretation. *Active Physics* is accessible to all students. The teacher is in the best position to make accommodations in time reflecting the needs of the students.

6. Physics Talk

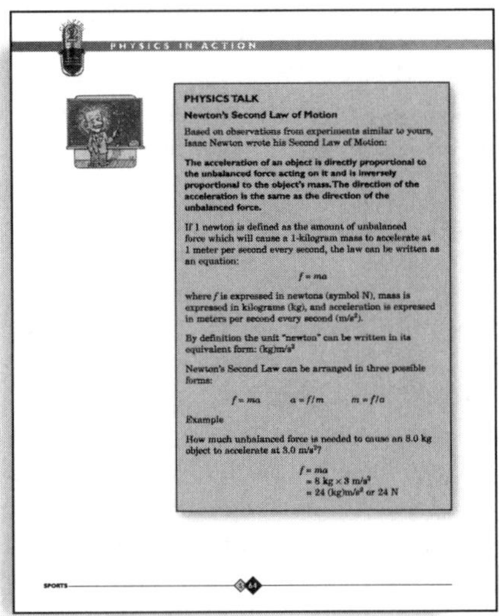
PHYSICS IN ACTION

PHYSICS TALK

Newton's Second Law of Motion

Based on observations from experiments similar to yours, Isaac Newton wrote his Second Law of Motion:

The acceleration of an object is directly proportional to the unbalanced force acting on it and is inversely proportional to the object's mass. The direction of the acceleration is the same as the direction of the unbalanced force.

If 1 newton is defined as the amount of unbalanced force which will cause a 1-kilogram mass to accelerate at 1 meter per second every second, the law can be written as an equation:

$$f = ma$$

where f is expressed in newtons (symbol N), mass is expressed in kilograms (kg), and acceleration is expressed in meters per second every second (m/s^2).

By definition the unit "newton" can be written in its equivalent form: (kg)m/s^2

Newton's Second Law can be arranged in three possible forms:

$$f = ma \qquad a = f/m \qquad m = f/a$$

Example

How much unbalanced force is needed to cause an 8.0 kg object to accelerate at 3.0 m/s^2?

$$\begin{aligned} f &= ma \\ &= 8 \text{ kg} \times 3 \text{ m/s}^2 \\ &= 24 \text{ (kg)m/s}^2 \text{ or } 24 \text{ N} \end{aligned}$$

SPORTS S 61

Equations are often the simplest, most straightforward, most concise, and clearest way of expressing physics principles. *Active Physics* limits the mathematics to the ninth grade curriculum. Students who have shied away from studying physics because of the mathematics prerequisites find that they are welcomed into *Active Physics*. **Physics Talk** is a means by which specific attention can be given to the mathematical equations. It also provides an opportunity to illustrate a problem solution or to derive a complex equation. For some students, there is a need to guide them through the algebraic manipulation which shows the equivalence of $F = ma$ and $a = F/m$. Where appropriate, this manipulation is explicitly shown. Finally, sample problems required for the chapter challenge will also be in **Physics Talk**.

7. For You To Read

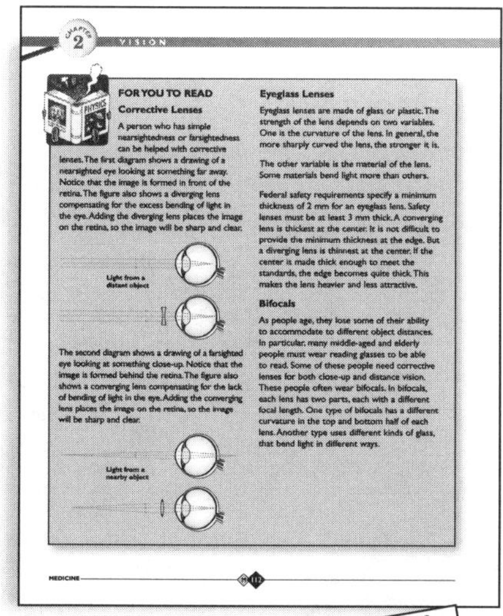

CHAPTER 2 VISION

FOR YOU TO READ

Corrective Lenses

A person who has simple nearsightedness or farsightedness can be helped with corrective lenses. The first diagram shows a drawing of a nearsighted eye looking at something far away. Notice that the image is formed in front of the retina. The figure also shows a diverging lens compensating for the excess bending of light in the eye. Adding the diverging lens places the image on the retina, so the image will be sharp and clear.

Light from a distant object

The second diagram shows a drawing of a farsighted eye looking at something close-up. Notice that the image is formed behind the retina. The figure also shows a converging lens compensating for the lack of bending of light in the eye. Adding the converging lens places the image on the retina, so the image will be sharp and clear.

Light from a nearby object

Eyeglass Lenses

Eyeglass lenses are made of glass or plastic. The strength of the lens depends on two variables. One is the curvature of the lens. In general, the more sharply curved the lens, the stronger it is.

The other variable is the material of the lens. Some materials bend light more than others.

Federal safety requirements specify a minimum thickness of 2 mm for an eyeglass lens. Safety lenses must be at least 3 mm thick. A converging lens is thickest at the center. It is not difficult to provide the minimum thickness at the edge. But a diverging lens is thinnest at the center. If the center is made thick enough to meet the standards, the edge becomes quite thick. This makes the lens heavier and less attractive.

Bifocals

As people age, they lose some of their ability to accommodate to different object distances. In particular, many middle-aged and elderly people must wear reading glasses to be able to read. Some of these people need corrective lenses for both close-up and distance vision. These people often wear bifocals. In bifocals, each lens has two parts, each with a different focal length. One type of bifocals has a different curvature in the top and bottom half of each lens. Another type uses different kinds of glass, that bend light in different ways.

MEDICINE M 112

ACTIVITY NINE: Tooth Tunes: The Inner Ear and Transducers

FOR YOU TO READ

Tooth Tunes

The apparatus you set up for this activity is called "tooth tunes."

Tooth tunes produce vibrations in the same way the speaker does. The diagram shows the path of these vibrations from the dowels to your inner ear and out again through vibrations of the eardrum.

[a] The tooth tunes has a coil of wire that vibrates when it is near the magnet.

[b] As the coil vibrates, it makes the dowel vibrate, too.

[c] These vibrations pass through your teeth and into your jaw and skull.

[d,e] These vibrations cause the tiny bones in the middle ear to vibrate. The oval window and the eardrum both vibrate. The vibrating inner ear lets you hear the music.

[f] The vibrating eardrum turns your ear into a speaker!

Conductive Hearing Loss

Tooth tunes show how sound is conducted from your teeth to the ossicles—the bones in your middle ear. These bones are surrounded by tissues in the middle ear.

As people age, the tissues surrounding the ossicles become less flexible. The ossicles' movement becomes restricted. They cannot transmit sound accurately from the eardrum to the oval window. This is called *conductive hearing loss*. The effect is something like pressing down on a stereo speaker while music is playing through it. The speaker can't vibrate freely, so the sound is distorted.

The Inner Ear and Neurosensory Hearing Loss

The inner ear is a *transducer*. A transducer changes energy from one form to another. You have already used transducers—you have used microphones, loudspeakers, oscilloscopes, and musical instruments. The inner ear is a transducer that changes sound energy (in the liquid in the inner ear) into electrical signals that travel on nerves to the brain.

The inner ear has two main parts:

1. three semicircular canals, which help control your sense of balance, and
2. the cochlea, which changes the sound to nerve impulses.

All are filled with liquid. They can be seen in the diagram on page M42. The cochlea is a small spiral about the size of the tip of your little finger.

MEDICINE M 55

The **For You To Read** inserts provide students with some reading at the ninth grade level. This section may be used to tie together concepts from the present activity or a set of activities. It may also be used to provide a glimpse into the history of the physics principle being investigated. Finally, **For You To Read** may provide background information which will help clarify the meaning of the physics principle investigated in **For You To Do**.

8. Reflecting On The Activity And The Challenge

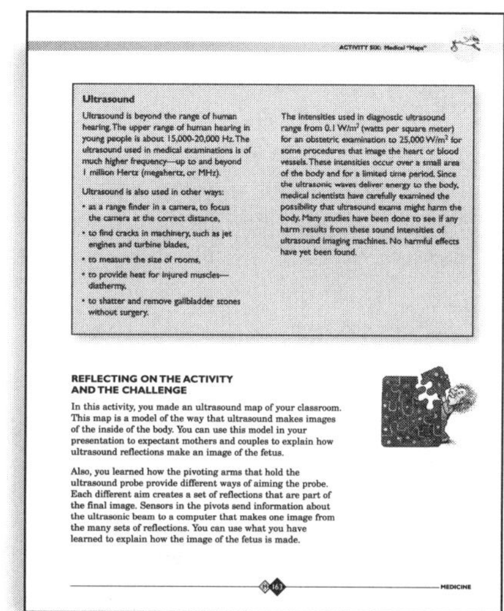

ACTIVITY SIX: Medical "Maps"

Ultrasound

Ultrasound is beyond the range of human hearing. The upper range of human hearing in young people is about 15,000-20,000 Hz. The ultrasound used in medical examinations is of much higher frequency—up to and beyond 1 million Hertz (megahertz, or MHz).

Ultrasound is also used in other ways:

- as a range finder in a camera, to focus the camera at the correct distance,
- to find cracks in machinery, such as jet engines and turbine blades,
- to measure the size of rooms,
- to provide heat for injured muscles—diathermy,
- to shatter and remove gallbladder stones without surgery.

The intensities used in diagnostic ultrasound range from 0.1 W/m^2 (watts per square meter) for an obstetric examination to 25,000 W/m^2 for some procedures that image the heart or blood vessels. These intensities occur over a small area of the body and for a limited time period. Since the ultrasonic waves deliver energy to the body, medical scientists have carefully examined the possibility that ultrasound exams might harm the body. Many studies have been done to see if any harm results from these sound intensities of ultrasound imaging machines. No harmful effects have yet been found.

REFLECTING ON THE ACTIVITY AND THE CHALLENGE

In this activity, you made an ultrasound map of your classroom. This map is a model of the way that ultrasound makes images of the inside of the body. You can use this model in your presentation to expectant mothers and couples to explain how ultrasound reflections make an image of the fetus.

Also, you learned how the pivoting arms that hold the ultrasound probe provide different ways of aiming the probe. Each different aim creates a set of reflections that are part of the final image. Sensors in the pivots send information about the ultrasonic beam to a computer that makes one image from the many sets of reflections. You can use what you have learned to explain how the image of the fetus is made.

M 163 MEDICINE

At the close of each activity, the student is often so involved with the completion of the single experiment that the larger context of the investigation is lost. **Reflecting On The Activity And The Challenge** is the opportunity for students to place the new insights and information into the context of the chapter and the chapter challenge. If the chapter challenge is considered a completed picture, each activity is a jigsaw piece. By completing enough of the **For You To Do** activities, the students will be able to fit the jigsaw pieces together and complete the challenge. This summary section ensures that the students do not forget about the larger context and continue their personal momentum toward completion of the challenge.

9. Physics To Go

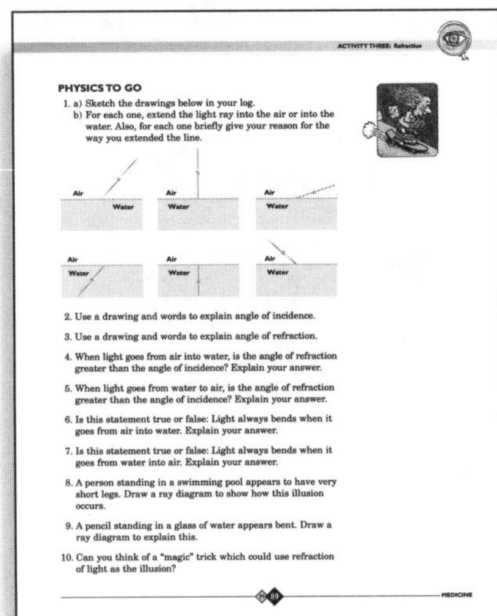

ACTIVITY THREE: Refraction

PHYSICS TO GO

1. a) Sketch the drawings below in your log.
   b) For each one, extend the light ray into the air or into the water. Also, for each one briefly give your reason for the way you extended the line.

2. Use a drawing and words to explain angle of incidence.
3. Use a drawing and words to explain angle of refraction.
4. When light goes from air into water, is the angle of refraction greater than the angle of incidence? Explain your answer.
5. When light goes from water to air, is the angle of refraction greater than the angle of incidence? Explain your answer.
6. Is this statement true or false: Light always bends when it goes from air into water. Explain your answer.
7. Is this statement true or false: Light always bends when it goes from water into air. Explain your answer.
8. A person standing in a swimming pool appears to have very short legs. Draw a ray diagram to show how this illusion occurs.
9. A pencil standing in a glass of water appears bent. Draw a ray diagram to explain this.
10. Can you think of a "magic" trick which could use refraction of light as the illusion?

M 89 MEDICINE

This section provides additional questions and problems that can be completed outside of class. Some of the problems are applications of the principles involved in the preceding activity. Others are replication of the work in the **For You To Do** activity. Still others provide an opportunity to transfer the results of the investigation to the context of the chapter challenge. **Physics To Go** provides a means by which students can be working on the larger chapter challenge in smaller chunks during the chapter.

10. Inquiry Investigation

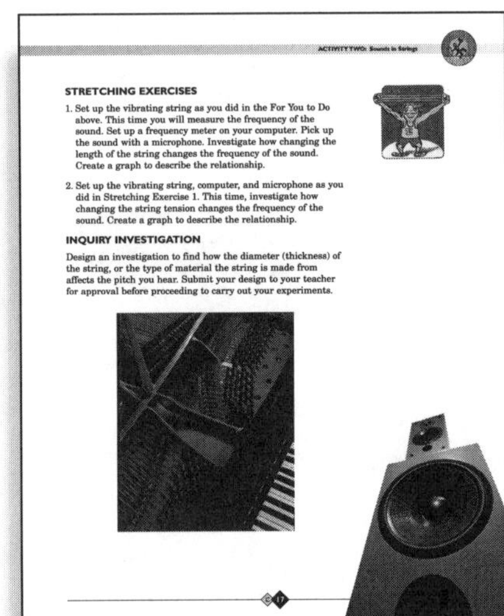

ACTIVITY TWO: Sounds in Strings

STRETCHING EXERCISES

1. Set up the vibrating string as you did in the For You to Do above. This time you will measure the frequency of the sound. Set up a frequency meter on your computer. Pick up the sound with a microphone. Investigate how changing the length of the string changes the frequency of the sound. Create a graph to describe the relationship.
2. Set up the vibrating string, computer, and microphone as you did in Stretching Exercise 1. This time, investigate how changing the string tension changes the frequency of the sound. Create a graph to describe the relationship.

INQUIRY INVESTIGATION

Design an investigation to find how the diameter (thickness) of the string, or the type of material the string is made from affects the pitch you hear. Submit your design to your teacher for approval before proceeding to carry out your experiments.

C 17

The outcome of good science instruction should be the ability of students to conceive of an experiment, design that experiment, complete the data collection, interpret the data and draw suitable conclusions based on the experiment. The nature of the daily immersion in activities in *Active Physics* often, by necessity, provides for detailed instructions in how to proceed. Inquiry is an opportunity to provide the right stimulus for students to try their hands at designing a specific experiment to answer a specific question. It affords students the chance to mirror the techniques and approaches that they have experienced in *Active Physics* and to expand the approach to secure new information. The Inquiry can be assigned as independent study or as a class extension to the lab.

11. Stretching Exercises

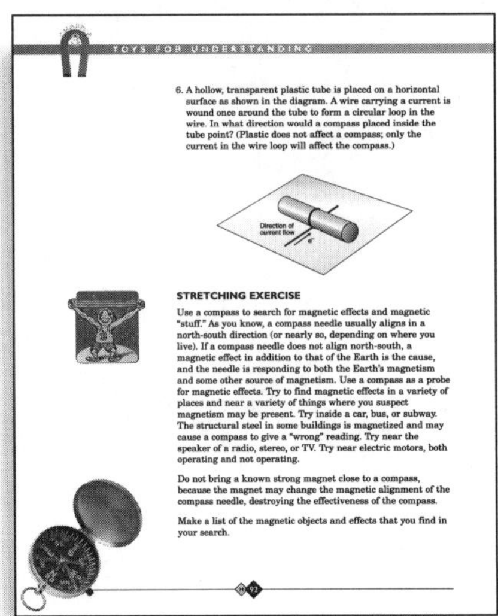

TOYS FOR UNDERSTANDING

6. A hollow, transparent plastic tube is placed on a horizontal surface as shown in the diagram. A wire carrying a current is wound once around the tube to form a circular loop in the wire. In what direction would a compass placed inside the tube point? (Plastic does not affect a compass; only the current in the wire loop will affect the compass.)

STRETCHING EXERCISE

Use a compass to search for magnetic effects and magnetic "stuff." As you know, a compass needle usually aligns in a north-south direction (or nearly so, depending on where you live). If a compass needle does not align north-south, a magnetic effect in addition to that of the Earth is the cause, and the needle is responding to both the Earth's magnetism and some other source of magnetism. Use a compass as a probe for magnetic effects. Try to find magnetic effects in a variety of places and near a variety of things where you suspect magnetism may be present. Try inside a car, bus, or subway. The structural steel in some buildings is magnetized and may cause a compass to give a "wrong" reading. Try near the speaker of a radio, stereo, or TV. Try near electric motors, both operating and not operating.

Do not bring a known strong magnet close to a compass, because the magnet may change the magnetic alignment of the compass needle, destroying the effectiveness of the compass.

Make a list of the magnetic objects and effects that you find in your search.

H 92

Some students express additional interest in a specific topic or an extension to a topic. The **Stretching Exercises** provide an avenue in which to pursue that interest. **Stretching Exercises** often require additional readings or interviews. They may be given for extra credit to students who wish to attempt a more in-depth problem or a tougher exercise.

12. Chapter Assessment

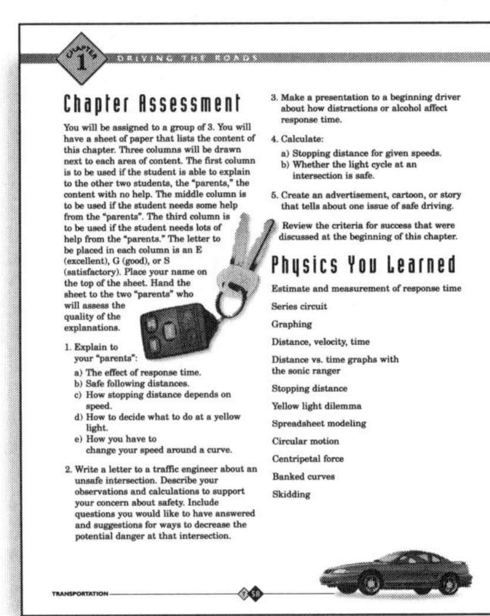

CHAPTER 1 DRIVING THE ROADS

Chapter Assessment

You will be assigned to a group of 3. You will have a sheet of paper that lists the content of this chapter. Three columns will be drawn next to each area of content. The first column is to be used if the student is able to explain to the other two students, the "parents," the content with no help. The middle column is to be used if the student needs some help from the "parents". The third column is to be used if the student needs lots of help from the "parents." The letter to be placed in each column is an E (excellent), G (good), or S (satisfactory). Place your name on the top of the sheet. Hand the sheet to the two "parents" who will assess the quality of the explanations.

1. Explain to your "parents":
   a) The effect of response time.
   b) Safe following distances.
   c) How stopping distance depends on speed.
   d) How to decide what to do at a yellow light.
   e) How you have to change your speed around a curve.
2. Write a letter to a traffic engineer about an unsafe intersection. Describe your observations and calculations to support your concern about safety. Include questions you would like to have answered and suggestions for ways to decrease the potential danger at that intersection.
3. Make a presentation to a beginning driver about how distractions or alcohol affect response time.
4. Calculate:
   a) Stopping distance for given speeds.
   b) Whether the light cycle at an intersection is safe.
5. Create an advertisement, cartoon, or story that tells about one issue of safe driving.

Review the criteria for success that were discussed at the beginning of this chapter.

Physics You Learned

Estimate and measurement of response time

Series circuit

Graphing

Distance, velocity, time

Distance vs. time graphs with the sonic ranger

Stopping distance

Yellow light dilemma

Spreadsheet modeling

Circular motion

Centripetal force

Banked curves

Skidding

TRANSPORTATION T 58

The **Chapter Assessment** is the return to the **Chapter Challenge and Criteria**. The students are ready to complete the challenge. They are able to view the challenge with a clarity that has emerged from the completion of the **For You To Do** activities of the chapter. Students are able to review the chapter as they discuss the synthesis of the information into the required context of the challenge. The students should have some class time to work together to complete the challenge and to present their project. In many physics courses, all students are expected to converge on the same solution. In *Active Physics*, each group is expected to have a unique solution. All solutions must have correct physics, but there is ample room for creativity on the students' part. This is one of the features that captures the imagination of students who have often previously chosen not to enroll in physics classes.

13. Physics You Learned

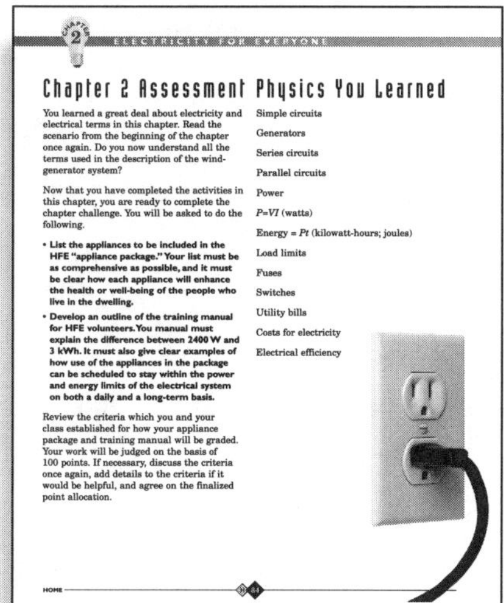

CHAPTER 2 ELECTRICITY FOR EVERYONE

Chapter 2 Assessment

You learned a great deal about electricity and electrical terms in this chapter. Read the scenario from the beginning of the chapter once again. Do you now understand all the terms used in the description of the wind-generator system?

Now that you have completed the activities in this chapter, you are ready to complete the chapter challenge. You will be asked to do the following.

- **List the appliances to be included in the HFE "appliance package." Your list must be as comprehensive as possible, and it must be clear how each appliance will enhance the health or well-being of the people who live in the dwelling.**
- **Develop an outline of the training manual for HFE volunteers. You manual must explain the difference between 2400 W and 3 kWh. It must also give clear examples of how use of the appliances in the package can be scheduled to stay within the power and energy limits of the electrical system on both a daily and a long-term basis.**

Review the criteria which you and your class established for how your appliance package and training manual will be graded. Your work will be judged on the basis of 100 points. If necessary, discuss the criteria once again, add details to the criteria if it would be helpful, and agree on the finalized point allocation.

Physics You Learned

Simple circuits

Generators

Series circuits

Parallel circuits

Power

$P=VI$ (watts)

Energy = Pt (kilowatt-hours; joules)

Load limits

Fuses

Switches

Utility bills

Costs for electricity

Electrical efficiency

HOME H 84

This small section at the end of the chapter provides a list of physics concepts and equations which were studied in the context of the **For You To Do** activities. It provides students with a sense of accomplishment and serves as a quick review of all that was learned during the preceding weeks.

14. Physics At Work

CHAPTER 3 SPORTS ON THE MOON

PHYSICS AT WORK

Linda M. Godwin, Ph.D.

NASA ASTRONAUT

It was while working on her Doctorate in physics at the University of Missouri in the late 1970s that Linda first thought about becoming a NASA Astronaut. Prior to that time, there had been only male Astronauts. When NASA began putting the word out that they were interested in breaking down the gender barriers for their scientific mission specialists, Linda responded.

Now she is a veteran of three space flights and has logged over 633 hours in space, including a six-hour space walk. Her six-hour space walk has been one of her greatest and most thrilling challenges. During a space walk she leaves the shuttle attached only by a tether, and goes out into space wearing and depending solely on the pressurized life-support space suit. Dr. Godwin went up on Atlantis with the third docking mission to the Russian space station Mir. She performed the space walk in order to mount experiment packages on the Mir docking module to detect and assess debris and contamination in a space station environment. Setting up equipment under the micro gravity environment, while wearing the life support apparatus, was very difficult. "The suit is over 500 pounds, and even though you really don't weigh anything, you still have all the properties of mass. So, in terms of starting or stopping it's like you're moving 500 pounds—all the inertia is still there. You just have to learn to move a little differently. For example, it's harder to stay in one place, because you can get this motion build up."

"Seeing the earth go by while up in space is just an incredible experience," says Linda. "Earth is so beautiful and peaceful. In the space craft we are orbiting her every 90 minutes, so we see a sunrise and a sunset every 45 minutes. At nighttime you see all the city lights and during daylight you see the oceans, clouds, land masses and weather like storms and lighting flashes. You get a sense of how we're all tied together. You can look down and see that little surface of air that we have shining through the horizon during a sunrise or sunset and you realize there isn't much of that either. It really makes you think about how fragile and vulnerable our planet is."

SPORTS S 162

ACTIVITY NINE: Visual Activity

PHYSICS AT WORK

Rafael Ortiz, Jr.

GIVING THE GIFT OF SIGHT

Rafael grew up in Newark, New Jersey and always dreamed of being a football star. He wanted to play for the Dallas Cowboys, but the course of his life was to take a different, although deeply fulfilling, turn instead. When he was a young teenager, the man next door, an optician, opened an optical store. Rafael began hanging out there after school, doing his homework, and talking to his neighbor. The optician became Rafael's mentor. Rafael found himself helping out a lot in the store and after a while he began working there part time and during the summers. "It was this neighbor who first taught me the physics of optics."

After graduating high school Rafael continued in the optical field and went to work for an optometrist, the eye specialist who examines patients, diagnosing sight problems and prescribing corrective glasses. "Each person has a unique eye problem that has to be individually studied. It's never the same, and each person must be treated uniquely." Rafael found that he loved giving people the gift of sight.

He now knew he wanted to become an optician and began working towards that goal. He found the apprenticeship program at LensCrafters where he went on to get his license. Today he is the general manager for one of LensCrafters largest stores. "As general manager I oversee three departments—the retail store, the lab, and the optometrist department."

Rafael particularly loves to make glasses for the children who do not see clearly. For example, he tells this story: "Recently there was a little three-year-old girl for whom we made glasses. When I put them on her, she turned around to her mom and said, 'Mommy I can see you,' and then she touched her mom's face. It was very moving." Rafael considers himself very fortunate to be in a position to help people to see.

MEDICINE

127

These sections highlight an individual whose work or hobby is illustrative of the **Chapter Challenge. Physics At Work** speaks to the authenticity of the **Chapter Challenges**. The profiles illustrate how knowledge of physics is important and valuable in different walks of life. The choice of profiles span the ethnic, racial, and gender diversity that we find in our nation.

Active Physics & National Science Education Standards

Active Physics was designed and developed to provide teachers with instructional strategies that model the following from *The Standards*:

Guide and Facilitate Learning

- Focus and support inquiries while interacting with students.
- Orchestrate discourse among students about scientific ideas.
- Challenge students to accept and share responsibility for their own learning.
- Recognize & respond to student diversity; encourage all to participate fully in science learning.
- Encourage and model the skills of scientific inquiry as well as the curiosity openness to new ideas and data and skepticism that characterize science.

Engage in ongoing assessment of their teaching and student learning

- Use multiple methods & systematically gather data about student understanding & ability.
- Analyze assessment data to guide teaching.
- Guide students in self-assessment.

Design and manage learning environments that provide students with time, space and resources needed for learning science

- Structure the time available so students are able to engage in extended investigations.
- Create a setting for student work that is flexible and supportive of science inquiry.
- Make available tools, materials, media, & technological resources accessible to students.
- Identify and use resources outside of school.

Develop communities of science learners that reflect the intellectual rigor of scientific attitudes and social values conducive to science learning

- Display and demand respect for diverse ideas, skills, & experiences of students.
- Enable students to have significant voice in decisions about content & context of work & require students to take responsibility for the learning of all members of the community.
- Nurture collaboration among students.
- Structure and facilitate ongoing formal and informal discussion based on shared understanding of rules.
- Model and emphasize the skills, attitudes and values of scientific inquiry.

Assessment Standards

- Features claimed to be measured are actually measured.
- Students have adequate opportunity to demonstrate their achievement and understanding.
- Assessment tasks are authentic and developmentally appropriate, set in familiar context, and engaging to students with different interests and experiences.
- Assesses student understanding as well as knowledge.
- Improve classroom practice and plan curricula.
- Develop self-directed learners.

Active Physics Addresses Key NSES Recommendations

Active Physics addresses the following science curriculum recommendations:

Scenario-Driven

In each thematic unit there are three chapters, each requiring approximately three to four weeks of class time. Each chapter begins with an engaging scenario or project assignment that challenges the students and sets the stage for the learning activities and chapter assessments to follow. Chapter contents and activities are selectively aimed at providing the students with the knowledge and skills needed to address the introductory challenge, thus providing a natural content filter in the "less is more" curriculum.

Flexibly Formatted

Units are designed to stand alone, so teachers have the flexibility of changing the sequence of presentation of the units, omitting the entire unit, or not finishing all of the chapters within a unit. Although intended to serve as a full-year physics course, the units of *Active Physics* could be adapted to spread across a four-year period in an integrated high school curriculum.

Multiple Exposure Curriculum

The thematic nature of the course requires students to continually revisit fundamental physics principles throughout the year, extending and deepening their understanding of these principles as they apply them in new contexts. This repeated exposure fosters the retention and transferability of learning, and promotes the development of critical thinking skills.

Constructivist Approach

Students are continually asked to explore how they think about certain situations. As they investigate new situations, they are challenged to either explain observed phenomena using an existing paradigm or to develop a more consistent one. This approach can be helpful in including situations to abandon previously held notions in favor of the more powerful ideas and explanations offered by scientists.

Authentic Assessment

For the culmination of each chapter, students are required to demonstrate the usefulness of their newly acquired knowledge by adequately meeting the challenge posed in the chapter introduction. Students are then evaluated on the degree to which they accomplish this performance task. The curriculum also includes other methods and instruments for authentic assessments as well as non-traditional procedures for evaluating and rewarding desirable behaviors and skills.

Cooperative Grouping Strategies

Use of cooperative groups is integral to the course as students work together in small groups to acquire the knowledge and information needed to address the series of challenges presented through the chapter scenarios. Ample teacher guidance is provided to assure that effective strategies are used in group formation, function, and evaluation.

Math Skills Development/Graphing Calculators and Computer Spreadsheets

The presentation and use of math in *Active Physics* varies substantially from traditional high school physics courses. Math, primarily algebraic expressions, equations, and graphs is approached as a way of representing ideas symbolically. Students begin to recognize the usefulness of math as an aid in exploring and understanding the world about them. Finally, since many of the students in the target audience are insecure about their math backgrounds, the course engages and provides instruction for the use of graphing calculators and computer spreadsheets to provide math assistance.

Minimal Reading Required

Because it is assumed that the target audience reads only what is absolutely necessary, the entire course is activity-driven. Reading passages are presented mainly within the context of the activities, and are written at the ninth grade level.

Use of Educational Technologies

Videos which capture students' attention explore a variety of the *Active Physics* topics. Opportunities are also provided for students to produce their own videos in order to record and analyze events. Computer software programs make use of various interfacing devices.

Problem Solving

For the curriculum to be both meaningful and relevant to the target population, problem solving related to technological applications and related issues is an essential component of the course. Problem solving ranges from simple numerical solutions where one result is expected, to more involved decision-making situations where multiple alternatives must be compared.

Challenging Learning Extensions

Throughout the text, a variety of **Stretching Exercises** are provided for more motivated students. These extensions range from more challenging design tasks, to enrichment readings, to intriguing and unusual problems. Many of the extensions take advantage of the frequent opportunities the curriculum provides for oral and written expression of student ideas.

Cooperative Learning

Benefits of Cooperative Learning

Cooperative learning requires you to organize and structure a lesson so that students work with other students to jointly accomplish a task. Group learning is an essential part of balanced methodology. It should be blended with whole-class instruction and individual study to meet a variety of learning styles and expectations as well as maintain a high level of student involvement.

Cooperative learning has been thoroughly researched and agreement has been reached on a number of results. Cooperative learning:

- promotes trust and risk-taking
- elevates self-esteem
- encourages acceptance of individual differences
- develops social skills
- permits a combination of a wide range of backgrounds and abilities
- provides an inviting atmosphere
- promotes a sense of community
- develops group and individual responsibility
- reduces the time on a task
- results in better attendance
- produces a positive effect on student achievement
- develops key employability skills

As with any learning approach, some students will benefit more than others from cooperative learning. Therefore, you may question as to what extent you should use cooperative learning strategies. It is important to involve the student in helping decide which type of learning approaches they prefer, and to what extent each is used in the classroom. When students have a say in their learning, they will accept to a greater extent any method which you choose to use.

Phases of Cooperative Learning Lessons

Organizational Pre-lesson Decisions

What academic and social objectives will be emphasized? In other words, what content and skills are to be learned and what interaction skills are to be emphasized or practiced?

What will be the group size? Or, what is the most appropriate group size to facilitate the achievement of the academic and social objectives? This will depend on the amount of individual involvement expected (small groups promote more individual involvement), the task (diverse thinking is promoted by larger groups), nature of the task or materials available and the time available (shorter time demands smaller groupings to promote involvement).

Who will make up the different groups? Teacher-selected groups usually have the best mix, but this can only happen after the teacher gets to know his/her students well enough to know who works well together. Heterogeneous groupings are most successful in that all can learn through active participation. The duration of the groups' existence may have some bearing on deciding the membership of groups.

How should the room be arranged? Practicing routines where students move into their groups quickly and quietly is an important aspect. Having students face-to-face is important. The teacher should still be able to move freely among the groups.

What Materials and/or Rewards Might be Prepared in Advance?

Setting the Lesson

Structure for Positive Interdependence: When students feel they need one another, they are more likely to work together--goal interdependence becomes important. Class interdependence can be promoted by setting class goals which all teams must achieve in order for class success.

Explanation of the Academic Task: Clear explanations and sometimes the use of models can help the students. An explanation of the relevance of the activity is importance. Checks for clear understanding can be done either before the groups form or after, but they are necessary for delimiting frustrations.

Explanation of Criteria for Success: Groups should know how their level of success will be determined.

Structure for Individual Accountability: The use of individual follow-up activities for tasks or social skills will provide for individual accountability.

Specification of Desired Social Behaviors: Definition and explanations of the importance of values of social skills will promote student practice and achievement of the different skills.

Monitoring/Intervening During Group Work

Through monitoring students' behaviors, intervention can be used more appropriately. Students can be involved in the monitoring by being "a team observer," but only when the students have a very clear understanding of the behavior being monitored.

Interventions to increase chances for success in completing the task or activity and for the teaching of collaborative skills should be used as necessary--they should not be interruptions. This means that the facilitating teacher should be moving among the groups as much as possible. During interventions, the problem should be turned back to the students as often as possible, taking care not to frustrate them.

Evaluating the Content and Process of Cooperative Group Work

Assessment of the achievement of content objectives should be completed by both the teacher and the students. Students can go back to their groups after an assignment to review the aspects in which they experienced difficulties.

When assessing the accomplishment of social objectives, two aspects are important: how well things proceeded and where/how improvements might be attempted. Student involvement in this evaluation is a very basic aspect of successful cooperative learning programs.

Organizing and Monitoring Groups

An optimum size of group for most activities appears to be four; however, for some tasks, two may be more efficient. Heterogeneous groups organized by the teacher are usually the most sucessful. The teacher will need to decide what factors should be considered in forming the heterogeneous groups. Factors which can be considered are: academic achievement, cultural background, language proficiency, sex, age, learning style, and even personality type.

Level of academic achievement is probably the simplest and initially the best way to form groups. Sort the students on the basis of marks on a particular task or on previous year's achievement. Then choose a student from each quartile to form a group. Once formed, groups should be flexible. Continually monitor groups for compatability and make adjustments as required.

Students should develop an appreciation that it is a privilege to belong to a group. Remove from group work any student who is a poor participant or one who is repeatedly absent. These individuals can then be assigned the same tasks to be completed in the same time line as a group. You may also wish to place a ten percent reduction on all group work that is completed individually.

The chart on the next page presents some possible group structures and their functions.

What Does Cooperative Learning Look Like?

During a cooperative learning situation, students should be assigned a variety of roles related to the particular task at hand. Following is a list of possible roles that students may be given. It is important that students are given the opportunity of assuming a number of different roles over the course of a semester.

Leader:

Assigns roles for the group. Gets the group started and keeps the group on task.

Organizer:

Helps focus discussion and ensures that all members of the group contribute to the discussion. The organizer ensures that all of the equipment has been gathered and that the group completes all parts of the activity.

Recorder:

Provides written procedures when required, diagrams where appropriate and records data. The recorder must work closely with the organizer to ensure that all group members contribute.

Researcher:

Seeks written and electronic information to support the findings of the group. In addition, where appropriate, the researcher will develop and test prototypes. The researcher will also exchange information gathered among different groups.

Encourager:

Encourages all group members to participate. Values contributions and supports involvement.

Checker:

Checks that the group has answered all the questions and the group members agree upon and understand the answers.

Diverger:

Seeks alternative explanations and approaches. The task of the diverger is to keep the discussion open. "Are other explanations possible?"

Some Possible Group Structures and Their Functions*

	Structure	Brief Description	Academic and Social Functions
Team Building	Round-robin	Each student in turn shares something with his/her teammates.	Expressing ideas and opinions, creating stories. Equal participation, getting acquainted with each other.
Class Building	Corners	Each student moves to a group in a corner or location as determined by the teacher through specified alternatives. Students discuss within groups, then listen to and paraphrase ideas from other groups.	Seeing alternative hypotheses, values, and problem solving approaches. Knowing and respecting differing points of view.
Mastery	Numbered heads together	The teacher asks a question, students consult within their groups to make sure that each member knows the answer. Then one student answers for the group in response to the number called out by the teacher.	Review, checking for knowledge comprehension, analysis, and divergent thinking. Tutoring.
	Color coded co-op cards	Students memorize facts using a flash card game or an adaption. The game is structured so that there is a maximum probability for success at each step, moving from short to long-term memory. Scoring is based on improvement.	Memorizing facts. Helping, praising.
	Pairs check	Students work in pairs within groups of four. Within pairs students alternate-one solves a problem while the other coaches. After every problem or so, the pair checks to see if they have the same answer as the other pair.	Practicing skills. Helping, praising.
Concept Development	Three-step interview	Students interview each other in pairs, first one way, then the other. Each student shares information learned during interviews with the group.	Sharing personal information such as hypotheses, views on an issue, or conclusions from a unit. Participation, involvement.
	Think-pair-share	Students think to themselves on a topic provided by the teacher; they pair up with another student to discuss it; and then share their thoughts with the class.	Generating and revising hypotheses, inductive and deductive reasoning, and application. Participation and involvement.
	Team word-webbing	Students write simultaneously on a piece of paper, drawing main concepts, supporting elements, and bridges representing the relation of concepts/ideas.	Analysis of concept into components, understanding multiple relations among ideas, and differentiating concepts. Role-taking.
Multifunctional	Roundtable	Each student in turn writes one answer as a paper and a pencil are passed around the group. With simultaneous roundtable, more than one pencil and paper are used.	Assessing print knowledge, practicing skills, recalling information, and creating designs. Team building, participation of all.
	Partners	Students work in pairs to create or master content. They consult with partners from other teams. Then they share their products or understandings with the other partner pair in their team.	Mastery and presentation of new material, concept development. Presentation and communication skills.
	Jigsaw	Each student from each team becomes an "expert" on one topic area by working with members from other teams assigned to the same topic area. On returning to their own teams, each one teaches the other members of the group and students are assessed on all aspects of the topic.	Acquisition and presentation of new material review and informed debate. Independence, status equalization.

* Adapted from Spencer Kagan (1990), "*The Structural Approach to Cooperative Learning,*" Educational Leadership, December 1989/January 1990.

Active Listener:

Repeats or paraphrases what has been said by the different members of the group.

Idea Giver:

Contributes ideas, information, and opinions.

Materials Manager:

Collects and distributes all necessary material for the group.

Observer:

Completes checklists for the group.

Questioner:

Seeks information, opinions, explanations, and justifications from other members of the group.

Reader:

Reads any textual material to the group.

Reporter:

Prepares and/or makes a report on behalf of the group.

Summarizer:

Summarizes the work, conclusions, or results of the group so that they can be presented coherently.

Timekeeper:

Keeps the group members focused on the task and keeps time.

Safety Manager:

Reponsible for ensuring that safety measures are being followed, and the equipment is clean prior to and at the end of the activity.

Group Assessment

Assessment should not end with a group mark. Students and their parents have a right to expect marks to reflect the students' individual contributions to the task. It is impossible for you as the instructor to continuously monitor and record the contribution of each individual student. Therefore, you will need to rely on the students in the group to assign individual marks as merited.

There are a number of ways that this can be accomplished. The group mark can be multiplied by the number of students in the group, and then the total mark can be divided among the students, as shown in the graphics that follow.

Activity:____________________

Group Mark: 8/10

Number in Group: 4

Total Marks: 32/40

Distribution of Marks

Student's Name	Mark	Signature
Ahmed	8/10	____________________
Jasmin	8/10	____________________
Mike	7/10	____________________
Tabitha	9/10	____________________

Another way to share group marks is to assign a factor to each student. The mark factors must total the number of students in the group. The group mark is then multiplied by this factor to arrive at each student's individual mark which best represents their contribution to the task, as shown below.

Activity:____________________

Group Mark: 8/10

Number in Group: 4

Mark Factors and Individual Marks

Student's Name	Mark Factor	Individual Mark	Signature
Ahmed	1.0	8/10	____________________
Jasmin	1.0	8/10	____________________
Mike	0.9	7.2/10	____________________
Tabitha	1.1	8.8/10	____________________
Total Mark Factor	4		

In any case, students must sign to show that they are in agreement with the way the individual marks were assigned.

You may also wish to provide students with an assessment rubric similar to the one shown which they can use to assess the manner in which the group worked together.

Assessment Rubric for Group Work: Individual Assessment of the Group

Individual's name: ______________________________

Names of group members: ______________________________

Name of activity: ______________________________

Circle the appropriate number: #1 is excellent, #2 is good, #3 is average, and #4 is poor.

1. The group worked cooperatively. Everyone assumed a role and carried it out.	1	2	3	4
2. Everyone contributed to the discussion. Everyone's opinion was valued.	1	2	3	4
3. Everyone assumed the roles assigned to them.	1	2	3	4
4. The group was organized. Materials were gathered, distributed, and collected.	1	2	3	4
5. Problems were addressed as a group.	1	2	3	4
6. All parts of the task were completed within the time assigned.	1	2	3	4
Comments:				

If you were to repeat the activity, what things would you change?

1

Home Chapter 1- Designing the Universal Dwelling

National Science Education Standards

Chapter Summary

Homes for Everyone establishes the scenario with a quest for a universal dwelling that meets the need for homes in diverse environments. Students are challenged to design a home that can be constructed quickly and simply at a remote building site and should use the least amount of materials to create the most living space. And, it should be energy-efficient!

To gain understanding of the science principles necessary to meet this challenge, students work collaboratively on activities in which they learn about energy transfer, solar energy, the iterative process of engineering design, and how to use collected data to refine designs. These experiences engage students in the following content identified in the *National Science Education Standards.*

Content Standards

Unifying Concepts

- Evidence, models and explanations
- Constancy, change, and measurement
- Form and function

Science as Inquiry

- Identify questions & concepts that guide scientific investigations
- Use technology and mathematics to improve investigations
- Formulate & revise scientific explanations & models using logic and evidence

Science and Technology

- Abilities of technological design
- Understanding about science and technology

Science in Personal and Social Perspectives

- Natural resources
- Environmental quality
- Science and technology in local, national, and global challenges

Physical

- Conservation of energy and increase in disorder
- Interactions of energy and matter

Key Physics Concepts and Skills

Activity Summaries	Physics Principles
Activity One: Factors in Designing the "Universal Dwelling" Examining characteristics of houses designed for a variety of geographic locations introduces students to the concept of form and function in a home. They then list features necessary for a universal dwelling.	• Form and function • Analyzing and interpreting data
Activity Two: What is the "Right Size" for a Universal Dwelling? After researching and analyzing data on living space in sample homes, students plan the design of their universal dwelling and calculate the necessary dimensions of each room based on its function. They conclude by drawing a floor plan.	• Analyzing and interpreting data • Models, measurements, and scale
Activity Three: The Shape of the Universal Dwelling Students examine their floor plans, applying knowledge of area, perimeter, and volume to decide if the planned living space is maximized while building materials are minimized. They then refine their plans to reflect what was learned from investigating size as compared to form and function of rooms in other dwellings.	• Applying measurement and data to predictions
Activity Four: Solar Heat Flow in the "Universal Dwelling" This activity confronts students with implications of shape and size on occupants of the home. Students construct a model of the home, then use a heat lamp and temperature probe to investigate interior light and heat during a simulated day and night. This also introduces the use of passive solar designs for light and heat in the home.	• Radiant energy • Energy transfer • Passive solar heating
Activity Five: The Role of Insulation... Students expand their understanding of solar heat by exploring the affect of different types of insulation in an experiment with hot and cold water. They apply data collected to plan how to maintain a stable temperature inside the home. Students read to learn about transfer of radiant energy through conduction and convection.	• Energy transfer • Heat conduction • Heating and cooling curves
Activity Six: Investigating Insulation Placement... Students collect and compare temperature data during simulated 24-hour cycles for different types, thickness, and placements of insulation in the ceilings and walls of their model homes. Interpretation of this data combined with new understanding of heat loss and gain is used to further refine design of the home.	• Energy transfer • Heat loss through conduction
Activity Seven: The Role of Windows... Light and ventilation are the focus of this activity as students plan and test placement, size, and materials of windows. As they continue experimenting with passive solar, they are challenged to again consider heat loss when an insulated wall is replaced with a window.	• Energy transfer • Heat loss through conduction • Passive solar heating • Passive solar lighting
Activity Eight: Investigating Overhangs and Awnings Students investigate the affect of the angle of the sun's rays in different geographic regions in a simulation with heat lamps and temperature probes. Overhangs and awnings are added to the house to compensate for increased interior temperature. Students then have the opportunity to further refine the design of their dwelling to maximize use of passive solar for light and heat.	• Energy transfer • Passive solar heating • Passive solar lighting

Equipment List For Chapter One

QTY	TO SERVE	ACTIVITY	ITEM	COMMENT
1	Individual	All	Calculator, basic	One per student best; one per group minimum
1	Individual	1	Card, 3x5	For Activity One, Physics To Go assignment
1	Group	4, 6, 7 ,8	Clock	
1	Group	4, 6, 7 ,8	Cutting tool	Scissor, “Exacto” knife or single edge razor blade
1	Individual	1	Foot ruler or yardstick	Loan to student for assignment, if necessary
1	Group	4, 6, 7 ,8	Heat lamp, approx. 250 watt, & 120-v fixture	Infrared reflector bulb, or standard clear bulb & reflector
1	Group	5	Hot water bath	Sufficient to hold 3 metal cans simultaneously
1	Group	5	Ice water bath	Sufficient to hold 3 metal cans simultaneously
1	Group	5	Insulating material (1 kind per group)	Sufficient amount to fill metal cans used for activity
1	Group	4, 6, 7, 8	Masking tape	Groups may share a roll
1	Group	4, 6, 7, 8	Meter stick	To measure distance from lamp to model home
1	Group	3	Piece corrugated cardboard, 8-1/2 x 11	To serve as backing when sticking pins in grid paper
1	Group	6	Piece corrugated cardboard, approx. 2 sq. ft.	To insulate ceiling and walls of model home
1	Group	4, 8	Piece tagboard, approx. 2 sq. ft.	A file folder will serve
8	Group	3	Pins	Common, florist or dissecting pins will serve
1	Group	8	Protractor	For measuring “sun” (heat lamp) angle
1	Group	4, 6, 7, 8	Ring stand and clamp	To mount and aim heat lamp
1	Class	7	Roll clear plastic wrap	Serves as window material for model home
1	Group	4, 6, 7, 8	Ruler, inch scale	Markings 1/8 inch or smaller
1	Group	5	Set of 3 metal cans having varying diameters	Such as small, medium, large coffee cans
1	Class	1	Set of photos of dwellings (optional)	To augment photos shown on text page H4
1	Group	3	Sheet 1-inch grid paper, 8-1/2 x 11	Substitute: Quad ruled 4 lines/inch, darken every 4th line
1	Individual	4, 5, 6, 7 ,8	Sheet graph paper	
1	Group	3	String, 20-inch loop	Students may measure and prepare loop
1	Group	4, 5, 6, 7 ,8	Thermometer or temperature probe	Celsius temperature in -10 to 110 range

Organizer for Materials Available in Teacher's Edition

Activity in Student Text	Additional Material	Alternative / Optional Activities
ACTIVITY ONE: Factors in Designing the "Universal Dwelling" p.H4	Floor Plan for a Home: Floor Area of a Home pgs. 20-21	
ACTIVITY TWO: What is the "Right Size" for a Universal Dwelling? p.H8	Floor Space for a Home pgs. 29-30	
ACTIVITY THREE: The Shape of the Universal Dwelling p.H13	Square Grid Paper p. 41	Activity Three A: Exploring Surface Area-to-Volume Ratio p. 42
ACTIVITY FOUR: Solar Heat Flow in the "Universal Dwelling" p.H19	Grid for Heating/Cooling Data p. 52	Activity Four A: How Does Location Affect Energy Demands? pgs. 53-54 Activity Four B: What Shape is Most Effective for Heat Storage? pgs. 55-57
ACTIVITY FIVE: The Role of Insulation... p.H24		Activity Five A: Transmission of Heat pgs. 65-66
ACTIVITY SIX: Investigating Insulation Placement p.H29	R Values for Insulation p. 75	
ACTIVITY SEVEN: The Role of Windows... p.H33	R Values for Windows p. 83	
ACTIVITY EIGHT: Investigating Overhangs and Awnings p.H37	Sun Location at Seasonal Times pgs. 91-93	

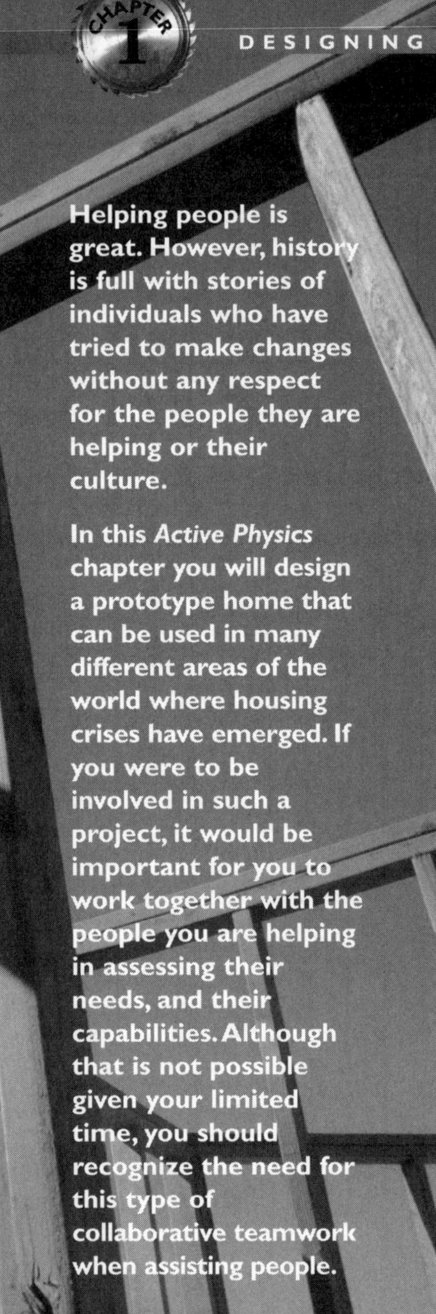

Scenario

Imagine you and your team members are part of an international group called Homes For Everyone (HFE). The purpose of your organization is to address the growing housing shortage in many areas throughout the world. You have recently been sent to work with a self-help community group in a far-away area. Here is a letter you might write home.

Dear Mom and Dad,

Greetings! I've finally settled into my new home. Sometimes I think that I'm not in another country but on another planet. Everything here is so different. Sorry about the water splotches on this letter. It's pouring rain outside, and the roof is leaking. I have to remind myself that at least I have a roof over my head. Many people here have lost their homes from the last hurricane and are crowded into their relatives' already crowded spaces.

We're trying to figure out what we can do to help with the housing situation here. We're still not sure what the solution is. Right now I'm trying to learn more about these people who have been so generous and gracious to me. When we arrived the whole village got together to greet our group. I felt so honored! I expect the same kind of welcome from my family when I return home!

Tomorrow we are going to start looking around. I'll keep you posted on what we discover and on our progress. Signing off for now. Miss you all!

Love,

Kim

HFE plans to design a "universal dwelling" to meet the need for homes in diverse environments. The group needs a design that can be constructed quickly and simply at the building site. The design should also use the least amount of materials to create the most living space. To make mass production possible, the dwelling design should be uniform, but you should be able to make simple changes to meet local conditions. It should be energy efficient in any climate.

Chapter and Challenge Overview

In this chapter, the students will be designing a home that will be energy-efficient, easily and inexpensively constructed, adaptable for many different climates, as well as being aesthetically pleasing.

In the beginning of the chapter the students will brainstorm as to the features, functions and other factors affecting the shape, size, and other attributes of a home. From there they will work their way through a designing process, while considering a number of different factors. Even though this is not meant to be an all-inclusive design, the students will get an appreciation for the need for looking at these issues when designing a home.

HOME

Challenge

After completing the eight activities in this chapter you will be challenged to do the following to present to the HFE Architectural Committee:

1. Develop scale drawings of the floor plan and all side views of the universal dwelling. Following are specifications for the drawings:
   a) The drawings should be done on a scale of 1 inch = 4 feet (1:48).
   b) The scale drawings should include all sides of the house, showing roof lines, roof overhangs, and placement and dimensions of all windows for a selected climatic region and culture.
   c) The scale drawings should show the floor plans of the living spaces and include specifications for the thickness of the wall, types of insulation and their thickness, and kinds and types of windows or ventilation openings.
   d) The plans should show the geographic orientation of the house (in which direction the house should face).

2. Write a two-page explanation which gives your reasons for the following:
   a) your choices for the shape and dimensions of the dwelling;
   b) the energy consideration that went into the design of the dwelling;
   c) the changes that could be made to the basic design to take into account different climates and cultures;
   d) the things you included to make your dwelling attractive.

Criteria

The HFE Architectural Committee will use criteria similiar to the ones below in evaluating your drawings and your written presentation. Discuss and decide as a class the exact criteria the committee should use.

- **(20%) The drawings and written presentation should meet all specifications listed in the Challenge.**
- **(10%) The drawings and written presentation should explain how you considered surface-to-volume ratio in your design.**
- **(20%) The written presentation should explain how the house will accommodate differing seasonal and climatic conditions in terms of heating and cooling. It should also show you have a basis for scaling the dwelling appropriate to the family and culture for which it is designed.**
- **(20%) The design of the roof and the placement and dimensions of windows should account for climatic, solar, and latitude considerations, and should show you have accounted for the advantages and disadvantages of windows.**
- **(20%) The placement and kind of insulation materials and thickness you choose should show you know the principles which make insulation effective.**
- **(10%) The appearance of your house and the interior layout should show consideration for fundamental human needs.**

H 3

Assessment Rubric for Challenge

The following rubric may be used to assess group work during Chapter 1. Each member of the group can evaluate the manner in which the group worked to solve problems with the challenge. This can constitute part of their mark, or can be incorporated in the criteria for evaluation.

This would be a peer evaluation. Emphasize that a mark with no comment is useless. Students must be able to justify their evaluation to the teacher.

Total = 12 marks

1. Low level – indicates minimum effort or effectiveness.
2. Average – acceptable standard has been achieved, but the group could have worked more effectively if better organized.
3. Good – this rating indicates a superior effort. Although improvements might have been made, the group was on task all of the time and completed all parts of the activity.

The following is a possible guideline for evaluation of the Challenge.

Place a check mark in the appropriate box. Each line may represent 5%. If you would rather, you could mark it holistically, where all the statements taken together earn a mark out of 30%, for example.

You may change the criteria, by adding or deleting any of the points determined by a class decision. For example, if you have a class that has had CAD training, those students might decide to put less emphasis on the actual scale drawings, and more emphasis on the written presentation.

Descriptor	**Values**		
1. The group worked cooperatively to design the HFE home.	1	2	3
2. Data was collected and recorded in an organized fashion in data tables in their logs.	1	2	3
3. The group was organized. Materials were collected and the problems were addressed by the entire group.	1	2	3
4. The two-page explanation was a good summary of the groups efforts, with input from all members.	1	2	3

For use with *Home*, Chapter 1

Descriptor	Yes	No
Scale drawings (30%)		
scale of 1:48		
show all sides of house, roof lines, roof overhangs		
show placement of windows including dimensions		
show floor plans of living space (thickness of walls, kinds of windows, etc.)		
geographic placement of home is clear		
drawing encompasses understanding of surface-to-volume ratio		
Written presentation (20%)		
clear statement for choice of shape and dimensions		
consideration of energy requirements for different climatic regions		
clear statement of changes to be considered depending on different climates, cultures and family		
any additional solar energy trapping ideas included		
Window and roof design (20%)		
clear statements of climatic, solar and latitude regions chosen		
clear statements as to pros and cons of chosen roof design		
clear statements for and against the choice of windows		
diagram reflects accurate understanding of placement and sizes of windows, and the area where they are located relative to the climatic region		
Insulation (20%)		
clear statements of type of insulation used		
clear statements of choice of insulation based on climatic region		
clear understanding of principles of insulative materials		
diagrams show accurate thickness of insulation		
Appearance (10%)		
appearance of home is pleasant		
interior layout reflects consideration of fundamental human needs		

What is in The Sun's Joules CD-ROM for Chapter 1?

The Sun's Joules CD-ROM is a comprehensive collection of information resources developed by the Center for Renewable Energy and Sustainable Technology (CREST), funded by the U.S. Department of Energy and directed by the National Renewable Energy Laboratory (NREL). It provides easy access to a great deal of information about new technological advances in utilizing energy resources. As a supplemental resource, it will provide enjoyable enhancement materials to the basic concepts and activities of the chapter. Its features include: a glossary with definitions of energy-related terms; an index with information on its main topic areas and a list of references for each of its topic areas.

One of the Main Menu items of the CD-ROM is entitled "Passive Solar" and contains a wealth of information that will directly help students in their designing of the Universal Home. Also, much of the information on the disc relates directly to the Stretching Exercises and Inquiry Investigations found in the chapter. For example, in Activity Seven the Stretching Exercise specifically asks students to find out about passive solar heating for homes and asks them a number of related questions.

What is in The Green Home CD-ROM for Chapter 1?

In The Green Home CD-ROM students are given the opportunity to walk through a digital home exploring important environmental and technology features that will help them in their Universal Home designs. They will therefore find this to be a valuable resource as they think about the many different types of design issues that they face in the chapter. For example one of the "topic" areas found in the walkthrough is entitled "Exterior Wall Construction" which is full of information and resources that will to help students in their inquires for Activity Five "The Role of Insulation."

There are also a number of interactive activities in which students manipulate various elements relating to one or more aspects of home design. Each activity has several input variables, for instance in the "Whole House Activity" students can explore the effects of house size, window configuration, window types, insulation, and location of the house (to name a few of the variables) on energy consumption. The Green Home CD-ROM is a wonderful enhancement resource to this chapter's challenge and activities.

What is in the Physics InfoMall for Chapter 1?

This entire book in *Active Physics* concerns the physics of the home. Many physics topics are discussed within this theme, and apply to the book as a whole more than to a single activity or chapter. These include energy conservation, alternate energy sources, and power. The Physics InfoMall CD-ROM contains many resources that address exactly these issues.

For example, look in the Textbook Trove at Madalyn Avery's *Household Physics: A Textbook for College Students in Home Economics*. Many topics from physics are discussed within the context of the home - ideal for this *Active Physics* book. Such topics include work, energy, and power; water supply and sewage disposal; heat and thermometers; heat transfer; refrigeration; air conditioning; and electricity. This book can provide information to augment *Active Physics.*

Another great resource on the CD-ROM is *Energy: Insights from Physics*, which contains sections specifically on home energy conservation and home heating. Other sections of this book should be equally useful. You can find out what a "degree-day" is, the effect on energy use, and how to calculate degree-days.

Chapter 11 of *The Fascination of Physics* describes why a fireplace can increase your home heating costs, not counting the cost of the firewood itself!

Articles describing use of energy can be found in the Articles and Abstracts Attic. For example, "Efficient Use of Energy," *Physics Today*, vol. 28, issue 8, discusses use of energy and what efficiency means. The topic is addressed again in *Physics Today*, vol. 33, issue 2 with "Efficient use of energy revisited." Since this topic is covered in chapters 1 and 2 of *Home* (and perhaps a bit in Chapter 3), these articles may be a great place to look. Keep in mind that these are not the only articles and information available on the InfoMall - this is just a place for you to start your search for information.

As you can well imagine, many of the resources on the InfoMall discuss the physics of the home, but often only as physics topics, leaving the home out of consideration. The references mentioned above are some of the resources that make the direct reference to the home, but the physics topics themselves are contained in most of the other resources on the CD-ROM; for example, energy is discussed in every physics textbook. However, some of the advanced books discuss the energy of subatomic particles without much development of the energy concept. With a little forethought, you can find any of these common topics discussed abundantly on the InfoMall.

Perhaps more than any other chapter in *Home*, Chapter 1 concerns itself with solar energy. Perform a search of the entire CD-ROM with the words "solar energy" and you will find hundreds of hits (over 400 in the Articles and Abstract Attics alone!). These include discussions of pro-solar, anti-nuclear energy; conversion of solar energy to electrical energy; and much more. Do this search and see what you find.

NOTES

1

ACTIVITY ONE
Factors in Designing the "Universal Dwelling"

Background Information

The main concept involved in Activity One is the calculation of the surface area of a two-dimensional object from measurements of the object's dimensions. Applied to determining the total surface area of the floor(s) of a home in Activity One, the shape of the object (floor) involved usually encountered will be a rectangle:

Area of a rectangle $(ft)^2$ = Length (ft) x Width (ft)

The foot (ft) is used as the unit of length in the above equation because the standard unit of measurement for expressing the floor area of a home in the U.S. is square feet $(ft)^2$.

Complex floor areas of homes may be "broken up" into simple rectangular sub-areas and the dimensions (length and width) of each sub-area can be measured. The surface area of each sub-area then can be calculated and then the total area of the home can be calculated by addition of the surface areas of all of the sub-areas.

The outcome of the calculations will depend on "rounding off" rules used in the process of measuring the lengths and widths of rectangular areas in a home. Also, principles of precision, accuracy and significant figures could be applied to calculation of the floor area of a home. However, the overarching principle suggested to be applied with students at this stage is "keep it simple." The main idea is for students to get a gross estimate of the floor area of their home as part of the sample represented by the homes of class members.

Equations for calculating the surface areas of other two-dimensional shapes which may be needed now and probably will be needed later are:

Area of triangle = 1/2 x Base x Height

Area of circle = π x $(\text{Radius})^2$

The surface areas of very complex two-dimensional shapes for which equations may be difficult or impossible to find can be determined in several other ways:

- The shape can be superimposed on a grid paper and the number of grid squares bounded within the perimeter can be counted while estimating, if necessary, fractional parts of grid squares "cut" by the perimeter line at the edges of the shape. Knowing the scale of the grid (how many square feet, for example, each grid square is "worth") the total surface area can be determined.
- The shape can be superimposed on a grid paper, "cut out" along the perimeter with scissors and then weighed on a sensitive balance (perhaps available from a chemistry teacher). Similarly, a grid square can be cut out from the paper and weighed (or, for more accuracy, 10 grid squares, dividing the weight by 10). Dividing the weight of the complex shape by the weight of one grid square will give the area of the shape in units of "grid squares."
- An instrument called a polar planimeter (not often found in schools) exists which gives a readout of the surface area of any shape when the instrument is used to trace the perimeter (some computer software may provide similar capability).

Active-ating the Physics InfoMall

In Physics To Go, the concept of "area" is important. Students sometimes have difficulty with this basic concept. A Compound Search on the entire InfoMall (which took less than 30 seconds!) using the words "area" and "student difficulties" uncovers area numbers of good references. CAUTION: The term "area" is often used to describe topics, as in "this area if physics" and will often result in search hits that do not apply to what you may be looking for.

For example, in the introduction to Arnold B. Arons' *A Guide to Introductory Physics Teaching* (in the Book Basement) it is said that students may "have never been asked to define area." All they have ever done is calculate areas of regular figures such as squares, rectangles, parallelograms, or triangles, using memorized formulas that they no longer connect with the operation of counting the unit squares, even though this connection may have been originally asserted. As a teacher, you cannot assume that students fully understand a concept such as area, but with the knowledge that some have difficulty, you may be prepared to address such difficulties.

As you may guess, most physics textbooks assume that students can calculate and understand areas, and for this reason most texts use the concept without explaining it. Nor do many of the books provide problems that explicitly allow students to practice calculations.

Planning for the Activity

Time Requirements

Allow approximately 30 to 40 minutes to carry the brainstorming activity to completion.

Materials needed

For the class:

- Optional: photos of a variety of dwellings to augment those shown in text.

For each student:

- 3x5 cards (for assignment)
- 1-foot ruler (loan for assignment if necessary)

Advance Preparation and Setup

None is required.

Teaching Notes

Before proceeding with the brainstorming activity, plan to reserve about 10 minutes at the end of the class period to give instructions for Physics To Go; the data which students will gather during Physics To Go is critical for tomorrow's class.

The success of the brainstorming activity strongly depends on each student understanding the rules and purpose. Therefore, it is suggested that the teacher read the procedure to the class and provide any necessary clarification. Further, the teacher should suggest that, within each group, one student should serve as recorder and another student should serve as leader. The leader's responsibility is to keep the group on task, observing the rules. The recorder's responsibility is to write down each characteristic given by group members. During the brainstorming session, you should "circulate," monitoring interactions within groups and, if necessary, clarifying rules. But you should not interject your ideas about characteristics of dwellings.

Set a time limit (perhaps 15 minutes) for brainstorming the initial list of 100 items, and have the students begin. When the time limit is reached, stop the brainstorming activity and direct groups to proceed to narrowing and separating the list into two lists, and to answer the questions; at the same time, announce that you will "cut off" work on For You To Do ten minutes before the end of class to allow time to give directions for Physics To Go.

CAUTION: Some students may be sensitive about having their homes compared to others (question 8 in Physics To Go). Emphasize that the information will be kept anonymous.

Distribute a 3x5 card to each student, and point out that the card is to be used to record data about each student's home as shown on Page 7. Stress that the data is needed for tomorrow's class. Use the overhead transparency of a house floor plan to show an example of how to measure and calculate the floor areas of living spaces. Be sure that all students have a ruler to use for measurements at home — if needed, a string knotted at each foot of length could be provided.

1

Activity Overview

This activity begins the chapter with the students examining different styles of houses from different areas of the world in order to get ideas of how they will design their HFE homes. When building a home, there are many different criteria to consider. This activity will get them thinking about these criteria.

Student Objectives

Students will:

- identify essential characteristics which all human dwellings have in common.
- identify characteristics of human dwellings which vary with environment.
- measure the dimensions of living spaces in the student's home.
- calculate the floor areas of living spaces in the student's home.

ANSWERS FOR THE TEACHER ONLY

What Do You Think?

Students will have an opportunity to be creative in their answers. Some of the things they should notice that are common are they provide shelter from water, sun and wind, all have roof openings, windows, supports for the roof, walls, prominent entrance, two stories, etc.

They are alike in that they have supports for the roof, walls, etc. They are different in that they are built of different materials. One is built on stilts, one is built into the side of a mountain, thatched roof in one, the size of each seems to be different, etc.

DESIGNING THE UNIVERSAL DWELLING

Activity One

Factors in Designing the "Universal" Dwelling

WHAT DO YOU THINK?

All humans have a basic need for shelter. Examine the pictures of dwellings shown on this page.

- **What are some common characteristics of all these dwellings?**
- **How are they alike? How are they different?**

Record your ideas about these questions in your *Active Physics log*. Be prepared to discuss your reponses with your small group and the class.

HOME 

FOR YOU TO DO

1. "Brainstorming" is a process in which you simply generate a large number of ideas. The rule of brainstorming is that all ideas should be accepted and no idea should be evaluated or thrown out. With your group, brainstorm a list of the characteristics of a "universal dwelling" for people anywhere in the world. In this case, set your team's goal at 100 different characteristics. Use the following questions to guide your brainstorming.
   - a) What are the functions of a home?
   - b) What features are essential to any home?
   - c) What are some of the factors that determine the size and shape of a home?
2. After brainstorming, narrow the lists down and develop two lists of ten or less items each. The first list should identify essential characteristics that should be present in all homes. The second list should identify special characteristics that are absolutely necessary for some environments, but that are non-essential in other environments.
   - a) Record the lists in your log using these two headings:
     - Essential characteristics of the universal dwelling.
     - Characteristics that must be modified for various climactic and cultural conditions.
3. Return to your group and answer the following questions in your log:
   - a) What things do you need to know about people, family sizes, and lifestyles in order to design a universal dwelling?
   - b) How large should a universal dwelling be? How could you make an educated guess?
   - c) How many of your "essential characteristics of the universal dwelling" require an energy input of some kind?

ANSWERS

For You To Do

1. a) Students' answers will vary. Functions may include: shelter from cold/warm environment; safety; protection from elements and undesirables; comfort; status; etc.

   b) Some of the features essential to any home might include: kitchen; bedrooms; able to cook, clean, heat, use warm water, etc.

   c) Many factors can be included. Some are: cost, location, local bylaws, types of material, climate, environment, type of ground, etc.

2. a) Student data

3. a) Students' answers will vary greatly, but expect some of the following: shift work, pets, number of people in family, whether there is an extended family, do they go on vacation a lot, are they involved in community activities, etc.

   b) Student will probably assign based on his/her own experience. Expect much variation.

   c) Some of the essential characteristics which may require energy input of some kind are: pumping of water, cooling/heating the house, hot water, electricity, gas or other form of heating energy, etc.

1

ANSWERS

Physics To Go

1. a) Student input.

   b) If the students live in cold climates, some of the features would include, double-pane windows, storm windows, insulated walls and ceilings, no windows on North side of house, heating of some kind, storm doors.... Sōme of the features seen on houses in hot climates would be insulation, but not as much; single pane windows, or only screens; weeping tiles in wet areas, house on stilts near swamps or large bodies of water, etc.

2. Students answers will vary, continue with the theme from previous question.

3. Student activity.

4. Student activity.

5. a) Student activity: e.g.: 16 feet by 26 feet

   b) Using above example
   Area = *l* x *w* therefore,
   Area = 16 x 26 = 416 sq. ft.

   c) Student observation.

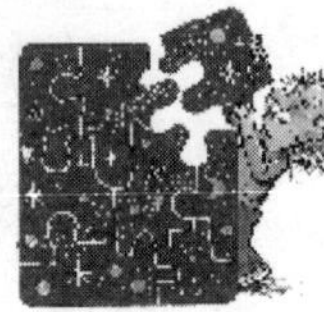

REFLECTING ON THE ACTIVITY AND THE CHALLENGE

You may think that this activity didn't move you very far toward meeting the challenge, but it really has gotten you started. Through interaction with others you have identified and shared ideas about the two basic aspects of dwellings for humans: function and form. Function involves the many things that a dwelling must do for people, and you have identified basic functions. Form involves the physical characteristics which a dwelling must have to support necessary functions, and you have started thinking about the size of a dwelling as perhaps the most basic part of form. Congratulations! You're on the way to meeting the challenge.

As you progress through this chapter, you and your group may find that you will need to modifications to your original plans. Don't be concerned about this, as this is typical of the planning and research process in which you are involved.

PHYSICS TO GO

1. a) Describe the weather in the area of the country in which you live.
   b) Describe some features of homes in your area that provide protection against the weather.
2. Choose another area of the country, or in the world, which has weather different from yours. Describe the weather in that area. Describe some features of homes in that area that provide protection against the weather.
3. A square foot (ft^2) is a unit of measurement of surface area. Using a ruler, draw an accurate diagram of a square foot. (You may have to tape two pieces of paper together.) Label the dimensions of width and length.
4. Use your diagram of a square foot. Estimate the number of square feet in the room in which you are presently located.
5. a) Measure the length and width (in feet) of the room in which you are presently located.
   b) To calculate the area of a rectangle you multiply the length by the width.
   $A = l \times w$
   Calculate the area of the room you are in.
   c) How close was your estimate in question 4 to the area you calculated?

6. A family has decided to install a new floor in the kitchen of their home. The kitchen floor is a rectangle 8 feet wide and 12 feet long. The new floor will be covered with tiles which are square pieces measuring 1 foot on each side. How many tiles will be needed?

7. The family described in question 6 has changed its mind and has decided to use a type of flooring material that is available in square pieces measuring 2 feet on each side. How many pieces will be needed?

8. To prepare for Activity 2, determine the total floor area of your own or someone else's living spaces. Measure the amount of floor space in the bedrooms, the living areas, the kitchen, bathroom(s), and any other areas. Include any closets in your measurement. Place the data you collect on a 3 × 5 card, using the format shown here. All the information will be kept anonymous.

The Total Floor Area of a Home

Combined area of bedrooms in square feet: ______

Combined area of kitchens/eating areas in square feet: ______

Combined area of living room, den, etc. in square feet: ______

Total area of all the above spaces in square feet: ______

Combined area of bathroom(s) in your home in square feet: ______

Total areas of all other living spaces in square feet: ______

GRAND TOTAL of all living spaces in square feet: ______

The number of people occupying the space: ______

STRETCHING EXERCISE

Do a survey in your neighborhood. Make a list of, or draw features of homes that are well-suited to the local climate.

ANSWERS

Physics To Go
(continued)

6. Each tile is 1 square foot, and, the total area is 96 square feet, therefore, the number of tiles is 96.

7. If each tile is now 2 ft on each side, each tile is now 4 sq. ft. Therefore, 96 sq. ft / 4 sq. ft, is 24 tiles needed to tile the floor.

8. Student activity.

Floor Plan for a Home

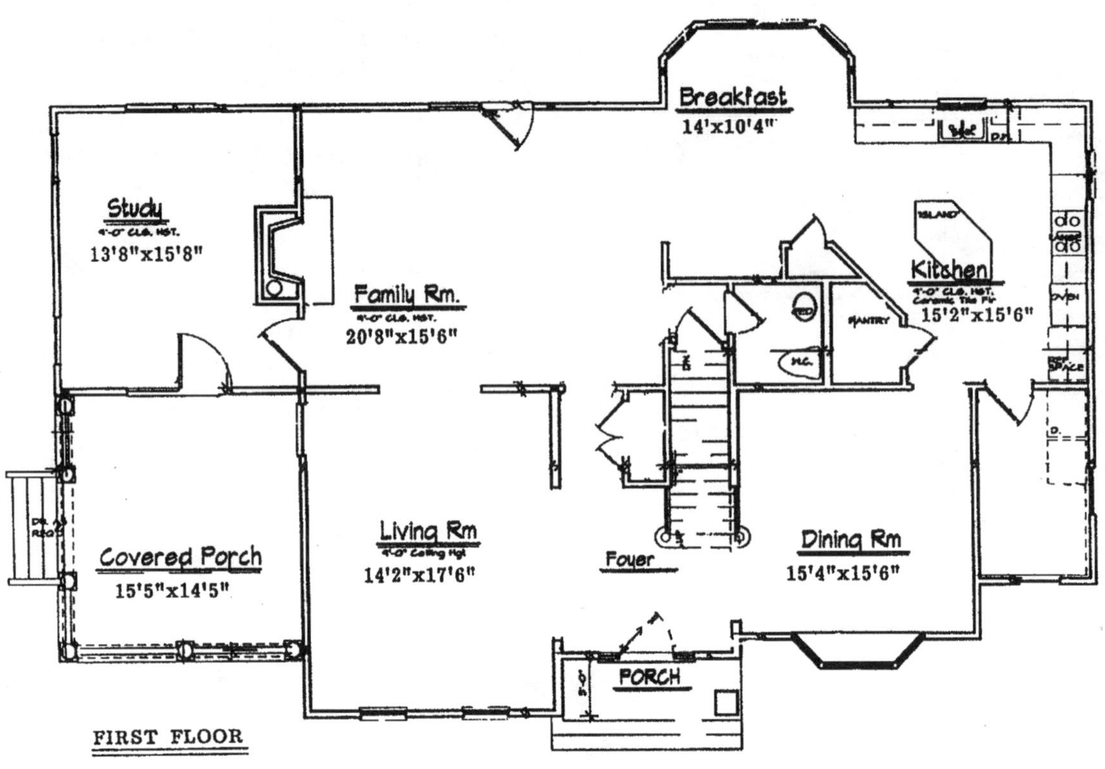

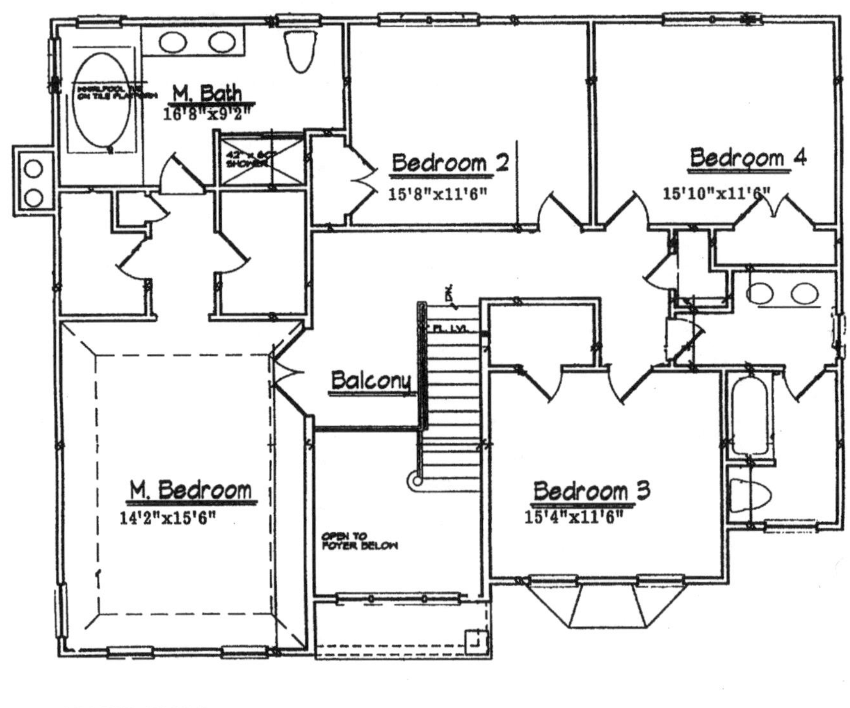

For use with *Home*, Chapter 1, ACTIVITY ONE: Factors in Designing the "Universal Dwelling"

Floor Area of a Home

The Total Floor Area of a Home

Combined area of bedrooms in square feet: ________
Combined area of kitchens/eating areas in square feet: ________
Combined area of living room, den, etc. in square feet: ________
Total area of all the above spaces in square feet: ________

Combined area of bathroom(s) in your home in square feet: ________
Total areas of all other living spaces in square feet: ________

GRAND TOTAL of all the living spaces in square feet: ________
The number of people occupying the space: ________

1

For use with *Home*, Chapter 1, ACTIVITY ONE: Factors in Designing the "Universal Dwelling"

The Total Floor Area of a Home

Combined area of bedrooms in square feet: ________
Combined area of kitchens/eating areas in square feet: ________
Combined area of living room, den, etc. in square feet: ________
Total area of all the above spaces in square feet: ________

Combined area of bathroom(s) in your home in square feet: ________
Total areas of all other living spaces in square feet: ________

GRAND TOTAL of all the living spaces in square feet: ________
The number of people occupying the space: ________

For use with *Home*, Chapter 1, ACTIVITY ONE: Factors in Designing the "Universal Dwelling"

©1999 American Association of Physics Teachers

ACTIVITY TWO
What is the "Right Size" for a Universal Dwelling?

Background Information

The main concept involved in Activity Two is a ratio, the "area per person" calculated by dividing the total surface area of the floor(s) of a home by the number of persons living in the home.

Area per person (ft^2/person) = Floor area (ft^2) ÷ Number (person)

Keep in mind that this ratio involves the interplay of two quantities, the floor area and the number of persons living in the home, and may be tricky. For example, it is possible that a big home having a very large floor area and many family members may have a smaller "area per person" ratio than a small home with few family members.

The class average of this ratio also is involved in this activity, and it is good to keep in mind that the average, or arithmetic mean (add all the values and divide by the number of values) is not always the best indicator of central tendency. It is possible, for example, that the class's average value of area per person may not be at all representative of the typical home for class members. This could happen if, for example, only a few homes had extremely large values compared to the rest.

If the class's average value of area per person does not seem meaningful, you could explore the possibility of using other indicators of central tendency such as the median (halfway between the smallest and largest values) or the mode (the most frequent value).

Once a decision is made about the desired value for the area per person ratio for a home, the total floor area needed can of course be calculated by multiplying the value of the ratio by the number of persons who will live in the home. Similarly, the range of floor areas of homes needed for various family sizes can be calculated by multiplying the area per person by the smallest and largest number of family members.

Active-ating the Physics InfoMall

One of the concepts in this Activity is the concept of scale. Again, this is an area where students have known difficulty. Arons has done much of the work on student understanding, and this concept is not excepted. Section IV of Arons article "Student patterns of thinking and reasoning, part one of three parts," (*The Physics Teacher*, vol. 21, issue 9) is on scaling and functional reasoning, such as how area and volume depend on linear dimensions. Arons returns to this topic in *A Guide to Introductory Physics Teaching* (in the Book Basement), in "Underpinnings" section 1.12.

For discussions on interpolation and extrapolation, you can perform a search using either of these as keywords. One of the hits is Chapter 11 of the textbook *Physics for the Inquiring Mind.* This is a short passage, but discusses some of the pros and cons of using limited data to form predictions.

Planning for the Activity

Time Requirements

Allow one class period for this activity. If you do the Stretching Exercise, allow at least one more class, or possibly two, depending on the resources available to you.

Materials needed

For the class:

- student data on 3x5 cards from Activity One, Physics To Go

For each group:

- calculator

Advance Preparation and Setup

Have some sample cards made up, with the calculation of the average number of square feet per person. Ave = Total sq. ft. / number of people.

Teaching Notes

Ask students to have ready to hand in the 3x5 card on which they have recorded data about their individual homes (be sure to announce that anonymity will be preserved). Collect the cards, and mix them up. Read the grand total for the living areas in square feet, and the number of people living in those homes. Guide the students through the For You To Do.

Activity Overview

In this activity, the students will be looking at floor plans, and calculating the space required for individuals. They will be applying mathematical understanding of area, and exploring the relationship between total living area or space, and number of individuals in the home.

Student Objectives

Students will:

- calculate the average number of square feet per person for a sample of homes represented in the student's class.
- recognize ranges in family size and the number of square feet per person in the class's sample of homes.
- use data on the class's sample of homes and family sizes to decide upon the size needed for a "basic" universal dwelling, and decide how the size of the dwelling will vary for large and small families.

DESIGNING THE UNIVERSAL DWELLING

Activity Two

What is the "Right Size" for a Universal Dwelling?

WHAT DO YOU THINK?

In some prisons in the United States, two inmates occupy an 8-foot by 10-foot cell. On the other hand, some people live in mansions of 10,000 to 20,000 square feet!

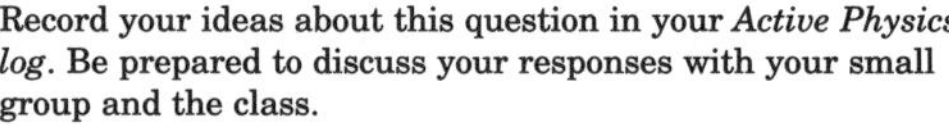

- **How much space do people need in their shelters to have a decent, humane life?**

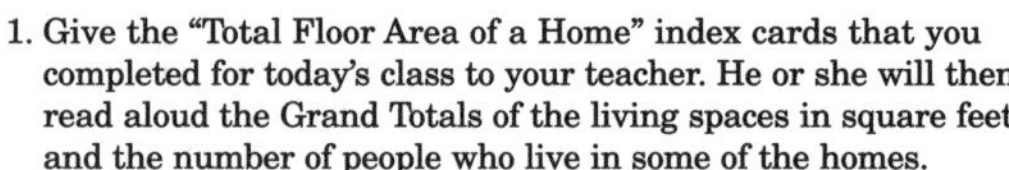

Record your ideas about this question in your *Active Physics log*. Be prepared to discuss your responses with your small group and the class.

FOR YOU TO DO

1. Give the "Total Floor Area of a Home" index cards that you completed for today's class to your teacher. He or she will then read aloud the Grand Totals of the living spaces in square feet and the number of people who live in some of the homes.
   a) Enter these numbers in your log.
   b) Calculate the average number of square feet per person for at least five of the homes in your community.

ANSWERS FOR THE TEACHER ONLY

What Do You Think?

Answers will vary according to the students' environment. For example, students who have lived in apartments all their life will have a different concept of space than the students raised on the wide open prairie on a ranch or a farm. This is a good opportunity to initiate a discussion regarding their preconceptions of living space.

ANSWERS

For You To Do

1. a) Student data.

   b) Ave = Total sq. ft. / number of people (for example: total square feet for one house is 1780 sq. ft and five people live there. Therefore, the average square feet per person is 1780 / 5. The average is 356 sq. ft. per person.

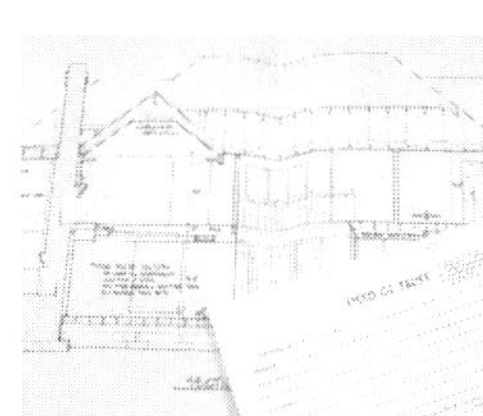

2. Discuss the answers to the questions below with your group and then record the answers in your log.
   a) How much total living space for all functions should your universal dwelling have per person?
   b) Could you design a universal dwelling that would combine some living space functions? If so, how might you do this?
   c) Will bathroom space be necessary for your universal dwelling? If not, explain how you might modify your dwelling if no indoor plumbing will be available. (Indoor plumbing is not available to many people in many countries.)
   d) What size family (number of people) and what total square footage will you use for designing your "basic" universal dwelling? Explain your group's reasoning for choosing these family and dwelling sizes.
   e) Decide on two additional sizes for your universal dwelling, the first to accommodate a larger family and the second to accommodate a smaller family. What will the square footage and family sizes of these versions be? What is your group's reasoning for deciding upon these specific larger and smaller sizes?

REFLECTING ON THE ACTIVITY AND THE CHALLENGE

Based upon the data that your class has collected, and your group discussions about what is needed in terms of living space for a universal dwelling, your group and other groups in the class have probably decided on universal dwellings of various sizes. This is another step toward completing the chapter challenge. You didn't just draw a size out of a hat. Your decision on size can be defended in terms of the data that you have collected about the sizes of homes of class members. You have also included necessary functions and various family sizes as factors in your decision.

There are probably a range of appropriate answers, but there is also opportunity to make changes and improvements as you proceed.

ANSWERS

For You To Do *(continued)*

2. a) Student data.

   b) Student data; Some students might have the bedroom and living room as one space (hide-a-bed).

   c) Student data; Some may realize that the toilet must be outside, as the smell inside the house might be rather noxious.

   d) Student data.

   e) Student data.

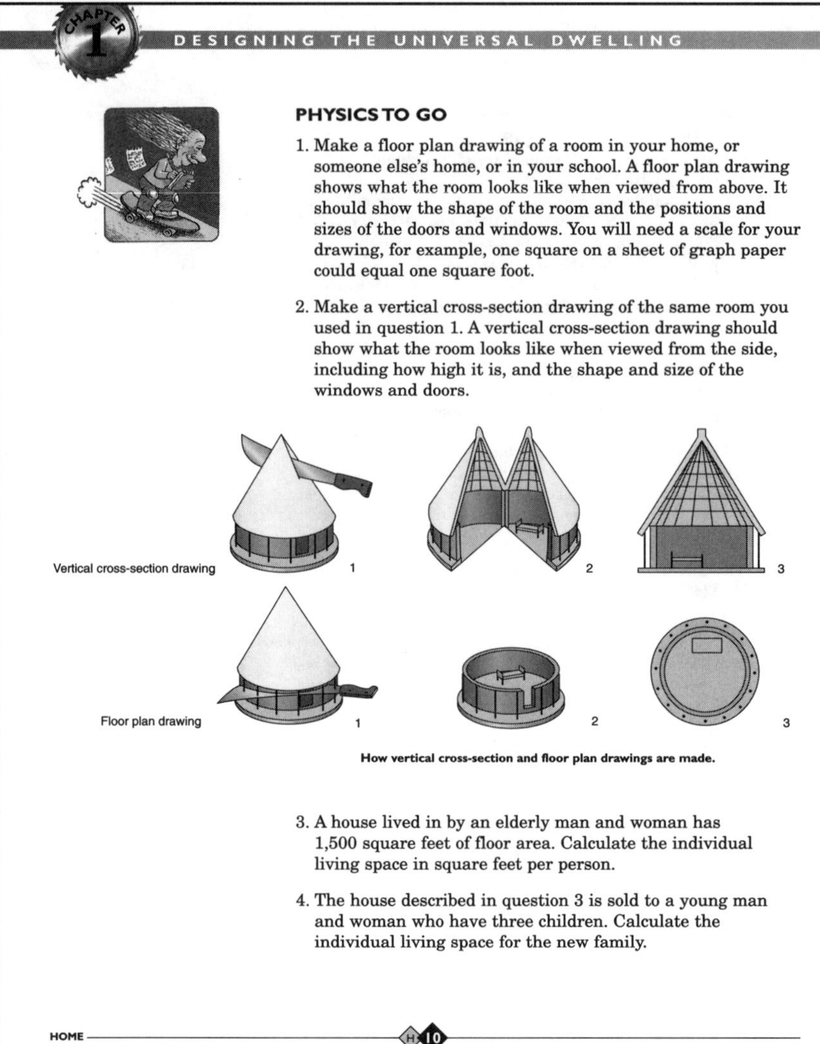

PHYSICS TO GO

1. Make a floor plan drawing of a room in your home, or someone else's home, or in your school. A floor plan drawing shows what the room looks like when viewed from above. It should show the shape of the room and the positions and sizes of the doors and windows. You will need a scale for your drawing, for example, one square on a sheet of graph paper could equal one square foot.

2. Make a vertical cross-section drawing of the same room you used in question 1. A vertical cross-section drawing should show what the room looks like when viewed from the side, including how high it is, and the shape and size of the windows and doors.

How vertical cross-section and floor plan drawings are made.

3. A house lived in by an elderly man and woman has 1,500 square feet of floor area. Calculate the individual living space in square feet per person.

4. The house described in question 3 is sold to a young man and woman who have three children. Calculate the individual living space for the new family.

ANSWERS

Physics To Go

1. Students' sketches.
2. Student activity.
3. 1500 sq. ft. / 2 people = 750 sq. ft. per person.
4. 1500 sq. ft. / 5 people = 300 sq. ft. per person.

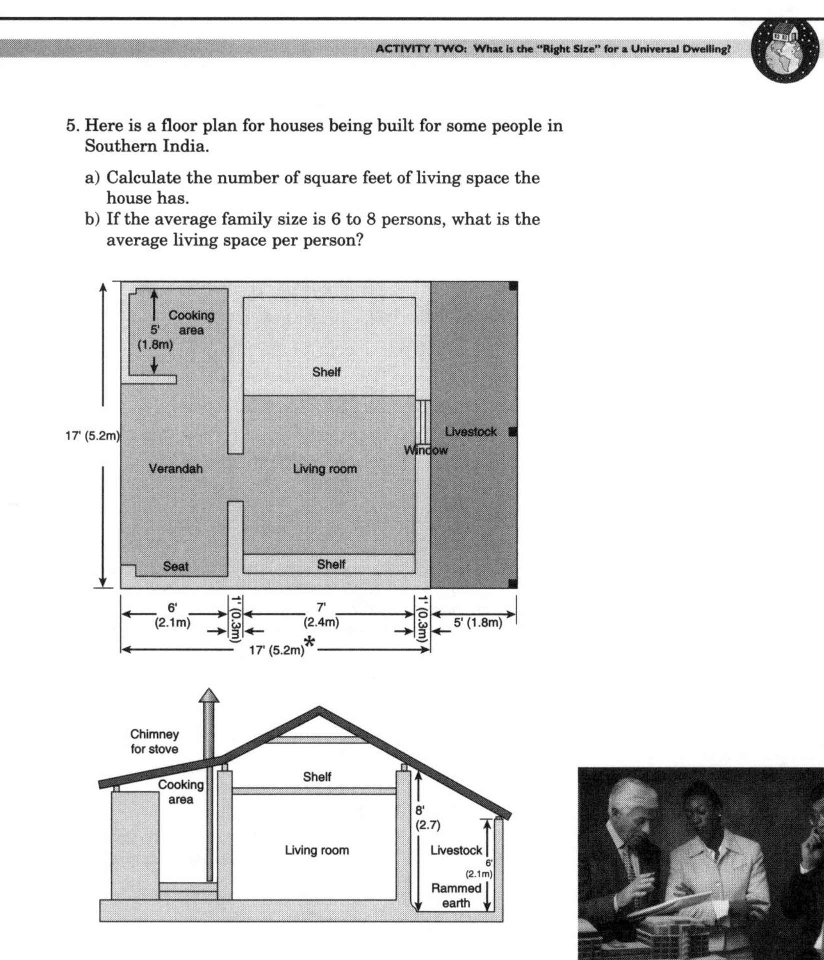

ACTIVITY TWO: What is the "Right Size" for a Universal Dwelling?

5. Here is a floor plan for houses being built for some people in Southern India.

   a) Calculate the number of square feet of living space the house has.

   b) If the average family size is 6 to 8 persons, what is the average living space per person?

Typical family house—vertical cross-section drawing.

H 11 HOME

* Incorrect measurement. The distance is 15' (4.5 m). See page 29 of the Teacher's Edition for additional measurement corrections.

Answers

Physics To Go *(continued)*

5. a) Area = l x w; Therefore, Area = 17' x 15' = 255 sq. ft.

   b) 221 sq. ft. / 6 people = 37 sq. ft. per person;
   255 sq. ft. / 6 people = 43 sq. ft. per person;
   255 sq. ft. / 8 people = 32 sq. ft. per person.

6. Look at the floor plan from Malawi of "a house that grows." It allows the homeowner to add rooms to the house as the household income or the family grow.

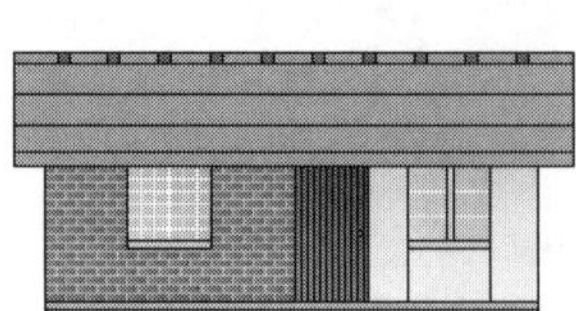

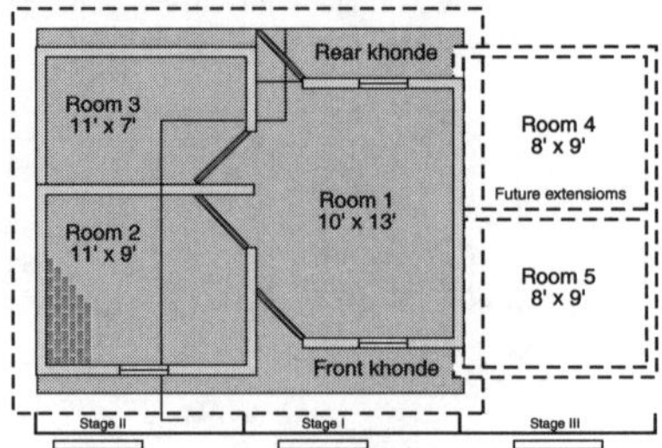

a) Calculate the number of square feet per person for a newly married couple who builds Stage I (Room 1).
b) The couple has two children and decides to build Stage II (Rooms 2 and 3). Calculate how may square feet there are per person for this family of four.
c) The couple has two more children and then builds Stage III (Rooms 4 and 5). Calculate the number of square feet per person for this family of six.

7. Make a floor plan drawing and a vertical cross-section drawing for your "universal" dwelling. Show the total square footage of each room and the total square footage of the dwelling. Include a scale for your drawing.

STRETCHING EXERCISES

1. Do research in your school library or on the Internet to find information on the size of the "average American home."

2. Locate information on the amount of living space used by an average person in another country.

ANSWERS

Physics To Go *(continued)*

6. a) Area of stage I = l x w = 13' x 10' = 130 sq. ft.

Ave = 130 sq. ft. / 2 = 65 sq. ft. per person.

b) Add the to the total area, Area of stage II = (l x w) + (l x w) = (11' x 7') + (11' x 9') = 306 sq. ft.

Ave = 306 sq. ft. / 4 = 79 sq. ft. per person.)

c) Add the to the total area, Area of stage III = (l x w) + (l x w) = (8' x 9') + (8 ' x 9') = 450 sq. ft.

Ave = 450 sq. ft. / 4 = 75 sq. ft. per person.

7. Student activity

Floor Space for a Home

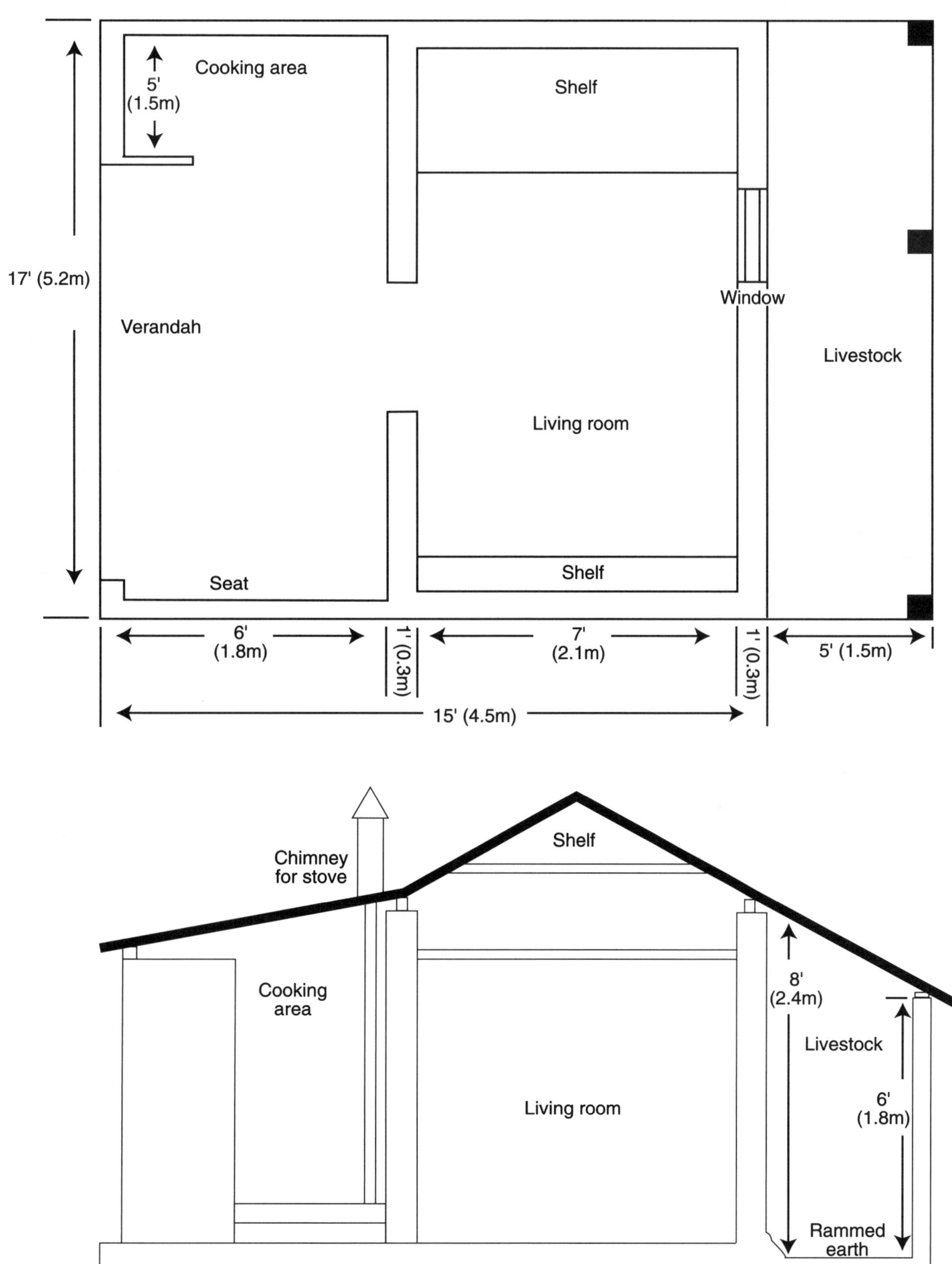

For use with *Home*, Chapter 1, ACTIVITY TWO: What is the "Right Size" for a Universal Dwelling?

Floor Space for a Home

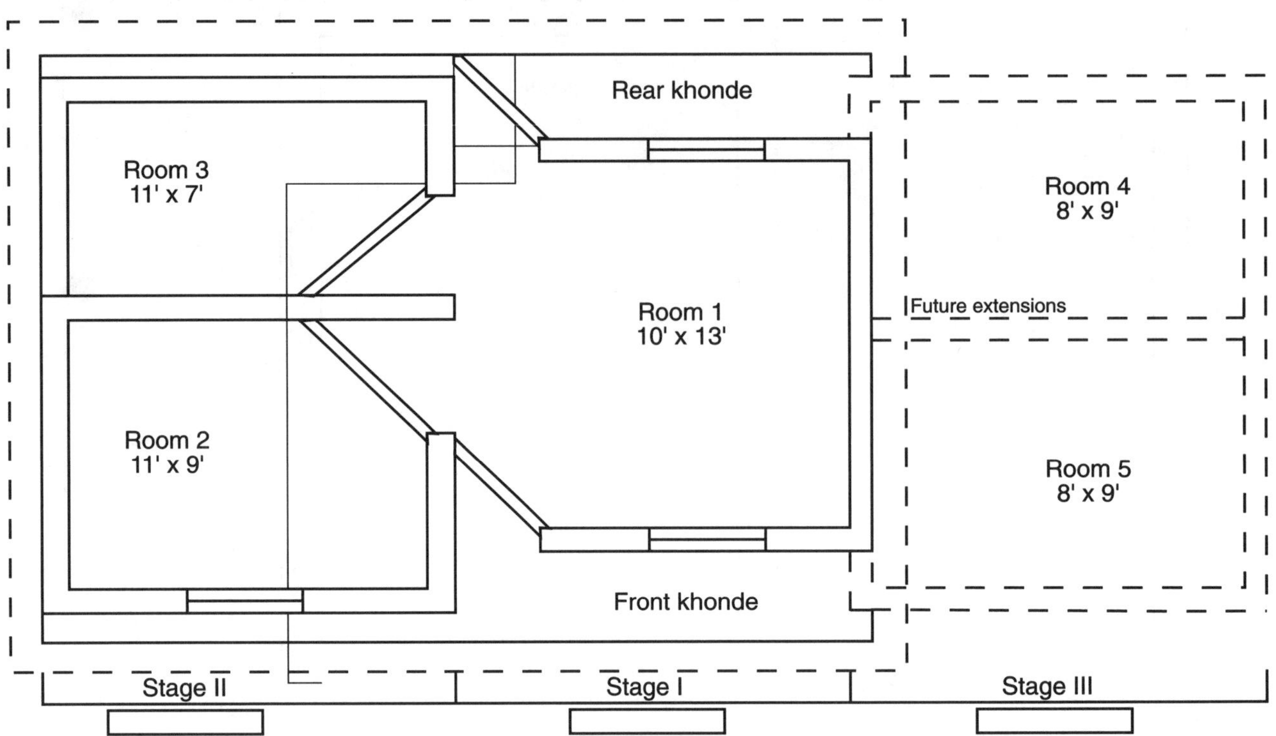

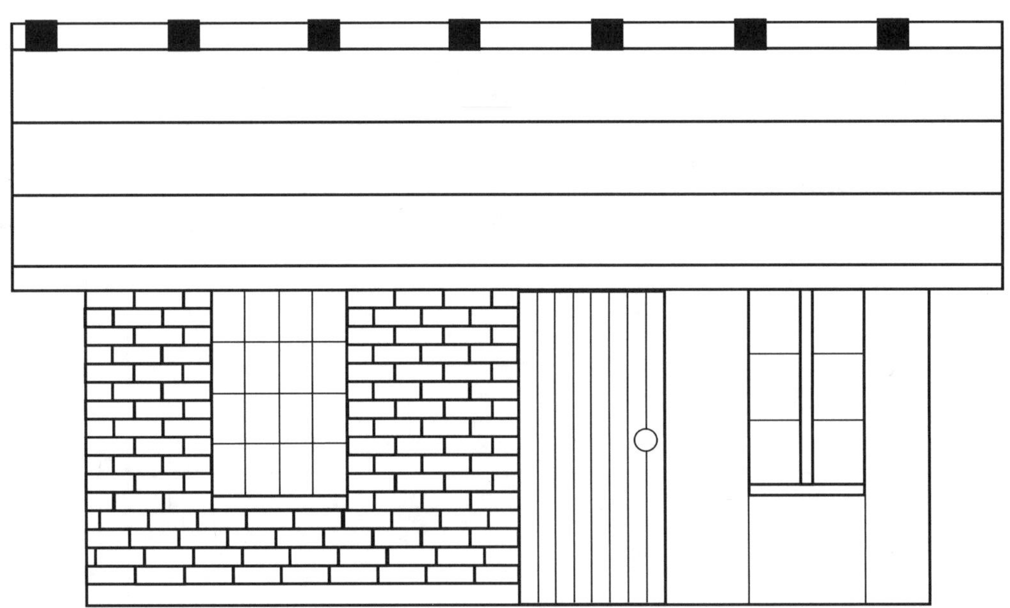

For use with *Home*, Chapter 1, ACTIVITY TWO: What is the "Right Size" for a Universal Dwelling?

NOTES

ACTIVITY THREE
The Shape of the "Universal Dwelling"

Background Information

Three mathematical relationships which affect the cost and performance of homes are introduced in Activity Three:

If the total floor area of a home is held constant, the total perimeter of the home (the total length of exterior walls) depends on the two-dimensional shape of the floor area.

The ratio of the exterior surface area of a home to the three-dimensional volume enclosed by the home, called the surface-to-volume ratio, depends on the three-dimensional shape of the home.

If the three-dimensional shape of a home is held constant, the surface-to-volume ratio of the home depends on the overall size of the home.

The dependence of shape on perimeter (area constant). For home designs limited to rectangular floor plans (four sides, all corners right angles) the smallest perimeter results for a square floor plan. For unlimited shapes the smallest perimeter for a given area is provided by a circular floor. Ideally, a circular house would require the least building material for exterior walls and, for vertical walls of standard height and thickness, would provide minimum surface area for heat escape through the walls.

The dependence of shape on surface-to-volume ratio. For home designs limited to three dimensional shapes resembling rectangular solids (rectangular surfaces on all sides) the smallest surface area for a particular enclosed volume (and, therefore, the smallest surface-to-volume ratio) results for a cubical shape. For unlimited shapes (assuming that a flat floor is desired) a hemisphere (dome) shape would have the least surface-to-volume ratio. Consideration of the three-dimensional shape of a home rather than only the two-dimensional shape of the floor plan allows optimization of building materials and heat loss; a dome, although complex to construct, would provide the least building materials and the least surface area for heat loss.

You may recall that the example in nature which demonstrates the sphere as having the least surface-to-volume ratio is the raindrop; the strong cohesive forces of water molecules cause the surface of a raindrop to shrink to the smallest possible size, resulting in a sphere.

The below equations apply to calculating the areas and volumes of three-dimensional shapes which are likely to be involved in this activity. The prism is included for cases where students may choose home designs which involve pitched or sloped roofs.

Volume of rectangular solid = Length x Width x Height

Surface area of sphere = 4 x π x $(\text{Radius})^2$

[divide by 2 for hemisphere]

Volume of sphere = 4/3 x π x $(\text{Radius})^3$

Surface area of cylinder including circular ends

= 2 x π (Radius) + [(Radius) + (Length)]

Volume of cylinder = π x $(\text{Radius})^2$ x Length

Volume of prism = Area of triangular side x Length of prism

= (1/2 x Base x Height) x Length

If dimensions are measured in feet of length, calculated areas and volumes will be in units of, respectively, square feet (ft^2) and (ft^3). In this application surface-to-volume ratio would have dimensions of "square feet per cubic foot" (ft^2/ft^3); mathematically, this dimension could be reduced to reciprocal feet (1/ft), but it has more meaning to retain the entire statement "square feet per cubic foot."

The dependence of surface-to-volume ratio on size. As shown immediately above in the discussion of units for expressing surface-to-volume ratio, the value of the ratio varies inversely with the fundamental dimensions, or scale of size, of a three-dimensional object of a given shape (see the Stretching Exercise for this activity in which this dependence is illustrated as a cube is scaled upward in size). Applied to a home design, this means, for example, that doubling all of the dimensions of the home (scaling upward by a factor of two) would decrease the home's surface-to-volume ratio by a factor of two. The "doubled" home would require more building materials, but not twice as much. Further, the larger home would have more heat loss through its surfaces than would a home half that size, but not twice as much. Therefore, some efficiency is gained with increased size. Similarly, there is a loss in efficiency upon scaling down; reducing the size of a home by a factor of two causes the surface-to-volume ratio to increase by the same factor.

The interplay between surface-to-volume ratio and scale of size is demonstrated in nature by the fact that small birds and mammals must ingest more food per unit of body volume each day—some consume many times their body weight each day—to offset the heat loss caused by the large surface-to-volume ratios of their small bodies. We humans, by comparison, don't need to eat as much on a "pound for pound" basis to maintain similar body temperature because, being of larger scale, our bodies have a comparatively smaller surface-to-volume ratio.

Active-ating the Physics InfoMall

In addition to the references mentioned earlier for area calculations, there is information on the InfoMall regarding student problems with area-to-volume ratios. If you perform a compound search for "area," "volume" and "ratio," you get too many hits. A good idea, as a first try, is to limit the search by indicating that the terms must appear in the same paragraph (alternately, you could limit which stores on the InfoMall are searched and reduce the number of hits as well). Among the hits is another from Arons, "Thinking, reasoning and understanding in introductory physics courses," *The Physics Teacher*, vol. 19, issue 3. Arons indicates that "The majority of U.S. college students in introductory physics courses have difficulty with this problem" of ratios.

Another hit from this list (*Physics: Foundations and Frontiers* in the Textbook Trove, look in the Biophysics section) tells how this area-to-volume ratio affects animals; smaller animals must have a high metabolic rate to keep their small volumes heated due to large heat loss through relatively large surface area. This compared well with Physics To Go, Step 9.

Planning for the Activity

Time Requirements

Allow at least 40 minutes for this activity, depending on how many different shapes are to be looked at and calculated.

Materials needed

For each group:

- 20-inch loop of string
- pins (8)
- 1-inch grid paper
- corrugated cardboard backing for grid paper

Advance Preparation and Setup

Have the materials available for the students, and depending on time restraints, have the 20 in. loops of string already closed and ready to use.

Teaching Notes

Introduce the term "optimize" and explain that the purpose of the For You To Do activity is to optimize the shape of the dwelling. Give the idea to the students that they should be "making the most with the least."

Some students may not understand the concept of surface area-to-volume ratio, and how it affects the design of the house. To help them understand, have them think of tents and how much material they would need as they increased the height of the walls, without increasing the floor space inside. They will come to see, as the tent gets higher and higher, there is greater surface area, and greater volume, but no difference in the floor space.

If 1-inch grid paper is not available, 1/4 inch grid or graph paper is okay. If using different grid paper, make the students aware of this change, and show how they can make 1-inch grid paper from different graph paper available.

NOTES

ACTIVITY THREE: The Shape of the "Universal Dwelling"

Activity Three

The Shape of the "Universal Dwelling"

WHAT DO YOU THINK?

Throughout the world, homes take on many different shapes.

• Why are most homes in the U.S. built in rectangular shapes?

Record your ideas about this question in your *Active Physics log*. Be prepared to discuss your responses with your small group and the class.

FOR YOU TO DO

1. Make a closed 20-inch loop of string. You will also need pins and 1-inch square grid graph paper attached to a sheet of cardboard as shown on page H14.

2. Carefully place 4 pins at the intersections of grid lines. Run the closed loop of string around the pins. Adjust the pins until you have constructed a rectangle on your grid paper. The loop should form a tight fit around the perimeter.

a) Count and record the number of one-inch squares that lie within this perimeter. Record your data in a table similar to the one shown on the following page.

HOME

Answers

For You To Do

1. Student activity.

2. a) Student activity and observations.

Activity Overview

In this activity, the students will look at the area of a house, and then compare it to the area needed for each individual in the house. They will determine the optimal size of floor space, while keeping the cost of the materials as low as possible.

Once they have looked at the floor space, they will look at the volume, and surface area. This is to aid them in determining more accurate costs for the building.

Student Objectives

Students will:

- explain how the surface area of a two-dimensional figure is related to its shape when the perimeter is held constant.
- calculate the surface-to-volume ratio of simple three-dimensional shapes.
- relate the shape of a dwelling to optimization of living space for a limited amount of building materials.

1

Answers for the teacher only

What Do You Think?

Answers will vary. Generally, when building with straight lumber, the easiest structure to build is one with 90° angles. Hence the "box" we are familiar with. An interesting discussion can develop from this if there are students from other countries, or who have traveled to other countries. Ask the students what is the most common structure, and what is the most common building material.

ANSWERS

For You To Do

(continued)

3. a) Student activity and observations.

4. a) All the rectangles should have equal perimeters.

   b) As the sides get longer and the perimeter stays the same, the area gets smaller.

   c) The size of rectangle which has the largest area of given perimeter is the square (5 x 5 x 5 x 5).

5. a) Student activity and observations.

   b) As the number of the sides increases, the enclosed area gets larger.

   c) Students' answers will vary. Some students will name large polygons (> 10 sides) as being the shape with the greatest area. However, it would become evident that as the shape approaches a circle, it becomes the shape with the largest area.

6. a) Students' answers will vary. The shape chosen should be a circle, as it takes the least amount of materials per maximum unit of floor space.

Perimeter	Length of Long Sides	Length of Short Sides	Area Inside Perimeter

3. By carefully moving the pins, construct at least five more rectangles.

   a) Record the results in the table in your log.

4. Use the data you collected to help you answer the following questions.

   a) Which rectangle has the greatest perimeter, or do they all have equal perimeters?

   b) What happens to the area of the rectangle as one pair of sides gets longer while the perimeter stays the same?

   c) Which rectangle seems to have the largest internal area?

5. With your partner, use your loop of string and graph paper to determine how triangular (3-sided), pentagonal (5-sided), hexagonal (6-sided), octagonal (8-sided), and other shapes compare to that of a square of the same perimeter.

   a) Record your results in a table. (You can determine the area of the shapes by counting the number of boxes in the graph paper enclosed by the string. You will probably need to count half-boxes as well.)

   b) What appears to happen to the enclosed area as the number of sides increase?

   c) What shape do you think will generate the largest area for a given perimeter?

6. Extend your two-dimensional knowledge to three dimensions. Since homes are surrounded by walls and not string, you must consider how the information about enclosing the largest possible area with a loop of string can be used in designing your home.

   a) If you only had a limited quantity of material for walls to enclose a home, which shape would give the most living area? Why?

7. Meet with the other members of your group and, using the information you have gathered from these activities, choose a design shape for your universal dwelling. Your group will also have to determine the ceiling height, number of stories, and surface area-to-volume ratio for your basic dwelling design.

   a) Record your group's decisions regarding these specifications in your log:

The shape of the universal dwelling will be:

The ceiling height of the rooms will be:

The living space of the dwelling in square feet will be:

The number of stories in the dwelling will be:

The volume of the dwelling will be:

REFLECTING ON THE ACTIVITY AND THE CHALLENGE

Your group has reached some tentative decisions about how many square feet of living space per person your "universal dwelling" should have. You have to be concerned about making sure that you provide enough living space. You also need to make sure that the building is not too expensive to produce. This means that a good design will not require a large building to contain the floor space.

In this activity, you explored how you may construct a dwelling with the required floor space, while keeping the dimensions of the building small and the amount of materials needed to construct the building as small as possible.

Now you have addressed the two most basic questions about the form of the universal dwelling: size and shape. You can defend your choice of shape in terms of keeping the cost of materials low. You are on your way to being able to present your plan to the Architectural Committee with confidence.

ANSWERS

For You To Do

(continued)

7. Student activity and observations.

1

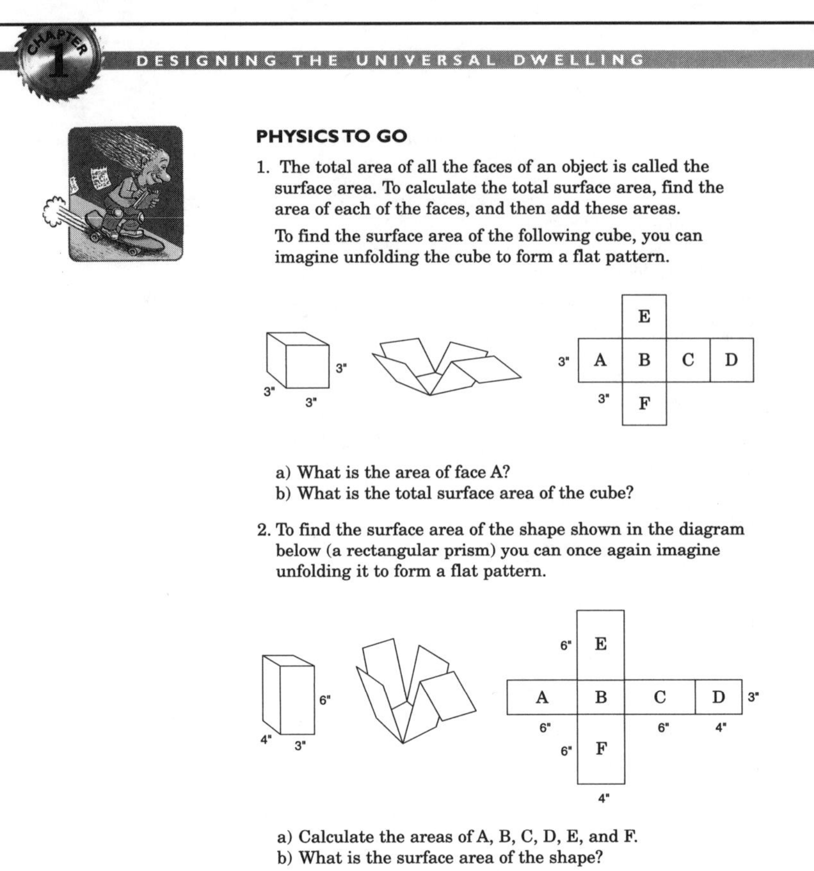

ANSWERS

Physics To Go

1.a) Face A has an area of 9 square inches.

b) Total surface area is 54 square inches.

2.a) Area A = 18 in^2; Area B = 12 in^2; Area C = 18 in^2; Area D = 12 in^2; Area E = 24 in^2; Area F = 24 in^2.

b) Total Area = 108 in^2.

ACTIVITY THREE: The Shape of the "Universal Dwelling"

3. Find the surface areas of the following:

a) 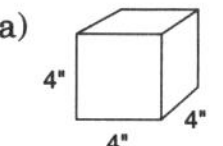 b) 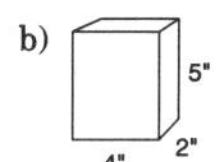 c) 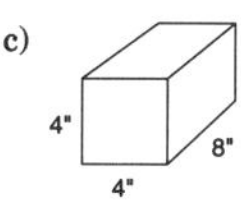

4. To calculate the volume of a rectangular shape you can use the following relationship:

   Volume = length × width × height

   Calculate the volume of each figure in question 3.

5. Find the surface area-to-volume ratio of each figure in question 3. (Divide the surface area by its volume.) Which figure has the greatest surface area-to-volume ratio? the lowest?

6. A house was designed with outside walls that form a square base 27 feet on each side.
   a) Calculate the perimeter (distance around) of the house in feet.
   b) Calculate the total floor area of the house in square feet.

7. A house was designed with an outside wall that forms a circle which has a radius of 17.2 feet.
   a) Calculate the circumference of (distance around) the house in feet. The equation for the circumference of a circle is Circumference = 2 × π × radius. You can use a value of 3.14 for π.
   b) Calculate the total floor area of the house in square feet. The equation for the area of a circle is Area = π × radius × radius.

H 17 HOME

Answers

Physics To Go

(continued)

3. a) 6 sides x 4" x 4" = 96 in^2.

   b) 2 sides x 4" x 2" = 16 in^2; 2 sides x 5" x 2" = 20 in^2; 2 sides x 4" x 5" = 40 in^2; Total = 76 in2

   c) 2 sides x 4" x 4" = 32 in^2; 4 sides x 4" x 8" = 128 in^2; Total = 160 in2

4. a) 4" x 4" x 4" = 64 in^3.

   b) 4" x 2" x 5" = 40 in^3.

   c) 4" x 4" x 8" = 128 in^3.

5. a) The surface area-to-volume ratio is surface area/volume = 96/64 = 1.5 to 1

   b) The surface area-to-volume ratio is surface area/volume = 76/40 = 1.9 to 1

   c) The surface area-to-volume ratio is surface area/volume = 160/128 = 1.3 to 1
   Figure b) has the greatest (1.9 to 1) and Figure c) has the least (1.3 to 1)

6. a) Perimeter is sum of all sides, therefore the perimeter is 27' x 4 sides = 108'.

   b) The total floor area is l x w = 27' x 27' = 729 square feet.

7. a) Circumference = 2 x π x r = 2 x 3.14 x 17.2 feet = 109.9 or 110 feet.

   b) Total floor area = π x r^2 = 3.14 x (17.2 feet)^2 = 928.9 or 929 square feet

1

ANSWERS

Physics To Go

(continued)

8. a) If we use the height of the walls to be 8 feet, then the area of the walls will be the circumference x height = 108 x 8 = 864 sq. ft., and the circular house will be circumference x height, 110 x 8 = 880 sq.ft. There is not a significant difference between the two.

   b) There are 200 more square feet in the circular house than in the square house. Yes, this is significant.

   c) As there is about 180 sq. ft. per person, there would be about four people in the square house and five people in the round house. It is very significant to the fifth person!

9. a) hut: 8 ft. x 8 ft. = 64 sq. ft., cabin: 16 ft. x 16 ft. x two floors = 512 sq.ft.

   b) hut: 8 ft. x 8 ft. x 6 surfaces = 384 sq. ft.
   cabin: 16 ft. x 16 ft. x 10 surfaces = 2560 sq. ft.

   Therefore, the ratio is 2560/384 or approximately 6.6 times (cabin to hut).

   c) Answer: hut: 8 ft. x 8 ft. x 8 ft. = 512 cu. ft.
   cabin: 16 ft. x 16 ft. x 32 ft. = 8192 cu. ft.

   Therefore, the ratio is 8192/512 or approximately 16 times (cabin to hut).

   d) hut: 384/512 = 0.75
   cabin: 2560/8192 = 0.3125

   Therefore, the hut would have the greatest possibility of losing heat through its surfaces.

10. Student activity.

8. Use numbers to compare the houses in questions 6 and 7.
   a) If the height of the outside walls of the two houses were equal, how would the amount of paint needed to cover the walls compare? How significant is the difference?
   b) How do the total floor areas of the two houses compare? How significant is the difference?
   c) If living space of at least 180 square feet per person is needed, how many persons could live in each house? How significant is this difference?

9. A research outpost for a scientist in a remote part of Alaska has a hut shelter which is a cube 8 feet on each side. The scientist sometimes visits a nearby family who lives in a two-story cabin also shaped as a cube. The cabin's dimensions are double the dimensions of the hut, measuring 16 feet on each side. Use the numbers to make the following comparisons:
   a) Compare the total floor areas of the two dwellings as a ratio. (The cabin has an upstairs level.)
   b) Compare the outside surface areas of the two dwellings including the bottom floor of each. Express the comparison as a ratio.
   c) Compare the volumes of the two dwellings as a ratio.
   d) Calculate the surface area-to-volume ratio for each dwelling. (Divide the outside surface area of each dwelling by its volume. The answers will be in units of square feet per cubic foot.) Which dwelling has the greatest possibility for heat loss through its surfaces per cubic foot of inside volume?

10. Using the information you gathered in this activity, modify your floor plan drawing and section drawing for your "universal" dwelling. Show the total square footage of each room and the total square footage of the dwelling. Include a scale for your drawing.

Square Grid Paper

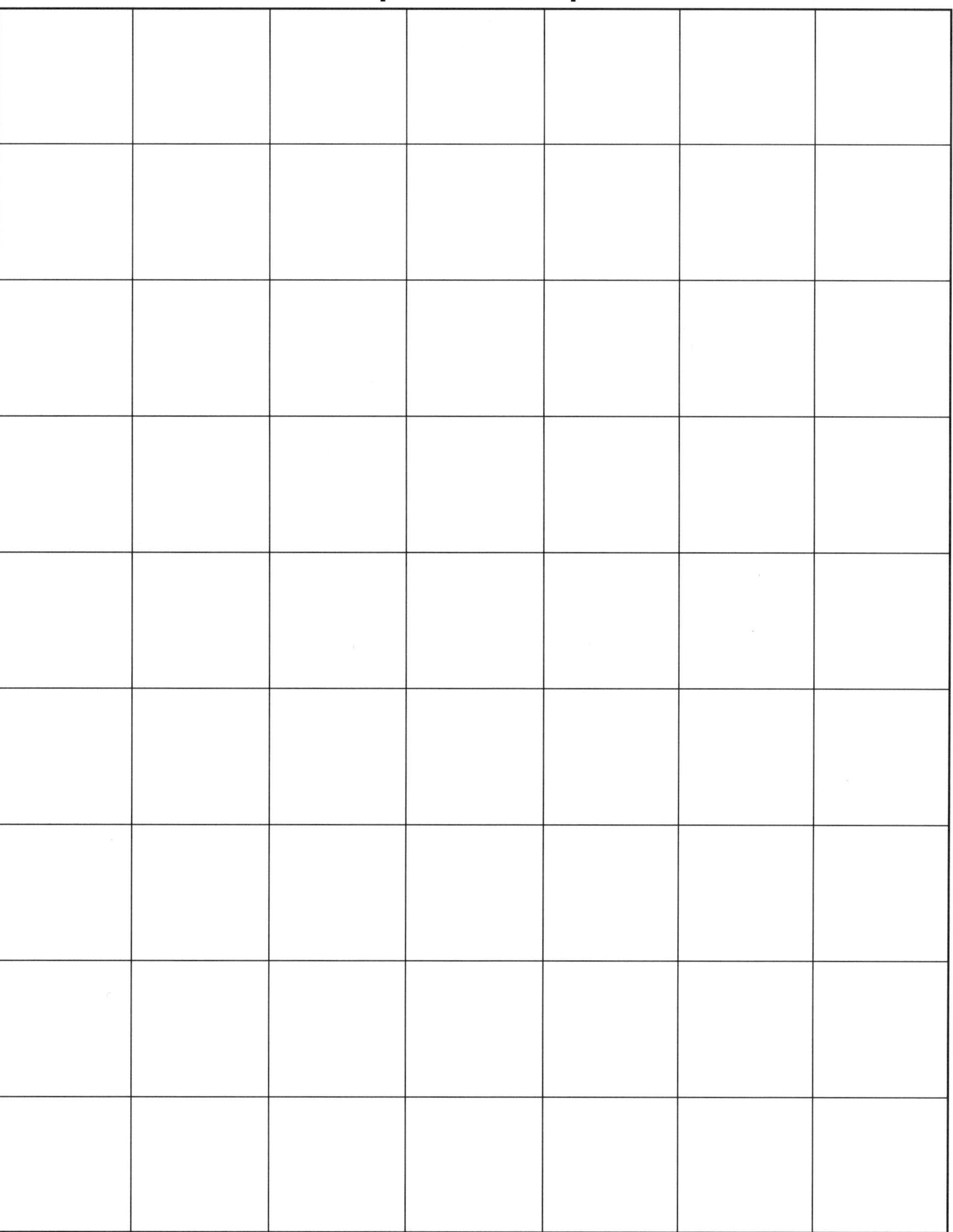

For use with *Home*, Chapter 1, ACTIVITY THREE: The Shape of the "Universal Dwelling"

Activity Three A

Exploring Surface Area-to-Volume Ratio

FOR YOU TO DO

1. The surface area-to-volume ratio changes with the scale of an object. Begin with a unit cube (1 x 1 x 1). This cube is one unit long on each side.

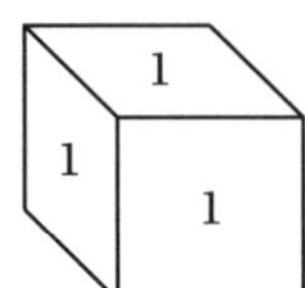

a) Calculate its volume.

b) Calculate its surface area.

c) What is its surface area-to-volume ratio?

2. This cube is two units long on each side.

a) Calculate its volume.

b) Calculate its surface area.

c) What is its surface area-to-volume ratio?

3. Calculate the surface areas, volumes, and surface area-to-volume ratios of three-, four- and five-unit cubes.

a) 3-unit cube: surface area: _______ volume: _______
surface area-to-volume ratio: _________

b) 4-unit cube: surface area: _______ volume: _______
surface area-to-volume ratio: _________

c) 5-unit cube: surface area: _______ volume: _______
surface area-to-volume ratio: _________

4. On a separate graph, plot the change in surface area-to-volume ratios against unit cube size.

5. If heat energy radiates equally out of each side of a cube, how does heat loss change as the cube increases in unit size? Why do small birds and mammals spend so much of their time eating? (You will revisit this question in Chapter Two.)

NOTES

1

ACTIVITY FOUR
Solar Heat Flow in the "Universal Dwelling"

Background Information

The concepts and skills introduced in Activity Four fall into two areas:

- producing a model of a three-dimensional object to a specified reduced scale of size.
- producing and interpreting a temperature versus time graph from temperature measurements made inside a model home which is first heated by an external source over time and then allowed to cool over time.

Modeling to a specified scale. The 1:48 scale specified for students to use for constructing their model homes in For You To Do was chosen to provide models of reasonable size for this and subsequent activities. It is the "shrink factor" which would allow, for example, that a home 48 feet long would have its length reduced to 1 foot in a model made this specified scale. As explained to students in the text, this also means that one inch on the model would represent 4 feet on the real home. The same scale can be expressed as 1/4 inch representing one foot:

1 foot: 48 feet = 12 inches : 48 feet = 1 inch : 4 feet = 1/4 inch : 1 foot

This is a standard choice of scale often used by architects and home designers who refer to it as a "one-fourth inch scale," carrying the silent meaning that one-fourth inch represents one foot in the real world. This particular scale offers the advantage that scale drawings of many homes, or rooms within large homes, will fit on standard sized sheets of paper; universally available 8-1/2" x 11" paper printed with a 1/4" grid is very handy for sketching plans to this particular scale. Other scales commonly used for home design include 1/8" and 1/16". Inexpensive computer software for do-it-yourself home designers are available for producing drawings to these common scales and may be useful for your students to render and refine plans for their universal dwellings. The technical education teachers at your school may be able to provide help in the area of computer-assisted drawing; this would be a good opportunity for interdisciplinary cooperation.

Heating/cooling curves. The background information presented here will apply to all of the activities remaining in this chapter. It is critical for you as the teacher to understand the principles presented here.

Before proceeding, is suggested that you read the For You To Read for Activity Five in the student text to refresh your knowledge of conduction, convection and radiation as heat transfer mechanisms; please do that reading now.

Having reviewed the three means by which heat is transferred in the reading suggested above, you, as the teacher, should have awareness that all three mechanisms will be involved when students heat and cool their model homes. During the heating phase, the heat from the lamp will be transferred primarily through infrared radiation to the outside surfaces of the model home which face the lamp . The heat next will conduct through the tagboard walls and roof to warm the inside surfaces which, in turn, will warm the air in contact with the surfaces. Finally, heat will be delivered to the thermometer at the center of the model home by convection through the air inside the model. The cooling phase will involve a similarly complex reverse chain of heat transfers involving all three mechanisms. Don't be fooled into believing that the heating and cooling processes in this exercise are simple, because they aren't. More than one mechanism is sure to be active at any given time; for example, final cooling of the outside surfaces of the home will be accomplished as the surfaces transfer heat to the air through simultaneous conduction by contact and emission of radiation.

For your background only, and not suggested to be treated with students, the rate of conduction of heat through a solid which would apply only to that part of the chain of heat transfers in this activity which involves the conduction of heat through the tagboard walls/roof is governed by the equation:

Rate of heat transfer through a material = $kA(\Delta T)/L$

where k represents the heat conductivity of the material, and A is the common area across which a temperature difference ΔT exists between surfaces of the material separated by thickness d.

The main factor which will affect the rate of heat transfer to and from the model home will be the difference in the temperature of the illuminated outside surfaces of the model and the temperatures of the inside surfaces and the air inside the model. The greater the temperature differences are at a particular time, the greater will be the rate of heat transfer at that time; the less the temperature difference, the less the rate of transfer.

Because the temperature difference between the outside and the inside of the model home diminishes during heating, the rate of heat transfer also can be expected to diminish. Therefore, the temperature versus time graph can be expected to climb rapidly at first, continue to climb with decreasing slope and then level off to plateau at an equilibrium temperature.

The equilibrium temperature, of course, is explained by the fact that, once the interior of the model home has been heated, it simultaneously cools, or loses heat, through the surfaces not exposed to the lamp because, for those surfaces, the inside temperature is higher than the outside temperature The equilibrium temperature is reached when the model is losing heat to the surrounding cool air at the same rate that it is receiving heated air from the lamp.

The cooling phase depends on the difference in the temperature of the air inside the model and the temperature of the air surrounding the model (the ambient temperature of the room). This temperature difference will diminish during cooling, so the cooling curve can be expected to fall rapidly at first, continue to fall with decreasing negative slope, and finally plateau at room temperature.

The key to interpreting the behavior of rates of heating and cooling over time is to focus on the slope of each temperature versus time graph. How the slope changes with time tells the story about how the rate of heating or cooling changes with time.

Be sure to have students carefully measure and record the position and orientation (distance and angle) of the heat lamp relative to the model home so that the setup can be replicated as called for in activities later in this chapter. It will be desirable that the heat input provided by the lamp will remain constant (not enter as a variable) in those future activities.

Active-ating the Physics InfoMall

The physics topics (solar energy and heat flow) in this activity were already discussed above. However, students are asked to construct graphs now. Search the InfoMall with the keywords "student difficult*" and "graph*". Note that the asterisks are wild-characters - "graph*" can be "graph", "graphs" and "graphing", for example. You will find several articles that discuss the difficulties students have interpreting graphs. However, most of the research done in this area (in physics, that is; math research may also report on general graphing difficulties, but math research does not appear on the InfoMall) is on kinematics. Nonetheless, the results may be enlightening. Students do not always understand what lines on a graph mean, and what slopes indicate, for example.

Planning for the Activity

Time Requirements

This activity can be completed within one period (40 - 50 minutes). Allow an extra 15 - 20 minutes if the students need to construct their houses. The graphing of the data may take up to 20 minutes to complete, or may be assigned for homework. If it is assigned for homework, ensure the students know how to label and plot the points on a graph. Allow 20 minutes to 30 minutes to guide the students in producing a graph from common data for the whole class if needed.

Materials needed

For each group:

- ruler, inch scale
- meter stick
- tagboard
- cutting tool
- masking tape
- heat lamp
- ring stand and clamp for lamp
- clock
- thermometer or temperature probe
- graph paper

Advance Preparation and Setup

Almost any heat lamp will do. A commonly available 250-watt clear infrared heat lamp with a built-in reflector is recommended; a 125-watt bulb of the same design will work, but will provide a lower rate of heating. If lamp fixtures with parabolic metal reflectors are available at the school, "Crystal Clear" (unfrosted) light bulbs available in 150, 200 and 300 watt sizes also will work (these bulbs, which have a straight filament aligned coincident with the bulb's axis of symmetry also are useful as intense "point" sources of light (filament viewed on end) for other laboratory activities.

Teaching Notes

The activities for this class session are very intensive. Student teams construct their scale model homes according to their prior specifications and then conduct the heating and cooling experiment on their model. You should have all materials they will need available and well-organized to ensure that the teams will be able to complete the activity. Begin the class by immediately having the student groups discuss What Do You Think?. Next, focus their attention on the model-building and heating/cooling phases of For You To Do. Check that the 1:48 scale of size is understood and encourage student to monitor time as they work so that they will complete the tasks.

CAUTION: Care should be taken when cutting the holes in the cardboard house. Also, remind the students to handle the thermometer carefully, and if it should break, to inform the teacher immediately.

Activity Four

Solar Heat Flow in the "Universal Dwelling"

WHAT DO YOU THINK?

Throughout one cloudless day in June, at 45° North latitude, over 300 million joules of solar radiation strike each square meter of area at the Earth's surface.

- **What is the relationship between how fast a building heats and how fast it cools? (Do buildings that heat quickly, cool slowly; or do buildings that heat quickly, cool quickly?)**

Record your ideas about these questions in your *Active Physics log*. Be prepared to discuss your responses with your small group and the class.

Activity Overview

In this activity the students will be performing experiments to simulate the heating of a building during the noonday sun, and cooling of the building at night (when the heat source is removed).

Student Objectives

Students will:

- construct a three-dimensional scale model of a universal dwelling to meet the design specifications of student groups.
- conduct a heat transfer experiment on the model.
- interpret heat transfer data collected from the experiment.

ANSWERS FOR THE TEACHER ONLY

1

What Do You Think?

Some students may think that some buildings will heat up quickly and cool down slowly, and vice versa. However, the rate of heating/cooling, has to do with the change in temperature between the building materials, and the environment. The rate of absorption is also dependent upon the types of materials with which the building is constructed, the texture of the building, how much glass is in the south side of the building, etc.

ANSWERS

For You To Do

1. Student activity.

2. Student activity.

3. Student activity.

FOR YOU TO DO

1. Using the resources that have been provided, construct a scale model of your universal dwelling using the design specifications for the basic unit. The model home should be built on a scale of 1:48. That means that one inch on the model will equal four feet, or 48", on the real home. In order to build the model quickly, build only the walls and roof of your home. Don't worry about putting a bottom (floor) on the model or placing windows and doors at this time.

2. Using the figure below, assemble a heat lamp, ring stand support and clamp, timer, measuring tools and thermometers. Conduct a timed heat-transfer experiment of 20 min. Place the nearest edge of the model 20 cm from the bulb of the heat lamp, with the lamp at approximately 45° from the center of the model home. (A 45° angle is halfway between the vertical and the horizontal.)

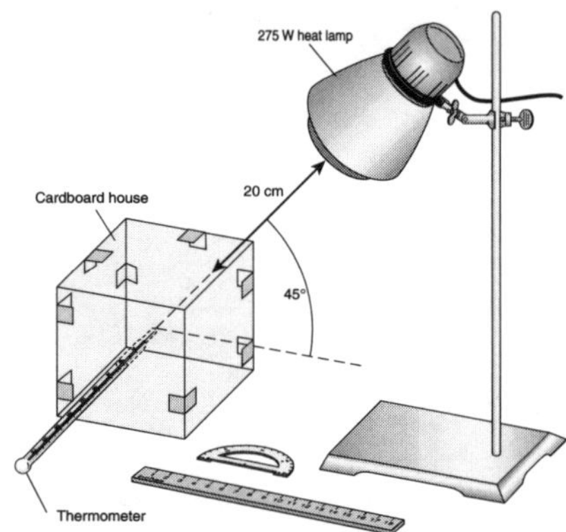

If the thermometer should break, *immediately* notify your instructor.

3. Carefully make a small hole in one wall. After making the hole, place the thermometer (or temperature probe) into one side of your model so that the bulb or probe is located in the dead center of the model. Be sure you can read the thermometer once it is in place!

4. When you have your model, the thermometer, and the heat lamp placed properly, have your teacher check it before you begin heating.
   a) Record the temperature of the thermometer before heating and record this as the temperature at 0 time.
   b) Turn on the heat lamp and, after 30 s, record the temperature.
   c) Continue this procedure for 10 min, recording temperature at each 30-s interval.

Caution: Heat lamps get very hot. Be careful not to touch the bulb or housing surrounding the bulb.

5. Turn off the lamp at the end of the 10-min heating phase.
   a) Continue to record the temperature every minute after the lamp is turned off for another 10 min.
   b) Calculate and record the change in temperature during each timed interval of heating and cooling.
   c) Graph your recorded data (temperatures against time) on the graph paper provided by your teacher. Your time axis should extend from 0 min (when you began) to 20 min (after the experiment was completed), and be placed on the x-axis.

6. Use the graph and the data you recorded to answer the following questions.
   a) What was the total temperature increase in your model home during the heating phase?
   b) What was the total temperature decrease in your model home during the cooling phase?
   c) Was the rate of temperature increase constant? How do you know?
   d) Was the rate of temperature decrease constant? How do you know?
   e) What time of day did the heating phase represent?
   f) What time of day did the cooling phase represent?
   g) What does your experiment suggest in regard to the potential of your model home to be heated by solar energy?

ANSWERS

For You To Do

(continued)

4\. a-c) Student activity and observations.

5\. a-b) Student activity and observations.

c) Student activity and observations. The graph should have fairly even heating and cooling. Depending on the types of materials, the heating curve and cooling curve should be approximately the same.

6\. a-b) Student data.

c) Student data. If the line is straight, it is a constant change.
If it is a curve, it is not a constant change.

d) Student data. If the line is straight, it is a constant change.
If it is a curve, it is not a constant change.

e) Heating phase represents the daytime heating.

f) Cooling phase represents the night.

g) Construction of the home can aid in increasing the amount of solar heating that can be utilized. Depending on the construction, the rate of heating will be increased or decreased, as needed depending on the climatic region in which the home is located.

1

ANSWERS

Physics To Go

1. Using a four feet to one inch scale, then one foot is represented by 1/4 inch on the scale.
2. Using the 1:48 inch scale, the size of the house would be 8.5 x 4 ft. by 11 x 4 ft. or 34 ft. x 44 ft.
3. One advantage is that the size of the scale drawings would be one half the size. This would allow a larger house to be put on ordinary paper.

REFLECTING ON THE ACTIVITY AND THE CHALLENGE

Over the past three activities you have made good progress in deciding upon the design specifications for your universal dwelling. In the last activity, you explored finding the "best fit" between living space and minimum surface area for your universal dwelling.

There are several reasons why you would want to keep surface area of the dwelling small, while keeping the interior as large as possible. One reason is that the materials for construction of the surface area of a building are expensive and a smaller surface area requires fewer materials. Another reason has to do with controlling the inside temperature of the building. In this activity, you constructed a model of your universal dwelling and investigated its heating and cooling properties.

The Architectural Committee probably will have some hard questions for you about your plans for heating and cooling the dwelling you are designing. That's because the greatest cost in operating most homes is for heating and cooling the home. This activity has given you some baseline information about how your dwelling design responds to the best kind of energy: free energy from the sun. It will be important for you to learn how to use solar energy to best advantage in the next activities. You do not want to design a building that is expensive to heat or cool.

PHYSICS TO GO

1. If four feet of length on a real home is represented by one inch on a scale model of the home, what length on the scale model would represent one foot on the real home?
2. A 1:48 scale drawing of the floor plan of a home must fit one $8\frac{1}{2} \times 11$ inch sheet of paper. What maximum length and width in feet can the home have?
3. Home designers sometimes use a 1:96 scale ($\frac{1}{8}$ inch represents 1 foot) when making drawings of home plans. What advantages would a 1:96 scale have over a 1:48 scale ($\frac{1}{4}$ inch represents 1 foot)?

4. If the heat lamp represented the sun at its noon position during the heating phase of the activity, which side of the model dwelling–north, south, east, or west–must have been facing the sun?
5. Describe how you would need to change the position of the heat lamp relative to the model dwelling to have the lamp represent the sun during the morning or afternoon.
6. Do you think that all of the radiation from the heat lamp that hit the model dwelling was absorbed by the dwelling? Give evidence to support your answer.
7. Explain how you think heat travelled from the inside surface of the model dwelling to the thermometer at the center of the model during the heating phase. Obviously, the heat had to travel through the air inside the model. How did it do that?

STRETCHING EXERCISES

1. Write down three questions that you would ask someone who uses solar heating or solar cooling for their home.
2. If you know of any people who use solar energy to heat their homes, or have designed ways to keep solar energy out to keep their homes cool, you may wish to talk with them about how they have done this. Ask them about the special things that they have done to control the effects of solar energy on their homes.

ANSWERS

Physics To Go

(continued)

4. The side of the model dwelling facing the sun would be south.
5. If you were facing the house, moving the lamp to the right would represent the morning sun, and moving the lamp to the left would represent the evening sun.
6. Not all of the radiation hit the house or was absorbed by the house, as the lamp shade heated up, as well as the area around the house (table top, air, any objects close by, etc.)
7. As particles are heated up, they increase their kinetic energy. This causes them to move faster and faster, until they bump into other particles. As the bumping increases, the energy is transferred from particle to particle. There is also convection currents which are set up inside the house, in which the heat is moved in "streams" or currents around the house.

ANSWERS

Stretching Exercises

1. Students' answers will vary. Some might include:
   - How much does it cost?
   - Describe how it works.
   - How does it work on cloudy days?
   - How does it work in the winter/summer?
   - How do you heat at night?
2. Student activity. Encourage students to seek out homes which are passively or actively solar heated. It is an opportunity to see how well it works in the area in which they live. Encourage the students to explore with the owners of the homes suggestions on how they might improve their home or ways in which it would work more efficiently in different climates.

Grid For Heating/Cooling Data

HEATING AND COOLING DATA

Time (min)	Empty house °C	Insulation Ceiling only °C	Insulation Full house °C	Windows °C	Summer °C	with Awnings °C	Winter °C
0.5							
1							
1.5							
2							
2.5							
3							
3.5							
4							
4.5							
5							
5.5							
6							
6.5							
7							
7.5							
8							
8.5							
9							
9.5							
10							
11							
12							
13							
14							
15							
16							
17							
18							
19							
20							

For use with *Home*, Chapter 1, ACTIVITY FOUR: Solar Heat Flow in the "Universal Dwelling"

Activity Four A

How Does Location Affect Energy Demands?

WHAT DO YOU THINK?

Some places have nearly the same temperature year-round. This may be hot, cold, or temperate. Other places have seasonal temperature changes. Where it is always cold and where there are noticeable seasonal changes, heating and/or cooling a dwelling is necessary. The amount of heat that must be used varies from day to night and from day to day. The range of temperatures and other conditions, such as amount of rainfall and sunshine, help determine how much heat is necessary.

- Using your assigned or chosen location, make a prediction about summer and winter climates. Imagine the people in the lowest economic category in this community.
- Do you think that they heat or air-condition their homes? What would they use as a source of fuel?

1

Record your ideas about these questions in your *Active Physics log*. Be prepared to discuss your responses with your small group and the class.

FOR YOU TO DO

1. Determine answers to the following questions for your team's location. Record your answers in your log.

a) What is the average high temperature in the middle of summer?

b) What is the average low temperature in the middle of summer?

c) What is the average high temperature in the middle of winter?

d) What is the average low temperature in the middle of winter?

e) What source of fuel for heat is most likely used by the poorest of the people there?

f) How many heating 'degree-days' are there in an average year? (There is one degree day for every degree Fahrenheit the average daily temperature is below 600F.) If you do any calculations, show your work in your log.

g) 'Cooling degree-days' are also kept track of, especially in more developed countries. How would you define one cooling degree-day? How many cooling degree-days are there in an average year?

h) Does the location you chose require a heating or cooling system? Write your answer in your log.

For use with *Home*, Chapter 1, ACTIVITY FOUR: Solar Heat Flow in the "Universal Dwelling"

PHYSICS TO GO

1. Find out how many heating degree-days there were in the last heating season in your local home town. (This information is available from the gas company that serves your area or from the people that supply the energy your family uses for heat.)

2. Determine how much energy your family used for heat last year. (If your family hasn't saved last year's bills, the company that supplies your energy can tell you, or they can give you a value for a 'typical' family.)

3. Calculate how much energy per degree day your family used for heating last year.

4. How much energy might be used annually for heat, by a family like yours, in the location your team is researching?

Activity Four B

What Shape is Most Effective for Heat Storage?

WHAT DO YOU THINK?

- Which shape of hot metal will cool more quickly: a sphere or a pancake?

Record your ideas about this question in your *Active Physics log*. Be prepared to discuss your responses with your small group and the class.

FOR YOU TO DO

1. Measure the mass and dimensions of a spherically and flat cylindrically shaped piece of the same type of metal. Record their values.

a) Mass of spherically shaped metal: _________g

b) Radius of spherically shaped metal: _________mm

c) Mass of flat cylindrically shaped metal: _________g

d) Radius of flat cylindrically shaped metal: _________mm

e) Thickness of flat cylindrically shaped metal: _________mm

1

2. Put on a pair of goggles. Place both samples in a 250 mL beaker with enough water to cover both samples.

3. Obtain two polystyrene cups. Place 50 mL of room-temperature water in each cup. (Note: The mass of 1 mL of water is 1 gm.) Measure the temperature of room-temperature water in each of your two polystyrene cups.

a) Record the temperature of the water.

DO NOT LET YOUR THERMOMETER REST IN THE POLYSTYRENE CUP WITHOUT EXTERNAL SUPPORT. UNSUPPORTED THERMOMETERS WILL TIP POLYSTYRENE CUPS OVER AND POSSIBLY BREAK.

4. Place the metal samples and water on a hot plate and bring to a boil.

5. After the water has come to a boil, using tongs, carefully remove the spherically shaped metal sample from the 250 mL beaker and place it in the first polystyrene cup. Start the stopwatch at this time.

6. Immerse your thermometer bulb in the water without letting it touch the metal. Stir the mixture in the polystyrene cup gently until the water increases by three degrees Celsius. Stop the stopwatch and record the time.

a) Calculate the amount of heat lost by the spherically shaped metal to the water and the amount of heat lost per minute per gram of material. (Heat lost by metal = heat gained by water = mass of water x specific heat of water x change in water temperature). The heat lost per minute per gram is found by dividing the heat lost by the mass in grams and the time in minutes.

7. Repeat steps 5 and 6 for the flat cylindrically shaped metal.

8. From your previous measurements, calculate the volumes, surface area, and surface area-to-volume ratio for each piece of metal. Show all your calculations in your log.

a) Volume of spherically shaped metal:

b) Surface area of spherically shaped metal:

c) Surface area-to-volume ratio of spherically shaped metal:

d) Volume of flat cylindrically shaped metal:

e) Surface area of flat cylindrically shaped metal:

f) Surface area-to-volume ratio of flat cylindrically shaped metal:

g) Describe how the surface area-to-volume ratio affects the rate at which heat is transferred. Write in your log how this applies to keeping heat from leaking away too fast.

PHYSICS TO GO

Do as many of the following as you can:

1. By treating your arms, legs, and torso as cylinders and your head as a sphere, estimate the dimensions, then calculate the surface area-to-volume ratio for your body. Repeat this for a baby (make approximations if you need to). Discuss the implications of your findings for retaining body heat. (Should a baby be kept more warmly dressed than an adult?)

2. Look at several water heaters at an appliance store or in advertising brochures. Take the necessary data to calculate surface area-to-volume ratios. Are some more effective at retaining heat than others? Is this related to brand? To capacity? (If you can get one or two other people to cooperate with you, you can get more data in less time!)

3. Look at several air-cooled, gasoline-powered engines, such as lawn mowers and chain saws. What is the biggest one (horsepower or cubic inches or liters) you can find? Do you know of any cars that have air-cooled engines? Do any airplanes have air-cooled engines? In your journal write about your discoveries and explain them in terms of this activity.

STRETCHING EXERCISES

1. Obtain a tall, cylindrical container such as a graduated cylinder or drinking glass. Fill it with different amounts of hot water and measure how fast the water cools. (Be sure to have a control to account for the fact that some of the heat will go to warming the container itself, and the more water you put in it the more energy goes into warming the container.)

2. Make a graph showing how heat loss depends on the surface area-to-volume ratio of the water. If you know how, determine the equation of this relationship.

1

ACTIVITY FIVE
The Role of Insulation: Investigating Insulation Types

Background Information

If you did not consult the teacher background information for Activity Four it is suggested that you do so now. The background information presented for Activity Four is needed for this activity and the remaining activities in this chapter.

The focus of Activity Five is thermal insulation, which in the thermodynamics context of this chapter, applies to the ability of materials to resist heat transfer by conduction. It is important that you and your students not confuse use of the term here with the electrical context in which the same term, insulation, applies to the ability of materials to conduct electricity.

The term insulation is used only informally among scientists and engineers who work in the area of thermodynamics. Instead, scientists use a physical property called "heat conductivity" to describe the ability of a material to conduct heat. The heat conductivity of a material expresses the amount of heat energy which flows per unit of time through a unit of cross-sectional area when a one-degree temperature difference exists between surfaces of one unit of thickness of the material (see the equation governing the rate of heat transfer through materials in the background information for Activity Four; heat conductivity is symbolized by "k" in that equation).

Values of heat conductivity have been measured for virtually all materials, and, in general, metals are found to be good conductors of heat while nonmetals are poor conductors. A scientist desiring to find a good thermal insulator would seek a poor conductor—a material having a low value of heat conductivity.

"R values" are included in one of the items for Physics To Go in this activity, and it is likely that you will need some knowledge about what R values mean. The industries which supply thermal insulating materials for the building trades have developed a relative scale of resistance to heat conduction called "R values," wherein "R" represents resistance in absolute (dimensionless) numbers. The higher the R value, the better the insulating quality. Insulating materials such as fiberglass wool batts and Styrofoam are manufactured in thicknesses tailored to the needs of builders (for example, batts of thickness to match the hollow space between 2 x 4 and 2 x 6 boards used to construct walls).

Homeowners and builders today can consult tables which recommend the R values needed in the walls, ceilings and floors of homes to provide efficiency for heating and cooling homes according to climatic region.

R values offer the easy-to-use advantage for consumers of being additive. For example, a homeowner in the northern part of the U.S. wishing to upgrade ceiling insulation from R-19 to the recommended value of R-38, can place a six-inch thickness of fiberglass wool batting having insulating value R-19 over the top of the existing insulation in the attic of the home.

Comparison of the heating and cooling curves generated by students in this activity should lead to two findings:

- different materials have different insulating effects.
- increasing the thickness of a particular insulating material has a generally inverse effect on the rate of flow of heat energy and, therefore, an increased insulating effect.

The inverse relationship between the rate of heat flow and the thickness of the material through which the heat is flowing suggests that, theoretically, no thickness of insulation will absolutely stop heat flow. Applying this to insulating a home, it is clear that cost and available space for insulation cause need for a trade-off: an acceptable level of heat loss must be decided upon in relation to the cost and ability to prevent heat loss through insulating.

Active-ating the Physics InfoMall

For alternate activities or demos, you can browse through the Demo & Lab Shop. Simply choose a book and find the section on heat. There are plenty from which to choose. Many of these have explanatory figures. Take a look.

Again, graphs may be a problem. Check out the references for Activity Four.

A search of the InfoMall discovers several good references on insulation. For example, *American Journal of Physics*, vol. 52, issue 7, contains "Cost per million BTU of solar heat, insulation, and conventional fuels." *The Physics Teacher*, vol. 16, issue 6, has "Insulation and the rate of heat transfer." Not to be outdone, *Physics Today* has two articles on the efficient use of energy, as discussed above (vol. 28, issue 8, and vol. 33, issue 2).

Simply search the entire CD-ROM with keyword "insulation" to find these and many other hits. One more example is the textbook *Physics Including Human Applications*, with Chapter 11 on Thermal Transport. This addresses conduction and convection. Do the search and browse some of the hits for yourself. You may find more than you can easily use!

Planning for the Activity

Time Requirements

Allow about 10 to 20 minutes for the discussion regarding the results from the previous activity.

Allow about 10 minutes to set up the apparatus, and the hot water bath. Twenty minutes is needed for the activity, and about another ten to twenty minutes to collect and interpret data. If desired, the class may share the results of the various kinds of insulating materials from each of the other groups.

Materials needed

For each group:

- insulating material (each group uses only one kind of material: sand, vermiculite, foam packing material, or fiberglass wool; vary the kinds of materials across groups)
- 3 empty metal cans of varying diameters (such as 1, 2, 3-pound coffee cans)
- thermometer or temperature probe
- hot water bath, sufficient size to hold cans simultaneously
- ice water bath, sufficient size to hold cans simultaneously
- graph paper

Advance Preparation and Setup

In order to get reliable results, collect the number of cans needed for your particular class size. Three different size identical cans per group are needed. Before the students arrive, have a model set up and ready to go to show the students how to do this activity.

Teaching Notes

In the previous class, heating and cooling experiments were conducted on the students' model homes. Begin this class by having each group report its results in terms of heat transfer (heating and cooling) for their model home. Discuss with the entire class the similarities and differences of results among groups.

Ask: "To what extent do you think the shape, styles and volumes of the houses were factors affecting the heating and cooling rates?
What other factors might influence heating and cooling rates in your model homes?"

Suggest that some groups may wish to consider design changes in light of the comparative results of groups.

Scientific inquiry can also be aided by working with the students to develop a proper procedure for this activity in order to achieve true scientific results. This can be done by having a discussion before the class, and establish the independent and dependent variables and which variables are being controlled in the experiment.

Discuss the heat transfer mechanisms described in the For You To Read with the class, and then have students complete What Do You Think? within their groups. Next, have students conduct For You To Do.

Remind the students of the safety concerns in the text book.

The transfer of heat is not dependent on whether there is heating or cooling as much as on the change in the temperature. Heat always moves from high temperatures to low temperatures. Therefore, the rate of heating or cooling is dependent on the temperature difference, and that it is not always exactly the same in heating in the hot water bath, and cooling in the ice bath.

At the end of class you may want to tabulate the class data so that the students can examine the comparative effects of different insulating materials. Discuss the results with the class and attempt to arrive at a generalization about the effects of two variables: insulation thickness and insulation quality. If the cans were not identical, ask the question, "If the sets of cans were not identical for all groups, would it be "fair" to compare the effects of the different kinds of insulation used by different groups?"

Activity Overview

The students will be evaluating properties of insulation, and its effect on temperature cooling with given variables (thickness, type of material, cooling/heating, etc.). They will be looking at the three ways in which heat energy is transferred - radiation, convection and conduction.

Student Objectives

Students will:

- explain how insulation retards heat flow in terms of conduction.
- explain how insulation retards heat flow in terms of convection.
- conduct an experiment to test how the thickness and kind of insulating material influence the rate of heat transfer.

ANSWERS FOR THE TEACHER ONLY

What Do You Think?

Students may give different answers based on preconceptions. For example, a student living in Arizona, will say that it is more important for summer cooling, however, a student from Alaska may say that it is more important for winter heating. Generally, the importance of insulation for heating is about as important as for cooling.

DESIGNING THE UNIVERSAL DWELLING

Activity Five

The Role of Insulation: Investigating Insulation Types

WHAT DO YOU THINK?

Insulation used in homes is usually a lightweight material that is designed to reduce the flow of heat energy through the walls or ceiling.

- **Is insulation in a home more important in the heat of summer or the cool of winter?**

Record your ideas about this question in your *Active Physics log*. Be prepared to discuss your responses with your small group and the class.

HOME H24

FOR YOU TO DO

1. Place the insulating material supplied to your team in each of the 3 cans. Insert a thermometer in the absolute center of each material.
   a) Measure the thickness of the insulation surrounding the thermometer in each can.
   b) Record the temperature shown by each thermometer.
2. Place the 3 cans in a hot water bath.
   a) Record the temperature of each can every minute for 10 min.

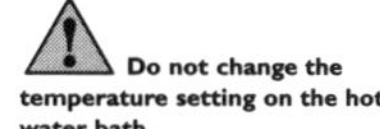

Do not change the temperature setting on the hot water bath.

3. Carefully check that the cans are not too hot to touch. Carefully remove the cans from the bath.
   a) Record the temperature each minute for another 10 min.

Use a cloth or paper towel to grasp the cans when removing them from the baths. Moisture may form on the outside—be careful that the can does not slip from your grasp.

4. Now place the 3 cans in an ice water bath and repeat the steps above.

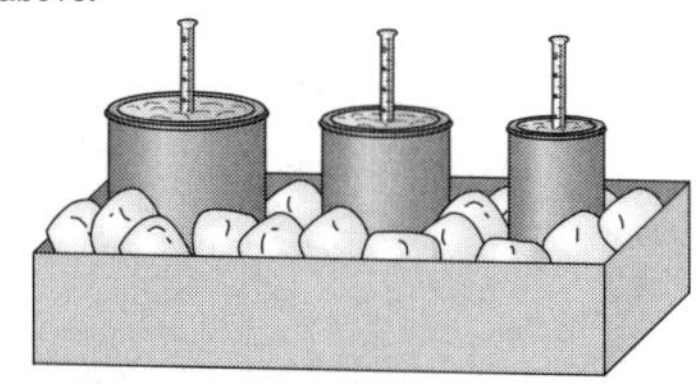

   a) Record the temperature in each can every minute for 10 min of cooling in the bath and for another 10 min after removing them from the bath.

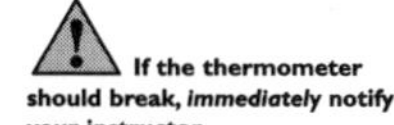

If the thermometer should break, *immediately* notify your instructor.

5. Display the data on a graph.
   a) Graph your heating and cooling data for each of the 3 cans on a single graph, labeling each appropriately.
6. Use your graph to answer the following questions:
   a) Compare the three graphs that you made. What differences do you note among the graphs?
   b) What do you conclude about the effectiveness of insulation in heating as opposed to cooling situations?
   c) What do you conclude about the effectiveness of using varying thickness of insulating material?

Answers

For You To Do

1. a-b) Student activity.

2. a) Student activity and observation.

3. a) Student activity and observation.

4. a) Student activity and observation.

5. a) Student activity and graphing.

6. a) Student data from their observations. They should note that there is a steeper curve with the least insulation.

   b) Students' answers will vary depending on the type of insulation. In general the students should notice that the effect of the insulation is about the same for heating and cooling.

   c) Generally, as you get thicker insulation, the effectiveness goes up. More is better. One variable to consider, is how much insulation is stuffed in, and students may note that if it is packed in too tightly, there is a reduction in the effectiveness. Discuss this with the students.

FOR YOU TO READ

Transmission of Heat Energy

You have most likely studied in prior science classes the three means by which heat energy is transmitted: conduction, convection, and radiation. As you read the descriptions of these means of transmission, try to recall experiments or investigations that you pursued if you studied this earlier.

In the case of conduction, the heat energy possessed by a material is transmitted to another material by direct contact of the materials with one another. The rapidly moving (and hence high energy) atoms in a red hot iron bar come in direct contact with, let us say, cold water. The heat energy of the iron atoms is conducted by physical contact directly to the water molecules, which, in turn, heat other adjacent molecules and so on, causing the heat energy to dissipate throughout the water, warming it in the process.

In convection, the molecules or atoms of a fluid (a liquid or a gas) which have more heat energy will move faster than the surrounding molecules of that material. As a result, they will move further apart and, therefore, become pushed by the colder, more closely packed molecules or atoms. As the hotter, lower-density molecules move through the colder surrounding material, they carry their heat energy (motion) with them, losing it along their path to other colder molecules by conduction. Convection then, is the transmission of heat energy from one place to another due to physical movement of a warmer fluid through a colder fluid (typically in response to the force of gravity).

Radiation is the third form of energy transmission. In this case, the electromagnetic radiation given off by high energy (hot) materials can be transmitted through objects, or even a vacuum, at the speed of light. When this energy strikes a material that can absorb it, the radiant energy causes the atoms or molecules of the material it strikes to move faster and the molecules now have more heat energy.

REFLECTING ON THE ACTIVITY AND THE CHALLENGE

Homes For Everyone (HFE) realizes that it is important to control the interior temperatures of their universal dwellings regardless of climate and location. It is important because of energy, comfort, and health concerns.

One of the criteria that the Architectural Committee will use to evaluate your plan is "the kind of insulation materials and thickness you choose should show you know the principles which make the insulation effective." That's exactly what this activity was about, so it will be very helpful in meeting the challenge.

PHYSICS TO GO

1. Explain how conduction, convection, and radiation were involved in both the heating and cooling phases of the model dwelling in Activity Four.
2. Which of the three ways of transferring heat was most directly involved in the investigation in Activity Five? Explain your answer.
3. In this activity you tested the effects of two variables on the transfer of heat. Identify the variables and explain what you learned about the effect of each on heat transfer.
4. If you wanted to reduce the amount of heat conducted through a particular kind of material to one-half the amount, what change in the thickness of the material would be needed? Also provide answers for reducing the transfer of heat to one-third, and one-fourth the amount.
5. Would insulating a home be more, less, or about equally important for keeping a home warm in a cold climate or keeping a home cool in a hot climate? Use evidence from the data for your answer.
6. Years ago, the answer to keeping warm during cold weather was to put on more clothes. Today, the answer can be to put on different clothes. Comment on these two ways of keeping warm in terms of the variables tested in this activity, and the evolution of clothing available for winter.
7. Find out what kinds and thickness of insulating materials are used in the walls and ceiling of your home. Your parents or building supervisor may have this information.
8. Go to a building supply store and examine various insulating materials. The insulating properties of these materials are given in "R values." Find out what an "R value" is.

ANSWERS

Physics To Go

1. Conduction is the transfer of heat from one particle to another. In Activity Four, the heat is transferred by conduction. This is when the outside molecules of the box transfer the heat to other molecules of the box, and eventually to the particles of air inside the box. Convection is the movement of heated particles, as some of the molecules are moving faster (more heat energy) than surrounding molecules. The heat is transferred from one area in the box to other areas in the box similar to the movement of water in a stream. Radiation is the transfer of heat in the form of electromagnetic radiation. Heat is transferred from one object to the next when electromagnetic radiation is absorbed by some materials. In this case the bulb is light and heat (electromagnetic radiation) and the energy is absorbed by the box.
2. Conduction is most directly involved in the transfer of heat as there is direct molecule to molecule transfer (hot water in direct contact with the can and other molecules in the insulation, etc.
3. One variable was the thickness of insulation. Generally, the thicker the insulation, the greater the insulative properties. The other variable is the temperature (either heating up or cooling down).
4. Student data. Probably reduce the amount of insulation to half. Students will be able to surmise from their data, based on the time it took to reach certain temperatures while heating or cooling.
5. Insulating the home would be about equally important for keeping the home warm in winter and cool in summer. One factor would be the cost of insulating the home. If the heat was bearable, the cost of insulating would too expensive.
6. The students, after comparing the results, might notice that some materials insulate better than others. Before some of the modern insulative materials were invented, all we could do was put on more layers. With modern insulation, the amount of mass is reduced by the type of material. Therefore, you can have better insulation with thinner insulation or smaller amounts of the materials.
7. In colder climates, walls generally have between 4 and 6 inches, and ceilings have between 6 and 20 inches.
8. The "R value" of a material is the relative insulative properties of different materials compared to a standard.

ANSWERS

Physics To Go

(continued)

9. The aluminum foil will increase the "R value" as it reflects the heat from the shiny surface. Therefore, the aluminum foil side should be facing the heat source. In colder climates the foil is facing inwards, and in hotter climates the foil is facing outwards.

10. Depends on the area. Check with local contractor or building inspector.

11. The amount of insulation is largest in the ceilings as hot air rises, and there will be a large amount of heat lost through the ceiling. The walls have the next largest amount, and the floors the least.

9. Some rigid insulating material has an aluminum foil surface bonded to the sheet. What purpose does this aluminum foil surface serve? How does it influence the "R value" of the material?
10. How much insulation is recommended for a home in your area of the country?
11. Is the amount of insulation recommended the same for floors, walls, and ceilings? Why?

STRETCHING EXERCISE

Design a beverage container to keep a cold drink cold, and a hot drink hot.

INQUIRY INVESTIGATION

Design an experiment to test the insulating effectiveness of natural material such as grass, dry mud, adobe brick, or stone. After your teacher approves your design, conduct the experiment.

ANSWERS

Stretching Exercise

Student activity. Look for innovative designs. Some of the considerations are : size, mass, portability, durability, cost, etc.

Activity Five A

Transmission of Heat

FOR YOU TO DO

1. Drip candle wax onto one end of a long nail. Put on a heat-proof glove and hold the end of the nail with tongs.

2. Carefully hold the other end of the nail in the candle flame. Observe what happens to the candle wax at the opposite end of the nail, as the nail heats up.

   a) Record your observations.

   b) Speculate on how the heat was transmitted from one end of the nail to the other.

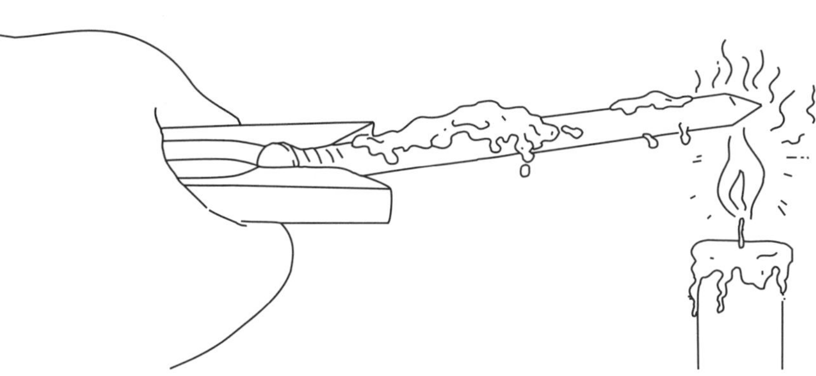

3. Obtain two identical-sized beakers or jars. Pour an equal amount of water into each beaker.

4. Cover one beaker with black paper, and the other with aluminum foil, with the shiny silver-side outwards.

5. Measure the initial temperature of the water in each beaker.

   a) Record the initial temperature in your log.

6. Set up both beakers equidistant from a heat lamp, or place the beakers in a sunny window. Allow the beakers to stand for one hour. Measure the temperature of the water in each beaker after the hour.

a) Record the final temperature of the water.

b) Speculate on how the heat from the lamp or the sun was transmitted to the water in the beakers.

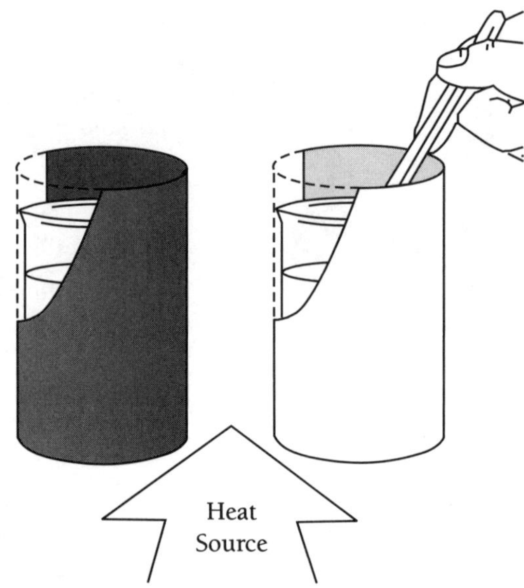

7. Fill a small plastic bottle with hot water. Add a few drops of food color to the bottle.

Seal the mouth of the bottle with aluminum foil attached to a string.

8. Fill a large tank with cold water. Carefully lower the plastic bottle into one corner of the tank. Let the water settle and then pull the foil lid off the bottle using the string. Observe what happens.

a) Record your observations in your log. You may wish to use a diagram.

b) Speculate on how the hot water was transmitted through the tank.

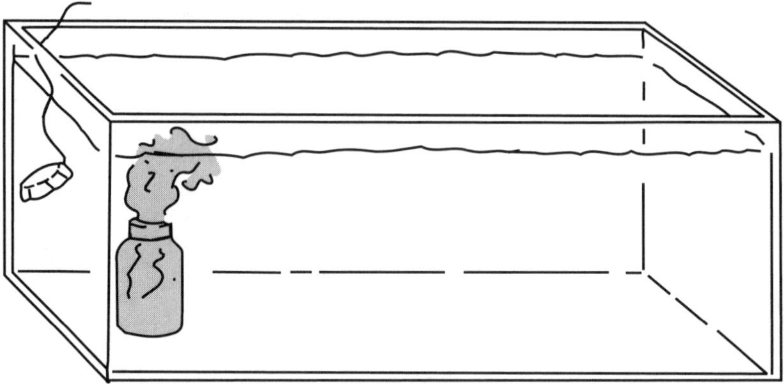

NOTES

ACTIVITY SIX
Investigating Insulation Placement in Your Universal Dwelling

Background Information

No new physics principles are introduced in Activity Six as students conduct an experiment to explore the effect of adding insulation to their model homes and repeat the heating/cooling procedure conducted on uninsulated models in Activity Four. The results of this activity should be able to be directly related to outcomes in Activity Five in which thickness was explored as a variable governing the effectiveness of insulating materials. However, some subtleties are involved which need your attention as the teacher.

Any departure from setting up the heat lamp in the same way as it was set up for Activity Four (same lamp intensity at the same distance and angle relative to the model home) will limit ability to compare results of this activity to the results of Activity Four. If a variety of heat lamps were used by different groups in Activity Four, each group should use the same kind (wattage and style) in this activity so that the heat output of the lamp will not enter as a variable. Since the angle of illumination also affects the heat delivered to a surface, it is desirable to use the same angle as in Activity Four. Finally, since the intensity of illumination provided by the lamp varies inversely with the square of distance, a small change in the distance between the lamp and the model home will cause a dramatic change in the heat delivered to the surface of the home. Therefore, it will be important to maintain the distance used in Activity Four. Need to replicate the setup of the heat lamp, and the cautions about changes in the setup just noted, will also apply to later activities in this chapter.

The sage saying "heat rises" has strong implications for insulating homes. While most homes have insulation in both exterior walls and ceilings (and sometimes in floors), ceiling insulation is generally regarded as the most important and effective procedure for preventing heat loss in homes. It is common practice today in residential home design to provide two or more times the insulating effect in ceilings than in walls. For example, for homes in the northern U.S., recommended minimum insulation values are R-19 for walls and R-38 or more for ceilings. It will be interesting to see if similar trends are reflected in students' data as they progressively insulate the ceiling and walls of their model homes.

The thickness of cardboard used as insulation in this activity probably would not be realistic in terms of the 1:48 scale of the model home. For example, a 1/4 inch thickness of cardboard scaled up to real world size would correspond to a 12 inch thickness. This would be a reasonable thickness for ceiling insulation in a home, but would be unrealistically large for wall thickness in conventional construction. Only in recent years have home designers begun using 2"x6" lumber as stud members in exterior walls to allow placing a greater thickness of insulation in the hollow spaces between studs than is allowed by 2"x4" studs. Of course, a lesser thickness of insulation for the model which would scale up to a reasonable real-world wall thickness could be provided by choosing a more effective insulating material than cardboard.

Active-ating the Physics InfoMall

For alternate activities or demos, you can browse through the Demo & Lab Shop. Simply choose a book and find the section on heat. There are plenty from which to choose. Many of these have explanatory figures. Take a look.

Again, graphs may be a problem. Check out the references for Activity Four.

A search of the InfoMall discovers several good references on insulation. For example, *American Journal of Phyiscs*, vol. 52, issue 7, contains "Cost per million BTU of solar heat, insulation, and conventional fuels." *The Physics Teacher*, vol. 16, issue 6, has "Insulation and the rate of heat transfer." Not to be outdone, *Physics Today* has two articles on the efficient use of energy, as discussed above (vol. 28, issue 8, and vol. 33, issue 2).

Simply search the entire CD-ROM with keyword "insulation" to find these and many other hits. One more example is the textbook *Physics Including Human Applications*, with Chapter 11 on Thermal Transport. This addresses conduction and convection. You may find more than you can easily use!

Planning for the Activity

Time Requirements

Allow about 40 minutes for this activity.

Materials needed

For each group:

- corrugated cardboard sheet
- model home built in Activity Four
- ruler, inch scale
- meter stick
- cutting tool
- masking tape
- heat lamp
- ring stand and clamp for lamp
- clock
- thermometer or temperature probe
- graph paper
- data from Activity Four.

Advance Preparation and Setup

Have the same setup ready from Activity Four. Have several pieces of cardboard ready so that the students are not waiting for one piece to be cut.

Teaching Notes

Start this class session by reminding students that they should seriously examine the Criteria for Evaluation at the beginning of the chapter. Point out that they can refine their plans for their universal dwelling throughout the next few lessons, and that the last day of the unit will be devoted to their presentations.

Have all student teams compare their findings from Activity Five. Each of the different materials used will show a different insulating effect. Two important ideas to develop in discussion of the findings are that:
1) those materials which trap air in small spaces within the insulating material retard conduction and convection best, and 2) there are diminishing returns past an optimum thickness of insulation. Elicit feedback on Physics To Go from Activity Five. Those students who completed the assignment should be able to relay information on "R values" and recommended thickness' of insulation for homes in your location.

Before having students begin For You To Do, discuss the importance of replicating the conditions used in Activity Four (the same heat lamp, at the same distance and angle) so that the only new variable introduced is the insulation added to the model dwelling. Also point out that data on window and wall areas of all students' homes as described in Physics To Go will be needed for tomorrow's class.

1

NOTES

ACTIVITY SIX: Investigating Insulation Placement in Your Universal Dwelling

Activity Six

Investigating Insulation Placement in Your Universal Dwelling

WHAT DO YOU THINK?

The density (mass per unit volume) of air decreases with temperature, leading to the common knowledge expression, "heat rises."

- **Why are attics of homes so hot on a summer day?**
- **What are these same attics like on a cold winter day?**

Record your ideas about these questions in your *Active Physics log*. Be prepared to discuss your responses with your small group and the class.

H29 HOME

Activity Overview

In the activity the students will be repeating the heating and cooling of their model homes, but using insulation this time. The students should notice a difference immediately, but if not, have them repeat the experiment using more cardboard this trial.

Student Objectives

Students will:

- identify and explain which surface in a house is vulnerable to the greatest heat loss in terms of conduction and convection.
- infer an optimum thickness for home insulation.
- identify limitations of using scale models in conducting experiments.

1

ANSWERS FOR THE TEACHER ONLY

What Do You Think?

Attics are hot due to the solar heating during the day. If there is little insulation, then the sun will heat up the attic quickly. Also, there is generally little circulation in the attic, and the air continues to heat up.

The same attics are cold because of the same reasons. That is, the attic is insulated against the heat from inside the home, but not the cold outside. Because the air outside is cold the heat that is trapped in the attic very quickly leaves the attic to the outside.

ANSWERS

For You To Do

1. Student activity.

2. a) Student activity.

   b) Student activity.

   c) Students should notice that there is a reduction in the transfer of heat to the inside during heating, and a reduction in the transfer of the heat to the outside from the inside during the cooling.

3. a) Again, there should be a reduction in the heat transfer.

4. a) Students' observations.

   b) Some of the differences may be due to the angles of the roofs, reflective properties of the roofs, quality of construction, etc.

   c) If 1 inch = 48 inches then 1:48 = 1/4:12. Therefore, the thickness on your house should be 12 inches.

   d) If you double the thickness, you should probably double the insulative value. Tripling the thickness should triple the insulative value. The students' answers will vary depending on their answers from Activity Five.

DESIGNING THE UNIVERSAL DWELLING

FOR YOU TO DO

1. Cut the cardboard as insulation so that it will fit snugly within the ceiling of your model home. Use masking tape to fix it in place.

2. Set up your experiment in the same manner as you did for Activity 4. Be sure to keep the lamp at the same distance (20 cm) and at the same 45° angle as in the first experiment.
   a) Construct a temperature vs. time graph of your data as you did in Activity 4.
   b) Compare this heat transfer experiment data with data from Activity 4 and interpret the results.
   c) How did insulating the ceiling affect the heating and cooling of your model?

3. Insulate the walls of your model in the same way as you did the ceiling. Repeat the heat transfer experiment.
   a) Compare and interpret these results with the first two experiments.

4. Use the results of Activities 4 and 6 to answer the following questions.
   a) Compare the results of your team's findings with those of the other teams.
   b) How do you explain the similarities and differences?
   c) Given the scale of your model home, to what thickness of insulation in a real home does your $\frac{1}{4}$ inch of cardboard insulation correspond?
   d) What effect do you predict would occur if you used twice the thickness of cardboard in your model? Three times the thickness? Defend your response with data from Activity 5.

HOME H30

REFLECTING ON THE ACTIVITY AND THE CHALLENGE

In this activity, you insulated your model home and then tested it to see what effects insulating will have on controlling the internal temperature of the home. The Architectural Committee will expect you to be able to show that you know where insulation is most effective in trapping energy. You now have gathered scientific data which you can use to show that you know where to place insulation most effectively in a home.

PHYSICS TO GO

1. In insulating a real home you probably wouldn't use cardboard as the insulating material as you did for the model dwelling. What materials might you use, and why?
2. What considerations, other than the effect of the insulation, might guide your choices of insulating materials for a home? Think about fire prevention.
3. Homes are usually designed to have about twice as much insulating effect in ceilings than in exterior walls. Why?
4. Could a vacuum be a good insulator? Explain why or why not, and under what conditions.
5. Compare and contrast the purpose of insulation in hot weather versus cold weather. Should placement of insulation be different for these different purposes?
6. Insulating materials for homes are rated on a relative scale of R values. Sheets or rolls of different kinds of materials in various thickness are available, and each has an assigned R value. The R values of two or more thickness can be added together to find the total insulating value of combined layers. What combinations of the following materials could be used to provide R-19 insulation for a wall and R-38 insulation for a ceiling?
   - R-8 expanded polystyrene board 2 inches thick
   - R-11 fiberglass wool $3\frac{1}{2}$ inches thick
   - R-30 fiberglass wool $9\frac{1}{2}$ inches thick

ANSWERS

Physics To Go

1. Cardboard is flammable, and would constitute a fire hazard. Also, the amount of cardboard needed would be rather costly, and it loses its insulative properties when wet. Materials used would be fiberglass insulation, Styrofoam®, plastics, etc. These are used because they are fire retarding, relatively water proof, resistant to mold, mildew and other odor-producing growths, relatively inexpensive, resistant to packing, even when wet retain their insulative properties.

2. See previous answer, as well as resistant to insects and small rodents. Ease of installation is also a good criteria.

3. The heat from the sun is more direct on the roof, than on the walls. From the inside of the house, the hot air rises, therefore, having insulation in the ceiling will prevent heat loss.

4. A vacuum is a good insulator when the heat is transferred only by conduction (molecule to molecule) or convection (moving currents of heat energy). If there is also the possibility of radiation (as in light or other forms of EMR), then a vacuum will do no good. Space is a vacuum, and there is radiation in space.

5. Students' answer will vary. The primary purpose of insulation in hot weather is to keep the heat out, and the cool in. In cold weather, it is to keep the heat in and the cold out. Placement of the insulation should be the same for both situations.

6. For the wall: in order to get at least R-19, the walls must be at least 6" thick. You could use 3 layers of R-8 polystyrene (R-value of 24); or R-11 fiberglass wool and R-8 polystyrene. For R-38, use R-30 fiberglass wool, and R-8 polystyrene, or 2 layers of R-8 plus 2 layers of R-11 fiberglass wool.

1

ANSWERS

Physics To Go

(continued)

7. Student activity and data for each a), b) and c)

7. In preparation for tomorrow's class work, collect the following information tonight at your home.
   a) Measure all the windows in your home and calculate the total number of square feet of window area of your home. Record your calculation.
   b) Measure all the exterior wall surface areas of your home, and calculate the total number of square feet (including the window areas) of exterior walls of your home. Record your calculation.
   c) Divide the total window area by the total wall surface area. Record your calculation.

STRETCHING EXERCISES

1. In constructing homes today, high, open (cathedral) ceilings are often part of the design plans for the living space. What advantages and disadvantages do high ceilings have with respect to heating and cooling considerations for the home?

2. Contemporary homes in America today are built with full basements, half buried basements, or are constructed on top of concrete slabs cast on the surface. What heating advantages and disadvantages do you believe would exist for each of these types of house foundation? Explain your responses for each type of foundation.

ANSWERS

Stretching Exercises

1. One advantage is that the heat is pulled to the ceiling away from the living area during summer months. One disadvantage is that the heating of the space is more expensive as the heat rises to the ceiling during the winter months.

   Often, many windows are associated with the high ceilings, and this causes problems during summer as more heat is entering the home, and in winter more heat is leaving the home.

2. Students' answers will vary. Homes built with in-ground basements, will have a greater living space, with less home above ground to insulate. Basements do not need as much insulation, as the ground acts as an insulator.) Basements are also necessary for the plumbing to remain in a heated environment.

R Values for Insulation: Manufacturers and Government Information

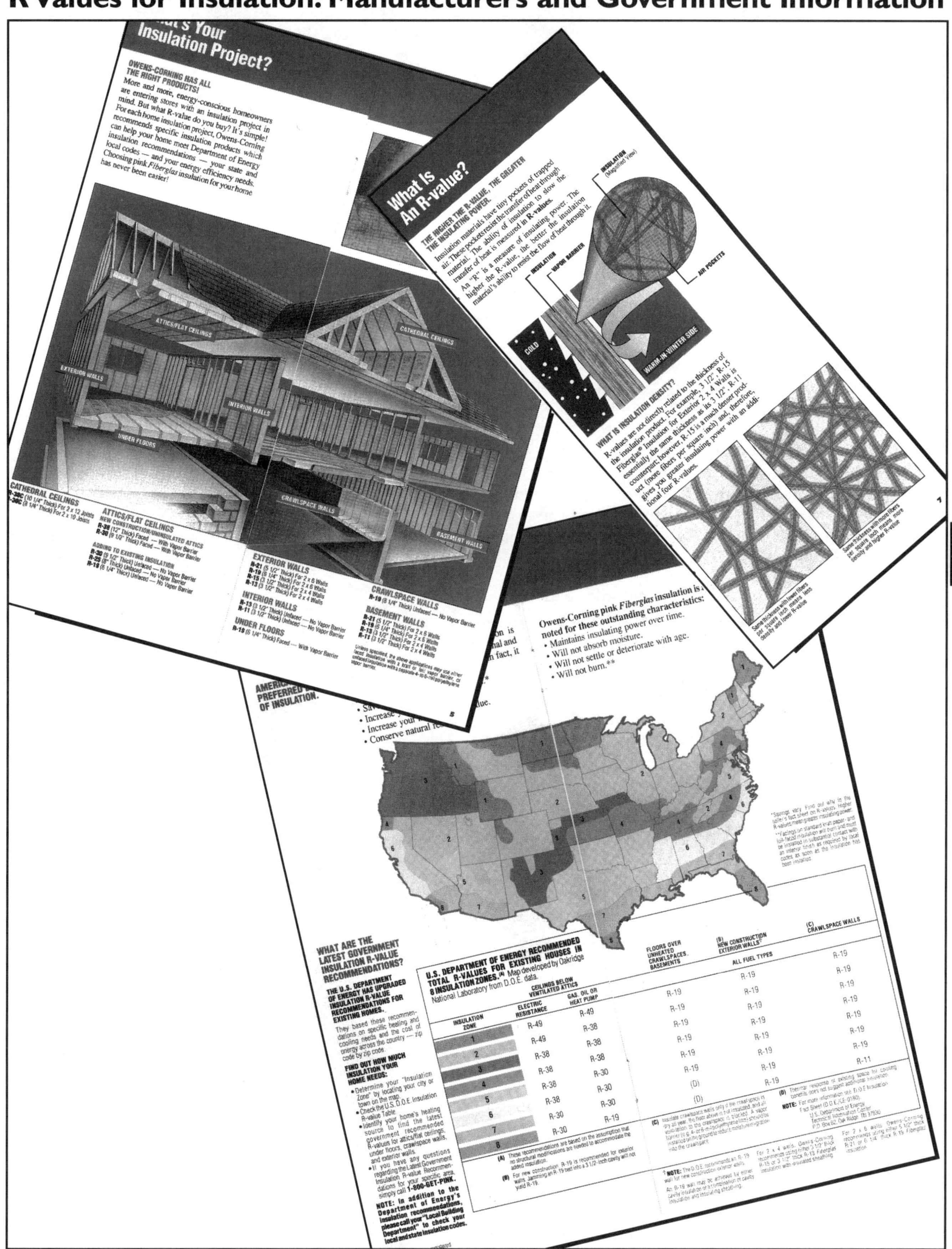

...at's Your Insulation Project?

OWENS-CORNING HAS ALL THE RIGHT PRODUCTS!

More and more, energy-conscious homeowners are entering stores with an insulation project in mind. But what R-value do you buy? It's simple! For each home insulation project, Owens-Corning recommends specific insulation products which can help your home meet Department of Energy insulation recommendations — your state and local codes — and your energy efficiency needs. Choosing pink *Fiberglas* insulation for your home has never been easier!

CATHEDRAL CEILINGS
R-38C (10 1/4" Thick) For 2 x 12 Joists
R-30C (8 1/4" Thick) For 2 x 10 Joists

ATTICS/FLAT CEILINGS
NEW CONSTRUCTION/UNINSULATED ATTICS
R-38 (12" Thick) Faced — With Vapor Barrier
R-30 (9 1/2" Thick) Faced — With Vapor Barrier
ADDING TO EXISTING INSULATION
R-30 (9 1/2" Thick) Unfaced — No Vapor Barrier
R-25 (8" Thick) Unfaced — No Vapor Barrier
R-19 (6 1/4" Thick) Unfaced — No Vapor Barrier

EXTERIOR WALLS
R-21 (5 1/2" Thick) For 2 x 6 Walls
R-19 (6 1/4" Thick) For 2 x 6 Walls
R-15 (3 1/2" Thick) For 2 x 4 Walls
R-13 (3 1/2" Thick) For 2 x 4 Walls

INTERIOR WALLS
R-13 (3 1/2" Thick) Unfaced — No Vapor Barrier
R-11 (3 1/2" Thick) Unfaced — No Vapor Barrier

UNDER FLOORS
R-19 (6 1/4" Thick) Faced — With Vapor Barrier

CRAWLSPACE WALLS
R-19 (6 1/4" Thick) Unfaced — No Vapor Barrier

BASEMENT WALLS
R-21 (5 1/2" Thick) For 2 x 6 Walls
R-19 (6 1/4" Thick) For 2 x 6 Walls
R-13 (3 1/2" Thick) For 2 x 4 Walls
R-11 (3 1/2" Thick) For 2 x 4 Walls

Unless specified, the above applications may use either faced insulation with a kraft or foil vapor barrier, or unfaced insulation with a separate 4- to 6-mil polyethylene vapor barrier.

5

What Is An R-value?

THE HIGHER THE R-VALUE, THE GREATER THE INSULATING POWER.

Insulation materials have tiny pockets of trapped air. These pockets resist the transfer of heat through material. The ability of insulation to slow the transfer of heat is measured in **R-values**.

An "R" is a measure of insulating power. The higher the R-value, the better the insulation material's ability to resist the flow of heat through it.

WHAT IS INSULATION DENSITY?

R-values are not directly related to the thickness of the insulation product. For example, 3 1/2", R-15 Fiberglas® Insulation for Exterior 2 x 4 Walls is essentially the same thickness as its 3 1/2", R-11 counterpart; however, R-15 is a much denser product (more fibers per square inch) and, therefore, gives you greater insulating power with an additional four R-values.

Same thickness with fewer fibers per square inch means less density and lower R-value

Same thickness with more fibers per square inch means more density and higher R-value

7

AMERIC... PREFERRED ... OF INSULATION.

...on is ...nal and ...n fact, it ...*

...lue.

- Sa...
- Increase y...
- Increase your...
- Conserve natural re...

Owens-Corning pink *Fiberglas* insulation is noted for these outstanding characteristics:

- Maintains insulating power over time.
- Will not absorb moisture.
- Will not settle or deteriorate with age.
- Will not burn.**

WHAT ARE THE LATEST GOVERNMENT INSULATION R-VALUE RECOMMENDATIONS?

THE U.S. DEPARTMENT OF ENERGY HAS UPGRADED INSULATION R-VALUE RECOMMENDATIONS FOR EXISTING HOMES.

They based these recommendations on specific heating and cooling needs and the cost of energy across the country — zip code by zip code.

FIND OUT HOW MUCH INSULATION YOUR HOME NEEDS:

- Determine your "Insulation Zone" by locating your city or town on the map.
- Check the U.S. D.O.E. Insulation R-value Table.
- Identify your home's heating source to find the latest government recommended R-values for attics/flat ceilings, under floors, crawlspace walls, and exterior walls.
- If you have any questions regarding the Latest Government Insulation R-value Recommendations for your specific area, simply call **1-800-GET-PINK.**

NOTE: In addition to the Department of Energy's insulation recommendations, please call your "Local Building Department" to check your local and state insulation codes.

U.S. DEPARTMENT OF ENERGY RECOMMENDED TOTAL R-VALUES FOR EXISTING HOUSES IN 8 INSULATION ZONES.(A) Map developed by Oakridge National Laboratory from D.O.E. data.

INSULATION ZONE	CEILINGS BELOW VENTILATED ATTICS: ELECTRIC RESISTANCE	CEILINGS BELOW VENTILATED ATTICS: GAS, OIL OR HEAT PUMP	FLOORS OVER UNHEATED CRAWLSPACES, BASEMENTS	(B) NEW CONSTRUCTION EXTERIOR WALLS† (ALL FUEL TYPES)	(C) CRAWLSPACE WALLS
1	R-49	R-49	R-19	R-19	R-19
2	R-49	R-38	R-19	R-19	R-19
3	R-38	R-38	R-19	R-19	R-19
4	R-38	R-38	R-19	R-19	R-19
5	R-38	R-30	R-19	R-19	R-19
6	R-38	R-30	R-19	R-19	R-19
7	R-30	R-30	(D)	R-19	R-19
8	R-30	R-19	(D)	R-19	R-11

(A) These recommendations are based on the assumption that no structural modifications are needed to accommodate the added insulation.

(B) For new construction, R-19 is recommended for exterior walls. Jamming an R-19 batt into a 3 1/2-inch cavity will not yield R-19.

(D) Thermal response of existing space for cooling benefits does not suggest additional insulation.

NOTE: For more information see D.O.E. Insulation Fact Sheet (D.O.E./CE-0180). U.S. Department of Energy Technical Information Center, P.O. Box 62, Oak Ridge, TN 37830

† NOTE: The D.O.E. recommends an R-19 wall for new construction exterior walls.

For 2 x 4 walls, Owens-Corning recommends using either 3 1/2" thick R-15 or 3 1/2" thick R-13 Fiberglas insulation with insulated sheathing.

For 2 x 6 walls, Owens-Corning recommends using either 5 1/2" thick R-21 or 6 1/4" thick R-19 Fiberglas insulation.

For use with *Home*, Chapter 1, ACTIVITY SIX: Investigating Insulation Placement in Your Universal Dwelling

ACTIVITY SEVEN
The Role of Windows... Placing Windows in Your Universal Dwelling

Background Information

The orientation of the model home with respect to geographic direction and the orientation of the sun in the sky is introduced in Activity Seven. The main thrust of this activity is that students add windows to their model homes and repeat the heating/cooling procedure used in Activity Four and Activity Six. The added specification is made that the model home will be oriented so that its south side faces the sun-simulating heat lamp. As in Activity Six which tested the effect of adding insulation to the home, the temperature versus time graphs produced from measurements taken during the heating and cooling phases are used to infer the effect of including windows in the model home.

As explained in the background information provided for Activity Six, it remains important for comparison of results across activities to maintain a constant setup for the heat lamp.

The 45° angle used for the orientation of the heat lamp in this series of activities takes on greater significance for this activity. That particular orientation matches the orientation of the sun in the sky at noon on the spring and autumn equinoxes (March 21 and September 23) for locations at 45 degrees north latitude; on those dates at such locations, the sun appears 45° above the south point of horizon at local noon. This is the median noon altitude of the sun throughout the year (the variation of the sun's altitude throughout the year will be discussed in the background information for Activity Eight). In the southern hemisphere, the sun appears in the northern sky at noon and the seasons are reversed.

The main property of windows which can be expected to affect heating and cooling results of this activity is the surface area of the windows. The radiant heat transmitted into the home through windows facing the sun should, in principal, be directly proportional to the window area. Similarly, heat loss through windows via conduction and radiation should be directly proportional to the total surface of windows regardless of the side of the house on which they are located. It is important to keep in mind that, during the heating phase of this activity, simultaneous gains and losses of heat will be occurring through windows.

This activity can be expected to produce the onset of greater diversity of results across groups than was the case for Activity Six. Even though a variety of sizes and shapes of model homes corresponding to groups' designs were used in Activity Six, the kind and amount of insulation added to the variety of models was the same across groups. Therefore, some uniformity in effects on heating and cooling rates probably was realized. Activity Seven, however, allows freedom for each group to choose the number, size and locations of windows to be added to their model and, therefore, the effects on heating and cooling rates should be expected to be as diverse as the choices made by students for windows. Overall, it can be expected students will find that windows on a southern exposure should offset some of the effect of the insulation added to the home in the previous activity to cause an increase the rate of heating; similarly, the rate of cooling can be expected to increase due to loss of some insulating effect.

Obviously, windows exposed to the sun during daylight hours can provide a profound heating effect through the process of radiation. This is true for windows not only on the south side of a home where the sun shines for most of each day, but also to a lesser, yet significant extent for windows placed on the east and west sides.

Less obvious to most people is that windows also cause very significant heat loss from homes through conduction and radiation. Despite tremendous efforts within the window industry to prevent heat loss (e.g., multiple panes of glass separated by layers of gas, thin coatings which reflect infrared radiation that would otherwise escape back into the home), it remains true that the window has not been made which matches the insulating quality of a well-insulated wall. A typical insulated wall is rated at R-19; windows range in insulating effect from about R-1 for a single pane of glass to less than R-5 for the best triple-glazed windows money can buy. Therefore, windows are a two-edged sword; they provide views, light, and solar heating, but their low insulating effects also cause problems with heating and air conditioning efforts.

Active-ating the Physics InfoMall

The textbooks mentioned at the beginning of this book (*Household Physics, and Energy: Insights From Physics*) contain chapters on heat, home energy conservation, home heating, solar radiation, solar heating, and home illumination. You are encouraged to look at these sections to see just how much information is available on this single CD-ROM.

Planning for the Activity

Time Requirements

Allow about 40 - 50 minutes for this activity.

Materials needed

For each group:

- model home built in Activity Four as modified in Activity Five
- clear plastic wrap
- ruler, inch scale
- meter stick
- cutting tool
- masking tape
- heat lamp
- ring stand and clamp for lamp
- clock
- thermometer or temperature probe
- graph paper

Advance Preparation and Setup

Have the students work within their teams to calculate the ratio of window-to-wall areas represented by the homes of students within each team. Circulate among the teams as the students work, moving the process along. Then turn the students' attention to need to make a decision about windows for each group's model home.

Teaching Notes

Before moving on to For You To Do, ask each group to give a brief report (anonymous, no names) on the ratios found for students' homes and the group's decision on windows for the universal dwelling. Point out in the instructions for For You To Do the conditions (cold winters, hot summers in the northern hemisphere) and allow that some groups may wish to adjust their initial decision about the number of windows and their placement. Also, remind students about the need to replicate the same heating conditions used in Activities Four and Five, this time introducing windows as a variable. Ask the entire class the question, "When you have completed this activity to gather data on the heating and cooling effects for a model home with windows, what data will you use for comparison? Will you use the data from Activity Four, a windowless home without insulation, or the data from Activity Five, a windowless home with insulation?" Discuss and decide as a class.

CAUTION: Remind students to be careful while cutting their windows.

NOTES

ACTIVITY SEVEN: The Role of Windows...Placing Windows in Your Universal Dwelling

Activity Seven

The Role of Windows...Placing Windows in Your Universal Dwelling

WHAT DO YOU THINK?

It is often said, "A window hasn't been made that is as good as a well-insulated wall."

- **Should all sides of the model dwelling have the same area of windows? Why or why not?**

Record your ideas about these questions in your *Active Physics log*. Be prepared to discuss your responses with your small group and the class.

H 33 HOME

Activity Overview

The students will continue their exploration into the heating and cooling of their home. In this activity, the students will place windows with a predetermined window-to-wall area ratio from their calculations in Activity Six.

Student Objectives

Students will:

- calculate the ratio of window-to-wall areas for typical homes.
- experimentally compare the heat transfer properties of a scale model of a home with and without windows.
- explain where windows should be placed in a home to optimize solar heating effects for various seasons and climates.

ANSWERS FOR THE TEACHER ONLY

What Do You Think?

In colder climates, there would be fewer windows on the north side of building than in a warmer country. However, in the warmer climate the opposite is true. There would be fewer windows on the south side than on the north side.

DESIGNING THE UNIVERSAL DWELLING

FOR YOU TO DO

1. Compile a chart in your group to summarize your calculations of window area to wall area ratios in your homes.
   a) What is the average window to wall area ratio for your group?

2. Use all the information and resources available to you. Decide upon the number, sizes, and placement of the windows for your model home. Remember, you want to provide for optimal lighting and ventilation and you also want to allow solar energy to enter the home and heat it when needed. However, you do not want to transfer large amounts of energy from the home to the outside when direct sunlight does not enter the window.
   a) Approximate the window to wall area ratio you plan to use in your model home.
   b) How does the window to wall area ratio for your model home compare to the average window to wall area ratio you calculated for your group? Explain why you chose the ratio you did.

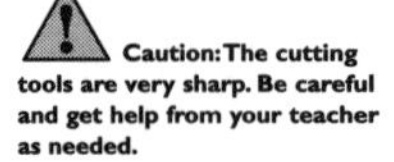

Caution: The cutting tools are very sharp. Be careful and get help from your teacher as needed.

3. Draw outlines of the windows to scale on the walls of your model and carefully cut out the windows with a cutting tool.

4. Use masking tape to tape transparent food wrap over the window cutouts.

5. Repeat the heat transfer experiment with the heat lamp on your model home. Place the heat lamp and model home so that the lamp is shining on the home at the same angle and at the same distance as in previous activities.
   a) Record and graph your findings as you did in previous activities.
   b) Compare your heating and cooling graphs for this activity with those in Activities Four and Six. How do the graphs differ? Explain your results.

HOME  H 34

ANSWERS

For You To Do

1. a) Student data.

2. a) Student data.

   b) Student data. Students' answers will vary, depending on their location, climate, apartment dwellers, people who live on farms, whether they like lots of natural lighting, etc.

3. Student activity.

4. Student activity.

5. a) Student activity.

   b) Students should notice that there is an increase in the heating and cooling curves, showing that there is a lot of energy lost through the windows.

REFLECTING ON THE ACTIVITY AND THE CHALLENGE

Virtually all dwellings have windows of one type or another to provide interior light and to provide for ventilation and temperature control. The windows in a home built today are extremely well-designed and engineered in comparison to those of 30 years ago. The problem your group faces is a complicated one. You wish to design and place windows in your Homes For Everyone (HFE) universal dwelling to provide for optimal lighting and ventilation, but you also know that windows have energy advantages and disadvantages. Windows, which can allow solar energy to enter the home and heat it when needed, lose heat through conduction, convection, and radiation to a much greater degree than the insulated walls.

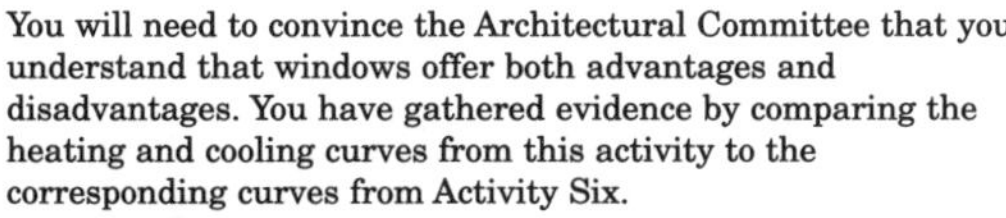

You will need to convince the Architectural Committee that you understand that windows offer both advantages and disadvantages. You have gathered evidence by comparing the heating and cooling curves from this activity to the corresponding curves from Activity Six.

PHYSICS TO GO

1. Heat can enter and leave a home through windows. How are conduction, convection, and radiation involved in
   a) the transfer of heat into a home through its windows?
   b) the transfer of heat out of a home through its windows?
2. The amount of heat gained or lost through a window is directly proportional to the surface area of the window.
   a) Compare the amount of heat expected to be transferred through a window 2 feet wide by 2 feet high to the amount expected for a window 4 feet wide by 4 feet high.
   b) Glass doors behave about the same as windows regarding heat transfer. Compare the amount of heat expected to be transferred through a glass patio door 8 feet wide by 6 feet high to the amount expected for a 2 feet by 2 feet window.

ANSWERS

Physics To Go

1. a) Conduction: Sun heats up the window glass, and window pane, then is transferred from the window to the inside of the home.

   Convection: Wind moves air by window and transfers heat to the window and air around the window.

   Radiation: Sunlight radiates through the window, and heats up the inside of the home.

   b) Conduction: The heat inside the home is transferred to the window and frame. It is then transferred by molecule to molecule contact to the outside.

   Convection: The warm air inside the home is moved to the cold air close to the windows, and then the heat is transferred outside.

   Radiation: Heat is radiated from the inside to the outside through the glass.

2. a) Find the area of both windows, then one would expect that the larger window would lose or gain proportionately. 2 x 2 = 4 sq. ft. and the larger 4 x 4 = 16 sq. ft. Therefore, the larger window loses (or gains) 4 times as much heat.

   b) 6 x 8 = 48 sq. ft. compared to the 4 sq. ft. window, therefore, the patio doors will lose (or gain) 48/4 or 12 times as much heat.

ANSWERS

Physics To Go

(continued)

3. Visit your local building supply store for this information. Generally as you increase the number of panes of glass in a window you increase the R value. Thermopane windows have different functions and construction depending on the climate in your region.

4. There is more dead air space in a wall as compared to the space in a window. The air in the window is free to move around inside the panes, and therefore can heat up more quickly than the dead air spaces in the walls. The walls also will not radiate heat as quickly as windows, as the heat energy must pass through the wall itself before getting to the trapped air. In a window the air is directly heated by radiation.

5. Curtains and shades provide a barrier to the different temperatures of the inside to the outside or vice versa. They provide a barrier to the radiation of the heat energy, as well as minimize the movement of air with different temperatures.

6. The sun does not shine on the north side of the home, so there is no advantage using those windows for heating. Also the prevailing winds are often from the north, and therefore will speed the process of heat loss.

7. The problems are associated with keeping the warm air out, and cool air in. This is just the opposite problem of the cold climate window problem. Windows are poor heat insulators, and therefore whether cooling or heating, the greater the surface area of windows, the greater the heat gain or loss.

3. Visit a building supply store in your community. Examine the windows available. Find out about the following:
   a) The R value of the cheapest and most expensive windows.
   b) The difference between thermopane and single pane windows.
   c) Why thermopane windows are built the way they are.
   d) What "low E" windows are, and how they function.
4. Even the highest quality windows do not have as much insulating effect as a well insulated wall. Explain why.
5. Window drapes and shades can provide privacy and beauty in a home. Explain how they may also be used to control heat transfer through windows.
6. Designs for energy-efficient homes in parts of the U.S. that have cold winters have very few if any windows on the north side of the home. Why?
7. People who live in warm climates often use air conditioners to cool their homes. What if any problems do windows present related to air conditioners?

STRETCHING EXERCISES

Find out about passive solar heating for homes. Answer the following:

a) How can adding more windows to a house serve to warm the house during the day?

b) How can you prevent heat from escaping from these extra windows during the night?

c) What can be used to store the heat that is collected during the day?

d) Where should windows for passive solar heating be placed to be most effective?

ANSWERS

Stretching Exercises

a) The solar heating of the carpets, floors and furniture.

b) Using shutters or blinds or curtains will prevent the heat loss to the outside at night.

c) Water is the best way to store heat. It has a very high specific heat capacity, and is easy to handle.

d) Windows used for passive solar heating should be placed on the south side of the home.

R Values for Windows: Manufacturers and Government Information

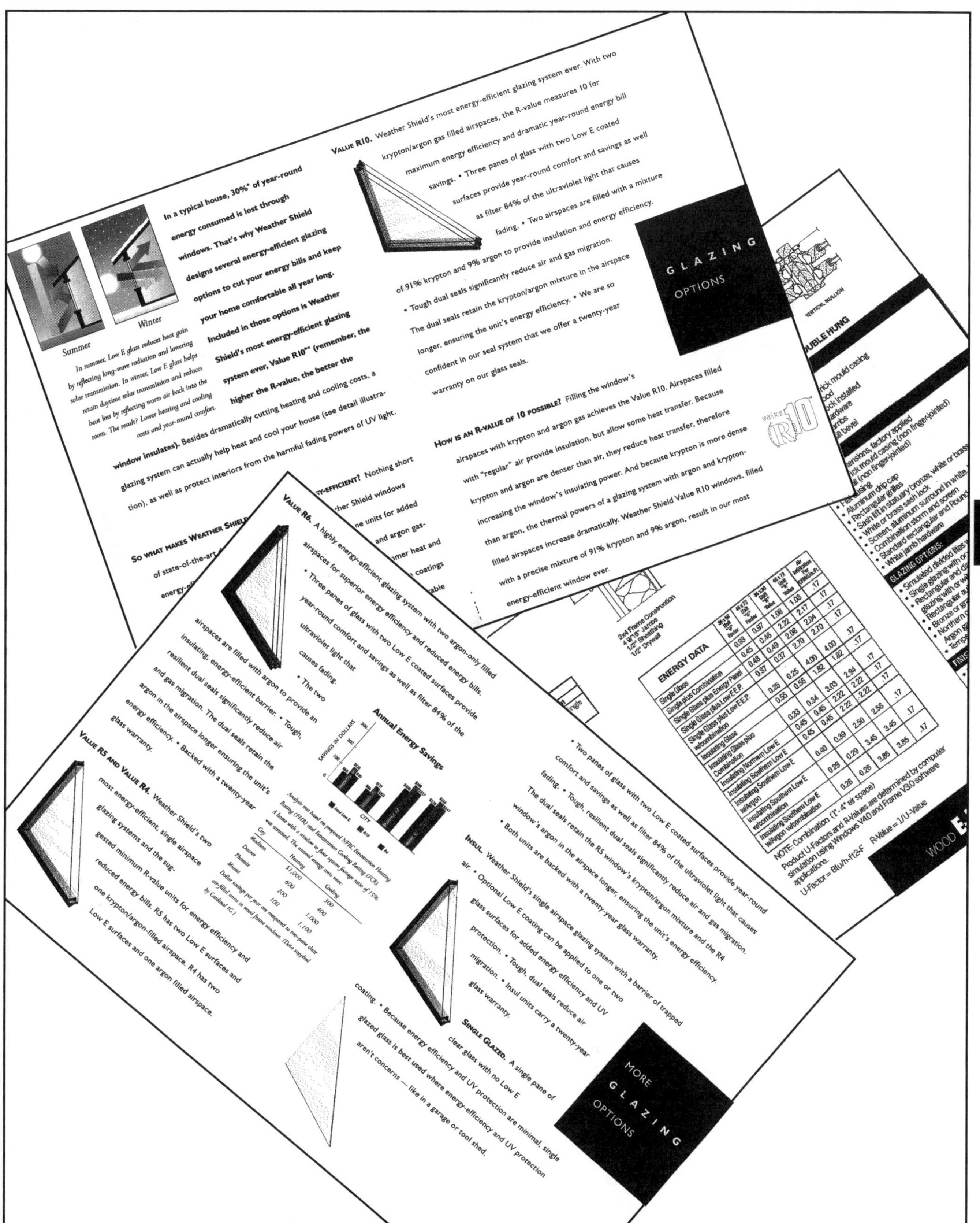

In a typical house, 30%* of year-round energy consumed is lost through windows. That's why Weather Shield designs several energy-efficient glazing options to cut your energy bills and keep your home comfortable all year long. Included in those options is Weather Shield's most energy-efficient glazing system ever, Value R10™ (remember, the higher the R-value, the better the window insulates). Besides dramatically cutting heating and cooling costs, a glazing system can actually help heat and cool your house (see detail illustration), as well as protect interiors from the harmful fading powers of UV light.

Summer Winter

In summer, Low E glass reduces heat gain by reflecting long-wave radiation and lowering solar transmission. In winter, Low E glass helps retain daytime solar transmission and reduces heat loss by reflecting warm air back into the room. The result? Lower heating and cooling costs and year-round comfort.

So what makes Weather Shield ... of state-of-the-art ... energy-ef...

...ergy-efficient? Nothing short ... ther Shield windows ... ne units for added ... and argon gas- ... rmer heat and ... coatings ... able

Value R10. Weather Shield's most energy-efficient glazing system ever. With two krypton/argon gas filled airspaces, the R-value measures 10 for maximum energy efficiency and dramatic year-round energy bill savings. • Three panes of glass with two Low E coated surfaces provide year-round comfort and savings as well as filter 84% of the ultraviolet light that causes fading. • Two airspaces are filled with a mixture of 91% krypton and 9% argon to provide insulation and energy efficiency. • Tough dual seals significantly reduce air and gas migration. The dual seals retain the krypton/argon mixture in the airspace longer, ensuring the unit's energy efficiency. • We are so confident in our seal system that we offer a twenty-year warranty on our glass seals.

GLAZING OPTIONS

How is an R-value of 10 possible? Filling the window's airspaces with krypton and argon gas achieves the Value R10. Airspaces filled with "regular" air provide insulation, but allow some heat transfer. Because krypton and argon are denser than air, they reduce heat transfer, therefore increasing the window's insulating power. And because krypton is more dense than argon, the thermal powers of a glazing system with argon and krypton-filled airspaces increase dramatically. Weather Shield Value R10 windows, filled with a precise mixture of 91% krypton and 9% argon, result in our most energy-efficient window ever.

value R10

Value R6. A highly energy-efficient glazing system with two argon-only filled airspaces for superior energy efficiency and reduced energy bills. • Three panes of glass with two Low E coated surfaces provide year-round comfort and savings as well as filter 84% of the ultraviolet light that causes fading. • The two airspaces are filled with argon to provide an insulating, energy-efficient barrier. • Tough, resilient dual seals significantly reduce air and gas migration. The dual seals retain the argon in the airspace longer ensuring the unit's energy efficiency. • Backed with a twenty-year glass warranty.

Annual Energy Savings

SAVINGS IN DOLLARS; CITY; Insul Low E; R10; R4

Analysis was based on proposed NFRC Fenestration Heating Rating (FHR) and Fenestration Cooling Rating (FCR). A home with a window to floor square footage ratio of 15% was assumed. The annual energy costs were:

City	Heating	Cooling
Madison	$1,000	300
Denver	600	400
Phoenix	200	1,000
Miami	100	1,100

Dollar savings per year are compared to two-pane clear air-filled units in wood frame windows. (Data supplied by Cardinal IG.)

Value R5 and Value R4. Weather Shield's two most energy-efficient, single airspace glazing systems and the suggested minimum R-value units for energy efficiency and reduced energy bills. R5 has two Low E surfaces and one krypton/argon-filled airspace. R4 has two Low E surfaces and one argon filled airspace. • Two panes of glass with two Low E coated surfaces provide year-round comfort and savings as well as filter 84% of the ultraviolet light that causes fading. • Tough, resilient dual seals significantly reduce air and gas migration. The dual seals retain the R5 window's krypton/argon mixture and the R4 window's argon in the airspace longer, ensuring the unit's energy efficiency. • Both units are backed with a twenty-year glass warranty.

Insul. Weather Shield's single airspace glazing system with a barrier of trapped air. • Optional Low E coating can be applied to one or two glass surfaces for added energy efficiency and UV protection. • Tough, dual seals reduce air migration. • Insul units carry a twenty-year glass warranty.

Single Glazed. A single pane of clear glass with no Low E coating. • Because energy efficiency and UV protection are minimal, single glazed glass is best used where energy-efficiency and UV protection aren't concerns — like in a garage or tool shed.

MORE GLAZING OPTIONS

VERTICAL MULLION

DOUBLE HUNG

2x4 Frame Construction
4 9/16" Jambs
1/2" Sheathing
1/2" Drywall

ENERGY DATA

	36 x 60 Unit "U" Factor	48 x 72 Unit "U" Factor	36 x 60 Unit "R" Value	48 x 72 Unit "R" Value	Air Infiltration Per cfm/lin.ft.
Single Glass	0.93	0.97	1.08	1.03	.17
Single plus Combination	0.45	0.46	2.22	2.17	.17
Single Glass plus Energy Panel	0.48	0.49	2.08	2.04	.17
Single Glass plus Low E E.P.	0.37	0.37	2.70	2.70	.17
Single Glass plus Low E E.P. w/combination	0.25	0.25	4.00	4.00	.17
Insulating Glass	0.55	0.55	1.82	1.82	.17
Insulating Glass plus Combination	0.33	0.34	3.03	2.94	.17
Insulating Northern Low E	0.45	0.45	2.22	2.22	.17
Insulating Southern Low E	0.45	0.45	2.22	2.22	.17
Insulating Southern Low E w/Argon	0.40	0.39	2.50	2.56	.17
Insulating Southern Low E w/combination	0.29	0.29	3.45	3.45	.17
Insulating Southern Low E w/Argon w/combination	0.26	0.26	3.85	3.85	.17

NOTE: Combination (1"- 4" air space)
Product U-Factors and R-Values are determined by computer simulation using Windows V4.0 and Frame V3.0 software applications.
U-Factor = Btu/h-ft2-F R-Value = 1/U-Value

WOOD

• Extensions, factory applied
• Brick mould casing (non finger-jointed)
• Sill (non finger-jointed)
• Flat casing
• Aluminum drip cap
• Rectangular grilles
• Sash lift in statuary bronze, white or brass
• White or brass sash lock
• Screen, aluminum surround in white
• Combination storm and screen
• Standard rectangular and Round...
• White jamb hardware

GLAZING OPTIONS:
• Simulated divided lites ...
• Single glazing with or ...
• Rectangular and di...
• Bronze or gr...
• Northern ...
• Argon g...
• Tempe...

For use with *Home*, Chapter 1, ACTIVITY SEVEN: The Role of Windows...

ACTIVITY EIGHT
Investigating Overhangs and Awnings

Background Information

Activity Eight has students explore how seasonal changes in the altitude of the sun may affect the heating and cooling of homes. Using the heat lamp to simulate the sun at its extreme noon altitudes during summer and winter, students again heat and cool their model homes with and without the addition of window awnings and/or roof overhangs to control the amount of light allowed to enter windows.

The sun's annual cycle of changing noon altitudes is caused by the fact that the Earth's spin axis is not perpendicular to the plane of Earth's orbit around the sun. Instead, the spin axis is tilted 23-½° away from the perpendicular to the plane of the orbit. The Earth maintains its tilted orientation, rotating daily as it completes its orbit in an amount of time which serves as the definition of one year on Earth. The tilt of Earth's orbit causes seasons. When the tilt causes the northern hemisphere to "lean" toward the sun it is summer; the sun appears higher in the sky at noon than it does at other times of year and radiation from the sun strike the earth's surface most directly, causing maximum heating of the surface for the year. When the northern hemisphere leans away from the sun, the sun appears lower in the sky, the heating effect is less and it is winter. Spring and autumn occur when the axis is tilted neither toward nor away from the sun, but sideways. The seasons are exactly reversed in the southern hemisphere, and observers at mid-southern latitudes see the sun residing above the north point on the horizon at noon.

The four special dates which mark the beginning of each season are helpful for keeping track of the sun's altitude throughout the year: the spring (or vernal) equinox on March 21, the summer solstice on June 21, the autumnal equinox on September 23 and the winter equinox on December 21. For observers in the U.S. noon altitude of the sun is maximum on the summer solstice and is minimum on the winter solstice, varying 47° (2 x 23-½°) in altitude (measured from the south point on the horizon) during the six month time interval from one solstice to the next. The altitude of the sun is a its median value on both equinoxes. The noon altitude of the sun varies sinusoidally throughout the year and, if necessary, can be predicted for any day of the year for any observer.

For purposes of home design involved in this activity, it is necessary to be able to calculate the extreme noon altitudes of the sun throughout the year (the altitude on each solstice) as viewed from the particular latitude at which the home is located. A diagram and narrative which explain how to accomplish the calculation is included in For You To Do for Activity Eight; a condensed version for you as the teacher is:

Calculate the complement of the latitude of the home (90° minus latitude).

Adding 23-½° to the complement of the latitude gives the sun's altitude above the horizon at noon on the summer solstice.

Subtracting 23-½° from the complement of the latitude gives the sun's altitude above the horizon at noon on the winter solstice.

By this discussion, it may be apparent that the 45° angle of the heat lamp used in prior activities can be thought of as having modeled the sun at noon on the equinoxes shining on a home located at 45° north latitude. This was an arbitrary choice by the authors and happens to correspond to locations in the northern contiguous U.S.

To allow comparison of results of this activity to the results of Activity Seven, it will be necessary for students to be careful not to introduce an undesired variable by changing the distance between the heat lamp and the model home when the lamp is being repositioned to illuminate the home at the solstice angles. The distance should be held constant at the same value used in earlier activities.

If your latitude is greatly different from 45° North, be aware that the 45° angle of the heat lamp used in prior activities did not represent the sun's noon altitude on the equinoxes for your location, but on dates other than the equinoxes.

Students should find it possible, as do home designers, to manipulate roof overhangs, awnings or other methods to shield windows from the sun during summer while allowing sunlight to enter windows during winter.

Active-ating the Physics InfoMall

Search the InfoMall with keywords "overhang*" or "awning*". You will find several hits with good information. One of these, again, is *Household Physics*. The section on Solar Heating (found, oddly, in the Air Conditioning the Home chapter) has an excellent graphic showing how awnings allow the winter sun to pass into the house, but prevent the summer sun from causing unwanted heating.

Planning for the Activity

Time Requirements

Again, this will be about 40 - 50 minutes. Allow extra time for students to try different kinds of awnings or overhangs if desired.

Materials needed

For each group:

- tagboard
- model homes built in Activities Four, Five, Six
- ruler, inch scale
- meter stick
- protractor
- cutting tool
- masking tape
- heat lamp
- ring stand and clamp for lamp
- clock
- thermometer or temperature probe
- graph paper

Advance Preparation and Setup

The data from Activity Six should point to the potential for using passive solar heating during winter months. However, a problem during summer months develops when south-facing windows may allow more solar energy to enter the home than would be desired. Elicit those conditions from students in a discussion of the results of Activity Six.

Teaching Notes

Ask for brief reports on student findings from Physics To Go for Activity Seven regarding single pane, thermopane and low e glass windows.

Announce that, in this activity, students will design roof overhangs or awnings for their universal dwelling which will shade the south-facing windows in the summer and yet allow maximum solar energy to enter the home during winter months. Use a world globe to point out the local latitude and determine the angle of the sun at summer and winter solstices for your location. Discuss the importance of maintaining the same distance between the heat lamp and the model home when adjusting the angle of the heat lamp during the For You To Do procedure, and begin the activity.

CAUTION: Be careful when using sharp instruments while cutting the overhangs.

NOTES

Activity Eight

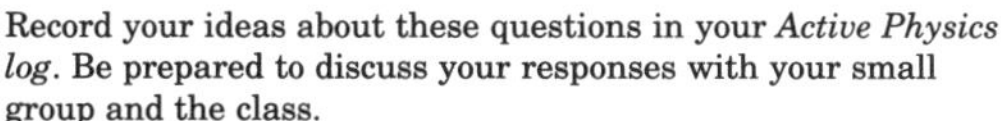

Investigating Overhangs and Awnings

WHAT DO YOU THINK?

Heating and air conditioning are the most expensive items for operating the average American home.

- **What can be done so that windows will let sun enter the dwelling when it is cold outside, and block sunlight from entering when it is hot outside?**

Record your ideas about these questions in your *Active Physics log*. Be prepared to discuss your responses with your small group and the class.

FOR YOU TO DO

1. Find the latitude of the location for which you are designing your model home.

ANSWERS

For You To Do

1. If you want an accurate reading, you can go to a good quality Atlas, or phone the local weather station. You could also ask any of the students, if they know how to get a reading of the latitude from the North Star at night.

Activity Overview

This Activity is the culmination of this chapter, where students will put the final variable on their home. Again, they are to be reminded of the importance of keeping all the other variables the same and only changing the one variable for this experiment.

Student Objectives

Students will:

- explain how the altitude and heating effect of the sun varies with seasons.
- design overhangs and awnings to control solar heating through the windows of a home during summer and winter.
- conduct a heat transfer experiment on a scale model of a home to test the effectiveness of overhangs and awnings for controlling solar heating with during summer and winter.

1

ANSWERS FOR THE TEACHER ONLY

What Do You Think?

Letting the sun in during the winter months is valuable in utilizing the sun's heat. However, it can be uncomfortable during the summer months. Therefore, people put up awnings, or have large overhangs on their roofs.

ANSWERS

For You To Do

(continued)

2. a) Student activity.

   b) Student activity.

3. Student activity.

4. a) Student activity and data.

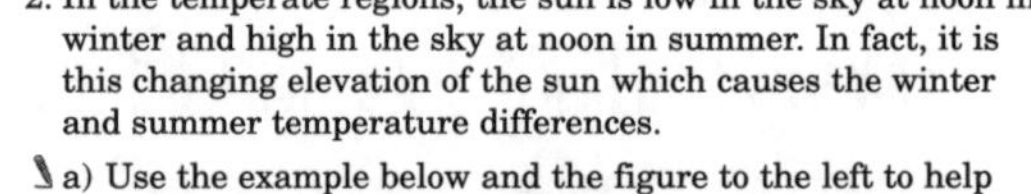

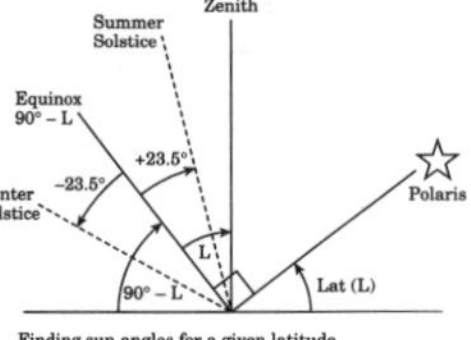

Finding sun angles for a given latitude

2. In the temperate regions, the sun is low in the sky at noon in winter and high in the sky at noon in summer. In fact, it is this changing elevation of the sun which causes the winter and summer temperature differences.

   a) Use the example below and the figure to the left to help you calculate the angle of the sun at noon at the winter and summer solstices in your area.

> Example:
> The latitude of St. Louis, Missouri, is 38 degrees North. Calculate the noon altitude of the sun as viewed from St. Louis on the equinoxes and solstices.
>
> Sun angle on equinoxes = (90 degrees) minus (latitude angle)
> $= 90° - 38°$
> $= 52°$
>
> Sun angle on summer solstice = (Sun angle on equinoxes) plus (23.5°)
> $= 52° + 23.5°$
> $= 75.5°$
>
> Sun angle on winter solstice = (Sun angle on equinoxes) minus (23.5)
> $= 52° - 23.5°$
> $= 28.5°$

   b) Use the same figure and example to help you calculate the angle of the sun at noon at the winter and summer soltices in the area for which you are designing a model home.

3. Set up your model home and the heat lamp as in previous activities.

4. Use a protractor and the sun angle data to adjust the heat lamp so that it matches the angle position of the sun at noon at the summer solstice.

   a) Measure, record, and graph the heating and cooling curves for your model home.

5. With the lamp turned on, place a small piece of tag board over one of the windows on the side of the model facing the heat lamp. Try different widths of tag board and the angles of attachment until you find the width and/or angle that will entirely block the lamp's light but still provide someone inside with a view. Use masking tape to attach tag board awnings and/or roof overhangs to your model.

6. Repeat the heat transfer experiment on your model home that is now fitted with awnings or overhangs for summer solstice conditions.

   a) Record and graph your data.

7. Do not change the awnings or overhangs on your model, but adjust the lamp so its position matches the angle of the sun at the winter solstice. Repeat the heat transfer experiment.

   a) Record and graph this data on the same graph.

   b) What differences do you note in the summer and winter solstice heating graphs? How do you explain the differences?

REFLECTING ON THE ACTIVITY AND THE CHALLENGE

One of the main requirements is that the universal dwelling must be able to be used in a wide variety of locations on Earth. Since the dwelling also depends on energy from the sun, you must include in your design the knowledge about how solar energy varies with location on the Earth. This activity has prepared you to answer questions which the Architectural Committee will ask about how your design allows for solar energy at different locations.

PHYSICS TO GO

1. Imagine yourself standing outdoors at noon at your home latitude. You are facing straight South toward the horizon. You are doing this on four special days during the year whose titles are listed below. For each special day give its date, explain its meaning in terms of seasons, and then predict the angle of the sun above the horizon.

   a) Vernal equinox
   b) Summer solstice
   c) Autumnal equinox
   d) Winter solstice

ANSWERS

For You To Do

(continued)

5. Student activity.

6. a) Student data.

7. a) Student activity and data.

   b) There should be an increase in the heating of the home in the winter scenario. This is due to more direct sun entering the window, where the inside is heated.

1

ANSWERS

Physics To Go

1. a) The vernal equinox is the position of Earth when the sun is directly over the equator. The plane of Earth's orbit is perpendicular to its axis. This is the spring, and in the northern hemisphere the days are getting longer and they are heating up. The date is close to March 21.

   b) The summer solstice is when the axis is tilted at a 23.5° angle where the northern hemisphere is tilted towards the sun. This gives us the longest days of the year, when the northern hemisphere is receiving more direct sunshine. The sun is directly over the Tropic of Cancer. The date is close to June 21.

   c) The autumnal equinox is the position of Earth when the sun is directly over the equator. The plane of Earth's orbit is perpendicular to its axis. This is the fall, and in the northern hemisphere the days are getting shorter and they are cooling down. The date is close to September 21.

   d) The winter solstice is when the axis is tilted at a 23.5° angle where the northern hemisphere is tilted away from the sun. This gives us the shortest days of the year, when the southern hemisphere is receiving more direct sunshine. The sun is directly over the Tropic of Capricorn. The date is close to December 21.

ANSWERS

Physics To Go

(continued)

2. a) 90° - 25° = 65°
   b) 90° - 30° = 60°
   c) 90° - 35° = 55°
   d) 90° - 40° = 50°
   e) 90° - 45° = 45°

3. 26° + 23.5° = 49.5°

4. On the summer solstice, the sun is directly over the Tropic of Cancer. The latitude of the Tropic of Cancer is 23.5°. Therefore, at noon on the summer solstice, the sun will be shining on the back of the house (see diagram lower right).

5. a) Students provide rough sketch. (see diagram lower right)

6. Awnings that can be retracted are good for those sides of the home. Therefore, in summer they can be extended, and in winter they can be drawn up. Another way is having trees or bushes that partially shade the window in summer. In winter when the leaves drop off, more light and more heat will get in. From the inside, curtains or shutters can be used in the hottest parts of the year.

7. It will depend on the area that the home is going to be built. If it is built in hot areas, then it would be worth the added expense.

8. Because the sun is close to the horizon, the awnings would not be very effective. Therefore, shades can be drawn, to let only as much as you want, or to shut out the heat altogether.

DESIGNING THE UNIVERSAL DWELLING

2. Latitudes in the continental U.S. vary from about 25° North to 50° North. Calculate the angle of the sun above the South horizon on the summer solstice for the latitudes listed below:
   a) 25° North
   b) 30° North
   c) 35° North
   d) 40° North
   e) 45° North

3. One town in the U.S. is 2,000 miles west of another town. At noon on the winter solstice at each town, the sun is observed to have an altitude of 26°. What is the latitude of each town?

4. The latitude of Mexico City, Mexico is 19° North. Do a calculation to show yourself that the sun will shine on the north side of a home in Mexico City at noon on the summer solstice. State a rule for locations in Earth's northern hemisphere where this can happen.

5. Sketch a design for a roof overhang or window awning that will always shade a south-facing window from the noontime sun during the six months between the vernal and autumnal equinoxes, but will allow the noon sun to shine on the entire window during the other six months of the year.

6. The sun shines on windows on the east and west sides of a home, too, but for only part of the day. What could be done to control heat gains and losses through those windows?

7. Do you think the added cost of building a roof overhang or using awnings on your model dwelling would be worth the additional expense? Why or why not?

8. Shades are more effective than awnings for blocking sun from entering windows on the east and west sides of buildings. Why is this so?

H 40

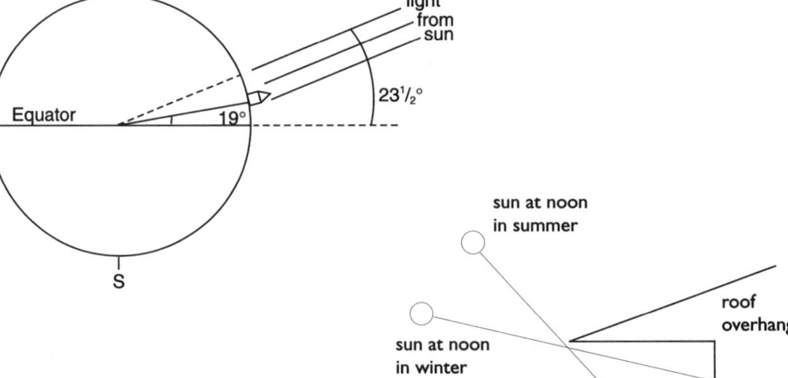

Sun Location at Seasonal Times

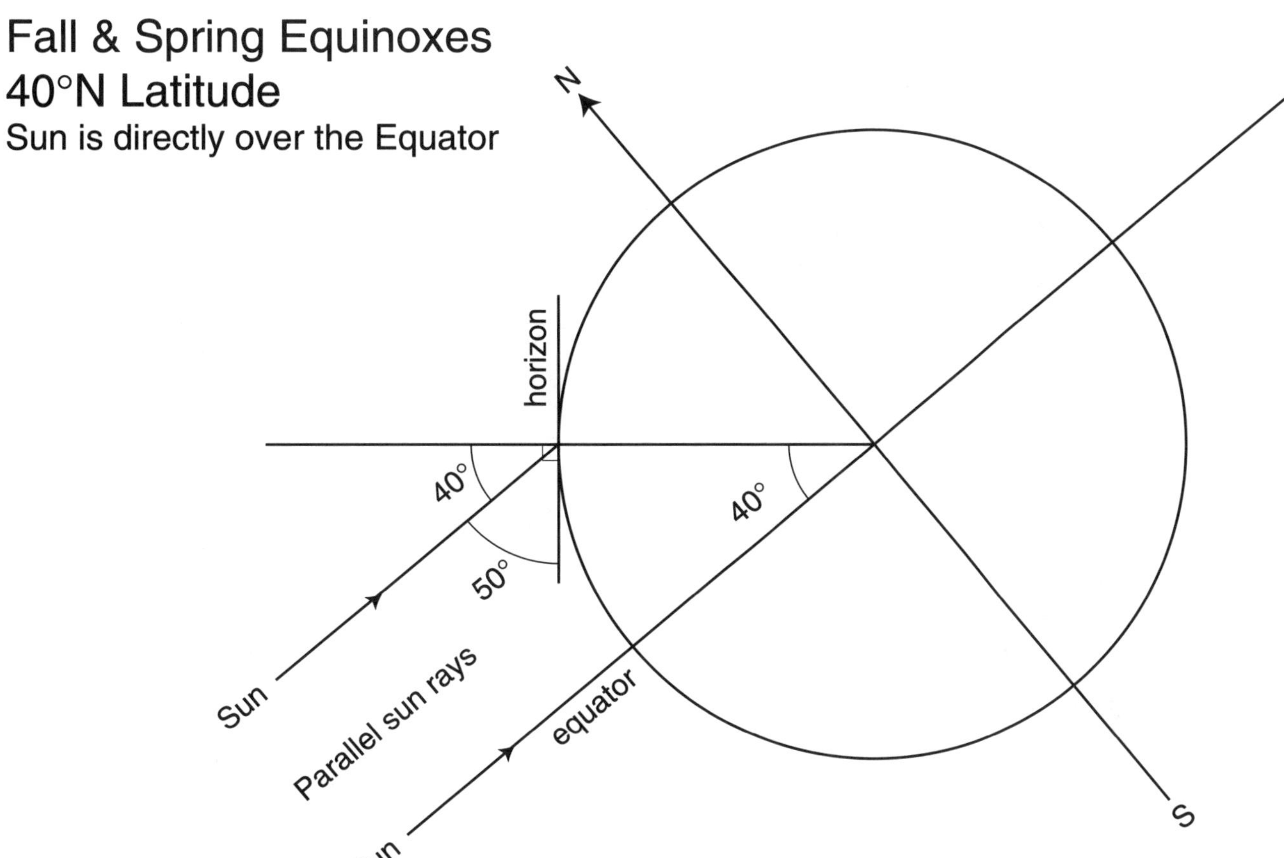

For use with *Home*, Chapter 1, ACTIVITY EIGHT: Investigating Overhangs and Awnings

Sun Location at Seasonal Times *(continued)*

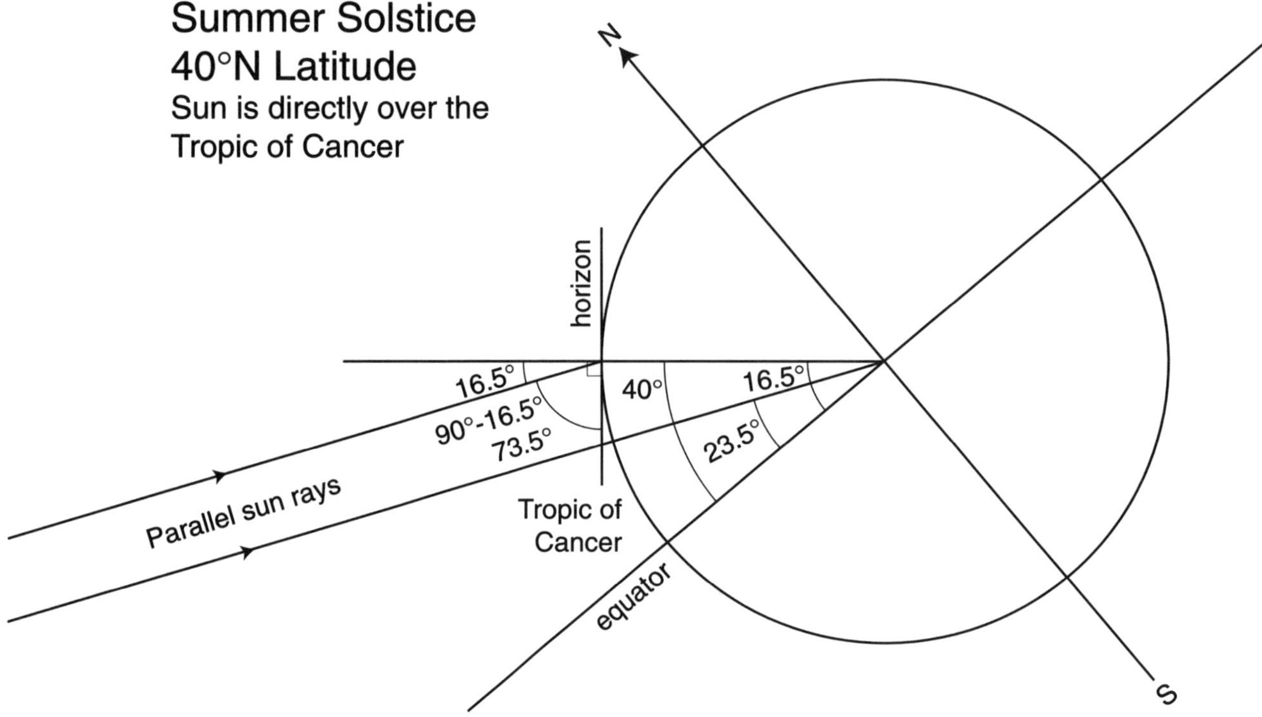

For use with *Home*, Chapter 1, ACTIVITY EIGHT: Investigating Overhangs and Awnings

Sun Location at Seasonal Times *(continued)*

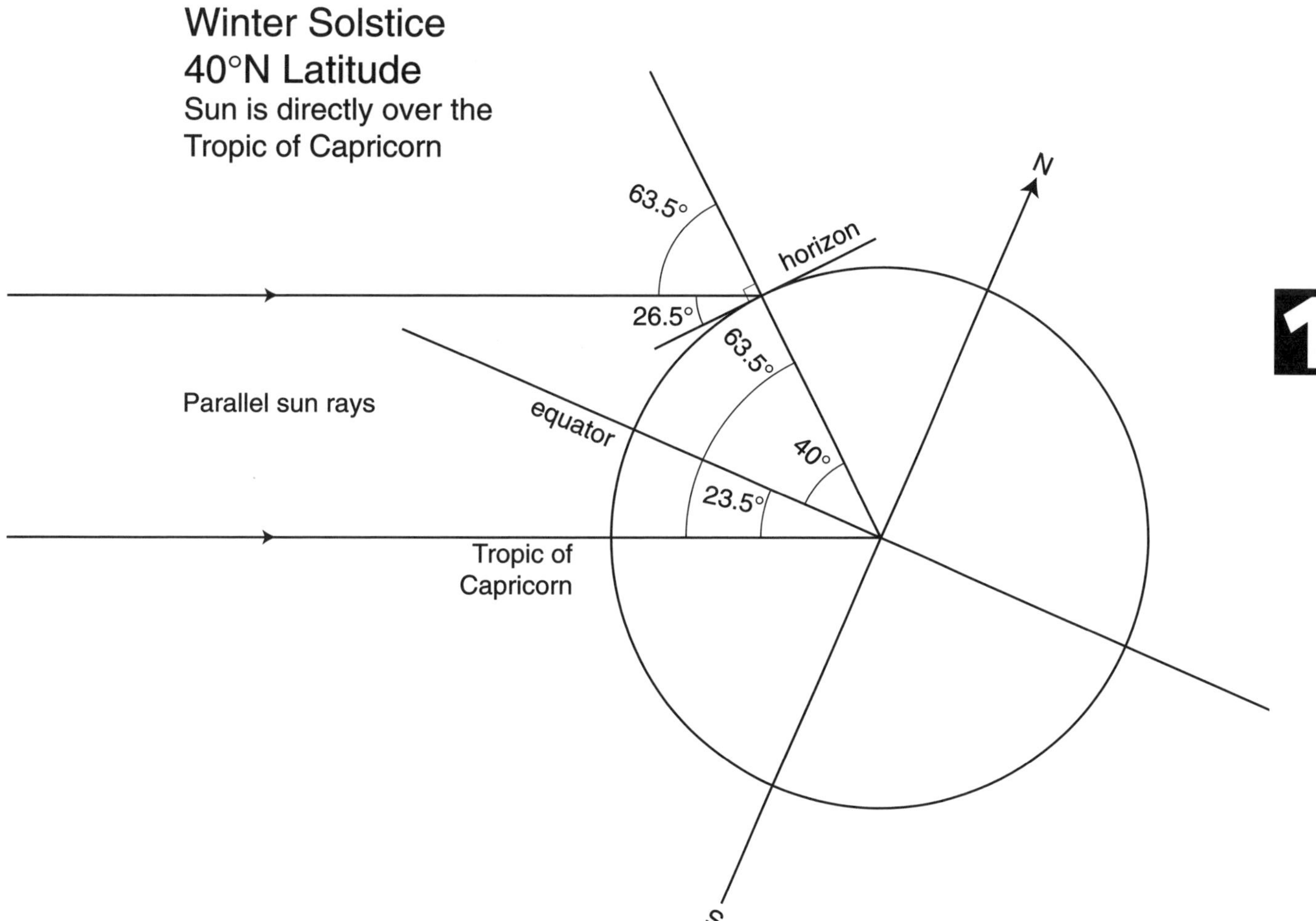

For use with *Home*, Chapter 1, ACTIVITY EIGHT: Investigating Overhangs and Awnings

NOTES

PHYSICS AT WORK

Ray Aguilera

HABITAT FOR HUMANITY

Ray is the construction manager at the Valley in the Sun, Arizona, Habitat for Humanity branch. Habitat for Humanity International is a non-profit organization that seeks to eliminate poverty, housing, and homelessness from the world. They do this by building and selling homes for no profit, to families who cannot get conventional financing. Homeowners also become partners in the process by contributing 500 hours of "sweat equity" toward the construction of their own home.

Our former president, Jimmy Carter, has been deeply committed to Habitat since 1984. Each year former President Carter and his wife, Rosalynn, join Habitat volunteers to build homes and raise awareness of the critical need for affordable housing.

Ray Aguilera was on his way to becoming a lawyer, when one summer he got a job building homes, and has never stopped. Ray gets a great deal of satisfaction from his work with Habitat. "I enjoy going from an empty lot and watching something magical grow out of it," he says.

Arizona has a different climate than many other places in the country and takes special considerations when planning homes. In this southwestern desert, the temperatures are often in the 100s and rarely very cold. For example, the foundations and footings for houses do not need as much concrete as other places because the soil conditions are so different. And, in Arizona, you never have to worry about winter frosts. "The most essential characteristic of building a house in Arizona," states Ray, "is to keep it energy efficient. We also strive to design houses that will blend in with the existing environment. In Arizona, we make more of an effort to keep the hot out and the cold in. To do this we use double-paned windows, and as much insulation as we can fit between the walls and in the attic."

Chapter 1 Assessment

You and your group have been investigating the design of your model universal dwelling for this entire chapter. You have learned a great deal about this problem and have explored possible solutions. You now have reached the point where you must finalize your plans and prepare your presentation for the hearing before the HFE Architectural Committee. Good luck!

Using the resources that you have been provided with, develop scale drawings of your model universal dwelling. Refer back to the challenge given at the beginning of this chapter to guide your group's activities. Your presentations will be strictly limited to five minutes, so make every drawing and sentence count!

Review the criteria you decided the HFE Architectural Committee should use in evaluating your drawings and your written presentation.

Physics You Learned

Surface area-to-volume ratio

Brief statements of conduction, convection, radiation

Heating curves and Cooling curves
- With opaque backgrounds
- With windows
- With insulation
- With awnings

Properties of insulation

Effect of thickness on insulation effectiveness

Brief review of latitude and solar position at equinox

Alternative Chapter Assessment

Select the best response for each statement or question.

1. Use the dimensions shown in the drawings of the outside walls of Houses A, B and C to compare the total floor areas of the houses in square feet. The drawings show views from above the houses.

House A

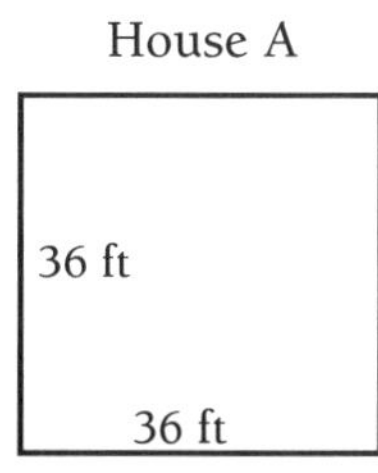

House B

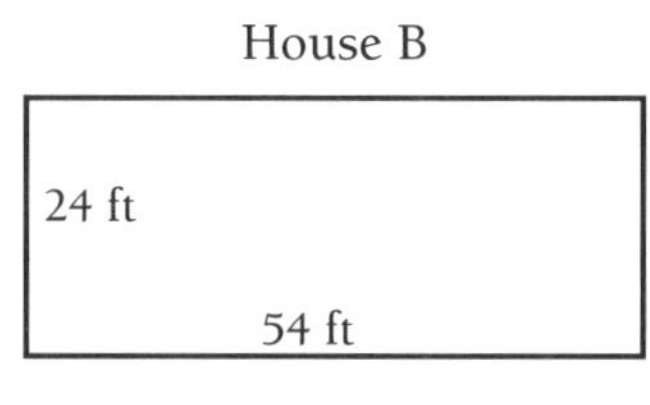

House C

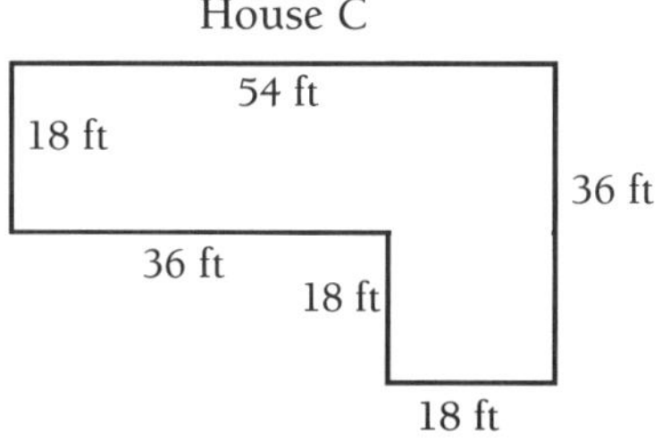

   a) House A has the greatest floor area.
   b) House C has the smallest floor area.
   c) House B's floor area is less than House A and Greater than House C.
   d) The floor areas of the three houses are equal.

2. In six months the angle at which sunlight strikes a location on Earth's surface at noon can change by a maximum of:
   a) 23.5°
   b) 45°
   c) 47°
   d) 90°

3. The vernal equinox occurs on:
   a) March 21
   b) June 21
   c) September 23
   d) December 21

4. The summer solstice occurs on:
   a) June 1
   b) June 21
   c) July 4
   d) July 21

5. The autumnal equinox occurs on:
   a) September 1
   b) September 23
   c) October 1
   d) October 31

6. The winter solstice occurs on:
   a) December 1
   b) December 21
   c) December 31
   d) January 1

7. During one minute in full sunlight the amount of solar energy striking a glass patio door 6 feet wide and 6 feet high compared to a window 2 feet wide and 2 feet high is:
   a) 3 times greater than the window.
   b) 4 times greater than the window.
   c) 9 times greater than the window.
   d) 16 times greater than the window.

8. To prevent heat loss from most homes the most insulation is needed in the:
   a) ceiling.
   b) outside walls.
   c) floor.
   d) doors and windows.

9. Three ways in which heat is transferred are:
   a) covention, convection and radiation.
   b) conduction, conversion and radiation.
   c) conduction, convection and irritation.
   d) conduction, convection and radiation.

10. Which unit of measurement would be correct expressing surface area?
    a) feet
    b) square feet
    c) cubic feet
    d) square feet per cubic foot

11. Which unit of measurement would be correct expressing volume?
    a) feet
    b) square feet
    c) cubic feet
    d) square feet per cubic foot

12. Which unit of measurement would be correct for expressing individual living space in a home having two or more family members?
    a) square feet per cubic foot
    b) persons per foot
    c) square feet per person
    d) cubic feet

13. Which unit of measurement would be correct for expressing the ratio of surface area to volume?
    a) square feet
    b) cubic feet
    c) square feet per person
    d) square feet per cubic foot

14. If the total distance around the outside walls of a house is limited to 120 feet, the shape formed by the walls to give the largest floor area at ground level would be a:
    a) square.
    b) rectangle.
    c) hexagon.
    d) circle.

15. If the total surface area of the ground floor of a home has been decided to be 1000 square feet, the three-dimensional shape for the home which would have the smallest surface area-to-volume ratio would be a:
    a) cube.
    b) rectangular solid.
    c) cylinder.
    d) hemisphere.

16. One-fourth of an inch on a 1:48 scale model represents how much real length?
    a) 3 inches
    b) 1 foot
    c) 4 feet
    d) 12 feet

17. A length of 8 feet should be made on a 1:48 scale model as a length of:
    a) 2 inches.
    b) 6 inches.
    c) 1/4 inch.
    d) 1/6 inch.

18. Radiation is the only way heat can transfer through:
    a) a glass window.
    b) outer space.
    c) a steel door.
    d) an insulated wall.

19. If other factors which affect the flow of heat through insulation stay constant, the effect of doubling the thickness of insulation in a wall or ceiling of a house should be to reduce the rate of heat flow through the insulation:
    a) by a factor of 2.
    b) by a factor of 4.
    c) to zero.
    d) not at all (no effect).

20. If other factors which affect the flow of heat through insulation stay constant, the effect of doubling the difference in temperature between the inside and the outside surfaces of an insulated wall should be to:
    a) have no effect on the rate of heat flow through the wall.
    b) increase the rate of heat flow through the wall by a factor of 4.
    c) reduce the rate of heat flow through the wall by a factor of 2.
    d) increase the rate of heat flow through the wall by a factor of 2.

Alternative Chapter Assessment Answers

1. d
2. c
3. a
4. b
5. b
6. b
7. c
8. a
9. d
10. b
11. c
12. c
13. d
14. d
15. d
16. b
17. a
18. b
19. a
20. d

NOTES

ELECTRICITY
FOR EVERYONE
CHAPTER
2

Home Chapter 2- Electricity for Everyone

National Science Education Standards

Chapter Summary

Homes for Everyone (HFE) again establishes the scenario, this time with the need for electricity for all homes. Wind is given as the universally available source for generating electricity. Students are challenged to write a manual that describes how to obtain electricity from the generator. They then must determine which electrical appliances can and should be provided for use in all homes built by Homes for Everyone.

To gain understanding of the content necessary to meet this challenge, students collaborate on activities in which they learn about electromagnetic motors, how electricity is generated, the use of wind to generate electricity, and the relative efficiency of different appliances. These experiences engage students in the following content identified in the *National Science Education Standards*.

Content Standards

Unifying Concepts

- Evidence, models and explanations
- Constancy, change and measurement

Science as Inquiry

- Identify questions & concepts that guide scientific investigations
- Use technology and mathematics to improve investigations
- Formulate & revise scientific explanations & models using logic and evidence

Science and Technology

- Abilities of technological design
- Understanding about science and technology

Science in Personal and Social Perspectives

- Natural resources
- Environmental quality
- Science and technology in local, national, and global challenges

Physical

- Motion and force
- Conservation of energy and increase in disorder
- Interactions of energy and matter

Key Physics Concepts and Skills

Activity Summaries	Physics Principles
Activity One: Generate Students investigate electrical energy and electric circuits with a simple hand generator, wires, and bulbs. Using the hand generator introduces the concept that electricity is the result of converting one form of energy into another.	• Energy conversions • Electricity • Mechanical energy • Simple circuits
Activity Two: Lighten Up An experiment in which students compare the relative brightness of light bulbs in series and parallel circuits and increases their understanding of energy flow necessary in generating electricity. They also learn that a generator has a limit of what it can support. Students also read to learn more about electrical energy.	• Energy conversions • Electricity • Mechanical energy • Series and parallel circuits
Activity Three: Load Limit To experience load limit, students add bulbs to their simple circuit until the load is exceeded. They then calculate the load limit of a household circuit and watts required by appliances, comparing these to the limits given in the challenge. This also introduces use of terms and equations for calculating power.	• Watts, voltage, currents • $P = IV$
Activity Four: Who's In Control? Students again assemble a parallel circuit to explore how switches control the flow of electricity to specific bulbs. They then propose and test strategies for using parallel circuits and switches to increase the number of bulbs on a circuit. Finally, they are introduced to circuit diagrams.	• Parallel circuits • Switches
Activity Five: Cold Shower Electricity used by water heaters is the focus of this activity, which also reinforces concepts of energy transfer. Students investigate the amount of energy in joules needed to raise the temperature of water, then calculate the efficiency of different water heaters. They also consider alternate solutions to the expectation for hot water in a home.	• Energy conversion • Power • Watts, joules • Specific heat
Activity Six: Pay Up Students compare different electric bills as they continue to explore concepts related to power consumption, efficiency of electrical appliances, and relative costs and benefits of specific electrical appliances. This activity also serves to review concepts units used to communicate about energy transformation.	• Heat energy • Electrical energy • Joules, watts • Energy flow and power • Electrical efficiency
Activity Seven: More for Your Money Students conduct an experiment in which they determine and compare the power consumed and the efficiency of three systems that could be used to heat water. They apply data collected to confirm their response to the challenge in which they recommend appliances for the universal home.	• Energy conversion • Energy flow and power • Electrical efficiency

Equipment List For Chapter Two

QTY	TO SERVE	ACTIVITY	ITEM	COMMENT
1	Class	4	Automatic switching devices, examples	Such as motion detector, photocell (for demonstration)
1	Group	1	Blinking bulb, miniature screwbase	Such as No. 406 or 407 available at electronics stores
3	Group	1,2,4	Bulb base for miniature screwbase bulbs	Any style to which wire leads easily can be connected
1	Group	3,5,6,7	Calculator, basic	One per student best; one per group minimum
1	Group	5	Calorimeter container	Styrofoam® cup will serve
1	Class	3	Circuit for demonstrating overload, 120-volt	See Advanced Preparation and Setup in TE for Activity Three
1	Class	5,7	Clock	
3	Group	2,4	Connecting wires, insulated	Preferably fitted with alligator clips
1	Group	1,2,4	DC Generator, hand-operated, with wire leads	"Genecon" brand recommended
1	Class	7	Electric hot plate, known wattage	Teacher measure wattage, if necessary
1	Group	5,7	Electric immersion heater, known wattage	Kind used by travelers for heating cup of water will serve
1	Group	5,7	Graduated cylinder, 100 ml	
3	Group	1,2,4	Light bulb, miniature screwbase	A "flashlight" bulb such as No. 13 (3.6 volt, 0.3 amp) or similar
1	Class	7	Microwave oven, known wattage	Teacher measure wattage, if necessary
1	Class	1	Pad of coarse grade steel wool	Each group needs only a short strand
2	Class	7	Pyrex® beaker, 1-liter capacity	
1	Group	7	Pyrex® beaker, 250 ml capacity	
1	Class	6	Set sample electric bills	From students (anonymously) or others
1	Class	5,7	Source of cold tap water	
1	Group	5,7	Stirring rod	
1	Group	4	Switch	Knife switch, single pole, single throw
1	Group	5,7	Thermometer or temperature probe	Celsius temperature in -10 to 110 range

Organizer for Materials Available in Teacher's Edition

Activity in Student Text	Additional Material	Alternative/Optional Activities
ACTIVITY ONE: Generate p.H46		Activity One A: Generator Principles p.124
ACTIVITY TWO: Lighten Up p.H50	A Water Model for Electricity p.133	
ACTIVITY THREE: Load Limit p.H55		
ACTIVITY FOUR: Who's In Control? p.H60	Circuit Diagrams p.150	
ACTIVITY FIVE: Cold Shower p.H64	Home Electrical Appliances: Power and Energy Use for a Family pgs.164-165	
ACTIVITY SIX: Pay Up p.H74	Sample Electric Bills for New York and Connecticut pgs.173-174	
ACTIVITY SEVEN: More for Your Money p.H79		

2

ELECTRICITY FOR EVERYONE

Throughout history people have tried to help other people. However, changes often have been made without any respect for the personal and cultural needs of those who are being assisted.

If you ever become involved in a self-help community group, it would be important for you to work together with the people you are helping in assessing their needs, and their capabilities. Although that is not possible given your limited time in class, you should recognize the need for this type of collaborative teamwork when assisting people.

Scenario

The Homes For Everyone (HFE) Architectural Committee has just accepted your design for a "universal" dwelling to meet the growing housing shortage in many diverse areas of the world. The organization would now like you to develop an appliance package that would help meet the basic needs for healthy, enjoyable living for the families who will reside in the universal dwellings.

The source of electrical energy chosen for this particular project is a wind generator. The following is a description of the wind-generator system chosen for HFE. Try to get a sense of the meaning of unfamiliar words. When the chapter is completed, you will understand these terms.

The wind-generator system chosen for HFE is a highly reliable, mass-produced model that has an output of 2400 W (2.4 kW). Experience has shown that in areas having only moderate average wind speed (6 to 8 km/h) the generator system will deliver a monthly energy output of about 90 kWh (kilowatt-hours) to the home, or about 3 kWh per day.

Direct current (DC) from the wind-driven generator is stored in batteries that allow storage of electrical energy to keep the home going for four windless days. The batteries deliver DC electricity, but most home appliances are designed to use alternating current (AC). An inverter changes the DC from the batteries into AC before it enters the home. A circuit breaker rated at 2400 W protects the batteries from overheating if too much energy is asked for at any single time. Finally, a kiloWatt-hour meter is provided to keep track of the amount of electrical energy that has been used. The result is that the dwelling will have the same kind of electricity delivered to it as do most homes in the U.S., but less electrical power and energy will be available than for the average homes in the U.S.

Chapter and Challenge Overview

Students will be studying electricity, first of all, through their own eyes by exploring how a light bulb works, and then producing a list of terms about electricity. This offers an opportunity for the teacher to catch any misconceptions that students may have regarding electricity.

Understanding about electricity will be the primary objective of the first few activities. The students will need to have a basic understanding of circuits, series and parallel circuits, safety and circuits, and switches. At this level, it is not necessary to go into a lot of detail when discussing electricity, but the teacher will be able to gauge what is too much for their students and what is a sufficient challenge for them.

The students will next have an opportunity to apply their understanding of electricity, in order to analyze transfer of energy in the heating of water, and ultimately the cost of using electricity. The hope is that they will be able to apply that knowledge and understanding to build their HFE home, and finally to their own lives.

Students will be analyzing the difference between an appliance that uses 1200 W of power, and one that uses 750 W of power. This is to enable them to understand cost-effectiveness, and areas in which they will be able to save electrical energy.

Finally, students will be analyzing electricity bills, in order to appreciate that the cost of electric energy is not simple, but affected by a variety of factors. Again, in understanding the cost of electricity, students will better appreciate the real cost of energy, and bring to their own lives some appreciation for the conservation of energy sources.

You may wish to point out that wind generators often were used to provide lighting for remote homes, especially farms, before rural electrification. You may also want to discuss the impact of the REA on life in rural America. If you wish to take the time, videos on wind generators are available; Hawkhill Associates, for example, has one. Data on the availability of wind in various locations is not necessary for executing the chapter. The availability of moderate wind is assumed for all locations. If you or your students wish to check on the wind in various locations, data is available. Data on annual mean wind speed for various locations in the U.S. is available in the *Climatic Atlas of the United States*. Daily wind data is available from telecommunications-based sources such as Weather Machine, available to schools on a subscription basis. Also, global wind data may be available from the same references used in earlier chapters.

HOME 

Challenge

You will use your experience with electricity in your home and what you learn in this chapter to decide which electrical appliances, powered by a wind generator, can and should be provided for the HFE dwellings.

1. Your first task is to decide what electrical appliances can and should be used to meet the basic needs of the people whose HFE dwelling will be served by a wind generator.

- **Use the list of appliances on pages H72 - H73, any additional information that you can gather about appliances, and the characteristics of the wind-generator system to decide what appliances to include in an "appliance package" for HFE.**
- **As part of your decision-making process, determine if it seems best to provide a basic appliance package that would be the same for all dwellings, or if packages should be adapted with "options" to allow for factors such as different family sizes, climates, or other local conditions.**
- **Describe how each appliance in your package will contribute to the well-being of the people who live in the dwelling.**

2. Your second task is educational. The people will need to be instructed how to stay within the power and energy limits of their electrical system as they use their appliances.

- **You must outline a training manual for volunteers who will be going into the field to teach the inhabitants about the HFE wind-generator system and the appliances. The volunteers have no special knowledge of electricity. Therefore, the volunteers need a "crash course" that will prepare them to teach the people to use their electrical system with success.**
- **Two factors will be especially important to teach: the power demand of the combination of appliances being used at any one time may not exceed 2400 W, and the average daily total consumption of electrical energy should not exceed 3 kWh.**

Criteria

The criteria for this challenge will be judged on the basis of 100 points. Discuss the criteria below, add details to the criteria if it would be helpful, and agree as a class on the point allocation.

- **The list of appliances to be included in the HFE appliance package must be as comprehensive as possible, and it must be clear how each appliance will enhance the health or well-being of the people who live in the dwelling.**
- **The outline of the training manual for HFE volunteers must explain the difference between 2400 W and 3 kWh. It must also give clear examples of how use of the appliances in the package can be scheduled to stay within the power and energy limits of the electrical system on both a daily and a long-term basis.**

Assessment Rubric for Challenge

This is a possible rubric for evaluating the Challenge in this chapter. It has some criteria, but it would be advantageous for the teacher to go over the criteria with the students, and have the students add any that may have been overlooked. Try to have the number of points be a multiple of 10, for ease of calculation of a mark out of 100. However, whatever the criteria, a mark of 100 can be given using percent.

Descriptor	5	4	3	2	1
Appliance Package					
comprehensive list of appliances					
appliances are energy-efficient					
appliances are useful (not frivolous e.g., electric can opener)					
choice of appliances is within the maximum power usage					
appliance package has options for different climates, family sizes, etc.					
appliance package has a description of benefit to people's well-being					
package is aesthetically pleasing					
Training Manual					
concise, simple language					
explains circuits					
explains AC and DC current					
explains series and parallel circuits					
explains power, current, and voltage					
explains the difference between 2400 W and 3kWh					
explains the need to stay within the power and energy limits both daily and long term					
Appearance of Manual					
easy to read					
professional quality					
well laid out					

For use with *Home*, Chapter 2

What is in the Physics InfoMall for Chapter 2?

When using the Physics InfoMall CD-ROM, it is easy to get in the "search" mode, where every time you want something, you engage the search engine. Don't forget that this InfoMall is also great for simply browsing. For example, this *Active Physics* book is all about the physics of the Home. Is there something on the InfoMall that we might expect to provide plenty of information? There is; Madalyn Avery's *Household Physics*. This chapter of *Active Physics* deals with electricity. A look at the table of contents from *Household Physics* uncovers several chapters that might be useful: Sources and uses of electricity, Magnetism, Electrostatics, Sources of electrical energy, Simple electromagnetic generators, Electrical measurements, Resistance in series and in parallel, Electric heating devices, Electric lights, Electric motors, Chemical effects of a current, Transformers, and House wiring. We should not be surprised when these appear as search results later. However, using the powerful search engine on the InfoMall is still a great method for becoming familiar with the contents of the CD-ROM.

If you are already familiar with using the search engine, you may wish to skip this paragraph and the next. The search engine for the InfoMall enables the user to locate almost any word or passage included in the more than 3,000 articles, 19 text-books, etc. If you use a Macintosh (remember - the CD-ROM works on both PC and Mac), you can search the entire database (that is, all stores) at once. This discussion was prepared using a Mac. If you use a PC, there will be minor differences but the database is identical. The same information can be found on either platform. There are two categories for searches: Simple and Compound. Simple searches look for a single word or phrase. Compound searches can locate multiple words or phrases that may not occur together. The Compound search also provides search options that are not available in the Simple search. Since a Compound search can always be done for a single word, it provides the same function as a Simple search. All searches in this discussion will be done using the Compound search.

The search option can be found under the "Functions" menu. When you select "Compound Search", you will get a window that has all the options you need for just about any search you are likely to want. Among these choices are database selection (which store or stores you want searched), category (perhaps only certain articles), and search words. You can enter any words or words you want the engine to search for. These words can be combined with the logical operators AND, OR, and NOT. That is, you can find passages that contain, for example, "wind" AND "generator" but NOT "politician". In addition, you can use an asterisk * as a wild character. That is, search word "fun*" will search for any word beginning with "fun", such as "fun", "funny", "funding", "fundamental", etc. Wild characters allow great freedom in searching, but as this example shows, you need to be careful. And finally, if your search is too broad, you will get "Too Many Hits" and you will have to restrict your search parameters to something that will not be found so many times on the CD-ROM. Such restriction techniques include searching in fewer stores, using fewer wild characters, or searching for less common words followed by a search of only the search hits. With a little practice, you should have very little trouble finding the information you desire.

The Scenario mentions a wind generator. It may be a good idea to have some under-standing of generators in general before jumping into this chapter. You never know what a students will ask, but "how does a generator work?" seems likely. To find an answer (or several answers) search the InfoMall for "generator*". The list of hits includes articles and chapters on such things as Van de Graaff generators and func-tion generators, but the list also includes information relevant to our needs. For example, there is a chapter on "Generation and Transmission of Electricity" in Philip DiLavore's *Energy: Insights from Physics* found in the Textbook Trove. Not surprisingly, Household Physics is also on this list. There are many items on this list, and you should check them out. Some will be relevant, others will simply be interesting.

The Physics InfoMall was created by physicists who are interested in how physics is taught and learned. Therefore, many of the references in the database relate to physics education. These can be especially helpful. Electricity is a great example of how helpful this can be. Perform a search using "student" AND "difficult*" AND "electric*" on the entire CD-ROM. This search initially provides "Too Many Hits" so it must be limited to Terms Must Appear in the Same Paragraph. This finds several references on the difficulties students have with concepts related to electricity. Knowing these difficulties will allow the teacher to expect them, and have ideas on how to overcome them. A similar search can be done using "misconcept*" in place of "difficult*". The results are not identical, so both searches should be tried. It may also be interesting to note that most of the search hits are journal articles. The remainder are from the Book Basement. None are from textbooks.

What is in the Sun's Joules CD-ROM for Chapter 2?

The Sun's Joules CD-ROM is a comprehensive collection of information resources developed by the Center for Renewable Energy and Sustainable Technology (CREST), funded by the U.S. Department of Energy and directed by the National Renewable Energy Laboratory (NREL). It provides easy access to a great deal of information about new technological advances in utilizing energy resources. As a supplemental resource, it will provide enjoyable enhancement materials to the basic concepts and activities of the chapter. Its features include: a glossary with definitions of energy-related terms; an index with information on its main topic areas and a list of references for each of its topic areas. Much of the information on the disc relates directly to the Stretching Exercises and Inquiry Investigations found in the chapter.

One of the main menu topic sections from the Sun's Joules is entitled "Wind Energy" and therefore corresponds very specifically to the context of the Scenario for Chapter Two in which students are challenged to write a manual that describes how to obtain electricity from a wind generator. It contains a wealth of information that will directly help students understand this energy source. Also, another nice enhancement for the chapter comes from one of the interactive activities found in the Photovoltaics section of the disc. In this exercise students drag appliances into or out of a house and observe the different energy consumption used for each appliance, making it a complimentary exercise for their Chapter Challenge.

What is in the Green Home CD-ROM for Chapter 2?

In the Green Home CD-ROM students are given the opportunity to walk through a digital home exploring important environmental and technology features that will help them in their understanding of generating electricity and energy consumption. They will therefore find this to be a valuable resource as they think about the many different types of appliances and the relative efficiency of different appliances as they complete their chapter challenge.

There are also a number of interactive activities in this CD-ROM in which students can manipulate various aspects of a house to see how different appliances, fixtures, designs and practices lead to different amounts of resource consumption. For example, they have the opportunity to compare the energy and economic performance of conventional incandescent lighting and compact fluorescent lighting.

Also, much of the information on the disc relates directly to the Stretching Exercises and Inquiry Investigations found in the chapter. For example the "Lighting Activity" will help students in the Stretching Exercise of Activity One which asks them to investigate different types of light bulbs. The "Indoor Water Use Activity" relates directly to the Stretching Exercise from Active Five in which students are asked to research ways to reduce the amount of electrical energy needed to provide hot water to a dwelling.

ACTIVITY ONE
Generate

Background Information

The physics principles involved in Activity One are:

- resistive heating by an electric current (light bulb effect).
- production of electricity using a generator.
- energy transformations including conservation of energy.

Resistive Heating. As students use a hand-operated generator to drive an electric current through light bulb filaments and a short strand of steel wool, the current heats the metal resulting in the release of heat and light. Although it is not intended to quantify this process with students at this stage, it is important for you to understand that the mechanical power input provided by the student to crank the generator [Power = work/time = (force x distance)/time] is transferred—less, of course, the power expended overcoming friction in the generator—to the filament as electrical power [Power = Current x Voltage = Current squared x Resistance]. In turn, the electrical power is released by the resistive filament in the forms of heat and light. Similar transformations will be treated quantitatively later in this chapter.

Generator. Throughout this chapter the generator is meant to be treated as a "black box" by students; that is, the generator is used to produce electricity without understanding how or why it works. You as the teacher will be more comfortable and better prepared to respond to student questions about the generator if you understand its principles of operation.

Background information about AC and DC generators provided for students from another part of the *Active Physics* course materials labeled Generator Principles is reproduced for you as the last section of this background discussion. The kind of generator used in this chapter is a DC generator, meaning that it produces direct (not alternating) current and voltage.

If you are not familiar with the operating principles of generators it is recommended that you study the Generator Principles section now.

The particular generator recommended for use in the Teacher's Guide for this and later activities in Chapter Three has a power output (current and voltage) which is generally proportional to the rate of cranking the handle (below a cranking rate which would damage the gears). The direction of the current reverses as the direction of rotation of the handle is reversed.

Energy Transformations. Perhaps the most profound thing to be learned about the generation of electrical energy in Activity One is found in the "feel" of operating the generator with and without it delivering current to an external device such as a light bulb. When the generator is cranked without delivering a current only minimal effort is needed. This is the effort needed to overcome mechanical friction within the moving parts of the generator. However, when the generator is cranked to deliver a current to the circuit, the effort becomes noticeably greater. This is where a subtle, yet highly profound phenomenon comes into action. The greater effort upon delivery of current to an external device happens because as soon as current begins to flow within the internal wire coil of the generator, that current, in the presence of magnets within the generator, causes the generator to act as an electric motor which wants to run backwards against the cranking action. This is known as the "back emf" (back electromotive force, or backward voltage) which always causes a generator to "fight back" any effort to make it produce an electric current. The harder and faster one may try to crank an operating generator, the more the generator fights back. Therefore, it is necessary to maintain as much input power to a generator as the desired output power; in fact, since friction always is present to be overcome, input power must always exceed output power. Electric generators do not produce free energy. For fullest understanding of this phenomenon you may also wish to consult a reference on the operating principles of electric motors.

For your information, light bulbs are filled with an inert gas to prevent oxidation of the metal (usually tungsten) filament. The strand of steel wool used in this activity oxides immediately because it is exposed to air.

The sun is the primary source of energy in the chain of transformations which culminates in a student cranking a generator to light a bulb.

Active-ating the Physics InfoMall

One of the strengths of the InfoMall is the enormous number of demonstrations that can be found in the Demo & Lab Shop. As an example, consider step 3 of For You To Do. Steel wool is used in a circuit. Are there demonstrations that could also be used? (Note that a demonstration should not replace the student activity, but can be used in addition.) Try a search for "steel wool". The second hit on the list includes one way to use steel wool as a fuse in a simple circuit with light bulbs. This appears in Arnold Arons' *A Guide to Introductory Physics Teaching*, found in the Book Basement. This was not in the Demo & Lab Shop. Suppose we want to force the issue and limit our search to only the Demo & Lab Shop, and search for "electricity". Try this, and you will not be disappointed. However, high on this list is the following: *LAB MANUAL: Recipes for Science: Misconceptions.* Quite by accident, we have found an item that did not appear in our search for student misconceptions about electricity (done previously, in the Scenario section). Why? The word "Student" was included in our search. If we eliminate that word, our search provides additional references for us. Try it.

Again, this illustrates one of the properties of the InfoMall - it is like a real mall. Sometimes you find just the right item for someone while shopping for something or someone else.

Physics To Go step 1 asks for a list of "electricity words." You can find a long list in the Keyword Kiosk. Simply go to the Kiosk and find the electricity and magnetism keywords. These are also good words for searching the InfoMall in order to find definitions.

Physics To Go also asks about light bulbs. A search for "light bulb*" provides many informative references that you may wish to read. Don't forget – the text on the InfoMall (together with graphics) can be copied and pasted directly into your own word processor for your own handouts.

Planning for the Activity

Time Requirements

This activity can be completed in less than one period. Allow the students to have sufficient time so that each student is allowed to experience what the cranking "feels" like under load and no load.

Materials needed

For each group:

- manual electric generator: a hand-operated DC generator capable of a maximum output of about 300 milliamps at 6 volts is recommended for this and several other activities in the remaining part of this and the next chapter. The "Genecon" manufactured by "Nakamura Scientific Co., Ltd." is recommended. It is available from several U.S. science supply houses. Generators are considered essential for student use in this and the next chapter, and batteries or power supplies should not be substituted for them.
- light bulb, miniature screwbase ("flashlight" bulbs): Just about any low voltage bulb will do; a No. 13 (3.6 volt, .30 amp) is a good choice.
- blinking bulb, miniature screwbase: a No. 406 or No. 407, available at electronics stores.
- bulb base for miniature screwbase bulbs: any kind.
- steel wool: coarse grade is easiest to "grab" with electrical clips; a little goes a long way.
- connecting wires, insulated

Advance Preparation and Setup

Have one set up to show the students how to set up the generator and the bulbs.

Teaching Notes

Do not give extensive directions for the FYTD activity because it is meant to be exploratory. Reading the objectives to the students will suffice to indicate to the students what to think about as they engage in the WDYT and FYTD activities. Ask students not to worry about how the generator works, just use it as a "black box" source of electricity.

Remind the students that electricity can be dangerous. Although the currents and voltages are not likely to be harmful, the possibility for harm is there for students who may have heart or other bio-electrical problems.

Some students are not familiar with what electricity is. They may try to explain that electricity is a "something" (a particle, molecule, or other substance) that is converted into light and that the thing goes away once it is converted into light (or heat). Don't try to explain everything during this first activity, but allow the students to discover what is electricity. The activities allow for this discovery of the nature of electricity.

AC Generator

The following figure shows the position of the rotating coil of an AC generator at instants separated by one-fourth of a rotation of the coil. Students should analyze your observations during the AC generator demonstration, and record their understanding of the drawing and the subsequent explanation in their journals.

It is easier to understand the creation of a current if we invent a set of invisible threads to signify the magnetic field of the permanent magnets. The very thin threads fill the space and connect the north pole of one magnet with the south pole of the other magnet. If the wire of the generator is imagined to be a very thin, sharp knife, the question you must ask is whether the knife (the wire) can "cut" the threads (the magnetic field lines). If the wire can "cut" the field lines, then a current is generated. If the wire moves in such a way that it does not "cut" the field lines, then NO current is generated.

For the purpose of analysing the generator in the figure of the rotating coil, you may want to build a small model of the rectangular coil so that you can move the model as a way to make sense of the drawings. The coil model can be constructed with three pens, or pencils held together with rubber bands. Rest the coil between two pieces of paper - the left paper is the north pole of a magnet; the right paper is the south pole of a magnet.

For the purpose of analysing the rotating coil figure, the four sides of the rectangular coil of the AC generator will be referred to as sides AB, BC, CD, and DA, corresponding to the lines from corners A to B, B to C, etc. Side DA is "broken" to allow extension of the coil to the rings. The "brushes" labelled 1 and 2, make sliding contact with the rings to provide a path for the induced current to travel to an external circuit (not shown) connected to the brushes. The magnetic field has a left-to-right direction (from the north pole to the south pole) in the space between the magnets in the rotating coil figure. It is assumed that the coil has a constant speed of rotation.

1. When the generator coil is in the position shown in the rotating coil figure (1), no current is being induced because all sides of the coil are moving parallel to the magnetic field. The AB wire and the CD wire do not "cut" the field lines. On Graph 1, plot a point at the origin of the graph, indicating the amount of induced current is zero at the instant corresponding to the beginning of one rotation of the coil.

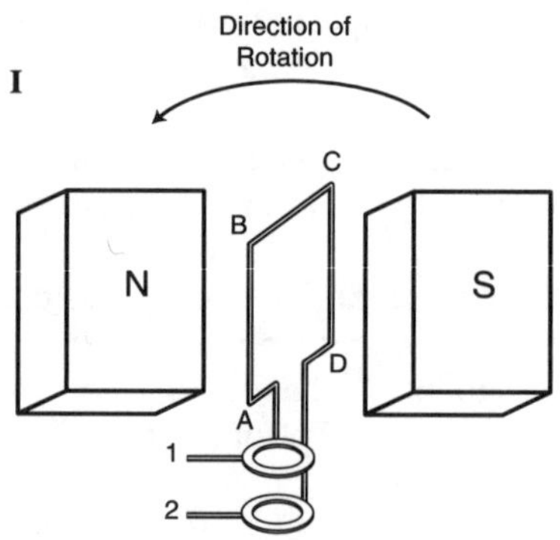

2. One-fourth turn later, at the instant shown in the rotating coil figure (II), the induced current is maximum because both sides AB and CD are "cutting" perpendicularly through the magnetic field. At this instant, the relative motion between the magnetic field and the coil is maximum. If the generator were connected to an external circuit, current would flow out of brush 1, travel around the circuit, and enter brush 2. The amount of current flowing in the circuit would be exactly the same as the induced current flowing around the coil as indicated by the arrows. On Graph 1, plot a point directly above the 1/4-turn mark at a height equal to the top of the vertical axis to represent maximum current flow in one direction.

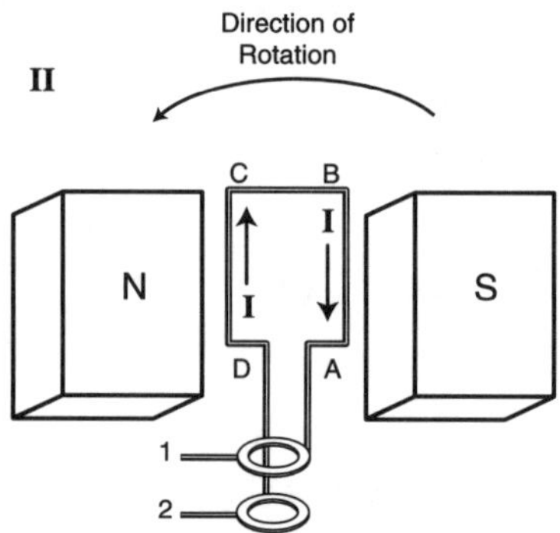

3. One-half turn into the rotation of the coil, at the instant shown in the rotating coil figure (III) on next page, the current again is zero because all sides of the coil are moving parallel to the magnetic field. Plot a point at the 1/2 mark on the horizontal axis to show that no current is being induced at that instant.

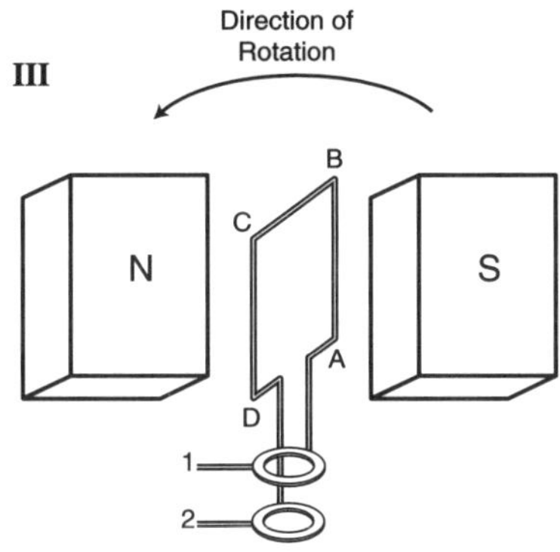

4. At the instant at which 3/4 of the rotation of the coil has been completed, shown in the rotating coil figure (IV), the induced current again is maximum because coil sides AB and CD again are moving across the magnetic field at maximum rate. However, this is not exactly the same situation as shown in the rotating coil figure (II); it is a different situation in one important way: the direction of the induced current has reversed. Follow the directions of the arrows which represent the direction of the current flow in the coil to notice that, at this instant, the current would flow to an external circuit out of brush 2 and would return through brush 1. On Graph 1, plot a point below the 3/4-turn mark at a distance as far below the horizontal axis as the bottom end of the vertical axis. This point will represent maximum current in the opposite, or "alternate," direction of the current shown earlier at 1/4-turn.

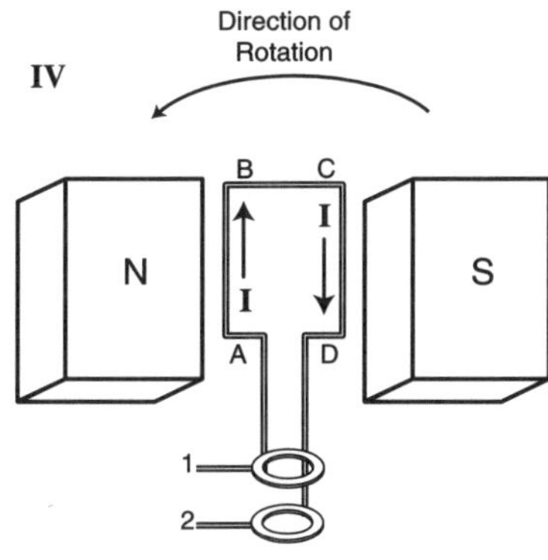

5. The rotating coil figure (1) is used again to show the instant at which one full rotation of the generator coil has been completed. Again, all sides of the coil are moving parallel to the magnetic field, and no current is being induced. Plot a point on the horizontal axis at the 1-turn mark to show that the current at this instant is zero.

6. You have plotted only 5 points to represent the current induced during one complete cycle of an AC generator. What about the points to be plotted that would represent the amount of induced current at each instant during one complete rotation of the generator coil? What is the overall shape of the graph? Should the graph be smooth, or have sharp edges? Sketch it to connect the points plotted on Graph 1.

7. Additional rotations of the generator coil would, if the same speed and resistance in the external circuit were maintained, result in the same graph, over and over.

DC Generator

The DC generator figure below shows the important parts of a DC generator. Students should analyze your observations during the DC generator demonstration, and record their understanding of the drawing and the subsequent explanation in their journals.

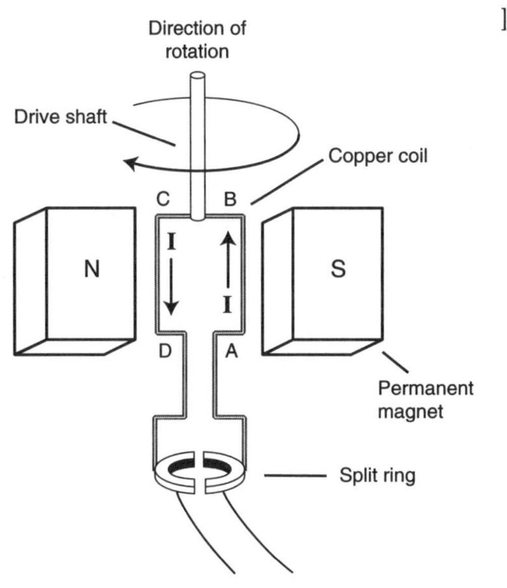

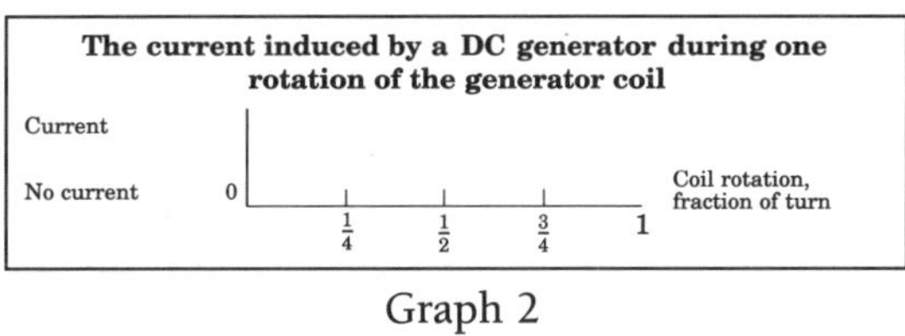

Graph 2

Graph 2 can be completed using the same pattern of analysis applied to the AC generator.

1. At the instant shown in the DC generator figure above, the induced current is maximum both in the generator coil and the external circuit to which the generator is connected (the external circuit is not shown). The instant corresponds to the rotating coil (II). Plot a point on Graph 2 directly above the 1/4-turn mark at a height equal to the top of the vertical axis to represent maximum current flow at that instant.

2. At the instant 1/4-turn earlier than the instant shown in the DC generator figure, corresponding to the zero mark of rotation, the current would have been zero because all sides of the coil would have been moving parallel to the direction of the magnetic field. Therefore, plot a point at the origin of Graph 2. Similarly, the induced current again would be zero at the instant 1/4-turn later than the instant shown in the DC generator figure; therefore, plot a point on the horizontal axis at the 1/2-turn mark.

3. Notice the arrangement used to transfer current from the generator to the external circuit for the DC generator. It is different from the arrangement used for the AC generator. The DC generator has a "split-ring commutator" for transferring the current to the external circuit. Notice that if the coil shown in the DC generator figure were rotated 1/4-turn in either direction, the "brush" ends that extend from the coil to make rubbing contact with each half of the split ring would reverse, or switch, the connection to the external circuit. Further, notice that the connection to the external circuit would be reversed at the same instant that the induced current in the coil reverses due to the change in direction in which the sides of the coil move through the magnetic field. The outcome is that while the current induced in the coil alternates, or changes direction each 1/2-rotation, the current delivered to the external circuit always flows in the same direction. Current that flows always in one direction is called direct current, or DC. Therefore, it is appropriate to plot a point on Graph 2 at a point directly above the 3/4 -turn mark at the same height at the point plotted earlier for the 1/4-turn mark.

4. As done for the AC generator, find out how to connect the points plotted on Graph 2 to represent the amount of current delivered always in the same direction to the external circuit during the entire cycle.

Generators will supply electricity to the homes that we build through HFE. The voltage of an AC generator varies from zero to a maximum then back to zero and then to a maximum in the other direction. You will hear people give one value for AC voltage in the same way that they give one value for a battery. A 1.5-volt battery or a 9-volt battery provides a steady, direct voltage. The 120-volt AC in your home varies as we have shown; the 120 volts is a type of average that allows us to compare different AC voltages.

NOTES

2

Activity Overview

This activity introduces students to electricity in a way that may not be familiar to them. They will be generating electricity using a hand generator. This will allow them to see the effect of cranking quickly or slowly, and to experience the "feel" of the cranking.

Student Objectives

Students will:

- trace energy transformations.
- identify the sun as Earth's ultimate energy source.
- begin developing a personal model for electricity.

ANSWERS FOR THE TEACHER ONLY

What Do You Think?

Students may refer to solar photovoltaic cells, or wind generators as being "free". However, there is no such thing as "free" energy. The First Law of Thermodynamics states that energy can neither be created nor destroyed, only converted from one form into another. Therefore, energy is never "free". Even with solar energy and wind energy (often referred to as renewable), the converter from solar (wind) to electrical energy for your home, must be built and costs money. The transmission from the point of generation to the point of use, costs money.

CHAPTER 2 ELECTRICITY FOR EVERYONE

Activity One

Generate

WHAT DO YOU THINK?

Electricity affects most parts of your life. You pay for it, over and over, in the form of electric bills and batteries. Also, most products that you purchase are manufactured by processes that use electricity, so you pay for electricity in indirect ways, too.

- **Is there any "free" electricity available and, if so, why pay for it?**

Record your ideas about this question in your *Active Physics log*. Be prepared to discuss your responses with your small group and the class.

HOME H 46

FOR YOU TO DO

1. You will be provided with a bulb, bulb base, connecting wires and a generator. Assemble the bulb, bulb base, connecting wires, and hand generator, and turn the crank of the generator to make the bulb light. Never turn the crank too fast. You can strip the gears!
   a) Draw a diagram of how you assembled the equipment for the bulb to light.
   b) Under what conditions will the bulb not light? Use words and a diagram in your answer.
   c) What are the effects of changing the speed or direction of cranking the generator?
   d) What are the effects of reversing the connections of the wires to the bulb or to the generator?

2. Replace the bulb that you have been using with a blinking bulb, the kind used in some toys, flashlights, and decorations. As before, use the generator to make it light, and keep cranking the generator to make the bulb go through several on and off cycles.
   a) Describe any difference that you can feel in cranking the generator when the bulb is on compared to when the bulb is off.
   b) How do you think that the blinking bulb works? What makes it go on and off?

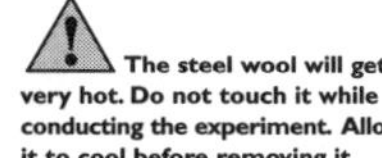
The steel wool will get very hot. Do not touch it while conducting the experiment. Allow it to cool before removing it.

3. Replace the blinking bulb with a strand of steel wool within the bulb socket. Crank the generator and observe what happens to the steel wool. Be careful not to touch the hot steel wool! You may push the steel wool with the point of a pencil to provide a better contact with the socket.
   a) Describe the appearance of the steel wool.
   b) What factors affect whether or not the steel wool glows, how much it glows, and for how long?
   c) What were the similarities and differences between the steel wool and the light bulbs as used above?

ANSWERS

For You To Do

1. a) Student activity and drawing.
   b) Students' answer will vary. However, the bulb will not light when the generator is not moving, or if they have the wires hooked up incorrectly. If there is a short the bulb will not light.
   c) The students should notice as they increase the speed of the generator, the bulb will get brighter. The direction should have no bearing on the brightness of the bulb. They will notice that when changing from one direction to the other, the bulb will go dim, out, and then bright again.
   d) There should be no effect.
2. a) The students will notice that the crank is harder to turn when the bulb is on than when the bulb is off.
   b) Students' answers will vary.
3. a) As the generator is cranked, the steel wool will start to glow.
   b) Students will notice that the harder they crank the generator, the more intense the glow of the steel wool. They may notice at some point that the steel wool starts to melt or break down. The steel wool will only glow for a short period of time.

ANSWERS

For You To Do

(continued)

4. a) Some students will not be able to answer this exactly. However, they should be able to understand that the cranking of the generator puts energy into the system. Understanding exactly this process is not necessary at this time. The energy is not free, but students may see it as free meaning rather that there is no monetary cost.

 b) Students' answer will vary. There is stored chemical energy in the arm muscles. They produce kinetic energy of movement of the crank. This kinetic energy is converted to electrical energy in the generator (see Background Information for details). The electrical energy is then converted into light and heat energy of the light bulb. Some students may also refer to the "lost" energy of friction and heat lost to the environment. (In essence it is not lost energy but rather energy that is converted into useless energy.)

 c) The source in this activity is the chemical energy stored in the arms. In a flashlight bulb, it is the chemical energy stored in the battery. The source of energy for the house lamp is dependent on the type of electric power plant (coal - chemical energy stored in the coal; nuclear power - nuclear energy in the fission or the breaking down of the atom into smaller particles, and giving off energy; gravitational potential energy that is stored in the water in a dam, mechanical energy of the wind; etc.)

ANSWERS

Physics To Go

1. Answers will vary. There will be others. If you do not know the definition, check out any senior-level physics text book.

ELECTRICITY FOR EVERYONE

4. Was the electrical energy that you used to "light things up" in this activity "free"? Did you get something for nothing? Using your observations in this activity, write a short paragraph to answer each of the following questions.
   a) What was the energy source for each part of the activity (bulb, blinking bulb, steel wool)? Was it free energy, at no cost?
   b) What forms of energy were involved in the activity, and in what order did the forms appear?
   c) How is the energy source used in this activity different from the source used to light a bulb in a flashlight, or in a house lamp?

REFLECTING ON THE ACTIVITY AND THE CHALLENGE

This activity has given you some experience with a process that is involved in the electrical system you will use for the HFE dwelling: using a generator to provide energy for electric light bulbs. The generator and the light bulbs used in this activity are scaled-down versions of the ones to be used for the dwelling, but they work in the same way. One additional feature will exist in the electrical system for the dwelling, the electrical energy from the generator will be able to be stored in batteries until it is needed to operate lights and other appliances.

Part of your challenge is to write a training manual to help instructors teach the inhabitants about their wind-generator system. You will probably want to include what you learned in this activity in your manual.

PHYSICS TO GO

1. Make a chart with two columns, the first one labelled "Word" and the other labelled "Meaning."
   a) In the first column make a list of "electricity words"—words that you have heard used in connection with electrical units of measurement, parts of electrical systems, or how electricity behaves.
   b) In the second column write what *you* think each word means, or describes.

HOME 

Word	Meaning
electricity	electrical energy
current	measure of amperage or flow of electrons
voltage	measure of potential difference (electromotive force)
ohms	measure of resistance
resistance	property of a substance which slows motion of electrons (sometimes referred to as non-conductivity)
conductor	allows the motion of electrons easily without resistance
insulator	impedes the movement of electrons
electrons	negatively charged particles which are free to move
switch	controls flow of electrons in a circuit
circuit	closed path where electrons flow from source (battery) to resistor (light bulb)

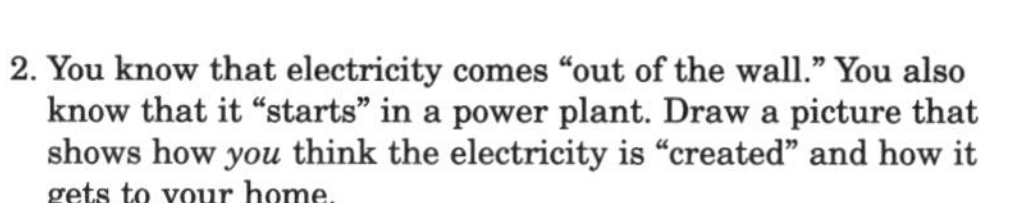

2. You know that electricity comes "out of the wall." You also know that it "starts" in a power plant. Draw a picture that shows how *you* think the electricity is "created" and how it gets to your home.

3. Explain what *you* think electricity is, how it behaves, and how it does what it does.

4. A variety of energy sources are used to operate light bulbs. Identify as many energy sources as you can which are used to power light sources.

5. The kind of light bulb you used in this activity is called "incandescent." Another kind of light bulb often used is called "fluorescent." Look up the meaning of the two words and explain how they are related to what glows to cause each kind of bulb to give off light.

6. "You don't get something for nothing." Explain how this expression applies to using a hand-operated generator to light a bulb.

STRETCHING EXERCISES

Some light bulbs are frosted on the inside, while others are clear. Some light bulbs have built-in reflectors to make them serve as a spotlight or a floodlight. Research different types of light bulbs. On a poster, describe how each is different, how each works, and where and why each is useful.

H 49 HOME

ANSWERS

Physics To Go

(continued)

2. Many possibilities for generation of electricity depending on the area. Hydroelectric dams, coal- and gas-fired power plants, nuclear plants are the most common. All of them will have similar paths from generator to home. The primary difference is how the electricity is generated. The students' diagrams should show how the electricity is generated, and then that it is transported to the consumer via power lines. Although most students have never been to a power generating station, a lot of them will have a basic understanding that the generator needs an input energy (water falling over a turbine), turning the generator, then passes through a series of invertors, and transformers increasing voltage to transmission levels (> 500 kilovolts), through a different series of transformers to step down the voltage to 240 V into our homes. With a coal-fired power plant, the coal is burned to heat up the water to steam, which is then used to drive the turbines. Nuclear power is using the nuclear reactor to generate heat to drive the turbines. Students at this level need not know the details, but if time or curiosity allows, a special project may be assigned as enrichment.

3. Students' answers will vary.

4. Students' answers will vary. The most common answers will be as listed previously, as well as batteries, car, RV batteries, gas-powered generators, solar panels, water wheels, geothermal power generators, etc.

5. Incandescent means that the light comes from the heating of filament which glows at certain temperatures. Fluorescence is the glowing of a substance when electromagnetic radiation of shorter wavelengths (such as UV light) hit the substance (tube lining) and emit light of a longer wavelength and greater visibility.

6. Although you are getting light without a monetary cost, you need to start out with some form of energy, (chemical stored energy in your muscles); use a converter (muscles), and convert the energy into a usable form (movement of the arm, and ultimately the crank of the generator). That kinetic energy is converted by the generator into electrical energy which is then passed through the light bulb which coverts it to light and heat energy.

2

Activity One A: Demonstration

Generator Principles

FOR YOU TO DO

Examine AC & DC Generators

1. Your teacher will explain and demonstrate a hand-operated, alternating current (AC) generator. During the demonstration, make the observations necessary to gain the information needed to answer these questions:

a) When the AC generator is used to light a bulb, describe the behavior in time of the brightness of the bulb when the generator is cranked.

(a) slowly, and (b) rapidly. Write your observations in your journal.

b) When the AC generator is connected to a galvanometer, describe the action of the galvanometer needle when the generator is cranked

(a) slowly, and (b) rapidly.

2. Your teacher will explain and demonstrate a hand-operated, direct current (DC) generator.

a) During the demonstration, make the observations necessary to gain the information needed to answer these questions:

b) When the DC generator is used to light a bulb, describe the behavior in time of the brightness of the bulb when the generator is cranked

(a) slowly, and (b) rapidly. Write your observations in your journal.

c) When the DC generator is connected to a galvanometer, describe the action of the galvanometer needle when the generator is cranked

(a) slowly, and (b) rapidly.

ACTIVITY TWO
Lighten Up

Background Information

The physics principles involved in Activity Two are:

- basic electrical theory.
- basic electrical units of measurement.
- series and parallel forms of electric circuits.
- dynamic rules of series and parallel circuits.

Basic electrical theory and basic electrical units. Explanations of basic electrical theory and units of measurement are presented in the For You To Read, of the student text for Activity Two. It is suggested that you complete that reading now.

Series and parallel forms of electric circuits. The diagrams of series and parallel circuits shown in Activity Two illustrate the most fundamental difference in the two kinds of circuits: only one possible path which a particular electron may take to traverse a series circuit, and multiple paths which an electron could take to complete a parallel circuit.

Students may come up with another possibility: a combination series/parallel circuit in which part of the circuit is series (one possible path) and another part of the circuit is parallel (two or more paths).

Both kinds of circuits have advantages which depend on the applications for which they are used. Parallel circuits are preferred for homes because, for example, when one light bulb on a circuit burns out the others are not affected. Also, parallel circuits provide the constant voltage needed for each parallel "branch" of a home circuit.

Dynamics and rules of series and parallel circuits. To enhance your background about what happens, and why, in series versus parallel circuits, it is suggested that you first read A Water Model for Electricity at the end of this background information and Physics To Go sections of the student text for Activity Two. When you have completed reading those sections, apply the rules below for series and parallel circuits to the quantitative examples presented in the sections.

A definition: 1 ohm is the amount of resistance which allows 1 amp of current to flow when 1 volt is applied.

Kirchoff's Law: All of the voltage (energy per unit of charge) applied to a circuit will be exactly dissipated in resistive parts of the circuit (that is, each unit of charge will have zero energy left when it has completed the circuit).

Ohm's Law: The total current (in amps) which will flow in a circuit may be calculated by dividing the voltage (in volts) applied to the circuit by the total resistance (in ohms) of the circuit.

Ohm's Law applies to both series and parallel (and other) circuits.

Rules applying to series circuits

The total resistance of a series circuit (R_T) is the sum of the individual resistances (R_1, R_2, R_3, . . .) in the circuit:

$R_T = R_1 + R_2 + R_3$

The total current in a series circuit (I_T) is equal to the current flowing in each resistor (I_1, I_2, I_3, . . .) in the circuit:

$I_T = I_1 = I_2 = I_3$

The total voltage (V_T, or energy per unit of charge) applied to a circuit is equal to the sum of the voltages dissipated in the individual resistors (V_1, V_2, V_3, . . .) in the circuit.

$V_T = V_1 + V_2 + V_3$

Further, Ohm's Law transposed as $V = IR$ may be applied to both entire circuit and to each resistor to show that the voltage dissipated by each resistor in a series circuit is proportional to its amount of resistance (that is, the larger resistors dissipate the most energy in this kind of circuit). Substituting IR for V in the right-hand terms of the above equation:

$V_T = I_1R_1 + I_2R_2 + I_3R_3$

Since $I_1 = I_2 = I_3$, the voltage dissipated at each resistor is proportional to the amount of resistance it represents in the circuit.

Rules applying to parallel circuits

The total current in a parallel circuit (I_T) is equal to the sum of the currents flowing in the individual resistors (I_1, I_2, I_3, . . .) in the circuit:

$I_T = I_1 + I_2 + I_3$

The total voltage (V_T, or energy per unit of charge) applied to a circuit is equal to the sum of the voltage dissipated by each resistor (V_1, V_2, V_3, . . .) in the circuit (see Kirchoff's Law above):

$V_T = V_1 = V_2 = V_3$

2

Substituting Ohm's Law in the form $I = V/R$ for each term in the equation $I_T = I_1 + I_2 + I_3$:

$V_T/R_T = V_1/R_1 + V_2/R_2 + V_3/R_3$

Since $V_T = V_1 = V_2 = V_3$ the above equation can be simplified through division by V to:

$1/R_T = 1/R_1 + 1/R_2 + 1/R_3$

Therefore, the reciprocal of the total resistance of a parallel circuit (R_T) is the sum of the reciprocals of the individual resistances (R_1, R_2, R_3, . . .) in the circuit.

Active-ating the Physics InfoMall

This activity immediately asks about light bulbs. We have already done the search for light bulbs in Activity One. You may wish to repeat the search now to find items specifically for this activity.

For You To Do step 2 mentions series and parallel circuits. A search for "series" AND "parallel" results in "Too Many Hits" again. If you limit this search, you can find many hits with wonderful information. For example, search for "misconcept*" AND "series" AND "parallel". The first hit is "Electricity Visualized: The Castle Project: Section 6: Circuits As Systems: What Makes Bulb Brightness Change?" from the Demo & Lab Shop. This contains activities that you may find useful. A little further down the list is "Potential difference and current in simple electric circuits: A study of students' concepts," from the *American Journal of Physics*, vol. 51, issue 5, 1983.

For You To Do step 2 also asks the students to make a prediction. The importance of the prediction should not be overlooked; indeed, predictions force students to examine their understanding of a phenomena and actively engage thought. If you were to search the InfoMall to find more about the importance of predictions in learning, you would find that you need to limit your search. Sadly, not much information exists on the InfoMall regarding predictions about electric circuits. To find information on the importance of predictions, we must turn to a topic that has been researched extensively; dynamics. Let's borrow from a search we perform in *Active Physics: Sports* and *Active Physics: Transportation:* A search for "prediction*" AND "inertia" resulted in several hits; the first hit is from *A Guide to Introductory Physics Teaching: Elementary Dynamics,* Arnold B. Arons' Book Basement entry. Here is a quote from that book: "Because of the obvious conceptual importance of the subject matter, the preconceptions students bring with them when starting the study of dynamics, and the difficulties they encounter with the Law of Inertia and the concept of force, have attracted extensive investigation and generated a substantial literature. A sampling of useful papers, giving far more extensive detail than can be incorporated here, is cited in the bibliography [Champagne, Klopfer, and Anderson (1980); Clement (1982); di Sessa (1982); Gunstone, Champagne, and Klopfer (1981); Halloun and Hestenes (1985); McCloskey, Camarazza, and Green (1980); McCloskey (1983); McDermott (1984); Minstrell (1982); Viennot (1979); White (1983), (1984)]." Note that students' preconceptions can have a large effect on how they learn something. It is important that they are forced to consciously acknowledge their preconceptions by making predictions.

The InfoMall can also be used for more entertaining purposes. In For You To Read, we are told that Ben Franklin named charges as positive or negative. One of the underused parts of the InfoMall is the Calendar Cart. If you search the Calendar Cart for "Franklin" you will find that on "07/11/1747 In a letter to Peter Collinson, Benjamin Franklin described a discovery that would lead to the invention of the lightning rod and introduced the terms 'positive' and 'negative' and 'to electrise plus or minus.'" and "09/01/1747 In a letter to Peter Collinson, a Fellow of the Royal Society in London, Benjamin Franklin used his ideas about the 'two states of Electricity, the plus and minus' to explain how a Leiden jar stores electrical charge."

We are also told in For You To Read that a lightning bolt transfers approximately one coulomb of charge. If you look in the Utility Closet, in *Many Magnitudes: A Collection of Useful and Useless Numbers* (within Physics Pfact Potpourri) you will find that the "charge transfer in lightning stroke" is about 25 coulombs. Not very different, but it makes lightning that much more impressive.

Physics To Go asks if household wiring is series or parallel. For an answer, search the InfoMall for "house" AND "series" AND "parallel" but limit it to "same paragraph" to avoid too many hits.

The Stretching Exercises ask about Thomas Edison and his inventions. While this information does not seem to be on the InfoMall, a search for "Edison" AND "inventions" provides an article from the *American Journal of Physics* that contains the references for many books that you could use to find a list of his inventions. This article, and an update, are "Book-length biographies of physicists and astronomers," *American Journal of Physics*, vol. 12, issue 1, 1944, and "Book-length biographies of physicists and astronomers - addendum," *American Journal of Physics,* vol. 16, issue 3, 1948.

Planning for the Activity

Time Requirements

The students will be able to complete this activity in one 40-minute period or less.

Materials needed

For each group:

- hand generator
- miniature bulbs (all identical), and bases, 2 or 3 sets
- connecting wires, insulated

Advance Preparation and Setup

Discuss the "electricity words" identified by students the previous day and ask some students to share some features of their personal models for electricity. You may wish to make notes about misconceptions which exist, for a later treatment.

Teaching Notes

The students should not need extensive instructions to proceed with the FYTD in this activity. The FYTD activity should not take much time, so plan to reserve time for with-class reading and discussion of For You To Read, and encourage students to begin Physics To Go.

Encourage students to try to turn the generator at the same speed throughout the activity, as it will help them to determine which variable is causing the brightness in the bulbs.

CAUTION: Remind the students they are working with electricity, which is dangerous under certain circumstances. Watch to make sure the students are not trying to "zap" other students. Students with heart problems may be affected by the currents from the generator.

Because this lab is over quickly, it is advisable that you get to each of the student lab groups before they are finished. This is to ensure that they are on task, and also to watch for proper and safe lab technique.

Some students may refer to electricity as the transforming of electricity into heat and light energy. Emphasize that it is the transfer of energy in one form (electric kinetic energy) to another form (thermal energy -- molecules are heated up as there are more and more collisions with the electrons). Students may ask for an explanation of what the difference is between series circuits, and parallel circuits. You may refer to the water provided or another method may be the analogy of the stream. The potential difference in the water is the change in height. With a series circuit, it is analogous to the river with several rapids in a single line. As the water flows past each of the rapids it loses some of its potential energy at each rapid (the voltage in the electric circuit). The amount of water before and after each rapid is the same, regardless of the number of rapids (the current in the electric circuit). With a parallel circuit, the river has different channels, with the potential energy before each channel the same, and the potential after each is the same. Therefore, the potential difference in the stream is like the voltage in the circuit. However, the current through the channels may be different, and some may have a large flow (current in the electric circuit), and some may have a small flow, but the total flow will be the same before and after.

Activity Overview

The students will be investigating what electricity is, and how it works, in a very simplified form. They do not need the depth of explanation in the background information.

Student Objectives

Students will:

- qualitatively describe current, resistance, voltage.
- define: coulomb, ampere, volt.
- compare series and parallel circuits.
- recognize generator output limit.
- extend a personal model of electricity.

ANSWERS FOR THE TEACHER ONLY

What Do You Think?

Students' answers will vary. Electric energy is transformed into heat or light energy when electrons with a large amount of kinetic energy collide with the atoms in the wire. As more and more collisions occur, the wire heats ups, and if it heats up enough, as in the filament of an electric light bulb, it will glow

CHAPTER 2 ELECTRICITY FOR EVERYONE

Activity Two

Lighten Up

WHAT DO YOU THINK?

Lights were the first electric appliances for homes.

- **How do light bulbs, and the electricity that makes them glow, work?**

Record your ideas about this question in your *Active Physics log*. Be prepared to discuss your responses with your small group and the class.

FOR YOU TO DO

1. Before you begin this activity, remind yourself about the "feel" of the generator and the brightness of the bulb when the generator was used to energize one bulb in Activity 1. Connect a single bulb to the generator and crank. Use your observations of a single bulb as a basis for comparison when you use two or more bulbs during this activity.

HOME H 50

ANSWERS

For You To Do

1. Student activity.

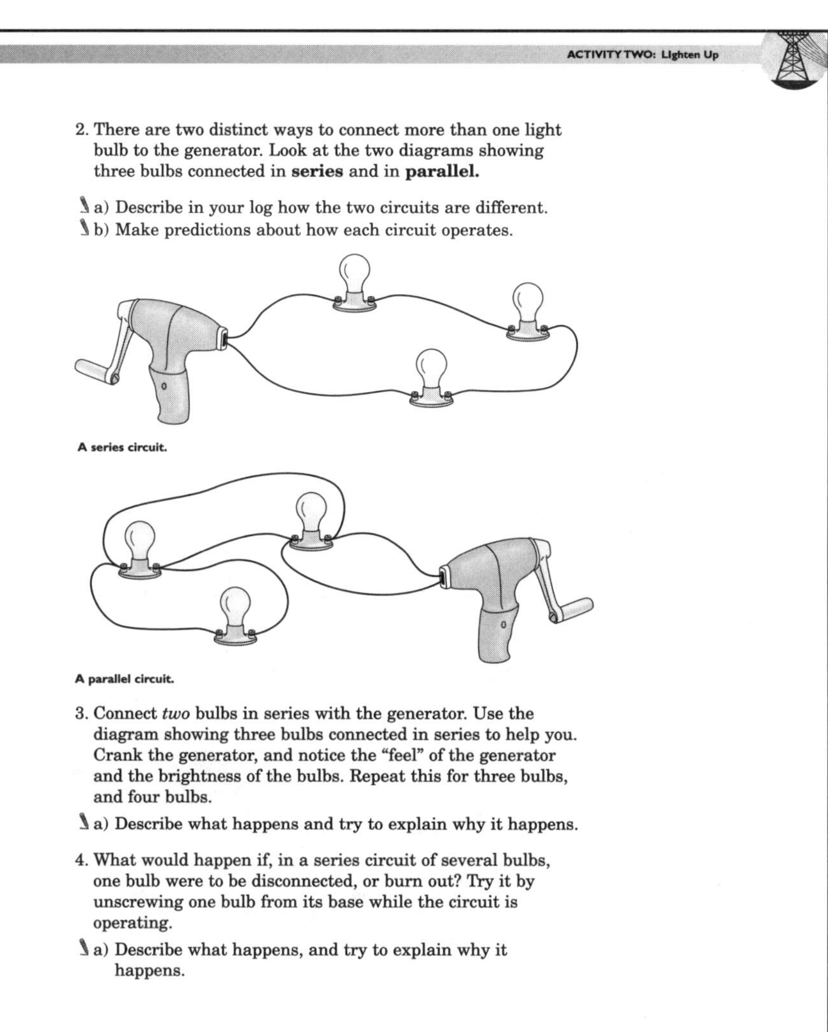

ACTIVITY TWO: Lighten Up

2. There are two distinct ways to connect more than one light bulb to the generator. Look at the two diagrams showing three bulbs connected in **series** and in **parallel.**

   a) Describe in your log how the two circuits are different.

   b) Make predictions about how each circuit operates.

A series circuit.

A parallel circuit.

3. Connect *two* bulbs in series with the generator. Use the diagram showing three bulbs connected in series to help you. Crank the generator, and notice the "feel" of the generator and the brightness of the bulbs. Repeat this for three bulbs, and four bulbs.

   a) Describe what happens and try to explain why it happens.

4. What would happen if, in a series circuit of several bulbs, one bulb were to be disconnected, or burn out? Try it by unscrewing one bulb from its base while the circuit is operating.

   a) Describe what happens, and try to explain why it happens.

H 51 HOME

ANSWERS

For You To Do *(continued)*

2. a) Student response. Some students may observe that there is only one path in a series, and more paths in the parallel circuit.

   b) Student response. Students' answers will vary.

3. a) In a series circuit, as you increase the number of the bulbs, the resistance increases. Therefore, as you increase the number of light bulbs, the cranking of the generator gets more difficult. You will also notice that you must crank the generator faster in order to light up more light bulbs. Again, the faster you crank the generator, the brighter the bulbs.

4. a) When you disconnect one of the bulbs, you actually break (open) the circuit, which stops the flow of electrons. No flow of electrons, no energy transformation.

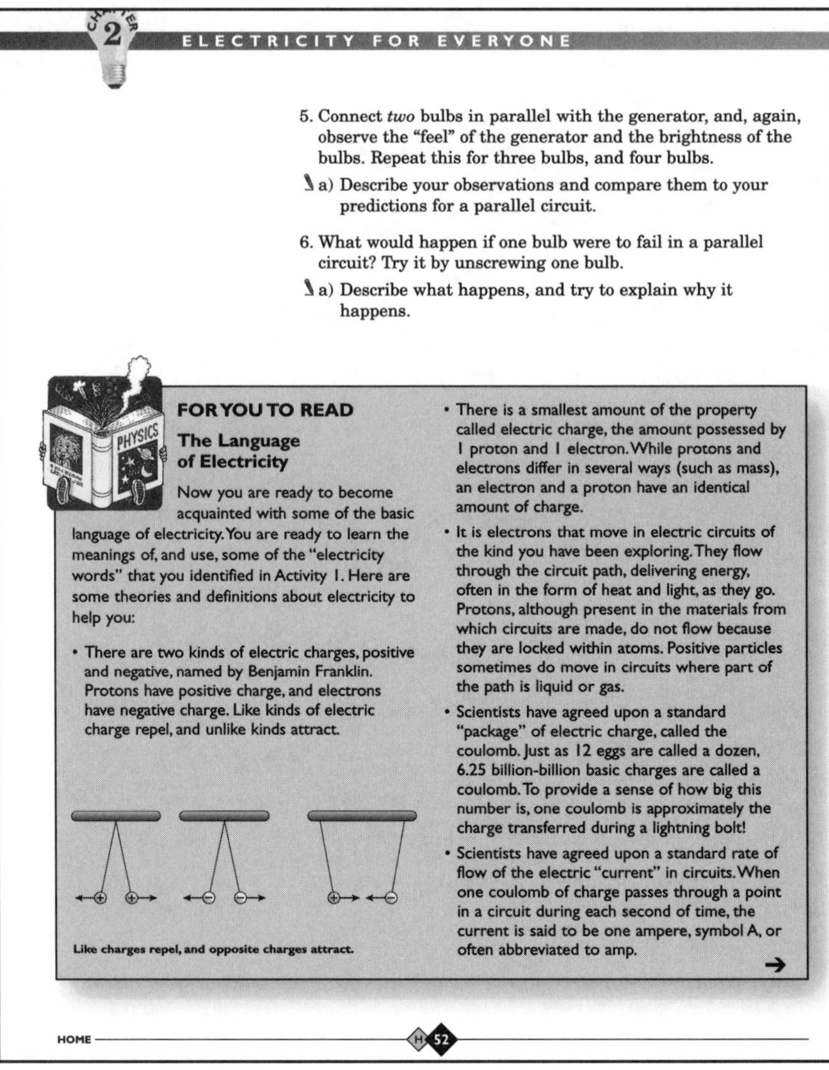

ELECTRICITY FOR EVERYONE

5. Connect *two* bulbs in parallel with the generator, and, again, observe the "feel" of the generator and the brightness of the bulbs. Repeat this for three bulbs, and four bulbs.
   a) Describe your observations and compare them to your predictions for a parallel circuit.

6. What would happen if one bulb were to fail in a parallel circuit? Try it by unscrewing one bulb.
   a) Describe what happens, and try to explain why it happens.

FOR YOU TO READ

The Language of Electricity

Now you are ready to become acquainted with some of the basic language of electricity. You are ready to learn the meanings of, and use, some of the "electricity words" that you identified in Activity 1. Here are some theories and definitions about electricity to help you:

- There are two kinds of electric charges, positive and negative, named by Benjamin Franklin. Protons have positive charge, and electrons have negative charge. Like kinds of electric charge repel, and unlike kinds attract.

Like charges repel, and opposite charges attract.

- There is a smallest amount of the property called electric charge, the amount possessed by 1 proton and 1 electron. While protons and electrons differ in several ways (such as mass), an electron and a proton have an identical amount of charge.
- It is electrons that move in electric circuits of the kind you have been exploring. They flow through the circuit path, delivering energy, often in the form of heat and light, as they go. Protons, although present in the materials from which circuits are made, do not flow because they are locked within atoms. Positive particles sometimes do move in circuits where part of the path is liquid or gas.
- Scientists have agreed upon a standard "package" of electric charge, called the coulomb. Just as 12 eggs are called a dozen, 6.25 billion-billion basic charges are called a coulomb. To provide a sense of how big this number is, one coulomb is approximately the charge transferred during a lightning bolt!
- Scientists have agreed upon a standard rate of flow of the electric "current" in circuits. When one coulomb of charge passes through a point in a circuit during each second of time, the current is said to be one ampere, symbol A, or often abbreviated to amp.

HOME H 52

ANSWERS

For You To Do *(continued)*

5\. a) The brightness should be about the same. Because the amperage will remain the same for each bulb as you add bulbs, then the brightness of each bulb will be the same. The students should not feel any difference in the cranking as they add bulbs.

6\. a) If one bulb were to fail, there would be no change in the brightness, and there should be little if any difference in the cranking.

- Different materials offer different resistance, or opposition, to the flow of electric current through them. Tungsten, from which light bulb filaments are made, has high electrical resistance. When current flows through it, the tungsten metal "robs" energy from the moving electrons and gets hot. Copper, by contrast, has low resistance; electrons transfer very little energy when flowing through copper. Electrical resistance is measured in ohms(Ω).
- Batteries or the hand generator provide energy to the electrons. These electrons are then able to light bulbs, heat wires, or make motors turn. The energy given to each coulomb of charge is measured in volts (V).

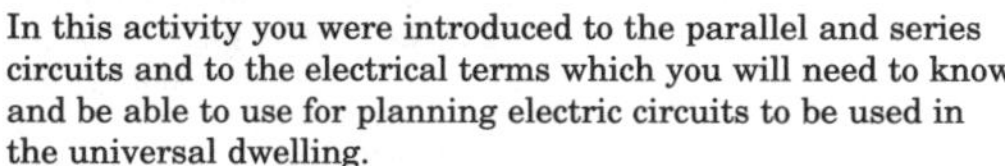

REFLECTING ON THE ACTIVITY AND THE CHALLENGE

In this activity you were introduced to the parallel and series circuits and to the electrical terms which you will need to know and be able to use for planning electric circuits to be used in the universal dwelling.

It is a fact that homes are "wired" using parallel circuits. Individual houses, apartments, mobile homes, or any other dwellings that receive electricity from a power company, have circuits of the parallel kind. Some older homes have as few as four circuits, and newer homes usually have many more. Each circuit in a home may have several light bulbs and other electrical appliances "plugged in," all in parallel. When electrical appliances are hooked up in parallel, if one is off or diconnected, the others can still be on. In a series circuit, if any appliance is disconnected, the other appliances cannot work. In your training manual, you will need to explain why the circuits in the universal dwelling are wired in parallel.

ANSWERS

Physics To Go

1. Students answers will vary. Expect students to choose parallel circuits, because of the multiple paths the current is taking. If one bulb burns out on a series circuit, it will turn the whole circuit off. Also, on a series circuit, every time you turn on a new appliance, or light, there would be a "dip" in the current, and the lights would become dimmer each time a new resistor was added to the circuit.

2. Depending on the type of generator, you will notice it has an upper limit on the current it will produce. Before the students arrive, the teacher should establish what the upper limit is.

3. Students will see that there is a limit to the number of appliances and light bulbs a circuit can accommodate. As they go through the next few activities, they will discover the limit of the number of electric devices allowed with a limited electric output.

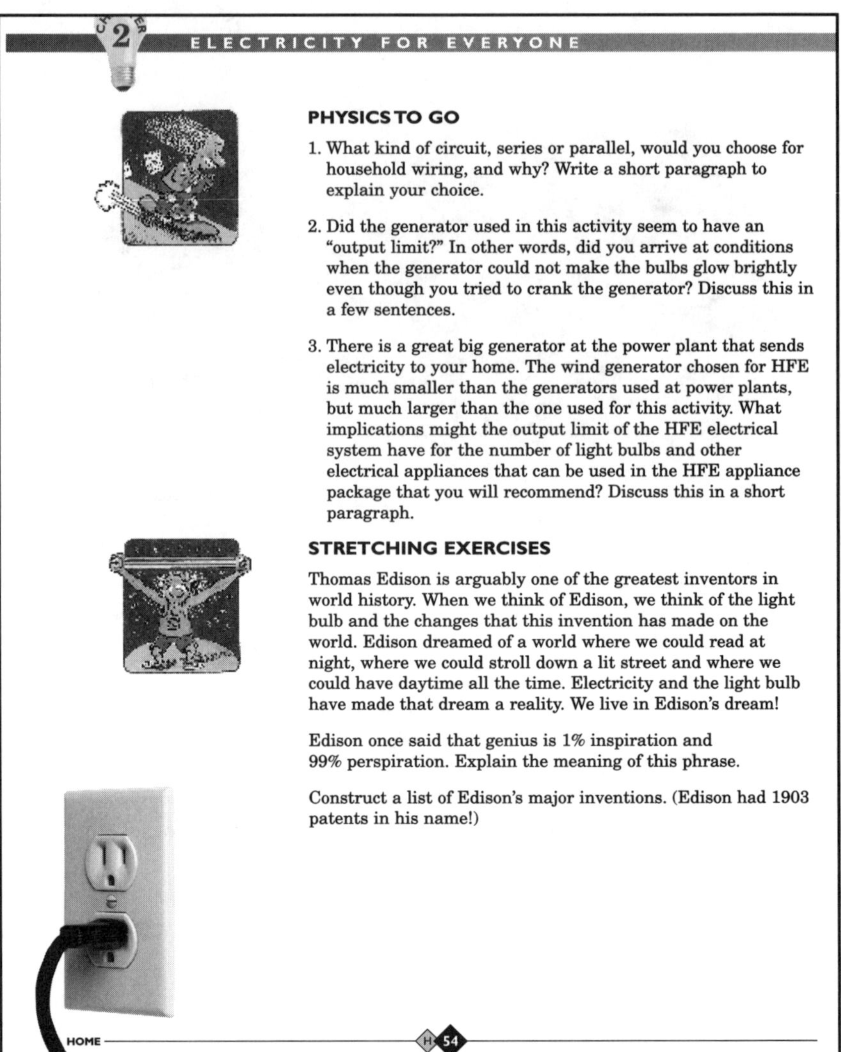

CHAPTER 2 ELECTRICITY FOR EVERYONE

PHYSICS TO GO

1. What kind of circuit, series or parallel, would you choose for household wiring, and why? Write a short paragraph to explain your choice.
2. Did the generator used in this activity seem to have an "output limit?" In other words, did you arrive at conditions when the generator could not make the bulbs glow brightly even though you tried to crank the generator? Discuss this in a few sentences.
3. There is a great big generator at the power plant that sends electricity to your home. The wind generator chosen for HFE is much smaller than the generators used at power plants, but much larger than the one used for this activity. What implications might the output limit of the HFE electrical system have for the number of light bulbs and other electrical appliances that can be used in the HFE appliance package that you will recommend? Discuss this in a short paragraph.

STRETCHING EXERCISES

Thomas Edison is arguably one of the greatest inventors in world history. When we think of Edison, we think of the light bulb and the changes that this invention has made on the world. Edison dreamed of a world where we could read at night, where we could stroll down a lit street and where we could have daytime all the time. Electricity and the light bulb have made that dream a reality. We live in Edison's dream!

Edison once said that genius is 1% inspiration and 99% perspiration. Explain the meaning of this phrase.

Construct a list of Edison's major inventions. (Edison had 1903 patents in his name!)

HOME H 54

ANSWERS

Stretching Exercises

As an extension to this activity, the students may want to choose one of Edison's inventions and give a report to the class. This can be done, by simply a written report, or visual, or even having the students reconstruct an invention. Students should submit a plan and discuss it with their teacher before building.

A Water Model for Electricity

Imagine a pump that can lift water from the ground to a height of 4 m (12 feet). This water can then be dropped to the ground and, on its way, it can turn the paddles of a water wheel. A rotating water wheel is a motor that can be used for many purposes. The water can be lifted again and, once again, can turn the water wheel. In a more complex system, the water can be lifted 16 meters and dropped through a series of different sized water wheels. Some of the wheels would spin fast and some would spin slowly-their speed would depend on their sizes. But all could be used as motors. The water would have to be lifted way up to 16 m again, but the energy we would get in our water wheel motors would be very useful.

In our electrical circuit, the hand generator gave the electrons energy. The electrons then "dropped" their energy in the three light bulbs. The electrons could, just as easily, have "dropped" their energy into electric motors that spin.

These models help you become more familiar with some of the electrical terms described earlier. If you turn the hand generator faster, you are providing more voltage to the electrons in the circuit. This is similar to raising the water to 16 m instead of 4 m. The number of amps is similar to the amount of water. Some light bulbs require more voltage to light (they have greater resistance) in the same way that some water wheels are harder to turn.

2

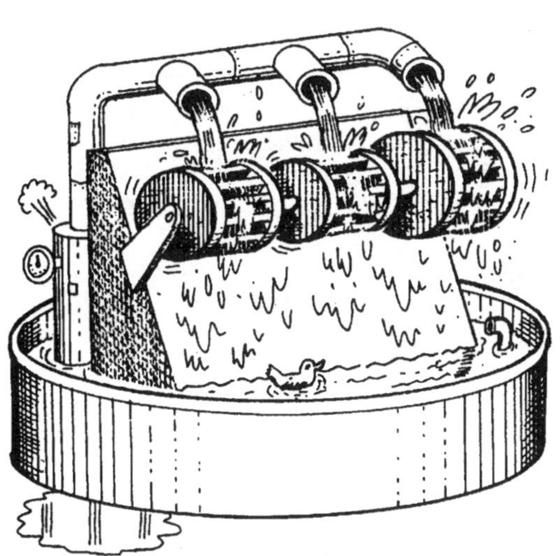

ACTIVITY THREE
Load Limit

Background Information

Principles involving power in a 120-volt AC household electric circuit are introduced in Activity Three. In particular, power calculations are applied to:

- the power consumed by individual appliances connected in a household circuit.
- the power limit, or "load limit," of a household circuit which is protected by a fuse or circuit breaker.

It is suggested that you first read the entire student text for Activity Three before proceeding in this background narrative. Please do that reading now.

The main focus of Activity Three is centered on the calculation of electric power presented in For You To Do as $P = IV$. Satisfy yourself that the units of measurement for the equation $P = IV$ are valid:

1 watt is defined as 1 joule/second

1 amp is defined as 1 coulomb/second

1 volt is defined as 1 joule/coulomb

Substituting the above definitions in the equation $P = IV$ gives:

joule/second = (coulomb/second) x (joule/coulomb) = joule/second

An alternate equation for calculating power is good for you to know in cases where current and resistance are known but voltage is not known. Need for the alternate equation probably will not arise in this activity, but may be useful later:

$P = I^2R$

As discussed in the teacher background information for Activity Two, the voltage applied to a parallel circuit is equal to the voltage dissipated in each parallel branch of the circuit. This makes it convenient for calculating the power dissipated by appliances in a home; the voltage applied to a household circuit is 120 volts AC and, since homes are wired so that each appliance on a circuit (e.g., each light bulb, TV set, radio, etc.) is the only device in its particular branch, the voltage dissipated by each device also is 120 volts AC. Therefore, if the power rating of an appliance is not known it can be calculated using one of the above equations if either the current or resistance for the appliance is known (or can be measured).

To calculate the load limit of a household circuit in watts it is necessary only to multiply 120 volts by the rating in amperes of the circuit breaker or fuse which projects the circuit. In most homes each circuit is protected by either a 15 amp or 20 amp circuit breaker or fuse. Using the equation $P = IV$, the load limit for a circuit having a 15 amp fuse would be 120 volts x 15 amps = 1,800 watts; for 20 amp protection the power would be 120 volts x 20 amps = 2,400 watts.

The relationship between the load limit of a household circuit and the power ratings of the appliances connected to the circuit is very simple:

$P_{limit} = P_1 + P_2 + P_3 + \ldots$

When the sum of the power ratings of the individual appliances connected to the circuit ($P_1 + P_2 + P_3 + \ldots$) exceeds the load limit (P_{limit}) the circuit breaker automatically shuts the circuit off to prevent overheating of the wires in the home.

For the HFE dwelling the power of the appliances operating at any time may not exceed the specified 2400 watt load limit.

Students who do the Stretching Exercise for Activity Three may discover that the load center in a home has some large circuit breakers which are rated at as much as 50 amps. Such circuit breakers control 240-volt AC devices such as kitchen ranges, hot water heaters or other high power devices. For your information, the power company provides a home with 240 volts and either 100 or 200 amp (60 amps for some old homes) capability for current. The 240 volts is applied in entirety to devices such as kitchen ranges and is divided into two 120-volt components which, in turn, are applied to the home's normal circuits. The combined current which can be carried simultaneously by all of the circuits in the home is determined by the 100 or 200 amp rating of the load center. The 240-volt aspect of household electricity will not be involved in the HFE dwelling.

Active-ating the Physics InfoMall

What Do You Think? asks about fuses and circuit breakers. Both of these can be searched for on the InfoMall. Suggested search words are "fuse*" or "circuit breaker*" where the asterisks have been included to allow for the singular and plural forms of the words.

For You To Do has a calculation and an equation for power. The InfoMall has many different avenues for exploring equations and calculations. You can go to the Equations Dictionary by clicking the button in the lower right-hand corner of the entrance screen (the button with equations all over it). This will give you a directory to choose from. When you have found the equation you can also ask for examples. Or you can browse through any of the textbooks, since most of them will have this equation. If you want homework-style problems, visit the Problems Place. You can choose from several collections of problems, including *Schaum's 3000 Solved Problems in Physics*. This would allow you to hand out problems and their solutions if you wish.

Physics To Go part 7 mentions horsepower. A search using "horsepower" quickly provides several definitions of "horsepower" along with the historical context and conversion factors.

Planning for the Activity

Time Requirements

Allow about 10 - 20 minutes for the demonstration.

Materials needed

For the class:

- 120-volt circuit for demonstrating overload (See Advance Preparation and Setup)

Advance Preparation and Setup

Arrange a tabletop array of 120-volt AC light bulbs in porcelain sockets, wired in parallel with lamp cord. The number of bulbs and their chosen (equal) wattage's must be sufficient to blow the fuse or circuit breaker that controls the 120-volt AC circuit used as the energy source. Preferably, the bulbs will be the only load on the circuit during the demonstration, and the fuse or breaker will be visible to the students. The latter can be accomplished by rigging a subpanel for a load center with a fuse and/or breaker and a cord and plug so that it can be plugged into a classroom outlet. It must be fused at less than the panel that feeds the classroom circuit. It would be best to demonstrate both a fuse and circuit breaker.

If you have a 15-A fuse (or circuit breaker), with 120-volt circuit, and 60-W light bulbs, and 100-W light bulbs, calculate the total wattage, for each type of bulb, and make sure you have enough sockets. ($P = IV$; $P = 15 \text{ A} \times 120 \text{ V} = 1800 \text{ W}$. Therefore, you would need 18 – 100-W light bulbs, or 30 – 60-W light bulbs. As this is large number of light bulbs, try using a smaller fuse, or use light bulbs, and a 1000-W hair dryer, and a 800-W kettle. Have the bulbs put a load of about 300, plug in the kettle and then plug in and turn on the hair dryer. Do this in different order, to see that it doesn't matter what the order is, it blows the fuse every time it is over the fuse rating.

If you have the time and equipment, place a voltmeter and an ammeter in the circuit to show the changes in the current, and the fact that the voltage stays the same.

Teaching Notes

Review from Activity Two that household circuits are parallel circuits and review the definitions of the coulomb and the ampere from the PTG in Activity Two. Do the demonstration, the FYTD, first, and then define the watt and the volt. Tread lightly when defining these terms, because prior background about work and energy cannot be assumed; you may wish to describe a joule as the work done when lifting a "quarter pounder" (the burger) one meter against gravity. The desired outcome is for students to have the idea that voltage is a measure of energy per unit of charge and that wattage is a measure of energy per unit time. Put it all together in the equation $P = IV$ using dimensional representation of the variables in the equation, and then set students to answering the questions in the FYTD.

To keep students aware that these activities contribute to knowledge needed for the Challenge be sure to link this activity to the load limit of the HFE electrical system. The power limit in the HFE system is 2400 watts. Be sure that students calculate the maximum current which the 120-volt system can accommodate at any one time.

To ensure the safety of the teacher and the students, do not leave the homemade circuit unattended. The household circuit of 15 A is more than enough to kill. As an added precaution, a GFCI plug should be used. If, as a teacher, you are uncomfortable with building your own circuit, ask for the electrician from your school district office to come out and build the circuit.

Students should come to understand that the current draw in any circuit is due to the resistance in the circuit. In keeping with Ohm's Law ($V = IR$), voltage is constant, and the resistance is a property of the substance (heating coils of a kettle for example). Therefore, by placing a 1200 W toaster with a resistance of 10 Ω, the amperage in a 120-volt circuit is 10 A. Show this by placing an ammeter in your circuit, and turning on the toaster. (Be sure to bring some bread and butter, to keep the students' attention.)

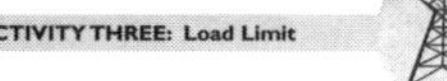

Activity Three

Load Limit

WHAT DO YOU THINK?

Everybody has at one time "blown a fuse" or "tripped" a circuit breaker.

- **What is a fuse or circuit breaker?**
- **Exactly what conditions do you think make a fuse "blow" or a circuit breaker "trip?"**

Record your ideas about these questions in your *Active Physics log*. Be prepared to discuss your responses with your small group and the class.

Activity Overview

This is a short demonstration activity, which should only take about 10 to 20 minutes. You may need to find out the size of the circuit breaker in your classroom from your building custodian. Make sure that the circuit you make in the classroom has a smaller amperage than the demonstration circuit.

Student Objectives

Students will:

- define: watt, insulator, conductor.
- apply $P = IV$
- measure the power limit of a 120-volt household circuit.
- differentiate between a fuse and a circuit breaker.
- understand the need for circuit breakers and fuses in a home.

ANSWERS FOR THE TEACHER ONLY

What Do You Think?

A fuse or a circuit breaker both operate on the principle that if the current surpasses the current allowed by the fuse, the fuse burns, or the breaker trips, opening the circuit. This is to prevent the overloading of a circuit, which would cause an increase in the heat energy in the circuit, and may lead to a fire.

For example, a 15 amp circuit breaker will trip when there is more than 15 amps on one circuit. This can happen if you have a toaster drawing 7 amps, and a kettle drawing 6 amps, (for a total of 13 amps), and someone plugs in the coffee maker which will draw 8 amps, adding to a total of 21 amps. The circuit will trip, causing you to go to the breaker box, and turn the breaker back on. With a fuse, the fuse will burn out, and would have to be replaced.

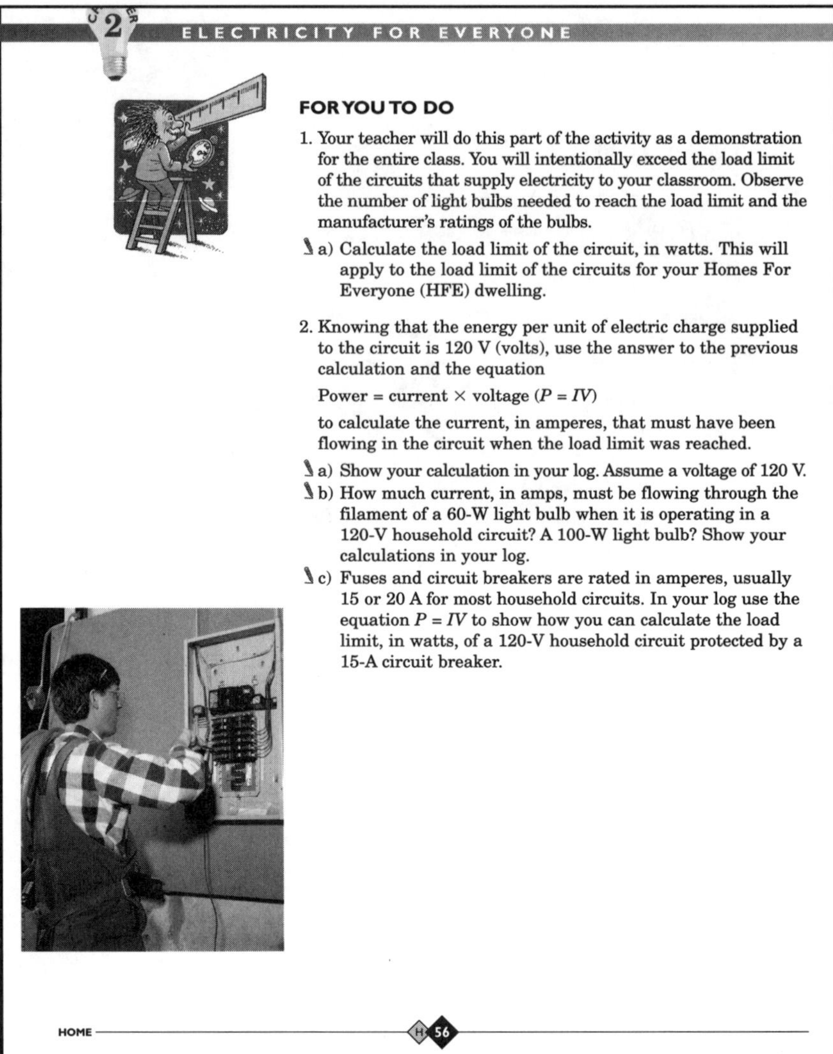

2 ELECTRICITY FOR EVERYONE

FOR YOU TO DO

1. Your teacher will do this part of the activity as a demonstration for the entire class. You will intentionally exceed the load limit of the circuits that supply electricity to your classroom. Observe the number of light bulbs needed to reach the load limit and the manufacturer's ratings of the bulbs.

   a) Calculate the load limit of the circuit, in watts. This will apply to the load limit of the circuits for your Homes For Everyone (HFE) dwelling.

2. Knowing that the energy per unit of electric charge supplied to the circuit is 120 V (volts), use the answer to the previous calculation and the equation

   Power = current × voltage ($P = IV$)

   to calculate the current, in amperes, that must have been flowing in the circuit when the load limit was reached.

   a) Show your calculation in your log. Assume a voltage of 120 V.

   b) How much current, in amps, must be flowing through the filament of a 60-W light bulb when it is operating in a 120-V household circuit? A 100-W light bulb? Show your calculations in your log.

   c) Fuses and circuit breakers are rated in amperes, usually 15 or 20 A for most household circuits. In your log use the equation $P = IV$ to show how you can calculate the load limit, in watts, of a 120-V household circuit protected by a 15-A circuit breaker.

HOME H 56

ANSWERS

For You To Do

1. a) The load limit of your circuit will depend on the fuse. For this part of the activity, count the number of bulbs (in W) and other appliances you have on the circuit when the circuit blows.

2. a) $P = IV$, and the $I = P/V$.

   b) $P = IV$, and the $I = P/V$, therefore, $I = 60\text{ W}/120\text{V}$ therefore, $I = 0.50$ A;

   $P = IV$, and the $I = P/V$, therefore, $I = 100\text{ W}/120\text{V}$ therefore, $I = 0.83$ A;

   c) $P = IV$, therefore, $P = 15\text{ A} \times 120\text{ V} = 1800\text{ W}$.

PHYSICS TALK

The power supplied to a circuit can be calculated using the following equation:

$P = IV$

where P is power in watts (W),

I is current in amperes (A), and

V is voltage in volts (V)

This equation may be rearranged to calculate the value of any of the terms.

$I = \frac{P}{V}$ $V = \frac{P}{I}$

Example:

A current of 0.83 A flows in a light bulb operating in a 120-V circuit. Calculate the power of the light bulb.

$$\begin{aligned} P &= IV \\ &= 0.83\text{ A} \times 120\text{ V} \\ &= 100\text{ W} \end{aligned}$$

REFLECTING ON THE ACTIVITY AND THE CHALLENGE

The load limit of the electrical system for the universal dwelling is set at 2400 W, as outlined in the chapter scenario. It is also established by the design of the windmill power plant that 120 V will be applied to circuits within the dwelling. In this activity you learned what load limit means, and how to relate it to current and voltage. If the people in the dwelling try to run appliances that require more than 2400 W, the fuse will blow. In your home, you can always choose a different line to run the extra appliances. With only one generator, this is not an option in the universal dwelling. This will have direct application soon when you begin selecting appliances to be used in the dwelling.

ANSWERS

Physics To Go

1. Load limit refers to the maximum amount of current which flows through the circuit. If it exceeds this maximum current, the fuse or circuit breaker will blow, stopping the flow of current. This is to protect the circuit from overheating. (Refer to teacher background for more information.)

2. Students' answers will vary. However, they should have several appliances with a similar calculation to the following:

   $P = IV$ using a toaster-oven rated at 1500 W.
   therefore, $I = P/V$;
   $I = 1500\ \text{W}/120\ \text{V} = 12.5\ \text{A}$)

3. Students' answers will vary. Students should take into consideration the time of day the appliance will be used, and what other appliances may be needed at the same time. For example, having a coffee perk rated at 600 W would be better to use than the drip coffee maker rated at 1100 W, if you were also making toast at the same time (toaster rated at 1100 W) with two 100 W light bulbs on at the same time.

4. $P = IV$, therefore $I = P/V$; therefore $I = 1200\ \text{W}/120\ \text{V} = 10\ \text{A}$)

5. First, find the total power rating for the circuit. $P = IV$; $= 20\ \text{A} \times 120\ \text{V} = 2400\ \text{W}$. Therefore, the total of the appliances must not exceed 2400 W: toaster and frying pan = 2200 W; toaster and blender and coffee maker = 1900 W; frying pan, blender and coffee maker = 2100 W; etc.

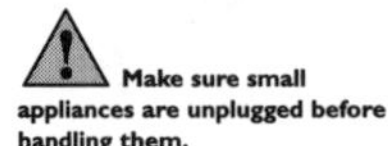

Make sure small appliances are unplugged before handling them.

PHYSICS TO GO

1. Explain in detail what load limit means, and include maximum current, in amperes, as part of your explanation.

2. Find out about the power rating, in watts, of at least six electrical appliances. You can do this at home, at a store that sells appliances, or by studying a catalog. Some appliances have the watt rating stamped somewhere on the device itself, but for others you may have to check the instruction book for the appliance or find the power rating on the original package. Also, your local power company probably will provide a free list of appliances and their power ratings on request. Bring your list to class.

   If the appliance lists the current in amps, you can assume a voltage of 120 V and calculate the power (in watts) by using the equation $P = VI$.

3. List three appliances you would include in the HFE appliance package that will be part of the chapter assessment. For each appliance, list the power demand. For each appliance, describe how it will contribute to the well being of the people living in the dwelling.

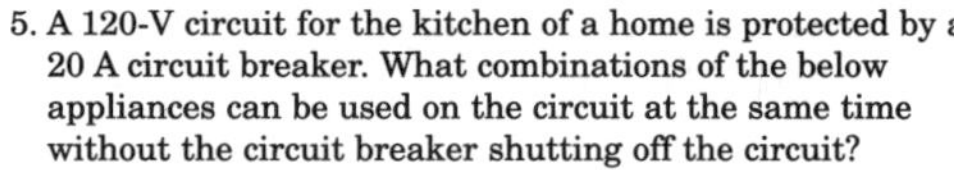

4. An electric hair dryer has a power rating of 1200 W and is designed to be used on a 120 V household circuit. How much current flows in the dryer when it is in use?

5. A 120-V circuit for the kitchen of a home is protected by a 20 A circuit breaker. What combinations of the below appliances can be used on the circuit at the same time without the circuit breaker shutting off the circuit?
   - 1000 W toaster
   - 1200 W frying pan
   - 300 W blender
   - 600 W coffee maker

6. How many 60-W incandescent light bulbs can be operated at the same time on a 120 V, 15 A circuit in a home? How many energy-efficient 22-W fluorescent bulbs can operate on a similar circuit?

7. Some electrical appliances are rated in horsepower (HP).

   1 HP = 746 W

   What amount of current flows in a 0.8 HP vacuum cleaner operating on a 120 V circuit?

8. Some electrical appliances are rated in amps. What is the power in watts of a 6 A appliance designed to operate on a 120 V circuit?

STRETCHING EXERCISE

Find out about the electrical system of your home or the home of a friend or acquaintance. **With the approval of the owner or manager, and with adult supervision,** locate the load center, also called the main distribution panel, for the electrical system. Open the panel door and observe whether the system uses circuit breakers or fuses. How many are there, and what is the ampere rating shown on each fuse or circuit breaker? You may find some larger fuses or breakers that control large, 240-V appliances such as a kitchen range (electric stove); if so, how many are there, what are their ampere ratings, and, if you can, determine what they control.

Warning: The inside of a load center is a dangerous area. Do not touch anything. Doing so could cause injury or death. Always have a qualified person help you.

In some load centers there is a list of what rooms or electrical devices are controlled by each fuse or breaker, but often the list is missing or incomplete.

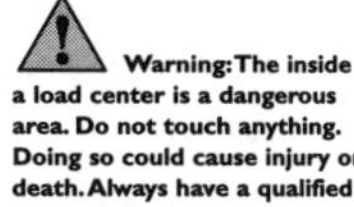

Do not touch any exposed electrical connections or wiring harnesses. Do not attempt to look into or insert anything into any wiring entry points on the panel. Do not reset any circuit breakers or attempt to change any fuses.

With the approval of the owner or manager, and with adult supervision, you can develop a list that indicates what each fuse or breaker controls. To do so, shut off one circuit and go through the entire house to find the lights and outlets that are "dead" (check outlets with a lamp that you can carry around easily). Those items that are "off" are controlled by that fuse or breaker. List them. Then repeat the same process.

Report your findings to your teacher in the form of a list or diagram of the house showing what is controlled by each fuse or circuit breaker.

ANSWERS

Physics To Go

(continued)

6. a) Total power: $P = IV$;
   P = 15 A x 120 V = 1800 W.
   Therefore, the number of light bulbs = 1800 W/60 W = 30 bulbs. For fluorescent bulbs 1800 W/22 W = 81 light bulbs (actually 81.8 light bulbs, but how would that .8 of a light bulb plug in?)

7. If one HP = 746 W, then the vacuum will have a power rating of 0.8 HP x 746 W = 597 W. The current that the vacuum draws is $I = P/V$ = 597 W/120 V = 5 A.

8. $P = IV$, therefore P = 6 A x 120 V = 720 W.

ANSWERS

Stretching Exercise

This is an excellent exercise, to help the student label the circuits in their house. One of the things the students may find, however, is that some of the circuits may be overloaded, and may have to be changed. Ensure that the students will be doing this with permission and supervision.

ACTIVITY FOUR
Who's in Control?

Background Information

Principles introduced in Activity Four include:

- using switches to control electric circuits.
- calculation of electric energy and its cost.

Switches. The "trick" involved with predicting the effect of placing a switch in a parallel circuit is to determine how the total current divides among the branches within the circuit. Refer to the circuit diagram in Activity Four, For You To Do in the student text. Visualize the current as a flow of electrons leaving the battery or generator and entering wire 1. The entire current will continue into wire 2 because there is no alternate path. A switch used to replace either wire 1 or wire 2 would control current flow to all bulbs.

At the far (left) end of wire 2 the current flow will divide into two parts, one part travelling through wire 11, bulb C and wire 12. Replacing either wire 11 or wire 12 would control only bulb C. The part of the current flow which leaves wire 2 and enters wire 3 is on its way to divide again at the next branch point. A switch replacing wire 3 would control both bulbs B and A.

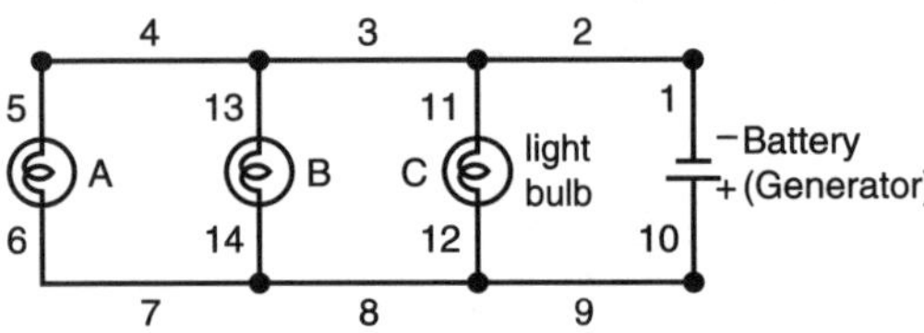

The current which flows through wire 3 divides into two parts, one part travelling through wire 13, bulb B and wire 14. A switch replacing either wire 13 or wire 14 would control only bulb B. The part of the current which leaves wire 3 to enter wires 4 and 5, bulb A, and wires 7 and 8 is on its way to recombine with the current flowing through bulb B. A switch replacing wire 4, 5, 7 or 8 would control only bulb A.

The currents flowing in wires 7 and 14 combine to flow into wire 8. A switch replacing wire 8 would control bulbs A and B.

The currents flowing through wires 8 and 12 combine to flow into wires 9 and 10 as the same amount of current that left the battery or generator to enter wires 1 and 2. A switch replacing either wire 9 or 10 would control all bulbs.

The kind of switch intended for Activity Four is a "single pole single throw" switch which simply "makes" or "breaks" a circuit. Special switches often used in homes include 3-way and 4-way switches used, for example, to control one light bulb for two or more switching locations. Details about how special switches work can be found in manuals available in the electrical departments of most home building centers.

Electric energy/cost. Please first read the Physics To Go and Physics Talk sections of Activity Four in the student text. The origin of the equation

Energy = VIt presented in Physics Talk is:

If, as defined, Power = (Energy)/(time)

Then, multiplying both sides of the above definition by time:

Energy = (Power) x (time)

Substituting appropriate electrical terms for power in the above:

Electric energy = $(IV)t$

Energy, regardless of its form, should be expressed in joules. To test the above equation, units are substituted in the right side of the equation for I, V and t:

joules
= (coulomb/second) x (joules/coulomb) x (second)

= joules

Unfortunately, the electric industry does not use joules as the unit of measurement for the energy it sells to customers. The industry uses kilowatt-hours (kWh). To understand this unit of measurement it is best to return to the definition of the watt as a unit of power:

Definition: 1 watt = 1 joule/second

Multiplying both sides of the definition by (second):

1 joule = 1 watt-second

Therefore, 1 watt-second is a unit of energy equivalent to 1 joule.

The electric energy industry deals with large amounts of energy, and the watt-second is too small for their purposes. Therefore, the industry scales power upward from watts to kilowatts (1,000 watts

= 1 kilowatt) and scales time upward from seconds to hours (3,600 seconds = 1 hour) resulting in:

1 kWh = (1,000 watts) x (3,600 seconds) = 3,600,000 watt-seconds = 3,600,000 joules

For Physics To Go students are asked to identify the power ratings of several appliances and estimate the amount of time each is used during one month. If time estimates are made in hours and power ratings of appliances are in watts, the monthly energy use in kWh will result if the power ratings in watts are divided by 1,000 to convert to kilowatts, and then the kilowatt ratings are multiplied by time in hours. This will lead to consideration of the cost of operating appliances based on the power company's cost per kilowatt hour in Activity Six.

Active-ating the Physics InfoMall

Again in this activity, we use circuits and make predictions. The InfoMall was searched for information related to both of these in earlier activities.

For You To Read discusses circuit diagrams. A quick search for "circuit diagram*" produces many hits with several graphics. In this case, the graphics were not searched for, only the words. But on the InfoMall, figures and graphics appear in blue and are hyperlinks to the graphic. If you do this search, simply scan the page for blue text, click on it, and the graphic will appear. These can also be copied and pasted into your own handouts. Finding the circuit diagram you want is unlikely, however, so these may serve best as examples of how to draw diagrams.

Planning for the Activity

Time Requirements

This activity will take approximately 20 minutes, provided the groups have all the materials they need at their station. Allow about 10 to 20 minutes to get around to all groups before they are allowed to turn on their circuit.

Materials needed

For the class:

- sample automatic switching devices (demonstrate)

For each group:

- hand generator
- miniature bulbs and bases (3) (same as for Activity Two)
- knife switch, SPST
- connecting wires, insulated

Advance Preparation and Setup

If time allows, you may want to demonstrate how a bi-metallic strip works as the heart of a thermostat, and demonstrate other automatic switching devices such as a mercury switch or a photocell. Discuss the conditions to which each responds.

For this activity, have the materials available in small packages or in separate bins. The actual design of the circuit will depend on the materials available. To save time, precut all wires, and label (1, 2, 3,...) The students would not have to do any cutting, and the circuits will all look the same and this will speed up the checking of the circuits. An example might be to cut wires number 1, 5, 6, 11, 12, 13, 14 all the same length, using one color, and wires 2, 3, 4, 7, 8, 9 all the same length, with a different color. Then instruct the students to get 8 of one color, and 6 of the other color.

2

Teaching Notes

Begin with a demonstration of automatic switching devices (see above recommendation). Ask students to offer explanations of the conditions which control the devices and what the devices must be doing to affect the electric circuits in which they are placed - how do they accomplish on/off actions? Then ask students to complete What Do You Think? to identify more ways that automatic switching is accomplished.

Before proceeding to For You To Do, plan to save some time at the end of the class period to discuss the Reflecting on the Activity and the Challenge and to be sure that the students understand how to complete Physics To Go.

Make sure the students are reminded of the dangers of electricity, and the precautions that must be taken. Under no circumstances, should the students be plugging their circuit into the wall outlets. This circuit is designed for low current, and plugging into a wall outlet could cause serious injury or death. There is also a fire hazard, as the wires will not be able to handle the load.

CAUTION: Students must not proceed until the teacher has checked the circuits.

Automatic switching devices may seem complicated, but once dissected, they are very simple. Show the students a number of different switching devices, and even allow the students to take apart some discarded switches. Go to an electronics store, or an electrician, for old switches. You may want to have an electrician or someone from the local power company, to come into class to demonstrate the hazards of electricity, and how to handle it safely.

NOTES

2

Activity Overview

The students will be investigating how switches work, and how to set up switches to operate a parallel circuit.

Student Objectives

Students will:

- explain how a variety of automatic electrical switches work.
- select switches and control devices to meet particular needs.
- insert a switch in a parallel circuit to control a particular lamp.

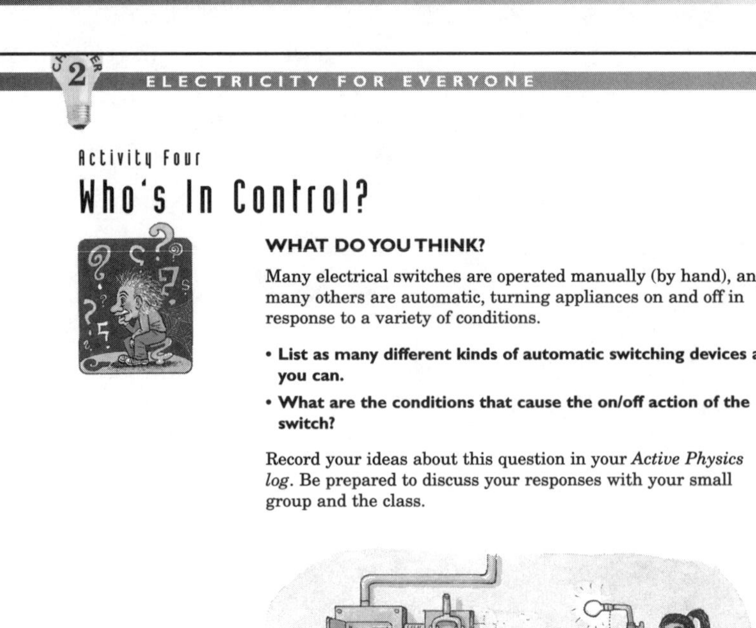

CHAPTER 2 ELECTRICITY FOR EVERYONE

Activity Four

Who's In Control?

WHAT DO YOU THINK?

Many electrical switches are operated manually (by hand), and many others are automatic, turning appliances on and off in response to a variety of conditions.

- **List as many different kinds of automatic switching devices as you can.**
- **What are the conditions that cause the on/off action of the switch?**

Record your ideas about this question in your *Active Physics log*. Be prepared to discuss your responses with your small group and the class.

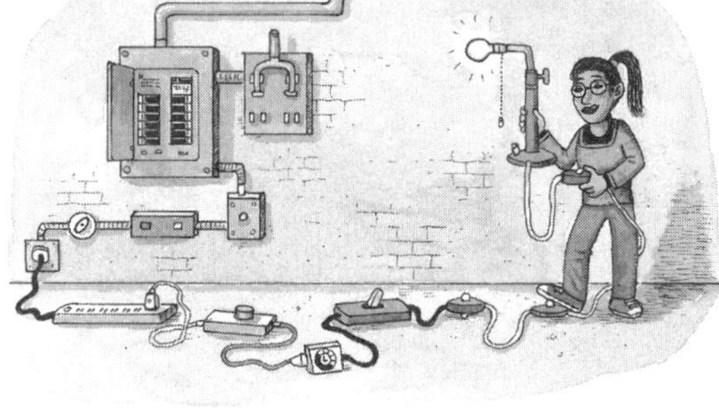

HOME H 60

ANSWERS FOR THE TEACHER ONLY

What Do You Think?

The number of switching devices the students list will be numerous. Some of them might include: street lights, timers for homes, timers on stoves, timers for traffic lights, thermostats in furnaces and air conditioners, signal lights in cars, automatic switches which turn on or off stoves, thermocouples, security systems which operate on infrared, or movement, voice activated microphones, etc. The switching on or off will often utilize an electromagnet, or photocell. With an electromagnetic switch, movement of the electromagnet, creates an electric current. This is attached to a relay. When an electric current runs through a relay, the current causes the relay switch to open or close (depending on the desired effect). This, then, activates the switch in another circuit to turn on your lights or stove or appliance.

FOR YOU TO DO

1. Assemble the circuit as shown in the diagram. (Each number corresponds to a different wire.)

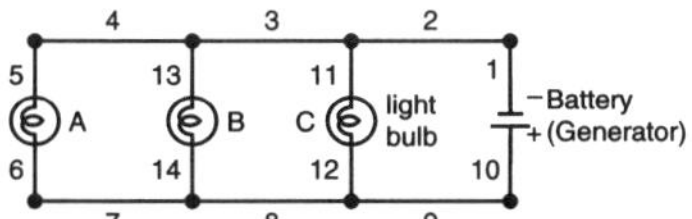

a) Draw a diagram of the circuit. Label the bulbs: A, B, C. (The bulb on the left should be A, the bulb in the middle B, and the bulb on the right C.)

Have your teacher approve your circuit before proceeding.

2. Compare the circuit you assembled with the one in the following diagram that shows the circuit that you used in Activity 2. This time you used additional wires, 14 wires in total. It is sometimes easier to place switches into circuits if you use a few additional wires in the circuit. Crank the generator to be sure that all bulbs operate in this circuit.

a) Identify the additional new wires on your circuit diagram.

b) What type of circuit (series or parallel) is represented in both diagrams?

3. Predict which wire could be replaced with a switch if you wished to turn all three bulbs on and off.

a) Record your prediction in your log.

b) Replace that wire with a switch. Does it work as predicted?

ANSWERS

For You To Do

1. a) Student activity

2. a) Students' answers will vary. You could refer to all the "inside" (1, 11, 13, 5, 6, 14, 12, 10) as new wires.

   b) Parallel circuit.

3. a) Students' prediction.

   b) A switch placed in wire 1, 2, 9, 10 would open the circuit to all three bulbs. See diagram.

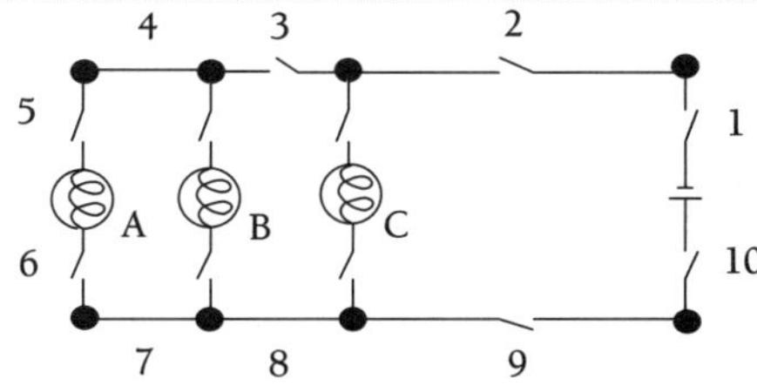

ANSWERS

For You To Do

(continued)

4. a) Students' prediction.

   b) A switch placed in wire 5, 6, would open the circuit to bulb A.

   c) Student's diagram.

5. i) a) Students' prediction.

   b) A switch placed in wire 13, 14, would open the circuit to bulb B.

   c) Student's diagram.

   ii) a) Students' prediction.

   b) A switch placed in wire 11, 12, would open the circuit to bulb C.

   c) Student's diagram. See diagram.

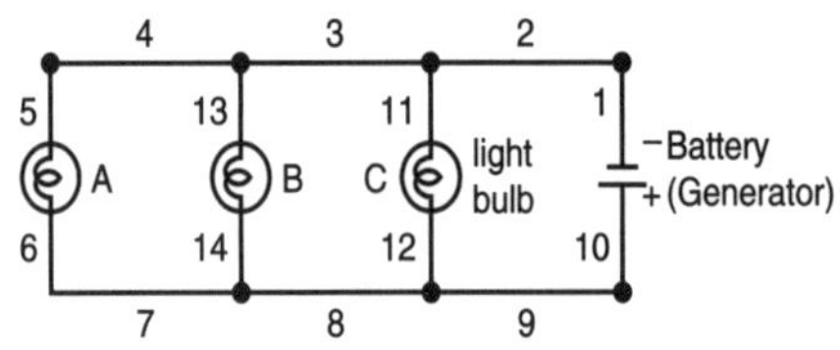

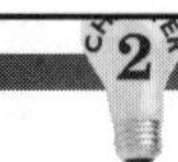

ELECTRICITY FOR EVERYONE

4. Predict which wire could be replaced with a switch if you wished to turn only bulb A on and off?
   a) Record your prediction in your log.
   b) Replace that wire with a switch. Does it work as predicted?
   c) Mark the location of the switch on the circuit diagram in your log by writing "Switch A" and drawing an arrow from the word "Switch A" to the place where the switch should be placed.

5. Repeat Step 4 for bulb B and then for bulb C.
   a) Remember to record your predictions.
   b) Replace the wire you chose with a switch. Are your predictions beginning to improve?
   c) Draw two addition diagrams to show the location of switch B and switch C.

FOR YOU TO READ

Switches

Regardless of how an electrical switch may be activated, most switches work in the same basic way. When a switch is "on," a good conductor of electricity, usually copper, is provided as the path for current flow through the switch. Then, the circuit containing the switch is said to be "closed," and the current flows. When a switch is turned "off," the conducting path through the switch is replaced by an air gap. Since air has very high resistance, the current flow through the switch is interrupted, and the circuit is said to be "open."

Circuit Diagrams

An electrical circuit can be represented by a simple line diagram, called a schematic diagram, or wiring diagram. You may have seen wiring diagrams for cars, stereo systems, or homes. They may appear complicated, but if you know what the different symbols represent, they are relatively easy to follow.

The wire that carries the electric current is represented by a straight line. If a wire crosses over another wire, a line crossing a straight line is shown. If the wires join, a heavy black dot is shown. A lamp or light bulb is shown by a loop in the center of a circle. A battery or a generator is represented by a number of unequal lines. A switch is a line shown at an angle to the wire. There are many other symbols that are used by electricians.

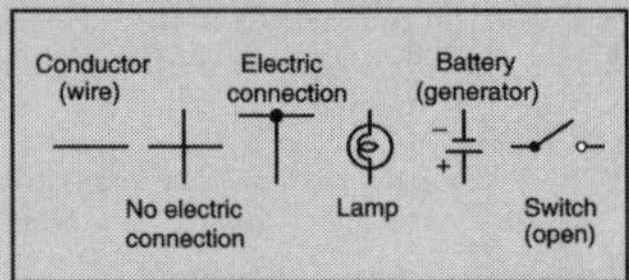

REFLECTING ON THE ACTIVITY AND THE CHALLENGE

Part of the problem you are facing with the electrical system for the HFE dwellings is to assure that the people who live in them will not exceed the 2400 W power limit of the system by having too many appliances in use at any one time. Depending on what you choose to include in the HFE appliance package, it may be necessary to use switching devices—automatic, manual, or both—to assure that the people who live in the homes will stay within the power limit as they use their appliances.

Perhaps you could also use automatic switches as "fail safe" devices to prevent accidentally using up too much electrical energy by, for example, forgetting to shut off lights that are not in use.

PHYSICS TO GO

1. In your log, describe several possibilities for using switching devices to address the power limit problem in your universal dwelling. Write your ideas in your log.
2. Electric switches are available which act as timers to turn appliances on and off at chosen times or for chosen intervals. Identify one or more ways a timer switch would be useful in an HFE dwelling.
3. Look at the wiring diagrams shown. Copy each into your log. Position and draw a switch in each circuit which would allow you to turn one light on, and leave two lights off.

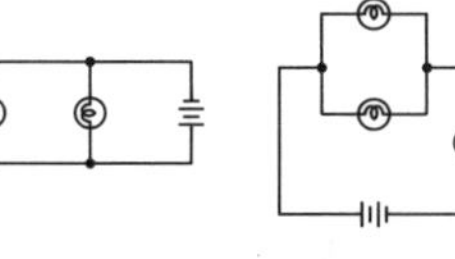

STRETCHING EXERCISES

Shop, in a store or catalog, for electrical switching devices controlled by a variety of conditions such as light/dark, high/low temperature, motion, etc. The devices may be either "built-in" to appliances (example: waterbed thermostat) or separate (example: a clock timer designed to control appliances plugged into it). Find as many different kinds of switching devices as you can, and note which ones may be useful for the HFE electrical system, and for what purpose. In your log, write a brief report on your findings.

Answers

Physics To Go

1. Some of the devices that could be used are timers, that automatically shut off small appliances or lights. For example, a switch could be installed in bathroom lights to automatically shut off after fifteen minutes (typically the length of time needed for a shower). Other examples may include switches which work towards warning that the power level limit is close. Another practical way can be listing appliances available and their power ratings, so that people in the home will know what is on and what can be turned on without blowing the breaker. Some other devices could use motion detectors that automatically turn on when someone enters a room, and turn off after a time limit or, no motion or "clap-on/clap-off.")
2. a) Answers will vary. See answer for #1.
3. See diagrams below and on next page.

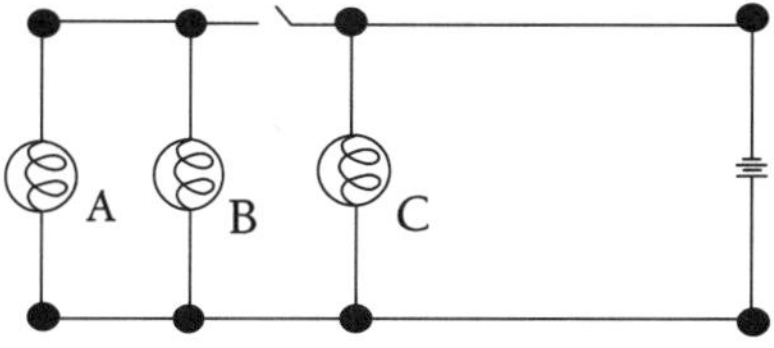

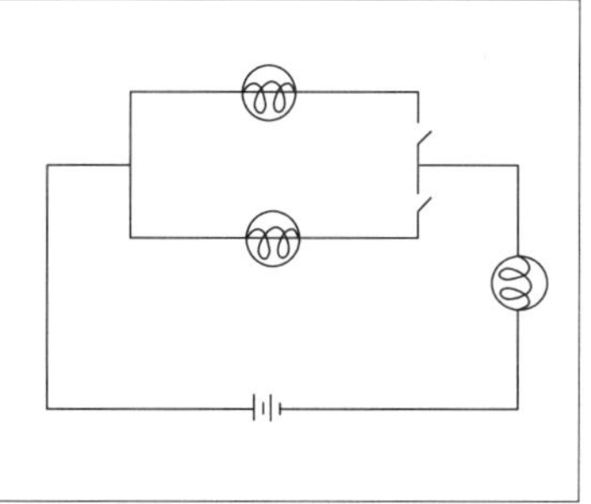

Answers

Stretching Exercises

Student report. Expect a variety of answers. The students will be looking for devices that will be useful in their HFE home. Look for energy-saving devices, timers, low wattage lights with timers, etc.

Circuit Diagrams

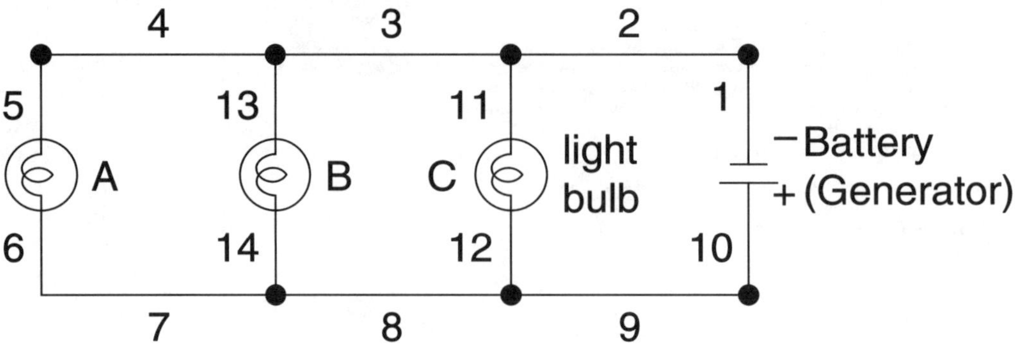

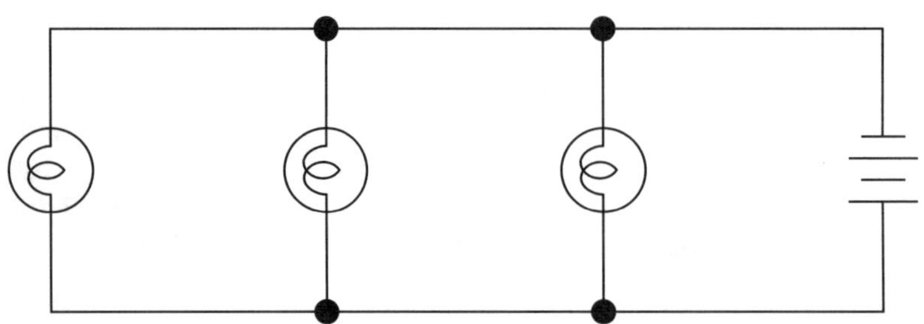

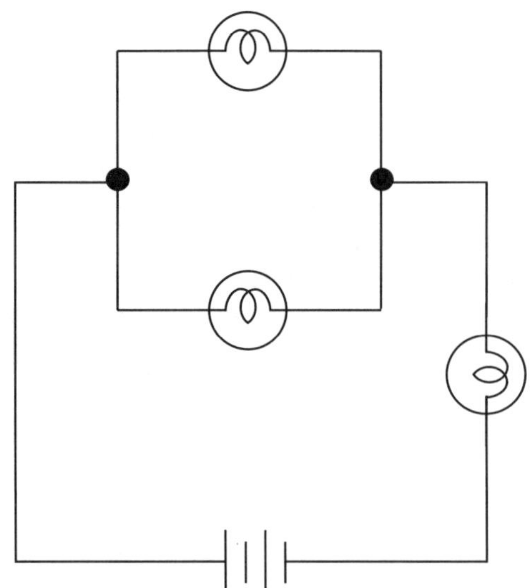

For use with *Home*, Chapter 2, ACTIVITY FOUR: Who's In Control?

NOTES

2

ACTIVITY FIVE
Cold Shower

Background Information

Activity Five combines principles of heating water with principles of electrical energy introduced in Activity Four of this chapter.

You may wish to review the following:

Heat lost = Heat gained in a transfer of energy between two objects.

Heat = $mc\Delta T$

Specific heat of water
= 4180 (joule)/(kilogram)(degree Celsius)

The purpose of this activity is to use an electric heater to transfer electrical energy to water in the form of heat, accounting for the electrical energy input and the heat received by the water.

The electrical energy delivered to the electric heater [a resistor having a known power rating (in watts) which is plugged into a 120-volt outlet for a measured amount of time in seconds] is:

Energy (joules) = Power (watts) x time (seconds)

The heat received by the water is:

Energy (joules) = mass (kilograms) x specific heat (joule)/(kilogram)(degree Celsius) x temperature change (degree Celsius)

In principle, the electrical energy expended in the heater should equal the heat received by the water. However, less than 100 % efficiency can be expected for the energy transfer due to heat loss from the system to the surrounding environment.

Active-ating the Physics InfoMall

For You To Do step 1 makes use of a calorimeter. A search for "calorimeter" provides many examples of calorimeters, together with diagrams. If you need a calorimeter, the Catalog Corner has Vernier, Central Scientific, and PASCO catalogs to choose from. This is a CD-ROM, however, so the catalogs are not exactly new. They can give you a great starting point, though.

Physics Talk discussed specific heat and resistors. Both of these topics are discussed at various level of detail in many places on the InfoMall. These are very good topics for which to prepare your own handouts, with examples and graphics included.

Physics To Go step 1 mentions conduction, convection, and radiation. While these terms may be familiar to your students, it might not be a bad idea to have some extra information ready, and you can easily find it on the InfoMall.

Planning for the Activity

Time Requirements

Allow about 10 - 15 minutes to set up the apparatus, and about 20 minutes to do the activity and record their results. If there is time, have the students run the activity with different quantities of water, in order to get a set of data to graph.

Materials needed

For each group:

- graduated cylinder
- cold tap water source
- thermometer or temperature probe
- resistive immersion heater of known wattage: Many are available, designed for labs at high cost, but the little portable heaters for making coffee in a hotel room do the job and are less expensive. A 200 watt, 120-volt AC one works fine when used with at least 300 mL of water.
- insulated calorimeter container: You can get fancy, but a Styrofoam® cup works about as well as anything. Just be sure the heater doesn't contact the wall of the cup. Use a ring stand and clamp to suspend the coil in the water without touching the cup.
- clock
- stirring rod
- calculator

Advance Preparation and Setup

Have students complete the What Do You Think?. Students may not know what specific heat capacity is. Briefly explain that SHC is referring to the amount of heat energy that is required to raise the temperature one degree Celsius of a specific quantity of water. The SHC of water is 4180 J/kg°C. This means 1 kg of water requires 4180 J of energy to raise the temperature 1°C. Emphasize to the students that it requires more energy to heat water than many other materials. Therefore, hot water for HFE dwellings presents a problem. Pose the For You To Do activity as an exploration of the viability of using the HFE electrical system for providing hot water for the universal dwellings. Plan to save some time at the end of class to assist students with the principles and calculations involved in the Physics To Go, and the Reflection.

Teaching Notes

Expect that students will need help with the energy and efficiency calculations involved in this activity.

Work through the Physics Talk with the students to establish that, since power is energy per unit time, energy can be thought of, and calculated, as power multiplied by time ($E = Pt$). Using the dimensions of the quantities, establish that watt-seconds are the equivalent of joules.

You will need to explain $(Q) = mc\Delta T$, where Q is the heat energy in joules, m is the mass in kilograms, c is the specific heat capacity of water (4180 J/kg°C), and ΔT is the change in temperature. This formula will help the students understand the quantity of heat energy required to heat water.

Be sure the students understand that, in principle, the energy lost by the hot resistor can be set equal to the energy gained by the cold water. Therefore, by calculating the heat energy lost by the resistor, ($E = I^2Rt$), and equating it to heat gained by the water, we can determine the amount of power required to heat a known quantity of water.

Again emphasize the need for safe practices when handling electric devices near water. Ensure that the students have properly assembled the calorimeters.

Reiterate the idea that there is not a 100% transfer of energy from the resistor to the water. They will calculate the efficiency of the transfer, and should be able to account for the "lost" energy!

Activity Overview

In this activity, the students will be measuring the effect of a resistor heating a quantity of water. From this data they will be able to determine the efficiency of the resistor heating water, and the energy required. After they have determined efficiency, they will be able to apply it to their own lives, and then to their HFE home.

Student Objectives

Students will:

- calculate the heat gained by a sample of water.
- calculate the electrical energy dissipated by a resistor.
- recognize and quantify an ideal mechanical/electrical equivalent of heat.
- calculate the efficiency of a transformation of electrical energy to heat.
- explore the power ratings and energy consumption levels of a variety of electrical appliances.

ANSWERS FOR THE TEACHER ONLY

What Do You Think?

Answers will vary. Amount of water, as you increase the mass, you increase the time of heating; current in the wire, heating increases as you increase the current ($E = I^2Rt$); resistance in the wire, as you increase the resistance, you increase the energy ($E = I^2Rt$); time, as you increase the time of heating, the temperature will increase; the type of wire or heating coil changes the resistance; the initial temperature, the lower the temperature, the longer it will take to heat up to a particular temperature.

Activity Five

Cold Shower

WHAT DO YOU THINK?

The entire daily energy output of an HFE generator would not be enough to heat water for an average American family for a day.

- **If an electrical heating coil (a type of resistor) were submerged in a container of water, and if a current were to flow through the coil to make it hot, what factors would affect the temperature increase of the water? Identify as many factors as you can, and predict the effect of each on the water temperature.**

Record your ideas about this question in your *Active Physics log.* Be prepared to discuss your responses with your small group and the class.

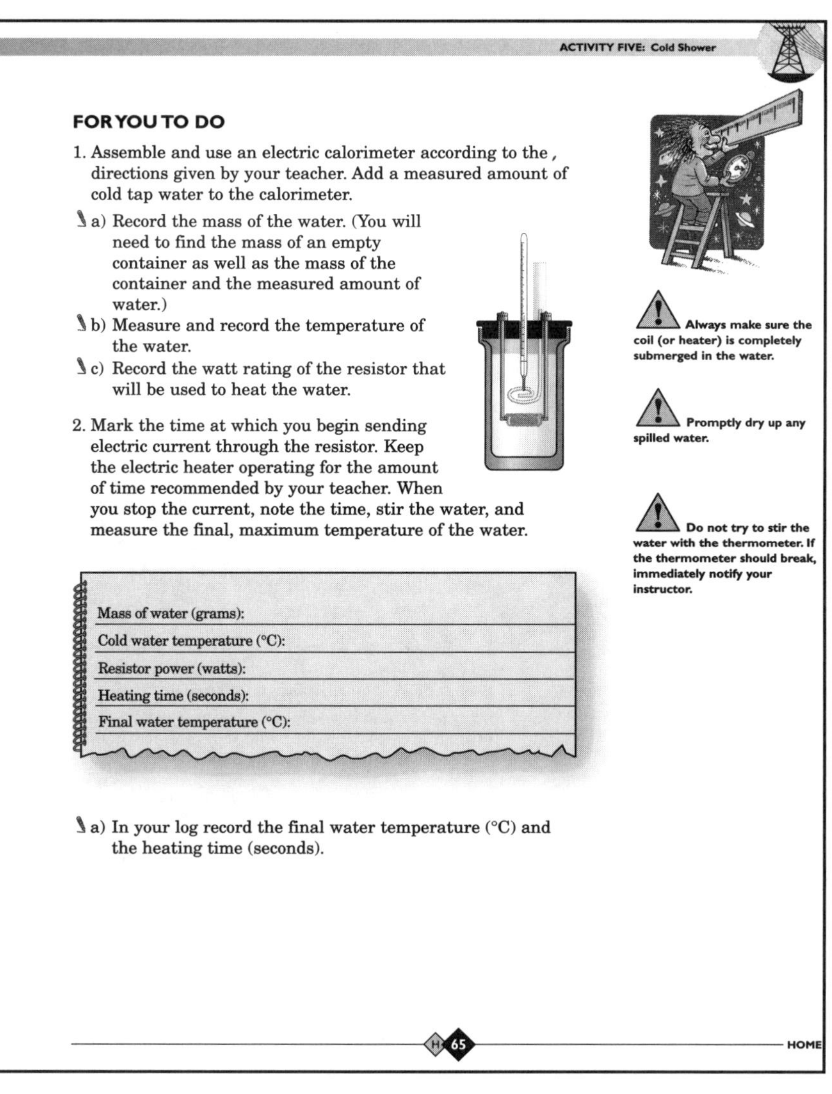

ACTIVITY FIVE: Cold Shower

FOR YOU TO DO

1. Assemble and use an electric calorimeter according to the directions given by your teacher. Add a measured amount of cold tap water to the calorimeter.
   a) Record the mass of the water. (You will need to find the mass of an empty container as well as the mass of the container and the measured amount of water.)
   b) Measure and record the temperature of the water.
   c) Record the watt rating of the resistor that will be used to heat the water.

2. Mark the time at which you begin sending electric current through the resistor. Keep the electric heater operating for the amount of time recommended by your teacher. When you stop the current, note the time, stir the water, and measure the final, maximum temperature of the water.

Mass of water (grams):
Cold water temperature (°C):
Resistor power (watts):
Heating time (seconds):
Final water temperature (°C):

   a) In your log record the final water temperature (°C) and the heating time (seconds).

Always make sure the coil (or heater) is completely submerged in the water.

Promptly dry up any spilled water.

Do not try to stir the water with the thermometer. If the thermometer should break, immediately notify your instructor.

H 65 HOME

Answers

For You To Do

1. a) Student observation and collected data.
   b) Student observation and collected data.
   c) Student observation and collected data.
2. a) Student observation and collected data.

ANSWERS

For You To Do

(continued)

3. a) Student data and calculation. The calculation should look like this (contrived data):

heat gained = $mc\Delta T$
= 0.045 kg x 4.180 J/kg°C x 35°C
= 65,835 J of energy.

4. a) Student data and calculation. The calculation should look like this (contrived data):

energy = Pt
= 1500 W x 90 s
= 135,000 J

5. a) Since the input energy (from the heater) of 135,000 J is greater than the output energy (heating of the water) of 65,835 J, we must conclude that some of the energy is "lost".

b) In fact, the energy is not lost (First Law of Thermodynamics), but converted into a useless form of energy, for the purposes of this experiment, that of heat to the environment.

6. a) Student data and calculation. The calculation should look like this (contrived data):

From the previous questions:

efficiency = input - output/input x 100%

= 135,000 J - 65,835 J/135,000 J x 100%

= 51%

3. The heat energy gained by an object can be found using the equation:

Heat energy = mass of object × specific heat of material × temperature change

Use the equation to calculate the heat energy gained by the water in the calorimeter. The specific heat of water is 4180 J/kg.°C.

a) Show your calculation in your log.

4. Power rating, in watts, is expressed as the amount of energy that something consumes per unit of time. Mathematically, power is expressed as

$$\text{Power} = \frac{\text{energy}}{\text{time}}$$

Then it is true that: Energy = power × time

Energy can be expressed in kilowatt-hours (kWh) if power is in kilowatts and time is in hours, OR energy can be expressed in joules, if power is expressed in watts, and time in seconds. Use the equation to calculate the electrical energy, in joules, consumed by the resistor in the calorimeter.

a) Show your calculation in your log.

5. The energy calculated from the temperature change of the water should be equal to the energy calculated from the power rating of the appliance and the time.

a) Compare these two values for the heat energy. If the values are not the same, what must you conclude?

b) Where could the "lost" energy have gone?

6. If all of the electrical energy did not heat up the water, then you know your system for heating water is less than 100% efficient. Calculate the efficiency of your water heating device. (Hint: If the appliance were 100% efficient, all of the electrical energy would have heated the water; if the appliance were 50% efficient, half of the electrical energy would have heated the water.)

a) Record your calculations in you log. How efficient was the calorimeter?

PHYSICS TALK

Energy, E, in joules, can be calculated using the following equation.

$$E = VIt$$

where V is voltage in volts,
I is current in amperes, and
t is time.

If time is given in seconds, energy units are watt-seconds or joules. If time is given in hours, energy units are watts-hours and can be converted to kilowatt-hours

Since $P = IV$, the equation above may be written as:

$$E = Pt$$

Example:

A 100 W electric heat coil is used to heat a cup of cold water for 8 min (8 min = (8 × 60)s) to make a hot chocolate drink. Calculate the energy used by the heat coil.

$$E = Pt$$
$$= 100 \text{ W} \times 480 \text{ s}$$
$$= 48{,}000 \text{ J (joules)}$$

Heat energy is measured in units of joules (J). The heat energy gained by an object can be found using the following equation.

Heat energy = mass of object × specific heat of material × temperature change

where heat energy is expressed in joules (J),
mass is in kilograms (kg),
specific heat in joules per kilogram degree Celsius (J/kg.°C),
temperature in degrees Celsius (°C).

You may also see this equation written as follows:

$$E_H = mc\Delta T$$

The symbol for specific heat is c. The symbol Δ represents a change in something, in this case, temperature.

To calculate the heat energy gained by a material, you must know the specific heat of the material. Different materials require different amounts of energy to raise the temperature of a given mass of the substance. Different substances have different capacities to hold heat. Water holds heat very well, whereas silver does not hold heat well. Water is said to have a higher specific heat than silver. The specific heat of a material is the amount of energy required to raise 1 kg of the material by 1°C.

The specific heat of water is 4180 J/kg.°C

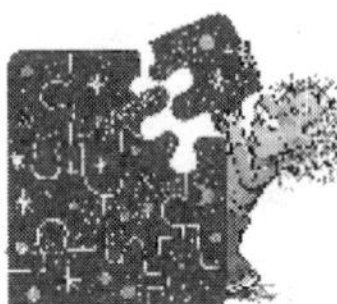

REFLECTING ON THE ACTIVITY AND THE CHALLENGE

In this activity your knowledge of how to calculate electric power consumption was extended to include how to calculate electric energy consumption. You also learned that heating water electrically requires a lot of energy and can be quite inefficient. All of this knowledge applies directly to the selections you will make for electrical appliances to be used in the universal dwelling.

PHYSICS TO GO

1. The calorimeter did not allow the water to trap 100% of the energy delivered to it by the resistor. Some of the heat energy probably escaped from the water. Identify and explain ways in which you think heat energy may have escaped from the water, reducing the efficiency of the calorimeter.
2. The calorimeter used in this activity can be thought of as a scaled-down, crude version of a household hot water heater. The efficiencies of hot water heaters used in homes range from about 80% for older models to as much as 92% for new, energy-efficient models. Identify and explain ways in which you think heat escapes from household hot water heaters, and how some of the heat loss could be prevented.
3. From what you have learned so far, discuss the possibilities for providing electrically heated water for Homes For Everyone (HFE). Is a standard water heater of the kind used in American homes desirable, or possible, for HFE? What other electrical options exist for accomplishing part or all of the task of heating water for HFE?
4. For most Americans, the second biggest energy user in the home, next to the heating/air conditioning system, is the water heater. A family of four that heats water electrically (some use gas or oil to heat water) typically spends about $35 per month using a 4500-W heater to keep a 160 L (40 gallon) tank of water hot at all times. The water is raised from an average inlet temperature of 10°C (50°F) to a temperature of 60°C (140°F), and the average family uses about 250 L (60 gallons) of hot water per day for bathing and washing clothes and dishes.

   In the above description, explain what each of the following numbers represents: 35, 4500, 160, 40, 10, 50, 60, 140, 250, 60.

ANSWERS

Physics To Go

1. Students answer will vary. Some of the ways in which the heat energy escaped will be through the insulation, through the top, heating the thermometer, residual heat left in the resistor, etc.
2. a) If you stand beside the hot water heater, you can feel the heat. Therefore, some of the heat is lost through the insulation. Some of the heat is lost up the chimney, from the bottom where the element or burner is, and through the pipes of the water which has been heated. Some of this could be prevented by increasing the insulation, more efficient burners, modifying the chimney to trap the heat (without the carbon monoxide), use cleaner fuel, insulating the pipes.
3. An electric water heater is rated at 4500 W. The amount of water used, will determine how long the hot water heater must run. There should be a more efficient method by which you can heat the water. Some other ways may be using a gas heater if it is available, or other fuel source such as heating on a wood stove. Students may come up with many different answers.
4. 35 - cost of running a hot water heater; 4500 - the rating of power, or the energy used in joules per second; 160 - liters of water; 40 - gallons of water; 10 - degrees Celsius, temperature of the water at the inlet to house; 60 - degrees Celsius, temperature of the hot water; 50 - degrees Fahrenheit, temperature of the water at the inlet to house; 140 - degrees Fahrenheit, temperature of the hot water; 250 - liters of hot water used by the average household; 60 - gallons of hot water used by the average household.

2

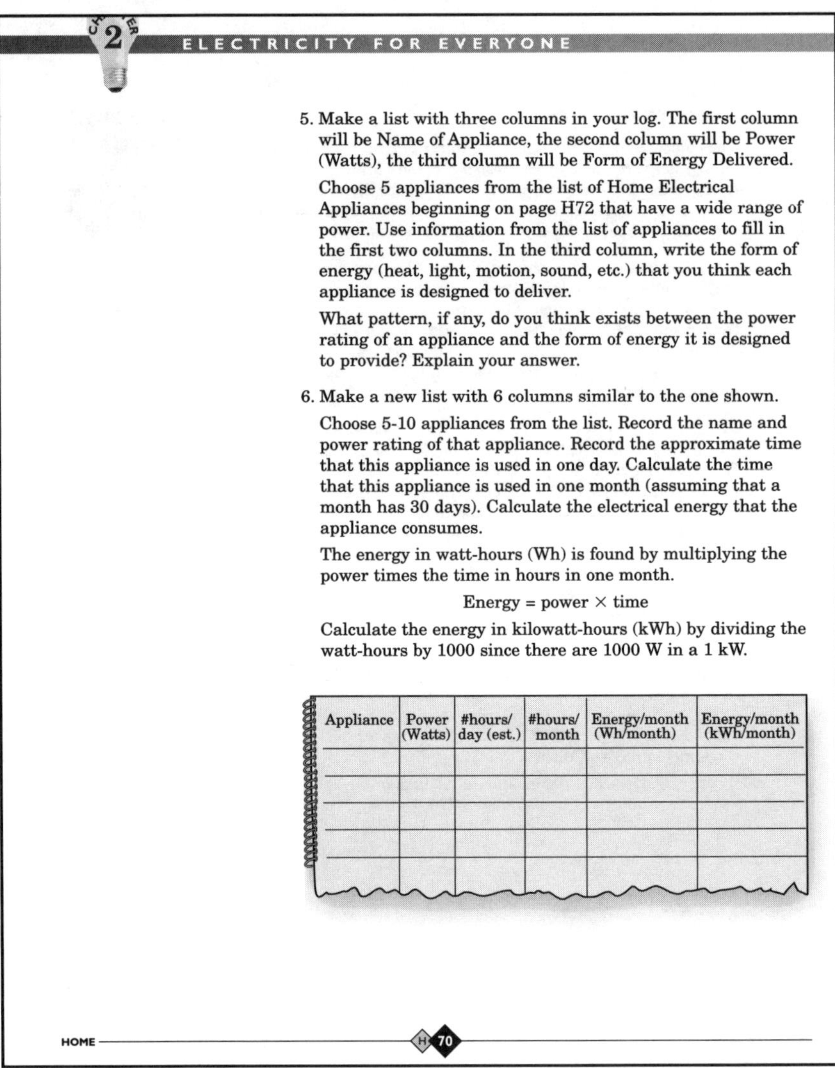

5. Make a list with three columns in your log. The first column will be Name of Appliance, the second column will be Power (Watts), the third column will be Form of Energy Delivered.

   Choose 5 appliances from the list of Home Electrical Appliances beginning on page H72 that have a wide range of power. Use information from the list of appliances to fill in the first two columns. In the third column, write the form of energy (heat, light, motion, sound, etc.) that you think each appliance is designed to deliver.

   What pattern, if any, do you think exists between the power rating of an appliance and the form of energy it is designed to provide? Explain your answer.

6. Make a new list with 6 columns similar to the one shown.

   Choose 5-10 appliances from the list. Record the name and power rating of that appliance. Record the approximate time that this appliance is used in one day. Calculate the time that this appliance is used in one month (assuming that a month has 30 days). Calculate the electrical energy that the appliance consumes.

   The energy in watt-hours (Wh) is found by multiplying the power times the time in hours in one month.

   $$\text{Energy} = \text{power} \times \text{time}$$

   Calculate the energy in kilowatt-hours (kWh) by dividing the watt-hours by 1000 since there are 1000 W in a 1 kW.

Appliance	Power (Watts)	#hours/ day (est.)	#hours/ month	Energy/month (Wh/month)	Energy/month (kWh/month)

ANSWERS

Physics To Go *(continued)*

5. Students answers will vary. The students may notice that if an appliance is designed for heating, it generally uses more energy.

6. Students answers will vary. One example row should look like the following:

Appliance	Power (W)	# hours/day	Energy/mo. (Wh)	Energy/mo. (kWh)
MW oven	1200	0.75	27,000	27

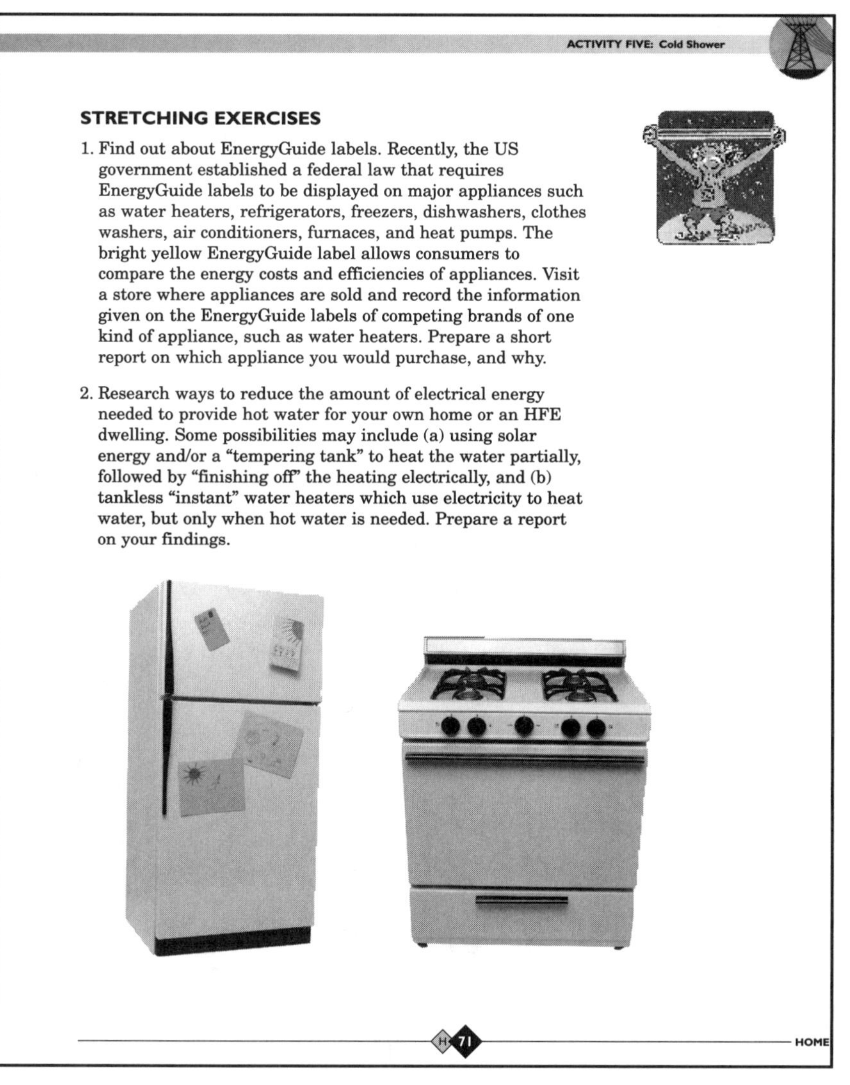

STRETCHING EXERCISES

1. Find out about EnergyGuide labels. Recently, the US government established a federal law that requires EnergyGuide labels to be displayed on major appliances such as water heaters, refrigerators, freezers, dishwashers, clothes washers, air conditioners, furnaces, and heat pumps. The bright yellow EnergyGuide label allows consumers to compare the energy costs and efficiencies of appliances. Visit a store where appliances are sold and record the information given on the EnergyGuide labels of competing brands of one kind of appliance, such as water heaters. Prepare a short report on which appliance you would purchase, and why.

2. Research ways to reduce the amount of electrical energy needed to provide hot water for your own home or an HFE dwelling. Some possibilities may include (a) using solar energy and/or a "tempering tank" to heat the water partially, followed by "finishing off" the heating electrically, and (b) tankless "instant" water heaters which use electricity to heat water, but only when hot water is needed. Prepare a report on your findings.

ANSWERS

Stretching Exercises

1. Student report. In the report look for the understanding of the EnergyGuide label. Have the students understand that one appliance may be rated lower than the other, but need to run it longer to do the same job. Also, some appliances will have a higher rating, (e.g., convection ovens), but don't necessarily need to be preheated to do the same job, and can do the same baking in less time with a lower temperature. The students need to understand the criteria for testing. For example, the freezer is less efficient when half empty, and will require more energy. Some appliances will not operate as efficiently in certain locations. For example, putting a refrigerator next to the furnace will cause the refrigerator to run longer, thereby cutting into the efficiency.

2. Students answers will vary.

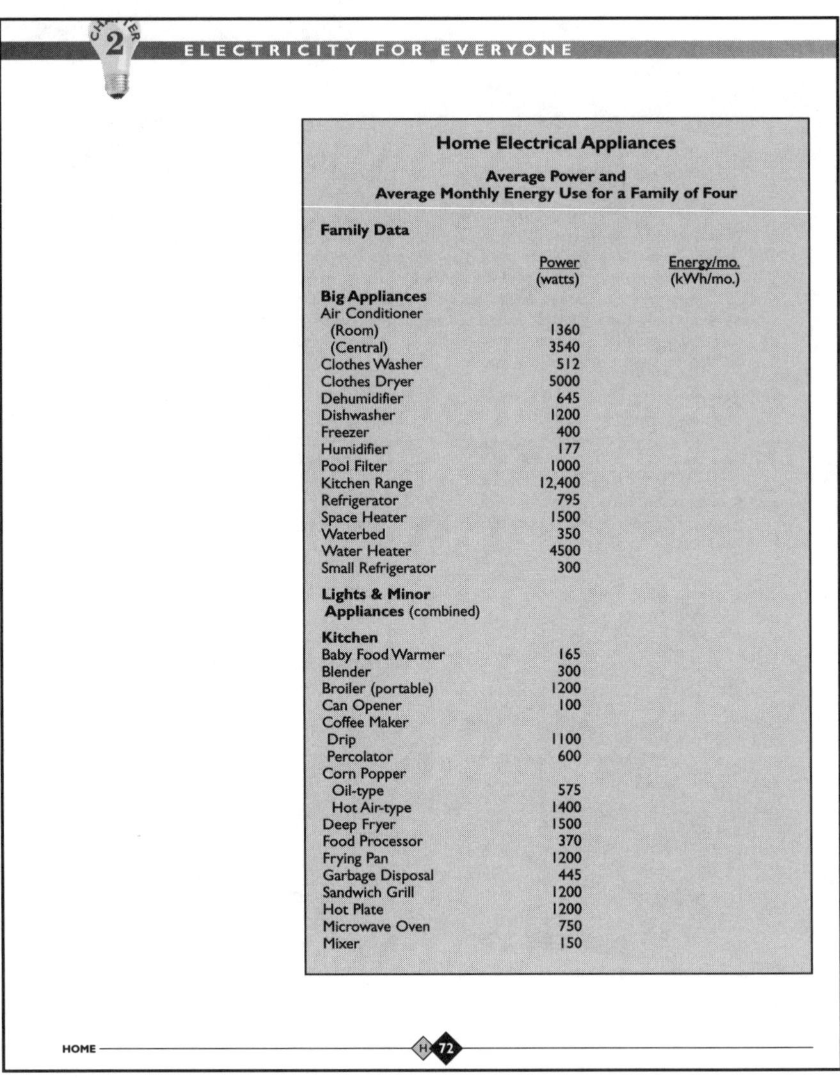

Home Electrical Appliances

Average Power and Average Monthly Energy Use for a Family of Four

Family Data

	Power (watts)	Energy/mo. (kWh/mo.)
Big Appliances		
Air Conditioner		
(Room)	1360	
(Central)	3540	
Clothes Washer	512	
Clothes Dryer	5000	
Dehumidifier	645	
Dishwasher	1200	
Freezer	400	
Humidifier	177	
Pool Filter	1000	
Kitchen Range	12,400	
Refrigerator	795	
Space Heater	1500	
Waterbed	350	
Water Heater	4500	
Small Refrigerator	300	
Lights & Minor Appliances (combined)		
Kitchen		
Baby Food Warmer	165	
Blender	300	
Broiler (portable)	1200	
Can Opener	100	
Coffee Maker		
Drip	1100	
Percolator	600	
Corn Popper		
Oil-type	575	
Hot Air-type	1400	
Deep Fryer	1500	
Food Processor	370	
Frying Pan	1200	
Garbage Disposal	445	
Sandwich Grill	1200	
Hot Plate	1200	
Microwave Oven	750	
Mixer	150	

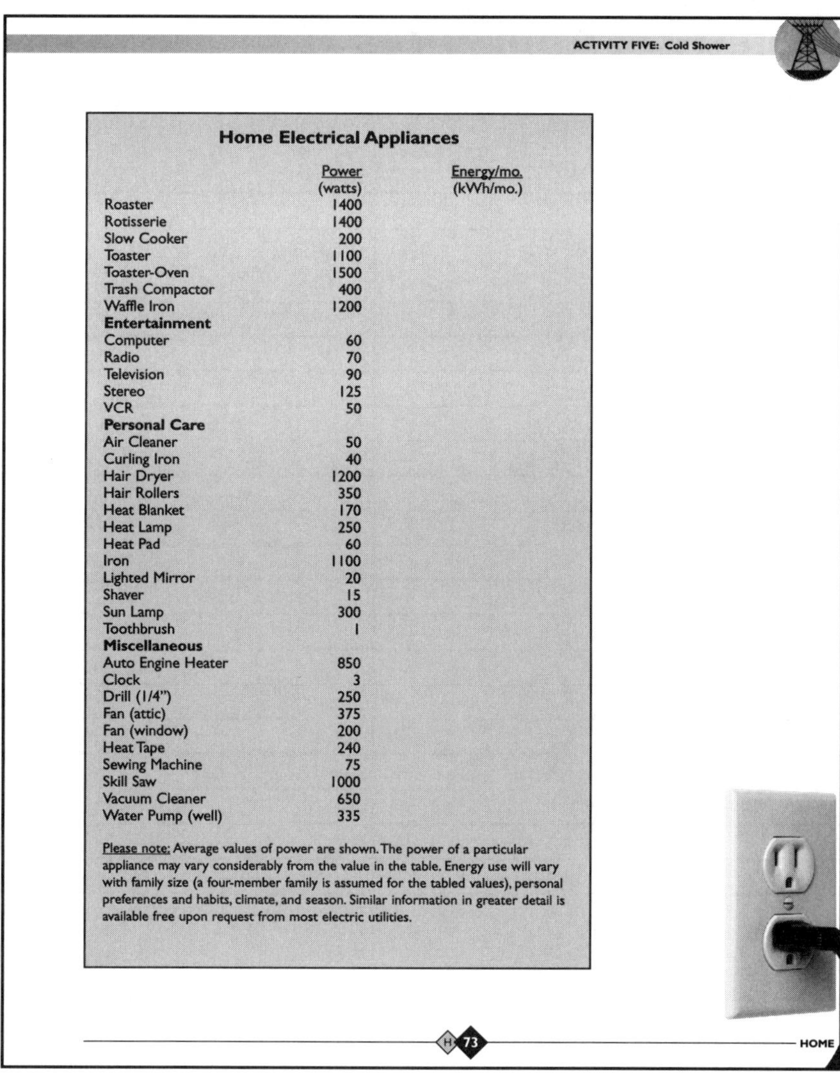

Home Electrical Appliances

	Power (watts)	Energy/mo. (kWh/mo.)
Roaster	1400	
Rotisserie	1400	
Slow Cooker	200	
Toaster	1100	
Toaster-Oven	1500	
Trash Compactor	400	
Waffle Iron	1200	
Entertainment		
Computer	60	
Radio	70	
Television	90	
Stereo	125	
VCR	50	
Personal Care		
Air Cleaner	50	
Curling Iron	40	
Hair Dryer	1200	
Hair Rollers	350	
Heat Blanket	170	
Heat Lamp	250	
Heat Pad	60	
Iron	1100	
Lighted Mirror	20	
Shaver	15	
Sun Lamp	300	
Toothbrush	1	
Miscellaneous		
Auto Engine Heater	850	
Clock	3	
Drill (1/4")	250	
Fan (attic)	375	
Fan (window)	200	
Heat Tape	240	
Sewing Machine	75	
Skill Saw	1000	
Vacuum Cleaner	650	
Water Pump (well)	335	

Please note: Average values of power are shown. The power of a particular appliance may vary considerably from the value in the table. Energy use will vary with family size (a four-member family is assumed for the tabled values), personal preferences and habits, climate, and season. Similar information in greater detail is available free upon request from most electric utilities.

Home Electrical Appliances

Average Power and Average Monthly Energy Use for a Family of Four

Family Data		
	Power (watts)	Energy/mo. (kWh/mo.)
Big Appliances		
Air Conditioner		
(Room)	1360	
(Central)	3540	
Clothes Washer	512	
Clothes Dryer	5000	
Dehumidifier	645	
Dishwasher	1200	
Freezer	400	
Humidifier	177	
Pool Filter	1000	
Kitchen Range	12,400	
Refrigerator	795	
Space Heater	1500	
Waterbed	350	
Water Heater	4500	
Small Refrigerator	300	
Lights & Minor Appliances (combined)		
Kitchen		
Baby Food Warmer	165	
Blender	300	
Broiler (portable)	1200	
Can Opener	100	
Coffee Maker		
Drip	1100	
Percolator	600	
Corn Popper		
Oil-type	575	
Hot Air-type	1400	
Deep Fryer	1500	
Food Processor	370	
Frying Pan	1200	
Garbage Disposal	445	
Sandwich Grill	1200	
Hot Plate	1200	
Microwave Oven	750	
Mixer	150	
Roaster	1400	
Rotisserie	1400	

For use with *Home*, Chapter 2, ACTIVITY FIVE: Cold Shower

Home Electrical Appliances

	Power (watts)	Energy/mo. (kWh/mo.)
Slow Cooker	200	
Toaster	1100	
Toaster Oven	1500	
Trash Compactor	400	
Waffle Iron	1200	
Entertainment		
Computer	60	
Radio	70	
Television	90	
Stereo	125	
VCR	50	
Personal Care		
Air Cleaner	50	
Curling Iron	40	
Hair Dryers	1200	
Hair Rollers	350	
Heat Blanket	170	
Heat Lamp	250	
Heat Pad	60	
Iron	1100	
Lighted Mirror	20	
Shaver	15	
Sun Lamp	300	
Toothbrush	1	
Miscellaneous		
Auto Engine Heater	850	
Clock	3	
Drill (1/4")	250	
Fan (attic)	375	
Fan (window)	200	
Heat Tape	240	
Sewing Machine	75	
Skill Saw	1000	
Vacuum Cleaner	650	
Water Pump (well)	335	

Please note: Average values of power are shown. The power of a particular appliance may vary considerably from the value in the table. Energy use will vary with family size (a four-member family is assumed for the tabled values), personal preferences and habits, climate, and season. Similar information in greater detail is available free upon request from most electric utilities.

For use with *Home*, Chapter 2, ACTIVITY FIVE: Cold Shower

ACTIVITY SIX
Pay Up

Background Information

Activity Six deals with the comparison of monthly electric bills and the cost of operating various electric appliances.

Several factors may account for differences in electric bills for different households, including but not limited to: family size, appliances used, different energy rates for different power companies.

As a direct extension of Activity Four, the cost of operating various electric appliances is calculated based on power ratings, time of use and cost per unit of energy. Students have gathered data on monthly energy used for several appliances in units of kWh/month. The monthly energy used per appliance multiplied by the billing rate in $/kWh gives the monthly cost of operating each appliance.

Active-ating the Physics InfoMall

This activity is pretty well self-contained. For fun, you can search the InfoMall for "electric bill". There are a small handful of hits for this search, and most of them are examples you may wish to use.

Of course, the CD-ROM is useful for this activity, but by now you know what you need to look up, and how to do it. If you need to know what a kilowatt-hour is, the InfoMall will provide the answer. If you want more problems for Physics To Go, simply look in the Problems Place.

Planning for the Activity

Time Requirements

This activity should take about 40 minutes to complete, including the Physics To Go.

Materials needed

For the class:

- sample household electric bills from students or others

For each group:

- calculator

Advance Preparation and Setup

Contact your local electric company for power bills. Ask for several different ones, and both residential and commercial. Alternatively, ask the students to bring in their monthly bills, from different times of the year if possible (make sure they first ask for permission from their parents, and black out any personal information). Collect them, then distribute them to the groups, providing a variety of bill types for each group.

Teaching Notes

Have students complete the What Do You Think? and then discuss their responses to the question. Be sure that it is clear to students that the two factors which determine the cost of operating any electrical appliance are (in addition to the rate established by the power company) the power rating of the appliance and the amount of time for which the appliance is used during a billing period.

Being sure to protect the anonymity of individuals, proceed to the analysis of the students' household electric bills in For You To Do.

NOTES

Activity Overview

Students will be analyzing electric bills from trends, cost per kWh, etc. From this they should get a better idea on how power is used, and whether it is used wisely. Taking this knowledge, they will apply it to their own HFE home, and hopefully, they will become more aware of how they can reduce the use of electricity in their own lives.

Student Objectives

Students will:

- analyze household electric bills, relating energy consumed, billing rate, and cost.
- compare the costs of operating a variety of electrical appliances in terms of power ratings, amount of time each appliance is used, and billing rate.
- appreciate energy consumption differences across cultures.

ANSWERS FOR THE TEACHER ONLY

What Do You Think?

Many factors are involved, and the students will provide answers based on the area in which they live. Some of the factors which affect the rate at which the power company charges for use of the electricity include: major industry close by; distance between populated centers; distance from power source; cost of the source; number of customers on the power grid; primarily urban or rural customers; how new or how old the grid is; etc. The two things which affect the amount of money charged is the power rating of the appliance, and how long it is operated in one month.

Activity Six

Pay Up

WHAT DO YOU THINK?

Eggs are priced by the dozen, and electricity is priced by the kilowatt-hour.

- **What factors determine the amount of money the electric company charges you for the use of an appliance?**

Record your ideas about this question in your *Active Physics log*. Be prepared to discuss your responses with your small group and the class.

HOME H 74

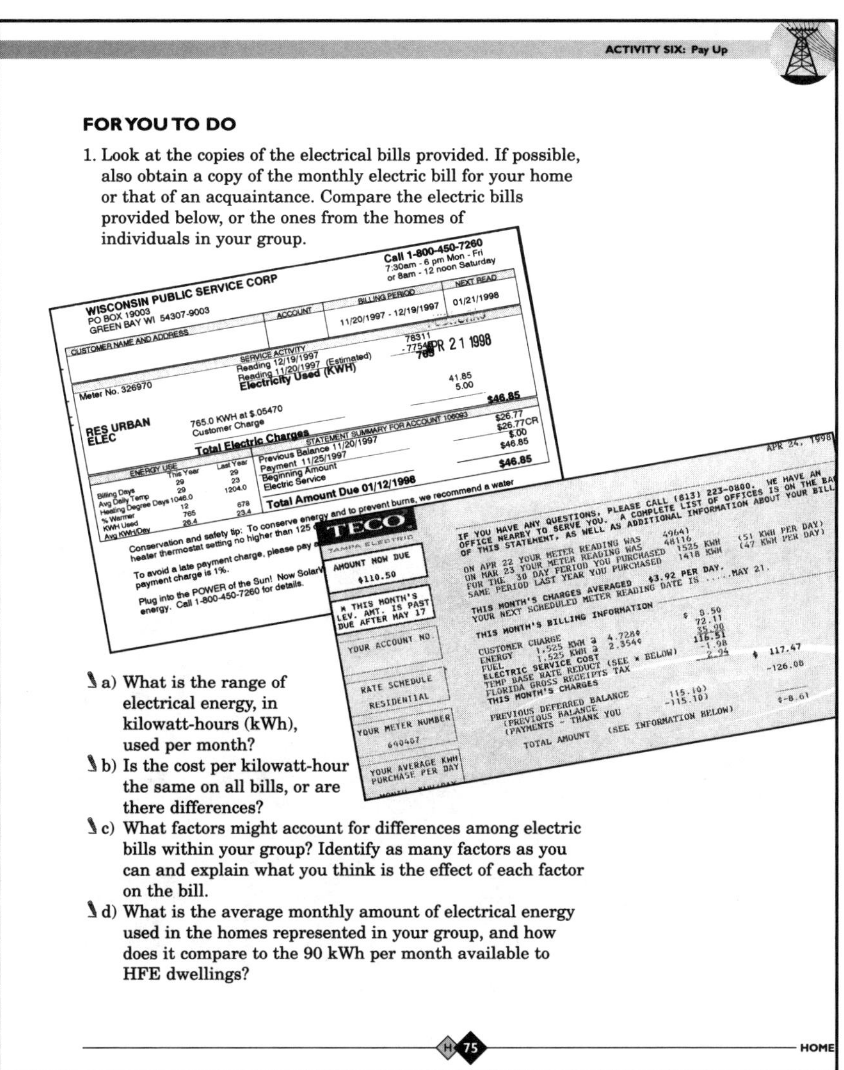

FOR YOU TO DO

1. Look at the copies of the electrical bills provided. If possible, also obtain a copy of the monthly electric bill for your home or that of an acquaintance. Compare the electric bills provided below, or the ones from the homes of individuals in your group.

a) What is the range of electrical energy, in kilowatt-hours (kWh), used per month?

b) Is the cost per kilowatt-hour the same on all bills, or are there differences?

c) What factors might account for differences among electric bills within your group? Identify as many factors as you can and explain what you think is the effect of each factor on the bill.

d) What is the average monthly amount of electrical energy used in the homes represented in your group, and how does it compare to the 90 kWh per month available to HFE dwellings?

Answers

For You To Do

1. a) This will vary with the type of bill.

b) The price will probably be different depending on whether it is commercial, residential, urban, rural, etc.

c) As mentioned in the What Do You Think?.

d) The average monthly bill would probably be many times larger than the 90 kWh per month available to the HFE homes.

ELECTRICITY FOR EVERYONE

2. In Activity 5, you estimated the time that an appliance is used, and the amount of energy required to use it for one month. Now you will calculate the expense of that energy. Combine the lists from the group members and calculate the expense of running the electrical appliances by using the following equation:

   Cost = Energy × Price per unit of energy

   The price for electricity can be taken from the electric bills that were provided.

   a) Record your calculations in your log.

3. Compare the cost of electricity in your town to other places in the United States. The "low" for electrical costs is approximately $0.03 (3 cents) per kWh. The "high" for electrical costs is approximately $0.16 (16 cents) per kWh.

   a) What are the high and low costs of the electrical bills which you examined?

   b) How might your consumption of electricity change if you had to pay for your own electrical bills?

FOR YOU TO READ

Determining Energy Consumption

The electrical energy consumed by appliances can be determined in different ways. If the power rating of an appliance is known, and if the power remains at a steady value while the appliance is in use (example: light bulb), the energy, in kWh, can be calculated by multiplying the power of the appliance, in kilowatts, by the time, in hours, for which the appliance is used (Energy = Power × Time).

Determining the energy consumed by some appliances, however, is tricky, because the appliances vary in power while they are in use. For example, a refrigerator may cycle on and off under the control of a thermostat. Therefore, it is not operating during all of the time it is "plugged in," and the calculation described above would lead to a misleadingly high value for the heater's energy consumption. For such appliances whose power varies throughout time, a kilowatt-hour meter is used to measure the total energy consumed, with variations in power throughout time taken into account. The same kind of meter, a kilowatt-hour meter, is used by the power company to measure the total electrical energy used in your home. The meter is mounted somewhere at your home so that it can be read by the power company's "meter reader" person.

Another way to determine the energy used by electrical appliances is to use the experience of power companies or corporations that sell electrical supplies. Extensive lists of appliances, their power ratings, and each appliance's average energy use per month by a typical family are available free from such sources.

ANSWERS

For You To Do *(continued)*

2\. a) Student data. Sample calculation: (microwave oven used 0.75 h/day)

Cost = Energy x price per unit of energy

= 27 kWh x $0.07/kWh

= $1.89

3\. a) Student response from data from electric bills.

b) Student response, but students will probably say their consumption will go down (hopefully!).

ACTIVITY SIX: Pay Up

PHYSICS TALK

The cost of operating an electrical appliance can be calculated using the following equation.

Cost = Energy × Price per unit of energy

where energy is in kilowatt-hours (1000 watt-hours = 1 kWh).

Example:

An electric coffee maker uses an average of 22.5 kWh of energy each month. If the family is charged 12¢/kWh for electricity, what is the average monthly cost of operating the coffee maker?

Cost = Energy × Price per unit of energy

= 22.5 kWh x $0.12/kWh

= $2.70

REFLECTING ON THE ACTIVITY AND THE CHALLENGE

In this activity you learned that the average American family's energy use exceeds the maximum available for our HFE dwellings. Imagine how your own standard of living would change if you were restricted to 90 kWh per month.

The challenge requires that you need to be thinking about two things at the same time as you select appliances for the universal dwelling: the power consumed by each appliance and the amount of time for which each appliance is used. Both need to be taken into account to stay within the power and energy limits of the HFE electrical system.

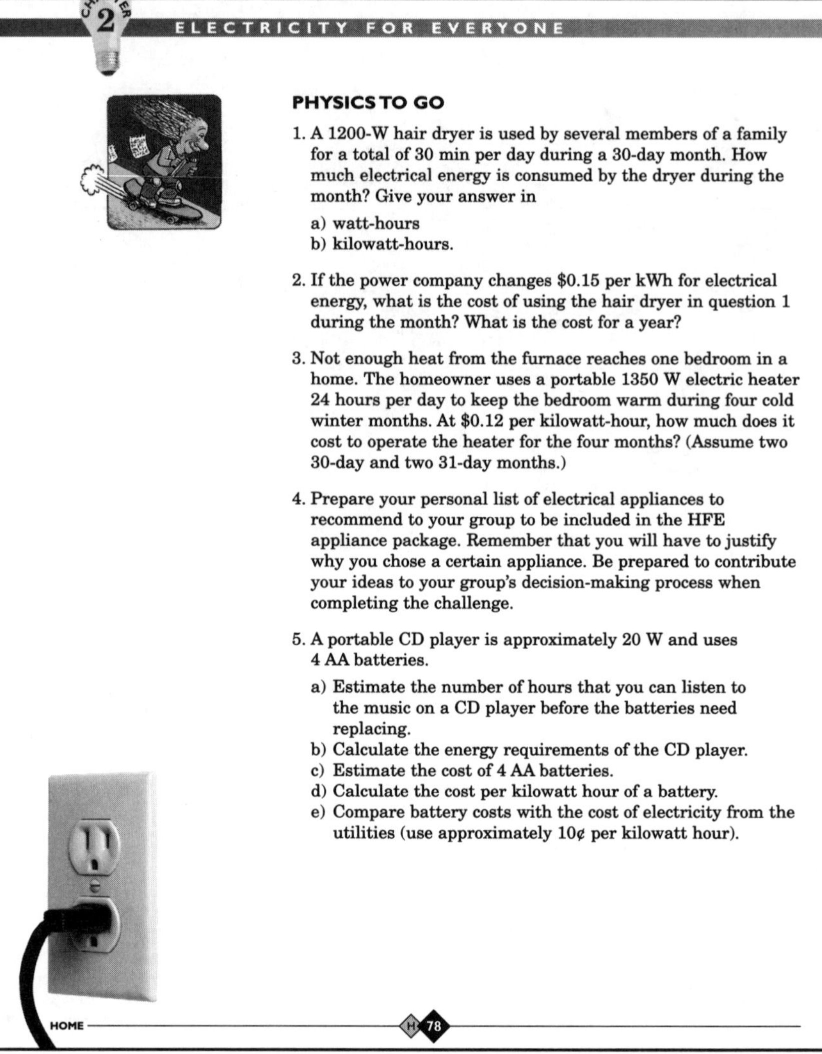

PHYSICS TO GO

1. A 1200-W hair dryer is used by several members of a family for a total of 30 min per day during a 30-day month. How much electrical energy is consumed by the dryer during the month? Give your answer in
   a) watt-hours
   b) kilowatt-hours.
2. If the power company changes $0.15 per kWh for electrical energy, what is the cost of using the hair dryer in question 1 during the month? What is the cost for a year?
3. Not enough heat from the furnace reaches one bedroom in a home. The homeowner uses a portable 1350 W electric heater 24 hours per day to keep the bedroom warm during four cold winter months. At $0.12 per kilowatt-hour, how much does it cost to operate the heater for the four months? (Assume two 30-day and two 31-day months.)
4. Prepare your personal list of electrical appliances to recommend to your group to be included in the HFE appliance package. Remember that you will have to justify why you chose a certain appliance. Be prepared to contribute your ideas to your group's decision-making process when completing the challenge.
5. A portable CD player is approximately 20 W and uses 4 AA batteries.
   a) Estimate the number of hours that you can listen to the music on a CD player before the batteries need replacing.
   b) Calculate the energy requirements of the CD player.
   c) Estimate the cost of 4 AA batteries.
   d) Calculate the cost per kilowatt hour of a battery.
   e) Compare battery costs with the cost of electricity from the utilities (use approximately 10¢ per kilowatt hour).

ANSWERS

Physics To Go

1. a) 30 days x 0.5 hours /day = 15 hours total

   Therefore, $E = Pt$
   = 1200 W x 15 h
   = 18,000 Wh

   b) In kilowatt hours, divide the Wh by 1000

   = 18,000 Wh/1000 Wh/kWh
   = 18 kWh

2. The cost for the month is 18 kWh x $0.15 /kWh = $2.70 /mo. The cost per year is multiplied by 12 = $2.70/mo. x 12 mo. = $32.40.

3. 1.350 kW x 24 h = 32.4 kWh. The cost for one day then is 32.4 kWh x $0.12 /kWh = $3.89 /day. For the 122 days, the cost of the heater is 122 days x $3.89 /day = $475.00.

4. Student activity, but the students should be listing low wattage appliances, and low wattage bulbs, etc.

5. a) Student response: Sample data = 10 hours.

   b) $E = Pt$
   = 20 W x 10 h
   = 200 Wh or 0.200 kWh

   c) Student response: sample cost of $2.00

   d) cost per kWh = $2.00 / 0.200 kWh = $10.00 per 4 batteries or $2.50 per battery.

   e) If you were to use the CD player for the same amount of time using the electricity from the utilities, the cost would be = 0.200 kWh x $0.10 /kWh = $0.02 for using the CD player for 10 hours.

Sample Electric Bill, NY

```
30-1285-0615-0010-7   OCT 16, 1998                 718-409-7100

79                          Service to: BARBARA ZAHM
                                    at: 88 HORTON ST 2FL

                          BILLING SUMMARY  AS OF 09/18/98

                        Amount due last bill...    $186.10
                        Payments through 09/16        NONE
                        Balance remaining......    $186.10

                        CURRENT ELEC CHARGES...    $122.11
                        CURRENT GAS CHARGES....     $36.22

                        TOTAL AMOUNT NOW DUE...    $344.43

                  BILLING DETAIL

ELECTRIC USE - RATE EL1  RESIDENTIAL

09/17/98 reading (Actual).......  50435
08/18/98 reading (Actual).......  -49688

Total KWH used in  30 days......    747

CHARGES FOR ELECTRICITY USED

Basic service charge:             $7.42
  (does not include usage)
          KWH     COST/KWH
First     250.0 @ 13.6720¢        34.18
Next      497.0 @ 14.6640¢        72.88
Fuel adjustment @   .3922¢         2.93
Sales tax @  4.000%                4.70

CURRENT ELECTRIC CHARGES       $122.11
```

AVERAGE DAILY ELECTRIC USE

■ = Actual, □ = Estimated
KWH ▥ = Other Customers This Period
35, 28, 21, 14, 7, 0
'97 S O N D J F M A M J J A S '98

DAILY AVERAGES

	KWH USED
THIS PERIOD:	24.90
SAME PERIOD LAST YEAR:	21.09

2

For use with *Home*, Chapter 2, ACTIVITY SIX: Pay Up

Sample Electric Bill, CT

ELECTRIC USE - RATE EL1 RESIDENTIAL

05/07/98 reading (Estimated)....	8190
04/08/98 reading (Estimated)....	-8168
Meter reading difference	22
Meter multiplier	x10
Total KWH used in 29 days......	220

CHARGES FOR ELECTRICITY USED

	KWH	COST/KWH	
Basic service charge: (does not include usage)			$7.18
First	220.0 @	13.6909¢	30.12
Fuel adjustment @		.6909¢	1.52
Sales tax @ 4.000%			1.55

CURRENT ELECTRIC CHARGES $40.37

AVERAGE DAILY ELECTRIC USE

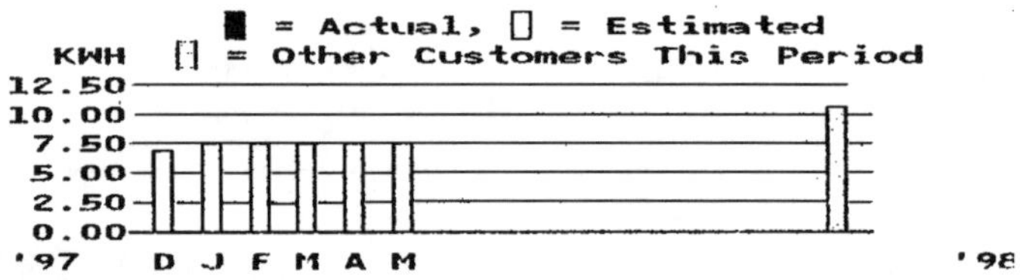

■ = Actual, □ = Estimated
KWH
[] = Other Customers This Period
12.50
10.00
7.50
5.00
2.50
0.00
'97
D J F M A M
'98

BILLING SUMMARY AS OF 05/08/98

Amount due last bill...	$39.95
Payments through 05/06	$39.95
Balance remaining......	NONE
CURRENT ELEC CHARGES...	**$40.37**
TOTAL AMOUNT NOW DUE...	**$40.37**

For use with *Home*, Chapter 2, ACTIVITY SIX: Pay Up

NOTES

2

ACTIVITY SEVEN
More for Your Money

Background Information

The efficiency of electric appliances is introduced in Activity Seven.

Three different heating appliances—a microwave oven, a hot plate and a heating coil—are used, one at a time, to effect equal temperature changes in standard samples (equal masses) of water in standard containers. The time to accomplish the temperature change for each heating device is recorded.

The electrical energy used by each appliance in joules is calculated by multiplying its power rating in watts by the heating time in seconds.

Since each appliance is used to accomplish the same heating task, the efficiencies of the appliances can be compared in an informal way on the basis of the energy used by each appliance; students perhaps will intuitively agree that the most efficent appliance is the one which used the least amount of energy to accomplish the task.

For your information and in case you wish to formalize treatment of efficiency for the appliances used for the particular task encountered in this activity:

Eff. (%) = [Heat gained by water (joules)/Energy used by appliance (joules)] x 100%

Active-ating the Physics InfoMall

Perhaps the most interesting use of the InfoMall in this Activity is exploring how microwave ovens work. Simply search for "microwave oven" and you will quickly find the answer.

Since this activity is about efficiency, you may note that one of the hits from this search is "Calibration and efficiency of microwave ovens," from *The Physics Teacher*, vol. 28, issue 8, 1990. (When you find this article, the citation on the InfoMall is incorrect - it lists it as vol. 25.) You may find this article interesting and you should check it out.

Planning for the Activity

Time Requirements

Allow at least 40 minutes for this activity. Depending on the appliances chosen, the activity may take a longer or shorter amount of time. Try this experiment, and evaluate what is the best quantity of water to use would be in order to get the best results in the shortest amount of time.

Materials needed

For the class:

- electric hot plate, known wattage
- microwave oven, known wattage on high setting
- Pyrex® beaker, 1 liter capacity (2)
- cold tap water
- graduated cylinder
- stirrer
- thermometer or temperature probe
- clock

For each group:

- Pyrex® beaker, 250 ml.
- electric immersion heater, known wattage
- graduated cylinder
- stirrer
- thermometer or temperature probe
- clock

Advance Preparation and Setup

Whether you do the FYTD as a demonstration or with students working in groups will depend upon the number of microwave ovens, hot plates and immersion coils available, and the power limit of the circuit(s) in your classroom. You will need to know the power ratings of the appliances used, and you may wish to measure them in advance. Also, you will need to know if the microwave oven power is steady as the oven operates or if the power cycles vary as it operates.

As it may be difficult to get to get enough microwaves and hot plates for all groups, the teacher may want to do the microwave and hot plate portions as a demonstration, and then allow the students to use the immersion coils.

Use a small quantity of water for the immersion heater activity, such as 1 cup (250 mL). Try this experiment before the students do it, to ensure that the results are sufficiently differentiated. The time for the microwave oven should be about two minutes to heat the water almost to boiling. The time for the hot plate, may be anywhere between 3 or 4 minutes up to ten minutes to get the same temperature change.

Teaching Notes

Have the students complete the What Do You Think?. This discussion could lead to the idea of a "payback" period. In other words, if it costs more for the energy-efficient bulb, how long does it have to be on at a smaller wattage, in order to make up the difference? This depends on the cost of power, the difference between the inefficient bulb and the efficient bulb, and the length that each will last. It would have to be stated also, that an energy-efficient bulb will probably last longer, as it will not burn as hot as the other bulb.

When doing this activity, one also must remember that, although the microwave heats more efficiently, and faster, the hot plate will keep the water hotter for longer periods of time. This is necessary in countries where boiling the water is necessary to kill microbes and other organisms which may cause disease. This gives the students another criterion with which to make their decision.

CAUTION: Safety concerns are that of operating any electrical appliance, as well as handling hot containers. Remind the students to be careful, and use oven mitts or tongs when handling the glassware. If the glass breaks, or if there are any cracks in the glass, remind the students to let the teacher know immediately.

NOTES

Activity Seven

More for Your Money

WHAT DO YOU THINK?

Some hot water heaters and furnaces for homes are more than 90% efficient.

- **If high-efficiency appliances cost more, are they worth the added cost?**

Record your ideas about this question in your *Active Physics log*. Be prepared to discuss your responses with your small group and the class.

FOR YOU TO DO

1. Place one liter of cold tap water in a beaker made of Pyrex glass. Make sure the outside of the beaker is dry so it does not slip from your grasp. Measure the temperature of the water.
   a) Record the temperature of the water in your log.
   b) Record the quantity of water in milliliters and grams. (1 mL of water has a mass of 1 g.)

HOME

ANSWERS

For You To Do

1. a) Student observation and data.
   b) Student observation and data.

Activity Overview

Students will be evaluating the efficiencies of different types of appliances that are designed to do the same job. This will be the culmination of the chapter, and therefore, allow them to choose the most energy efficient appliances for their HFE home.

Student Objectives

Students will:

- measure and compare the energy consumed by appliances.
- measure and compare the efficiencies of appliances.
- choose an appropriate appliance for efficiency, based on tests performed.

ANSWERS FOR THE TEACHER ONLY

What Do You Think?

In the long term they are worth the extra cost. Energy-efficient appliances also save on the environment as the power companies do not have to produce as much electricity, and therefore, the companies do not have to use non-renewable resources and pollute as much to keep up with the demand.

ANSWERS

For You To Do

(continued)

2. a) Student activity.

   b) The longer you wait to take the temperature, the more heat energy will leave the water and be transferred to the surroundings.

3. a) Student observation and data.

4. a) Student observation and data.

2. Place the beaker of water in a microwave oven of known power, in watts. Mark the time at which the oven is turned on at its highest power level. After two minutes, stop the time measurement. Carefully check that the beaker is not too hot to grasp and remove the beaker from the oven, stir the water, and check the water temperature, all as quickly as possible.

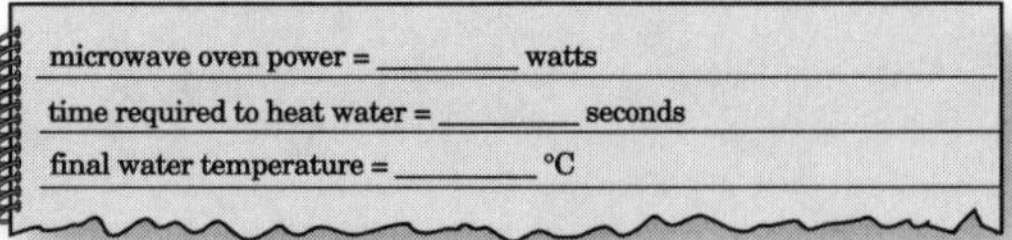

a) Record the following in your log:

b) Why is it important to complete the temperature measurement as quickly as possible?

3. Prepare an identical Pyrex beaker containing the same amount of cold tap water, preferably at the same original temperature as the water used above.

a) Record the mass and temperature of the water in your log.

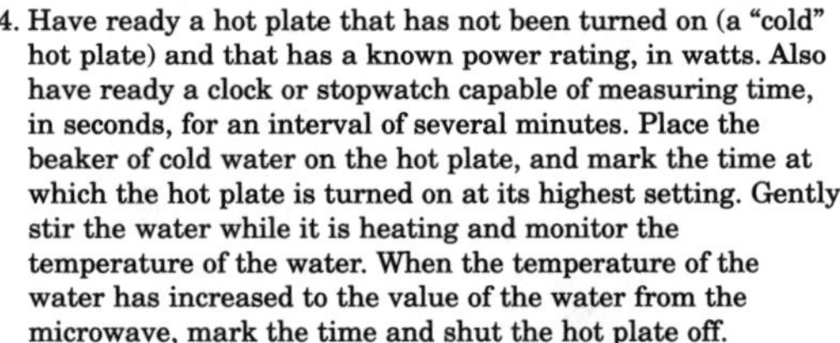

4. Have ready a hot plate that has not been turned on (a "cold" hot plate) and that has a known power rating, in watts. Also have ready a clock or stopwatch capable of measuring time, in seconds, for an interval of several minutes. Place the beaker of cold water on the hot plate, and mark the time at which the hot plate is turned on at its highest setting. Gently stir the water while it is heating and monitor the temperature of the water. When the temperature of the water has increased to the value of the water from the microwave, mark the time and shut the hot plate off.

a) Record the power of the hot plate, the time required to heat the water, and its final temperature in your log.

5. Repeat the process a third time with the coil.
   a) Record all your observations in your log.
6. Energy (in joules) = Power (in watts) × Time (in seconds)

   Calculate the energy used by each appliance to cause equal temperature increases in equal amounts of water.
   a) Show your calculations in your log.
   b) Which appliance is the "winner"? Choose a way to express a comparison of the performance of the three appliances.
   c) Was the method used to compare the three appliances fair? How could the fairness be improved?
   d) The beaker that served as the container for the water also was heated by the three appliances. Did it affect the outcome of the comparison? Might another kind of container be more or less effective to use with either appliance; for example, might using a metal pan as the container on a hot plate make the hot plate perform more efficiently?

REFLECTING ON THE ACTIVITY AND THE CHALLENGE

You know that the electrical appliances used in the universal dwelling cannot exceed 90 kWh per month of energy consumption. In this activity you discovered that some appliances are more efficient than others. That is, a highly efficient appliance can accomplish a task while using less electrical energy than a low-efficiency appliance for the same task. Obviously you will want to make a careful selection for each kind of appliance based on efficiency so that HFE inhabitants can have the greatest possible benefit from the electrical system.

ANSWERS

For You To Do

(continued)

5. a) Student observation and data.

6. a) Students will have their own data. Here is a sample data and calculations:

   Microwave: $E = Pt$

   $= 750 \text{ W } 120 \text{ s}$

   $= 90 \text{ kWs}$

   Hot plate: $E = Pt$

   $= 1200 \text{ W } 600 \text{ s}$

   $= 720 \text{ kWs}$

   Immersion coil $E = Pt$

   $= 1000 \text{ W } 180 \text{ s}$

   $= 180 \text{ kWs}$

   b) The winning appliance will be the appliance which has the lowest energy rating. In this case it is the microwave at 72 kWs.

   c) Probably not, as the microwave oven does not lose a lot of residual heat, compared to the hot plate. The immersion coil will not lose a lot of the heat to the surroundings either. But that is what makes these more efficient.

   d) Using different utensils will change the results somewhat, as there is a more efficient heat exchange with some metals than with glass. Glass, as the students found out before, is not a good conductor of heat.

2

ANSWERS

Physics To Go

1. Again, some utensils will be better for different purposes. For example, using a small pot on a large burner, will waste more heat than if it were on a small burner. Students will have more variations of this same theme.

2. The microwave oven is obviously the more efficient. However, in some third world countries, the need for clean water is as valuable as energy itself. Therefore, there is a need for looking at all alternatives when choosing appliances for the HFE home.

3. To calculate the actual efficiencies of the appliances, you would start with the same quantities of water, and heat them up for the same amount of time and measure the change in temperature. Calculate the heat energy, using $Q = mc\Delta T$, and then measure the efficiency.

4. a) $E = Pt$
   = 1500 J/s x 180 s
   = 270,000 J)

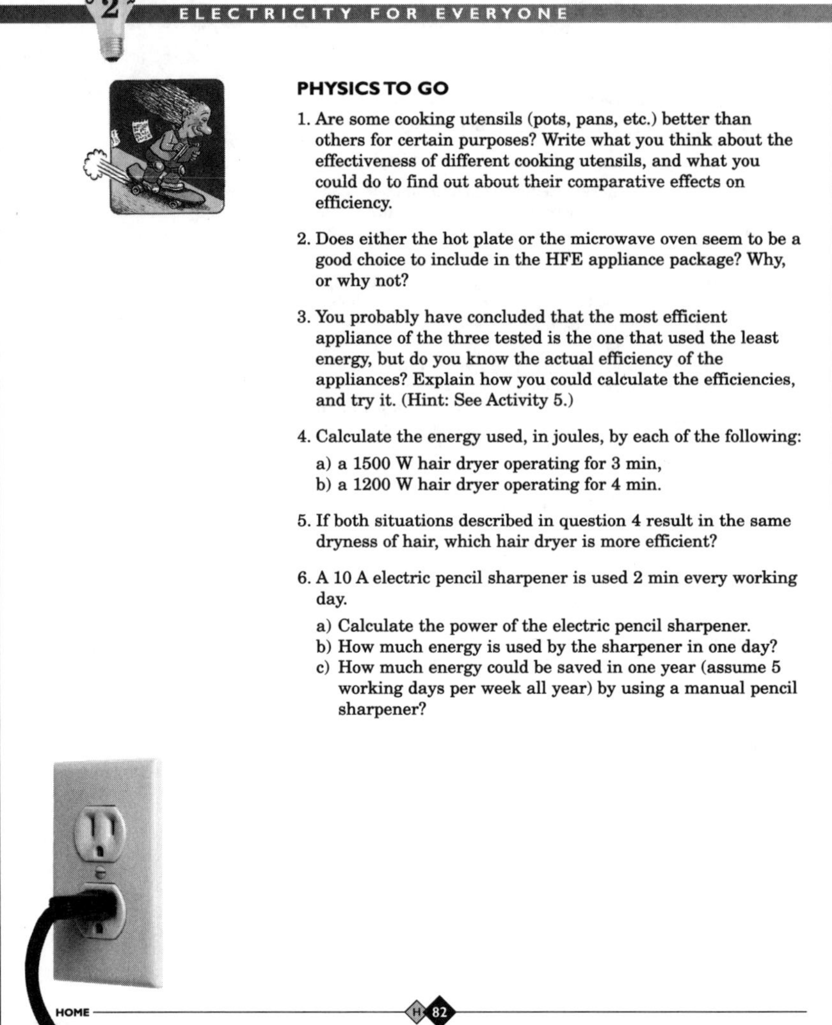

ELECTRICITY FOR EVERYONE

PHYSICS TO GO

1. Are some cooking utensils (pots, pans, etc.) better than others for certain purposes? Write what you think about the effectiveness of different cooking utensils, and what you could do to find out about their comparative effects on efficiency.

2. Does either the hot plate or the microwave oven seem to be a good choice to include in the HFE appliance package? Why, or why not?

3. You probably have concluded that the most efficient appliance of the three tested is the one that used the least energy, but do you know the actual efficiency of the appliances? Explain how you could calculate the efficiencies, and try it. (Hint: See Activity 5.)

4. Calculate the energy used, in joules, by each of the following:
   a) a 1500 W hair dryer operating for 3 min,
   b) a 1200 W hair dryer operating for 4 min.

5. If both situations described in question 4 result in the same dryness of hair, which hair dryer is more efficient?

6. A 10 A electric pencil sharpener is used 2 min every working day.
   a) Calculate the power of the electric pencil sharpener.
   b) How much energy is used by the sharpener in one day?
   c) How much energy could be saved in one year (assume 5 working days per week all year) by using a manual pencil sharpener?

HOME H 82

   b) $E = Pt$
   = 1200 J/s x 240 s
   = 288,000 J)

5. a) The 1500-W hair dryer is more efficient.

6. a) $P = IV$ (where I is the current = 10 A, and V is voltage = 120 V)
   = 10 A x 120 V
   = 1200 W)

   b) $E = Pt$
   = 1200 J/s x 120 s
   = 144,000 J)

   c) Energy for one day = 144,000 J
   Energy for one year = 144,000 J/day x 52 weeks x 5 days /week = 37,440,000 J/year.
   One other way to look at it is 37,440,000 Ws.

   Convert this to kWh:

   37,440,000 /1000 = 37,440 kWs;
   37,440 kWs / 3600 s/h = 10.4 kWh.

HOME 

PHYSICS AT WORK

The Schultzes

LIVING CLEAN AND FREE

Bob-o Schultze and his family live "off-the-grid," miles from the nearest electrical power line. Their 2,400 square foot home in northern California includes two computers, a dishwasher, a microwave oven, a washing machine, and a satellite television. It is entirely powered by clean, free, renewable energy.

"Living off-the-grid does not require any major lifestyle changes," explains Mr. Schultze who has been living without traditional energy for over 30 years. "It takes no more technical sophistication or work than the basic upkeep of any house or car."

The Schultzes use three natural power sources: water, wind, and sun. There is a hydroelectric facility in a creek on the property, a wind machine behind the house, and photovoltaic facilities on tracks following the sun. All three feed into one large industrial, deep-cycle, 6-V battery and there is never an electric bill. "We are fortunate to have a great site, but every site has at least one source of natural, renewable, energy and most have two. The sun is always an option and if conditions allow for a wind machine, which must be 20-30 feet higher than anything within 500 feet, the power of the wind can also be harnessed."

"I was inspired by the Grateful Dead" explains Bob-o whose name was created from Robert by children many years ago and has stuck. "I moved to a very rural area—30 miles from any electrical power—and I wanted my music. I started using regular D batteries, which drained very quickly, then a car battery, which drained almost as quickly, and then I developed a hydroelectric plant."

All of the appliances in the Schultze's home are the most energy efficient available. "Compact fluorescent light uses only 25% of the power of standard lighting—and simply turning things off when they are not being used can save 500 Watt-hours a day," says Bob-o, emphasizing that energy should be conserved regardless of its source. "We use nine to ten kiloWatt-hours per day, and the average for a family of four is about thirty. As more people become aware of the finite nature of traditional energy sources, the use of renewable energy will increase," claims Bob-o. The Schultzes are just a little ahead of many people in this regard.

2

ELECTRICITY FOR EVERYONE

Chapter 2 Assessment

You learned a great deal about electricity and electrical terms in this chapter. Read the scenario from the beginning of the chapter once again. Do you now understand all the terms used in the description of the wind-generator system?

Now that you have completed the activities in this chapter, you are ready to complete the chapter challenge. You will be asked to do the following.

- **List the appliances to be included in the HFE "appliance package." Your list must be as comprehensive as possible, and it must be clear how each appliance will enhance the health or well-being of the people who live in the dwelling.**
- **Develop an outline of the training manual for HFE volunteers. You manual must explain the difference between 2400 W and 3 kWh. It must also give clear examples of how use of the appliances in the package can be scheduled to stay within the power and energy limits of the electrical system on both a daily and a long-term basis.**

Review the criteria which you and your class established for how your appliance package and training manual will be graded. Your work will be judged on the basis of 100 points. If necessary, discuss the criteria once again, add details to the criteria if it would be helpful, and agree on the finalized point allocation.

Physics You Learned

Simple circuits

Generators

Series circuits

Parallel circuits

Power

$P=VI$ (watts)

Energy = Pt (kilowatt-hours; joules)

Load limits

Fuses

Switches

Utility bills

Costs for electricity

Electrical efficiency

Alternative Chapter Assessment

Select the best response for each statement or question.

1. Which property of a material describes the amount of heat required to increase the temperature of 1 kilogram of the material by 1° Celsius?

   A. Heat conductivity.

   B. Insulating effect.

   C. Specific heat.

   D. Heat of vaporization.

2. A light bulb transforms electrical energy into:

   A. heat only.

   B. mechanical energy.

   C. light only.

   D. heat and light.

3. A generator transforms:

   A. electrical energy into mechanical energy.

   B. heat into mechanical energy.

   C. mechanical energy into electrical energy.

   D. mechanical energy into heat.

4. The output energy of a generator:

   A. is much greater than the input energy.

   B. is slightly greater than the input energy.

   C. is equal to the input energy.

   D. is less than the input energy.

5. The ohm is a unit of electrical:

   A. current.

   B. energy per unit of charge.

   C. resistance.

   D. power.

6. The volt is a unit of electrical:

   A. current.

   B. energy per unit of charge.

   C. resistance.

   D. power.

7. The ampere, or amp, is a unit of electrical:

   A. current.

   B. energy per unit of charge.

   C. resistance.

   D. power.

8. The watt is a unit of electrical:

   A. current.

   B. energy per unit of charge.

   C. resistance.

   D. power.

9. The equation $P = IV$ is used to calculate electrical:

   A. current.

   B. energy per unit of charge.

   C. resistance.

   D. power.

10. Electrical energy can be calculated by multiplying:

    A. current x voltage.

    B. power x resistance.

    C. current x power.

    D. power x time.

11. The kilowatt-hour is a unit of electrical:

    A. energy.

    B. voltage.

    C. power.

    D. current.

12. Both a joule and a watt-second are units of:

    A. energy.

    B. voltage.

    C. power.

    D. current.

13. The cost of operating a 1000-watt heater for 24 hours when electricity costs 10 cents per kWh equals:

    A. $0.10

    B. $2.40

    C. $240

    D. $2,400

14. Which of the items listed below require the most energy for an average American family?

    A. food mixers.

    B. water heaters.

    C. televisions sets.

    D. lights.

15. One ampere, or amp, equals:

    A. one joule per coulomb.

    B. one ohm per volt.

    C. one joule per second.

    D. one coulomb per second.

16. One volt equals:

    A. one joule per coulomb.

    B. one ohm per volt.

    C. one joule per second.

    D. one coulomb per second.

17. One watt equals:

    A. one joule per coulomb.

    B. one ohm per volt.

    C. one joule per second.

    D. one coulomb per second.

18. One kilowatt-hour equals:

    A. 1 joule.

    B. 1,000 joules.

    C. 3,600 joules.

    D. 3,600,000 joules.

19. The maximum current for a 120-volt circuit rated at 2,400 watts is:

    A. 20 amps.

    B. 0.05 amps

    C. 288 amps.

    D. 288,000 amps.

20. If the current flow in a 120-volt vacuum cleaner is 5 amps the power of the vacuum cleaner is:

    A. 0.042 watts.

    B. 24 watts.

    C. 600 watts.

    D. 600 kilowatts.

Alternative Chapter Assessment Answers

1. C
2. D
3. C
4. D
5. C
6. B
7. A
8. D
9. D
10. D
11. A
12. A
13. B
14. B
15. D
16. A
17. C
18. D
19. A
20. C

NOTES

3

Home Chapter 3- Toys for Understanding

National Science Education Standards

Chapter Summary

Homes for Everyone (HFE) identified a need to educate children about electricity and how it is generated. HFE wants to approach this with toys. Students are challenged to prepare a kit, with materials and instructions, that children use to build a toy with a motor and/or generator. This toy will serve as a tool to illustrate how the electric motors in home appliances work or how electricity can be produced from an energy source such as wind, moving water, or some external force.

To gain understanding of the science concepts of energy conversions necessary to meet this challenge, students are engaged in activities to learn about electricity and magnetism. These experiences engage students in the following content from the *National Science Education Standards.*

Content Standards

Unifying Concepts

- Evidence, models and explanations
- Form and function

Science as Inquiry

- Identify questions & concepts that guide scientific investigations
- Use technology and mathematics to improve investigations
- Formulate & revise scientific explanations & models using logic and evidence

Science and Technology

- Abilities of technological design
- Understanding about science and technology

History and Nature of Science

- Historical perspectives

Science in Personal and Social Perspectives

- Natural resources
- Science and technology in local, national, and global challenges

Physical

- Motion and force
- Conservation of energy and increase in disorder
- Interactions of energy and matter

Key Physics Concepts and Skills

Activity Summaries	Physics Principles
Activity One: The Electricity & Magnetism Connection Students investigate the relationship between electricity and magnetism by testing the effect of a magnetic field on current-bearing wire and on a compass.	• Electricity • Magnetism • Magnetic fields
Activity Two: Electromagnets Using the hand generator to construct an electromagnet is the first step in this continued investigation of the relationship between electricity and magnetism. Students test the strength and find polarity of electromagnets made with different core materials.	• Electromagnets • Solenoids
Activity Three: Detect and Induce Currents Students construct a Galvanometer as they learn that a compass can detect the presence of a magnetic field. They use the Galvanometer to create a current similar to the process used by Faraday and Henry, manually alternating the motion of a magnet.	• Galvanometers • Induced currents
Activity Four: AC & DC Currents The use of human energy to produce electricity is replaced in this activity by a rotating coil motor. While using this motor, students test and describe the voltage in this induced current. They learn the difference between how AC and DC currents are generated. Students also learn to sketch output wave forms.	• Energy conversion • AC and DC currents • Electrical waves
Activity Five: Building an Electric Motor Students construct, operate, and explain the workings of a DC motor. This enables them to measure and express the efficiency of energy transfers. They also read to learn more about the discoveries that led to the generators and motors we use today to obtain useable power and electricity.	• Electricity • Magnetism • Energy transfer
Activity Six: Building a Motor/Generator Toy In this final activity, students apply what they have learned about the workings of an electromagnetic motor and how both AC and DC currents are generated. They must use given materials to design, construct, and demonstrate the physics of a motor or generator.	• Energy conversion • Electricity • Magnetism • AC and DC currents • Energy conversion • Energy flow and power • Electrical efficiency

3

Equipment List For Chapter Three

QTY	TO SERVE	ACTIVITY	ITEM	COMMENT
1	Class	4	AC generator, large demonstration type	For demonstration
1	Group	3	Bar magnet	
1	Group	3	Cardboard tube, approx 5 cm diameter	Toilet tissue roll will serve
2	Group	3, 5, 6	Connecting wire, insulated	Preferably fitted with alligator clips
1	Class	4	Copper pipe, 3/4" diameter x approx. 6 ft length	Available at plumbing supply outlets
1	Class	4	Cow magnet (or other cylindrical magnet)	To provide easy fit with 3/4" pipe
1	Group	1	Current-limiting resistance	To protect battery or power supply, if necessary
1	Group	5, 6	D-cell	To power basic motor
1	Class	4	DC generator, large demonstration type	For demonstration
1	Group	1	DC source, high current (5 amps or more)	Automobile battery may work best
1	Group	2	Drinking straw	
1	Group	2, 3, 5	Enamel-coated wire, approx. 10 m total per group	Thin (#24 or #26) wire also called "magnet wire"
1	Class	4	Galvanometer, demonstration-type	For demonstration
1	Group	2, 3, 5	Hand-operated generator (or variable power supply)	"Genecon" brand generator recommended
1	Group	1	Horizontal surface having hole for wire to penetrate	Drilled piece if cardboard or plywood will serve
1	Group	1	Insulated copper wire, approx. 2-m length	Such as #12 stranded wire for household circuits
1	Group	3	Light bulb & base, miniature screwbase	A "flashlight" bulb (such as No. 13) and base
1	Class	4	Light bulb & base, 120-volt	To show generator output during demonstration
1	Class	6	Magnet	For use in building motor/generator
1	Group	1, 2	Magnetic compass	Use a minimum of one per group
1	Group	2	Nail or rivet, iron or soft steel	Avoid high residual magnetism
10	Group	2	Paper clips, small	To serve as weights to be lifted by electromagnet
2	Group	5	Refrigerator magnets	Any small magnet
1	Group	5	Rubber band	To secure safety pins to D-cell
2	Group	5	Safety pins, large	Components of basic motor
1	Group	2, 3, 5	Sandpaper patch	For removing enamel insulation from ends of wire
1	Class	4	Stepladder	To access upper end of vertical copper pipe
1	Group	5	Styrofoam® cup	To serve as base for basic motor
1	Class	4	Supports to orient copper pipe vertically	Bottom end approx. 1 ft above floor
1	Group	3, 5	Tape	Small amounts of any kind of tape will do
1	Group	5	Test tube	To serve as cylindrical form for winding wire

Organizer for Materials Available in Teacher's Edition

Activity in Student Text	Additional Material	Alternative / Optional Activities
ACTIVITY ONE: The Electricity & Magnetism Connection p.H88		
ACTIVITY TWO: Electromagnets p.H93		
ACTIVITY THREE: Detect and Induce Currents p.H97		Activity Three A: Twin Coil Swings p. 226
ACTIVITY FOUR: AC & DC Currents p.H102	Current Induced by AC and DC Generators pgs. 238-239	Activity Four A: Falling Magnet p. 237
ACTIVITY FIVE: Building an Electric Motor p.H109		
ACTIVITY SIX: Building a Motor/Generator Toy p.H113		

Scenario

In this *Active Physics* chapter, you will try to help educate children through the use of toys. With your input, the Homes for Everyone (HFE) organization has developed an appliance package that will allow families living in the "universal dwelling" to enjoy a healthy and comfortable lifestyle. The HFE organization would now like to teach the children living in these homes, and elsewhere, more about electricity and the generation of electricity. They hope that this may encourage interest in children to use electricity wisely, as well as encourage development of alternative sources for electrical energy by future generations.

The HFE organization will work with a toy company to provide kits and instructions for children to make toy electric motors and generators. These toys should illustrate how electric motors and generators work and capture the interest of the children.

In an effort to help others, people often make changes or introduce new products without considering the personal and cultural impact on those whom they are trying to assist. If you ever become involved in a self-help community group, such as HFE, it would be important for you to work together with the people you are assisting to assess their needs, both personal and cultural. Although that is not possible given your limited time in class, you should recognize the need for collaborative teamwork in evaluating the impact of any new product on an established community.

Chapter and Challenge Overview

In this chapter, the students are applying some of the principles they have learned about electricity and applying it to the building of a toy. Although the toy is designed for children, it is important for the students to focus on the learning that is taking place. A generator can be a motor, and vice versa. The students need to realize that the chapter is designed to get them to apply a particular concept (electromagnetism) to a real life situation. It is hoped that the students will gain a greater respect for physics and be able to apply their knowledge in developing their overall appreciation of science.

A specific design for a DC motor which also could serve as a generator is not presented until the final activity of this chapter. Earlier, perhaps right away, you may wish to have students search for alternate designs - references on science projects would be good sources. Also, you may wish to make a rule on whether motor/generator kits available from hobby stores or toy kits will be allowed; greater benefit may result from having students build the device from "junk."

An understanding of the principles of an electric motor or generator, must be brought forward to the students. However, quantitative analysis is not necessary at this stage. Some aspects of the quantitative forces may be used as an alternative project for enrichment.

HOME

Challenge

Your task is to prepare a kit of materials and instructions that the toy company will manufacture. Children will use these kits to make a motor or generator, or a combination electric motor/generator. It will serve both as a toy and to illustrate how the electric motors in home appliances work or how electricity can be produced from an energy source such as wind, moving water, a falling weight, or some other external source.

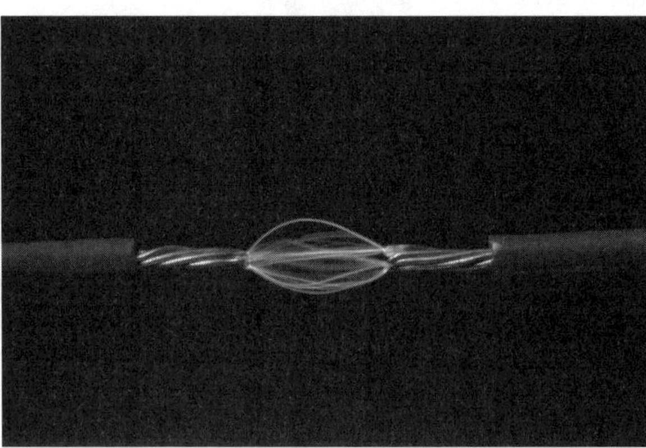

Criteria

Your work will be judged by the following criteria:

- **(30%) The motor/generator is made from inexpensive, common materials, and the working parts are exposed but with due consideration for safety.**
- **(40%) The instructions for the children clearly explain how to assemble and operate the motor/generator device, and explain how and why it works in terms of basic principles of physics.**
- **(30%) If used as a motor, the device will operate using a maximum of four 1.5 V (volt) batteries (D cells), and will power a toy (such as a car, boat, crane, etc.) that will be fascinating to children.**

OR

- **(30%) If used as a generator, the device will demonstrate the production of electricity from an energy source such as wind, moving water, a falling weight, or some other external source and be fascinating to children.**

Assessment Rubric for Challenge

The following is a possible guideline for evaluation of the Challenge.

Place a check mark in the appropriate box. If you would rather, you could mark it holistically, where all the statements taken together earn, for example, a mark out of 30%.

You may change the criteria, by adding or deleting any of the points, determined by a class decision.

Descriptor	Yes	No
Construction of motor/generator (30%)		
made from simple, inexpensive materials		
easy to assemble (or already assembled)		
working parts are exposed		
safe device		
creative and imaginative		
Instructions (40%)		
well-written		
clear and concise		
explanation of how it works is clear		
simple explanation of the physics involved		
includes safe operating instructions		
clearly stated as motor or generator (or both)		
provides evidence of testing with children		
clear understanding that there is no "creation " of electricity, but transformation		
A) Motor - toy (30%)		
will operate on maximum of four 1.5 V batteries		
will operate a toy		
is fascinating to children		
is durable in the hands of children		
toy shows character and imagination		
OR B) Generator (30%)		
clear understanding as to difference between motor and generator		
demonstrates the production of electricity from an energy source		
is fascinating to children		
is durable in the hands of children		
generator shows character and imagination in the transformation of energy		

For use with *Home*, Chapter 3

3

NOTES

What is in the Physics InfoMall for Chapter 3?

Although this chapter is called "Toys for Understanding," this chapter is not really about toys, but about motors and generators. And we will want to use the Physics InfoMall CD-ROM to gather information about these.

After entering the InfoMall, click on "Functions" from the menu bar and select "Compound Search." This will bring up a window which will allow you to specify the search you wish to do. (Caution: this information is generated on a Macintosh, and may vary slightly from what you will find on a PC. The same CD-ROM works on both platforms, and the database is the same. The interface is a little different.) Click the "Search under databases" button and select all databases, (it is sometimes faster to de-select the Keyword Kiosk, since it often provides information you may not want) then click "Apply." Enter "dc generator" in the uppermost box followed by clicking "OK." The search will take less than a minute, and will return all occurrences of the words "dc generator." The first hit on the list of search results is pretty good. You should check them out - they are on the InfoMall in their entirety. And the text is all live, meaning you can print it, copy it, and even paste it into your own hand-outs. This first hit even has reasonably good graphics

Since this entire chapter deals with electricity, it is a good idea to find out what problems students have with learning about electricity and electrical circuits. Perform a search using "student" AND "difficult*" AND "electric*" on the entire CD-ROM. This search initially provides "Too Many Hits" so it must be limited. One method is to limit it with Terms Must Appear in the Same Paragraph. This finds several references on the difficulties students have with concepts related to electricity. Knowing these difficulties will allow the teacher to expect them, and have ideas on how to overcome them. A similar search can be done using "misconcept*" in place of "difficult*". The results are not identical, so both searches should be tried.

Another idea for a search comes from realizing that the word "student" in the previous searches is almost redundant; we should not expect to find "difficulties" or "misconceptions" in the same paragraph with "electricity" very often unless we are talking about students. In addition, getting rid of the word "student" also gets rid of the "Too Many Hits" problem, so we can search entire articles again. If you perform the searches without "student" you will find many additional references, including a passage from the "Current Electricity" chapter of *A Guide to Introductory Physics Teaching* found in the Book Basement: "Research has been showing that the most basic concepts underpinning simple direct current (d.c.) circuits offer very serious difficulties to many students and that certain misconceptions are widely prevalent [Arons (1982); Cohen, Eylon, and Ganiel (1983); Fredette and Clement (1981)]. As in the case of static electricity, the learning problems are aggravated by the remoteness of the underlying phenomena from direct sense perception. The observable effects are not easily linked to abstractions such as "electrical charge," "current," and "energy." Since students are aware that batteries "run down" and that one "uses" household electricity, they believe that "something is used up" in electric circuits, and, to many of them, the most reasonable thing to be "used up" is "electricity" itself.

Another hit from this search is "LAB MANUAL: Recipes for Science: Misconceptions." You should check this out.

We searched above for "dc generator." What if we search now for "motor"? You might expect many, many hits. And you might expect that many of those hits are useless. Try it anyway. The very first hit is from *Household Physics* from the Textbook Trove, and is a great source of information, including a discussion of the theory of electric motors. We should not be surprised that this book shows up on our search, since this *Active Physics* book is about the Home. Look through the rest of the hits. Some even have nice graphics and homework problems you can use.

ACTIVITY ONE
The Electricity and Magnetism Connection

Background Information

The physics phenomenon involved in Activity One is the magnetic field surrounding a long, straight wire carrying a direct current.

Magnetic field near a current-carrying straight wire. Before providing background information about the magnetic field near a current-carrying straight wire, two definitions are offered which apply to magnetic fields in general:

Definition: The direction of a magnetic field at a particular location is the direction that the north-seeking pole of a magnetic compass would point if the compass were placed at the location.

Definition: The strength of a magnetic field, in Tesla, at a particular location is the force, in newtons, that a long, straight wire carrying a current of one ampere would experience per meter of wire length when the wire is placed at the location so that the length of the wire is oriented perpendicular to the direction of the magnetic field.

1 Tesla = 1 newton/(ampere)(meter) = 1N/am

Magnetic field strength is a vector quantity since it has both direction and magnitude.

As will be indicated by the compass in For You To Do, Activity One, the magnetic field near a long, straight wire carrying a direct current has a circular shape which is concentric on the wire as shown below:

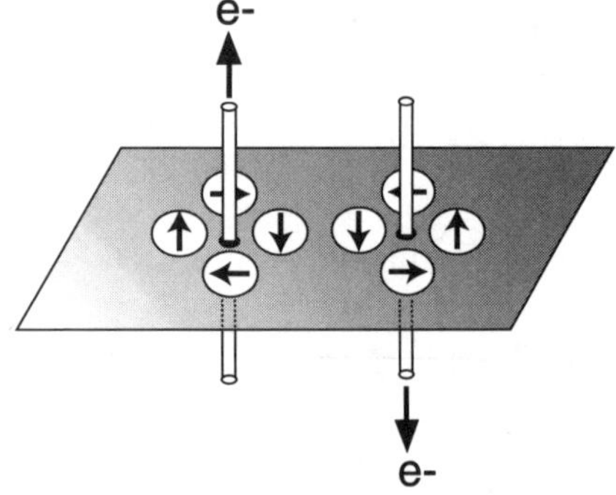

The direction of the magnetic field depends on the direction of the current flow; if the flow of electrons is reversed, so is the direction of the magnetic field around the wire. CAUTION: Some physics textbooks use the flow of positive charges (generally called conventional current) as the direction of current flow; this text uses the flow of [negative] electrons which travel around a circuit from the negative terminal of the energy source to the positive terminal.

A convenient rule for determining the direction of the magnetic field surrounding a straight wire in relation to the direction of the current in the wire is shown below as a left-hand rule:

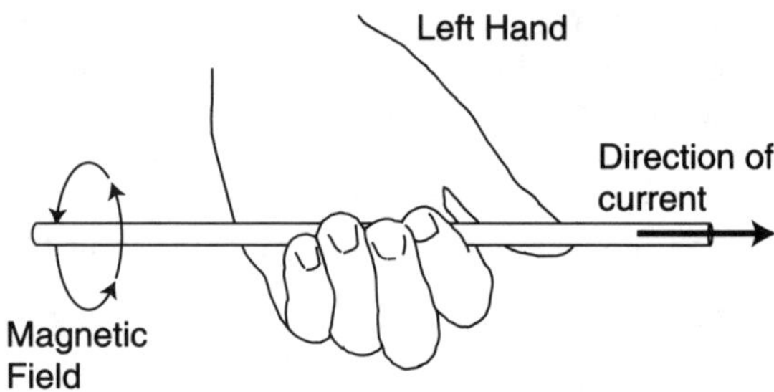

Left-hand rule for the direction of the magnetic field surrounding a straight current-carrying wire. Use the left hand to grasp the wire with the extended thumb pointing in the direction of the current in the wire. The fingers point in the direction in which the magnetic field surrounds the wire.

The strength of a magnetic field near a straight current-carrying wire. The strength of the magnetic field near a straight wire varies directly with the amount of current flowing in the wire and inversely with the distance from the wire. The equation is:

$B = m0I/2pd$

where B is the field strength in Tesla, $m0$ is the permeability of air or vacuum which has the value 4p x 10-7 newton/amp2, I is the current in amps, and d is the distance from the wire in meters.

Active-ating the Physics InfoMall

One of the topics in this activity is the magnetic field. While students often have difficulties learning about fields, this is one area that was not studied widely in time for inclusion on the Physics InfoMall. Some studies have been done more recently, so there is some information to be found, but little of it is on the CD-ROM. Still, you may wish to try a few searches to see what information does exist in this database.

A good search for this activity (with results that we will want in later activities) is "current" AND "compass." You should limit this search to Within Paragraph. Some of the results are great, including this passage, this time taken from the Electromagnetism chapter of *A Guide to Introductory Physics Teaching:* found in the Book Basement: "Very few students will conduct a meaningful investigation without guidance, however. The homework assignment should guide them Socratically into: (1) investigating the compass deflection both above and below the current-carrying wire; (2) investigating the effect of reversing the connection to the battery terminals; (3) ascertaining the pattern of the effect all the way around the wire-not just above and below; (4) qualitatively noting the effect of changing the distance between the wire and the compass needle; (5) qualitatively studying the strength of the effect on the compass needle (held at fixed distance from the wire) when additional bulbs are inserted in the circuit either in series or in parallel with an initial single bulb; (6) studying the effect of introducing an additional battery in series with the first; (7) forming, from synthesis of the observations, the right-hand rule mnemonic for the direction of magnetic field around the current-carrying wire."

What is this "right-hand rule" just mentioned? To find out, conduct a search on the list of hits from the previous search. To do this, simply change the Search Category to "Search Hits" and have the engine look for "hand rule" (after all, we don't want to leave out the left-handed versions). A quick look through these hits provides plenty of useful information, again including graphics. Don't forget to reset the search options before your next search!

Planning for the Activity

Time Requirements

If the students have to make the apparatus, allow about twenty minutes to set up the lab. It should then take about 20 - 30 minutes to complete the lab activity.

Depending on available equipment, this may be done either as a demonstration or in groups.

Materials needed

A demonstration or in groups:

- heavy-gauge (approx. #12) insulated copper wire vertically arranged to penetrate a horizontal surface such as a piece of cardboard.
- magnetic compass, 1 or more.
- DC power supply or automobile-type battery capable of producing high current (5 amps or more).
- protective resistance to limit current.

Advance Preparation and Setup

Try this activity in advance to be sure the field produced by the current deflects the compass to indicate a field concentric on the wire. Parallel currents in a bundle of wire (formed by looping one long wire) may be used to enhance the effect.

Adjust the current at each station in advance, and emphasize to students that they should not change the amount of current. Show students how to safely change the direction of the current.

Teaching Notes

Present the WDYT question to the students. The student responses may be explored in class discussion and noted on the board, or individually recorded by students and a discussion at the end of the lesson.

If there are not enough stations for each group, have each group come to the power supply (FYTD #5), while the other groups work on mapping the magnetic field (FYTD #2-4) of the bar magnet.

Again, a warning regarding the power supply is in order. The settings must not be changed. Warn them of the danger of any electric source, and that electricity is not something to take for granted. If there are any students with serious heart problems, they should probably not handle the equipment.

Students sometimes will refer to the poles of a magnet, in the same sense as the poles of an electrical charge. Whereas, the electric charges of positive and negative can be isolated, the north and south poles can never be isolated. As you break a bar magnet in half, you end up with two N-S magnets, not a magnet with a north pole at both ends and a magnet with a south pole at both ends.

Activity Overview

In this activity, the students will be observing the effects of a current on a compass. This will lay the foundation for developing an understanding of the relationship between electricity and magnetism.

Student Objectives

Students will:

- describe electric motor effect and generator effect in terms of energy transformations.
- use a magnetic compass to map a magnetic field.
- describe the magnetic field near a long, straight current-carrying wire.

TOYS FOR UNDERSTANDING

Activity One

The Electricity and Magnetism Connection

WHAT DO YOU THINK?

Generators produce electricity. Motors use electricity.

- **What is the significance of motors and generators to your standard of living? That is, how would your life be different if you had no motors or generators?**

Write your answer to this question in your *Active Physics log.* Be prepared to discuss your ideas with your small group and other members of your class.

FOR YOU TO DO

1. Set up the equipment as shown in the diagram, or as directed by your teacher.

2. The needle of a compass is a balanced magnet. It can be used as a magnetic field detector. If any magnet is present, the compass will respond. It usually aligns itself with Earth's magnetic field. With no current flowing in the wire, verify that the compass always points in the same direction, North, no matter where it is placed on the horizontal surface.

   a) Sketch the compass direction at different places on the horizontal surface in your log.

Copper wire

Magnetic compass

HOME  H 88

ANSWERS FOR THE TEACHER ONLY

What Do You Think?

Answers will vary. Some answers may include: no electricity; no TVs; video games; hair dryers; etc. Look for thoughtful answers where the students may refer to life before electricity was commonplace, and some may look at it as though they were camping or living at a cabin without power. Without motors, some students may reflect that they would have to return to the steam engine, or even earlier, where horse power, and muscles power, provided all the advantages that are enjoyed by people today. Some may refer to the advantages found in the kitchen (blenders, mix masters, coffee grinders, etc.).

ANSWERS

For You To Do

1. a) Student activity.

2. a) Student data. The compass should point in the same direction regardless of where on the horizontal surface it is placed. (Note: If some students don't see these results, it may be that they are close to a large power supply in the walls or floors of your school. This can be a teaching moment, where you can have the students try to locate the supplies.)

3. Bring another type of magnet, such as a bar magnet, into the area near the compass needle.
   - a) Describe your observations in your log.
   - b) What happens to the dependable north-pointing property of a compass when the compass is placed in a region where magnetic effects, in addition to Earth's magnetic field, exist?

4. You will now make a map of the magnetic field of the bar magnet. Place the magnet on another piece of paper and trace its position. Place the compass at one location and note the direction it points. Remove the compass.
   - a) Put a small arrow at the location from which you removed the compass to signify the way in which the compass pointed.
   - b) Place the compass at a second location about at the tip of the first arrow. Remove the compass and place another small arrow in this location to signify the way in which the compass pointed.
   - c) Repeat the process at an additional 20 locations to get a map of the magnetic field of a bar magnet. Tape the piece of paper of the map in your log.

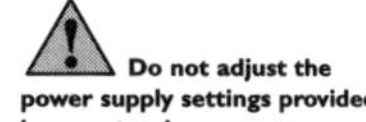

Do not adjust the power supply settings provided by your teacher.

5. Return the compass to the horizontal surface surrounding the wire. Observe the orientation of the compass. Send a current through the wire. The direction of the flow of electrons which make up the current in the wire is from the negative terminal of the power supply to the positive terminal. Move the compass to different locations on the horizontal surface, observing the direction in which the compass points at each location. Make observations on all sides of the wire, and at different distances from the wire.
   - a) Record how the compass was oriented when the bar magnet was removed.
   - b) Describe any pattern that you observe about how the compass behaves when it is near the current-carrying wire. Use a sketch and words to describe your observations in your log.
   - c) From your observations, what effect does the electric current appear to have on the wire?

ANSWERS

For You To Do

(continued)

3. a) The students should note that the compass needle will point either towards the magnet or away depending on whether the north or south pole of the magnet is pointed towards the compass.

   b) At that particular spot, the magnetic field of the magnet will be larger than the magnetic field of Earth. The students can see this measurable effect by moving the magnet farther way, until it no longer has the effect of "pulling" the compass pointer.

4. a) Student data.

   b) Student data.

   c) The students should note a pattern like the diagram below:

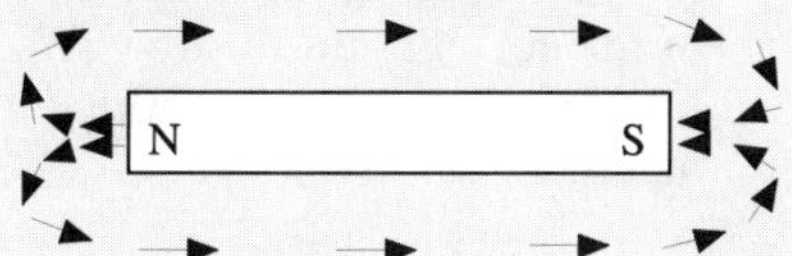

5. a) Student data.

   b) Student data. Students should have a sketch showing the compass pointing in a circular path around the current-carrying wire.

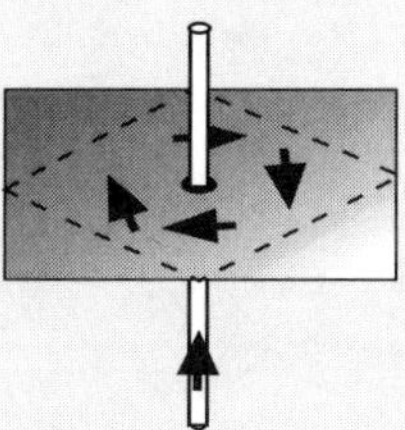

   c) The electric current appears to create a magnetic field. The compass indicates the direction of the magnetic field.

ANSWERS

For You To Do

(continued)

6. a) The students will note that the direction of the compass will be opposite to the previous question. Diagram will be opposite.

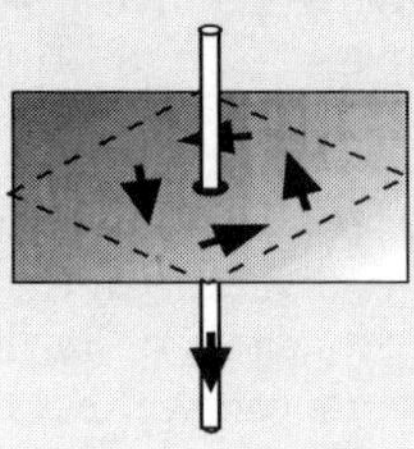

b) Students' answers will vary. Most will state that if the current is going up, the magnetic field will be directed clockwise. If the current is going down, the magnetic field is directed counter-clockwise. If they use the left-hand rule, they should say that the thumb points in the direction of the current and the fingers point in the direction of the magnetic field.

6. Reverse the direction of the current in the wire by exchanging the contacts of the power supply. Repeat your observations.
   a) Describe the results.
   b) Make up a rule for remembering the relationship between the direction of the current in a wire and the direction of the magnetism near the wire (i.e. when the current is up, the magnetic field . . .). Anyone told your rule should be able to use it with success. Write your rule in your log. Include a sketch. (Hint: One of the rules that physicists use makes use of your thumb and fingers.)

REFLECTING ON THE ACTIVITY AND THE CHALLENGE

This activity has provided you with knowledge about a critical link between electricity and magnetism, which is deeply involved in your challenge to make a working electric motor or generator. The response of the compass needle to a nearby electric current showed that an electric current itself has a magnetic effect which can cause a magnet, in this case a compass needle, to experience force. You have a way to go to understand and be able to be "in control" of electric motors and generators, but you've started along the path to being in control.

PHYSICS TO GO

1. If 100 compasses were available to be placed on the horizontal surface to surround the current-carrying wire in this activity, describe the pattern of directions in which the 100 compasses would point in each of the following situations:
   a) no current is flowing in the wire,
   b) a weak current is flowing in the wire,
   c) a strong current is flowing in the wire.
2. If a vertical wire carrying a strong current penetrated the floor of a room, and if you were using a compass to "navigate" in the room by always walking in the direction indicated by the north-seeking pole of the compass needle, describe the "walk" you would take.

ANSWERS

Physics To Go

1. a) All the compasses will be pointing towards the north.

   b) The students would notice that the compasses that are closest to the wire, will be pointing in a circular path surrounding the wire, in agreement with the left-hand rule. As the compasses get further and further away, they would then point towards the north.

   c) The students should notice that all of the compasses should be pointing in a circular path.

2. The path you would take would be in a circular path around the current-carrying wire. If the direction of the current is up, then the path would be clockwise. If the current is down, then the path would be counter-clockwise.

3. Use the rule which you made up for remembering the relationship between the direction of the current flowing in a wire and the direction of the magnetic field near the wire to make a sketch showing the direction of the magnetic field near a wire which has a current flowing:

   a) downward,

   b) horizontally.

4. Physicists remember the orientation of the magnetic field of a current by placing their left thumb in the direction of the electron current and noting whether their fingers of the left hand curve clockwise or counterclockwise. Copy the following diagrams into your log. Use this rule to sketch the direction of the magnetic field in each case.

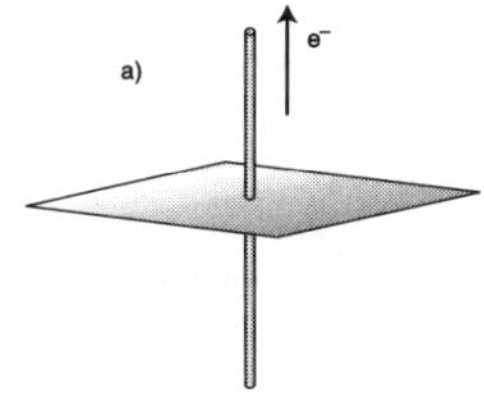

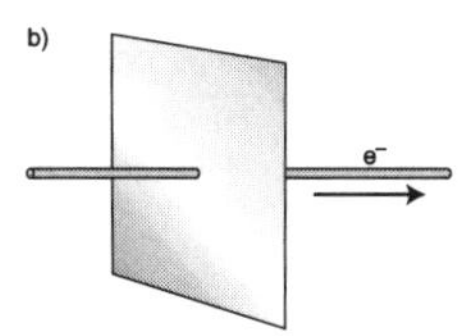

5. Imagine that a second vertical wire is placed in the apparatus used in this activity, but not touching the first wire. There is room to place a magnetic compass between the wires without touching either wire. If a compass were placed between the wires, in what direction would the compass point if the wires carry equal currents:

   a) which are in opposite directions,

   b) which are in the same direction.

5. a) In this diagram, the compass will appear to go back and forth between north and south poles.

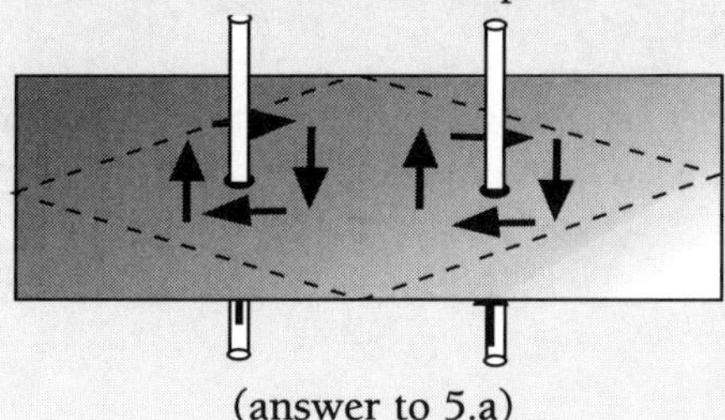

(answer to 5.a)

b) In this diagram, the compass will point in one direction (top of page.)

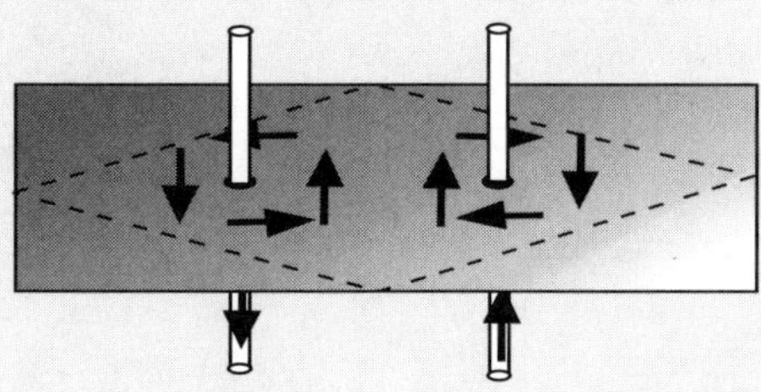

Answers

Physics To Go

(continued)

3.a)

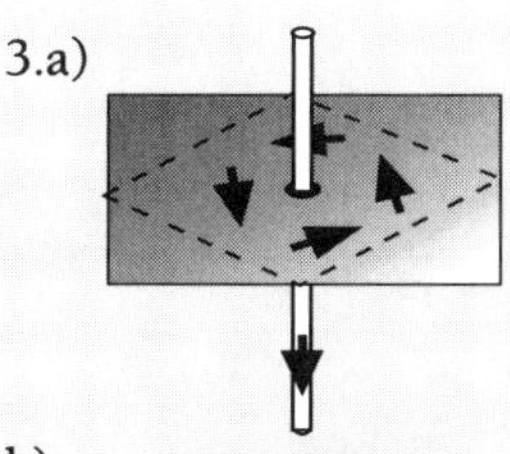

b)

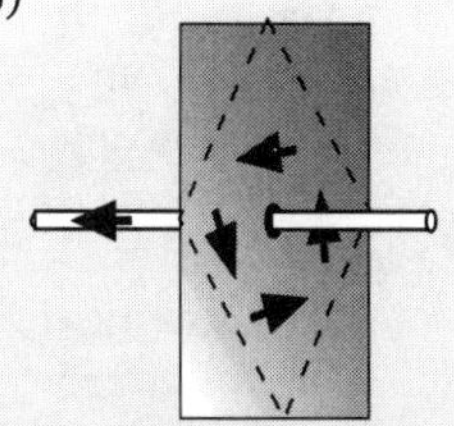

4.a)

b)

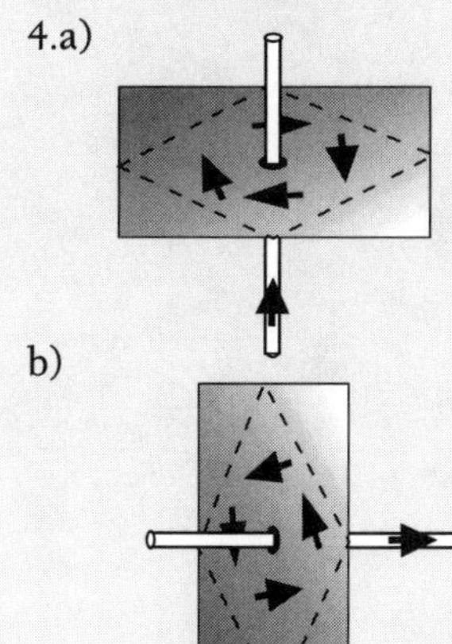

ANSWERS

Physics To Go

(continued)

6. The compass will point to the left hand side of the page. If the students don't see this, make a large loop of wire, and have them use the first left-hand rule to see the direction of the compass. They should note the wherever you put the compass inside the loop, it will point in the same direction. The compass will point in the same direction outside of the loop also. This will help them understand the next left-hand rule in the following activity.

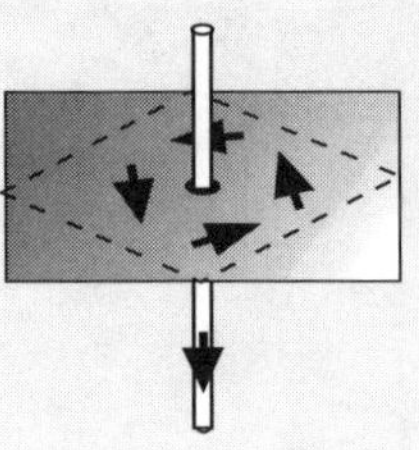

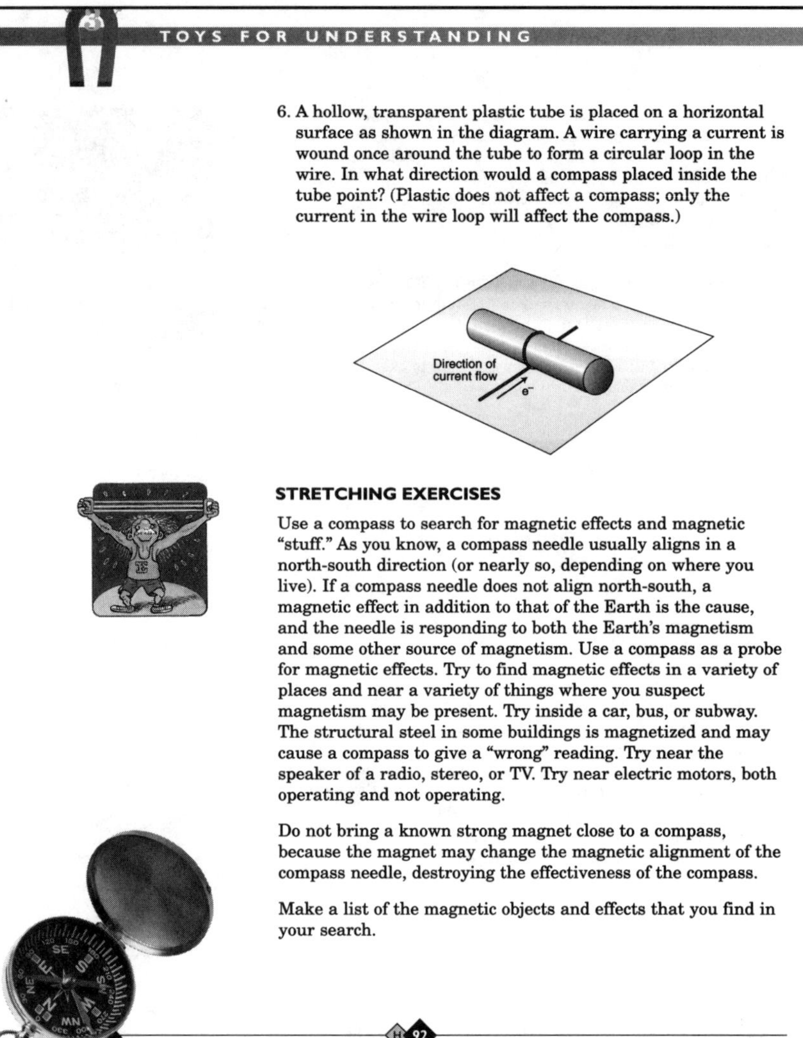

ANSWERS

Stretching Exercises

Students will enjoy this activity, as they will find that there are many different sources of magnetism even within their own house. Most electrical appliances will cause the compass to move, but may not show an accurate reading due to AC current.

NOTES

3

ACTIVITY TWO
Electromagnets

Background Information

The physics phenomenon involved in Activity Two is the magnetic field of a solenoid.

A wire wound into the shape of a solenoid as shown in For You To Do, Activity Two and carrying a direct current behaves similar to a bar magnet with the ends having north and south poles. Considering short segments of the wire of the solenoid as straight pieces of wire, the direction of the magnetic field of each segment can be found using the left-hand rule introduced in the teacher background information for Activity One. The combined effect of the magnetic fields of segments summed over the entire solenoid results in a magnetic field for the solenoid as shown below:

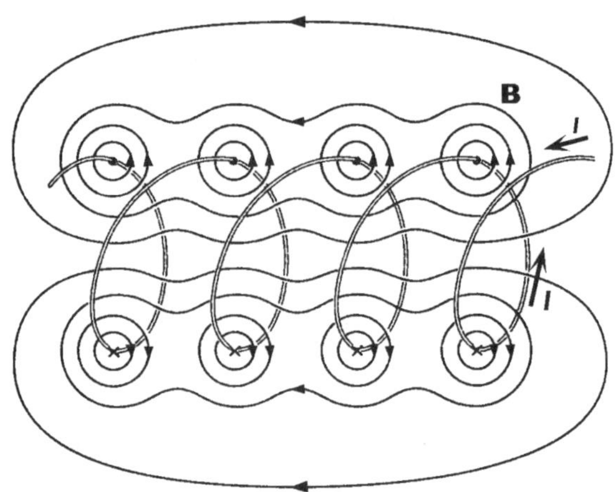

Left-hand rule for the polarity of a solenoid. A convenient rule for determining the magnetic polarity of a solenoid in relation to the direction of the current in the solenoid is to use the left hand to grasp the solenoid with the fingers pointing in the direction in which the current circles the windings. The extended left thumb points to the north pole of the solenoid.

The strength of the magnetic field near the center of a solenoid. The strength near the center (inside) a solenoid varies directly with the number of turns of wire, directly with the current flowing in the wire, and inversely with the length of the solenoid. The equation is:

$$B = m_0 NI/L$$

where B is the magnetic field strength in Tesla, m_0 is the permeability of air or vacuum (if the core is air or vacuum) in newtons/amp^2, N is the number of windings, I is the current in amps, and L is the length of the solenoid in meters.

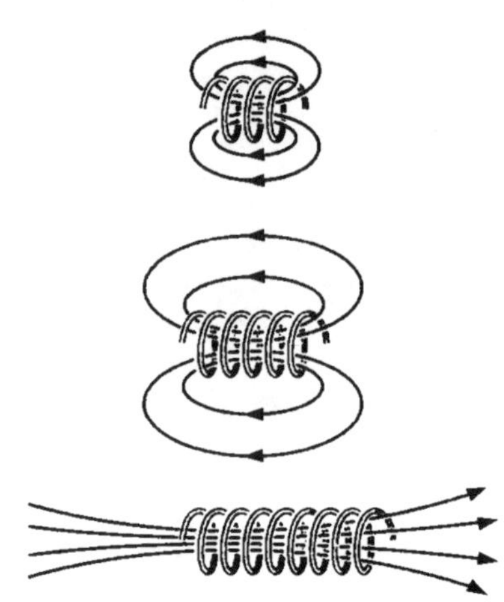

The effect of core material on the strength of a solenoid. If a ferromagnetic material such as iron (viz., a material having high tendency to become magnetized) is used as the core of a solenoid the magnetism of the core greatly adds to the strength of the magnetism. In such a case the constant m_0 in the above equation is replaced by the magnetic permeability, m, of the core material which commonly increases the magnetic effect by a factor of thousands.

Iron can be treated so that when used as a core material for a solenoid its magnetism "turns on and off" in concert with the electric current in the solenoid.

Notice in the diagram of the solenoid's field that inside the core of the solenoid the field lines are close together and point toward the right; outside the solenoid the field lines are farther apart and point toward the left. If a current-carrying wire were used as a probe to sample the magnetic field strength it would show that the field is stronger inside the solenoid than outside. This allows development of an alternate model for expressing the strength of a magnetic field in terms of the number of field lines which penetrate a unit of area oriented perpendicular to the direction of the field; the greater the "density" of lines penetrating a unit of area, the greater the magnetic field strength.

In the teacher background for Activity One the strength of a magnetic field was defined in terms of the force on a current-carrying wire oriented perpendicular to the direction of the field:

1 Tesla = 1 newton/ampere-meter

The magnetic field line model provides an alternate definition of field strength:

1 Tesla = 1 Weber per square meter

= 1 Wb/m^2

where the Weber (Wb) represents the number of magnetic field lines (and is called the "magnetic flux") and m^2 is the area penetrated by the flux [in more advanced treatments, the area is expressed as a vector; this will not be done here].

Symbolically, the alternate definition is expressed as:

$B = F/A$

where B is the magnetic field strength in Tesla, F is the magnetic flux (number of field lines) in Weber, and A is the area in m^2 .Therefore, the strength of a magnetic field may be expressed in two equivalent ways:

1 Tesla = 1 newton/ampere-meter
= 1 Weber/square meter

(Better to visualize magnetic fields penetrating small areas, physicists sometime prefer to express magnetic field strength in yet another unit, the "gauss" 1 Weber/m^2 = 10,000 gauss)

Active-ating the Physics InfoMall

A search for "electromagnet" will not be disappointing for this activity. Try it for yourself.

In For You To Do, step 3, students are asked to make a prediction. The importance of the prediction should not be overlooked; indeed, predictions force students to examine their understanding of a phenomena and actively engage thought. If you were to search the InfoMall to find more about the importance of predictions in learning, you would find that you need to limit your search. Sadly, not much information exists on the InfoMall regarding predictions about electromagnets. However, we can borrow from a search performed in *Active Physics: Sports* and *Active Physics: Transportation*: A search for "prediction*" AND "inertia." Try it. The prediction itself is important. Too often when we observe something new, we think "that's what I thought would happen" and learn nothing. By consciously recognizing our preconceptions, we have a chance to change the misconceptions.

The Stretching Exercise asks about magnetic levitation. A search for "magnetic levitation" produces a wonderful hit from "Large-scale applications of superconductivity," *Physics Today*, vol. 30, issue 7, 1977.

Planning for the Activity

Time Requirements

The class should be conducted in 40 - 50 minutes. If there is time, you may have the students do several different solenoids, to get enough data to see the relationship to the number of windings, and the relative strength of the electromagnet. Allow another class period to do the Inquiry Investigation.

Materials needed

Prepared solenoids with taps for varying the number of turns and a variety of core materials are available from science suppliers and may be used; however, greater impact may result from students winding their own solenoids. For the "homemade" version shown, you will need:

For each group:

- enamel-coated copper wire, approx. 1 m length
- drinking straw
- nail or rivet not having strong residual magnetism
- paper clips (10)
- hand generator (or power supply with a variable current)
- sandpaper for removing insulation from the wire ends
- magnetic compass

Advance Preparation and Setup

Demonstrate the magnetic field of a bar magnet and a solenoid, noting similarities. Apparatus for demonstrating the fields on an overhead projector are available from several science supply houses, and employ iron filings, or transparent compasses to visualize the fields.

Teaching Notes

Begin the lesson pursuing the students' understanding of electromagnetism. As an extension of What Do You Think?, demonstrate the fields of a bar magnet and solenoid (see Materials needed, above). For the solenoid, it would be helpful to use a diagram to show that the field can be inferred by considering short wire segments of the solenoid as straight conductors, each having a surrounding circular field which contributes to the total field of the solenoid (see Background Information). Be sure to include in the demonstration the obvious, but important, characteristic that the electromagnet can be turned on and off, while the bar magnet's magnetism can't.

Ask students which factors may be changed to affect the strength of the electromagnet or the bar magnet, and use this to establish the purpose of the For You To Do activity.

Here you may wish to establish, as a matter of definition, that the north pole of an electromagnet (or any magnet) is that pole which repels the north-seeking pole of a compass needle [this, of course, dictates that Earth's North Magnetic Pole is a south pole! - be prepared to deal with this if you bring this up, because it is likely that a student will come up with it].

Also, you may wish to share the second left-hand rule for remembering which is the north pole of a solenoid. This will be useful for students when in the next activity they wind a coil to make a galvanometer, and when later they wind armatures for motor/generators.

CAUTION: Remind students they are working with electricity, and caution must be taken. Anytime there is electricity running through a resistor wire, there can be a buildup of heat if the current is on for extended periods of time. Using a generator will help as students will not want to crank it for long periods of time. However, if you are using a power supply, make sure that the students will turn it off after use, and not leave it on for long periods of time or while they are writing up the lab activity.

NOTES

3

NOTES

Activity Two

Electromagnets

WHAT DO YOU THINK?

Large electromagnets are used to pick up cars in junk yards.

- **How does an electromagnet work?**
- **How could it be made stronger?**

Write your answer to this question in your *Active Physics log*. Be prepared to discuss your ideas with your small group and other members of your class.

FOR YOU TO DO

1. Wind 50 turns of wire on a drinking straw to form a solenoid as shown in the diagram on the next page. Use sandpaper to carefully clean the insulation from a short section of the wire ends to allow electrical connection of the solenoid to the generator.

ANSWERS

For You To Do

1. Student data.

Activity Overview

Students will be building their own electromagnet, using simple materials. They will discover the variables which give an electromagnet the force necessary to pick up large objects. There may be a need for some discussion about permanent and temporary magnets.

Student Objectives

Students will:

- describe and explain the magnetic field of a current-carrying solenoid.
- compare the field of a solenoid to the field of a bar magnet.
- identify the variables of an electromagnet and explain the effects of each variable.

ANSWERS FOR THE TEACHER ONLY

What Do You Think?

Electromagnets are the result of a changing electrical current in a wire surrounding a soft iron core. The greater the current flowing through the wire, or the greater the number of coils around the core, the greater the magnetic force will be.

ANSWERS

For You To Do

(continued)

2. a) Student data. The compass needle will orient either towards or away from the solenoid.

   b) If the compass needle points towards the solenoid, that will be the "south" pole (north-seeking pole). If the compass needle points away from the solenoid, that will be the "north" pole.

3. a) Change the wires to the different terminals of the generator.

   b) Students may also predict that reversing the direction of the generator will have the same effect.

4. a) Student data.

5. a) Students should notice that the solenoid causes the compass needle to point in the same direction as before without the nail inside the straw. There may be a visible increase in the strength of the electromagnet now.

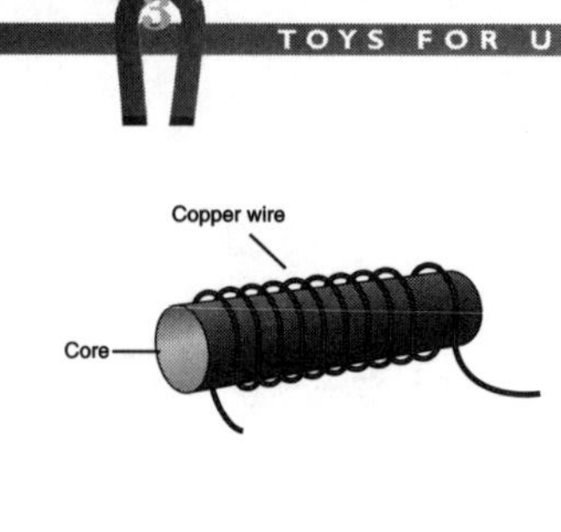

2. Carefully connect the wires from the generator to the wire ends of the solenoid. Bring one end of the solenoid near the magnetic compass and crank the generator to send a current through the solenoid. Observe any effect on the compass needle. Try several orientations of the solenoid to produce effects on the compass needle.
   a) Record your observations in your log.
   b) How can you tell the "polarity" of an electromagnet; that is, how can you tell which end of an electromagnet behaves as a north-seeking pole?

3. Predict what you can do to change the polarity of an electromagnet.
   a) Write your answer in your log.
   b) Test your prediction.

4. Use the solenoid wound on the drinking straw as an electromagnet to pick up paper clips.
   a) Record your observations in your log.

5. Carefully, slip a nail into the drinking straw to serve as a new core. Again, test the effect on a compass needle.
   a) Record your observations in your log.

6. Use the solenoid wound on the nail to pick up paper clips.
   a) Record your observations in your log.
   b) What evidence did you find that the choice of core material for an electromagnet makes a difference?

7. Predict what will happen when you increase the current running through the coiled wire solenoid. This can be done by increasing the speed at which you crank the generator.
   a) Write your answer in your log.
   b) Test your prediction by measuring how many paper clips can be picked up.

8. Predict what will happen when you increase the number of turns of wire forming the solenoid.
   a) Write your answer in your log.
   b) Test your prediction by measuring how many paper clips can be picked up.

6. a) Student data.

   b) There is an increase in the magnetic field, due to the iron core. The evidence is the number of paper clips will be larger than before.

7. a) Student data.

   b) As the students increase the speed of the generator, there will be an increase in the number of paper clips picked up. If you have a variable current power source, you may be able to show the effect is linear by graphing the number of paper clips picked up versus the current in the power source. (Depending on your power source, the effect may be hard to see. Try this before the students attempt it.)

8. a) Student data.

   b) Again, there should be a noticeable increase in the number of paper clips picked up as you increase the number of turns. Continue to use the nail as the core, and increase the number of turns by at least 20 turns. Again, the results may be graphed.

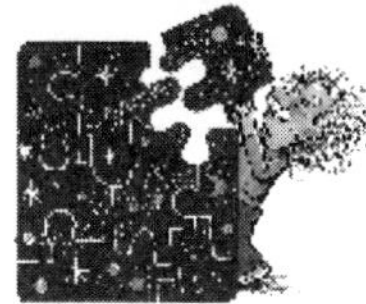

REFLECTING ON THE ACTIVITY AND THE CHALLENGE

An electromagnet, often constructed in the shape of a solenoid, and having an iron core, is the basic moving part of many electric motors. In this activity you learned how the amount of current and the number of turns of wire affect the strength of an electromagnet. You will be able to apply this knowledge to affect the speed and strength with which an electric motor of your own design rotates.

PHYSICS TO GO

1. Explain the differences between permanent magnets and electromagnets.
2. The diagram shows an electromagnet with a compass at each end. Copy the diagram and indicate the direction in which the compass needles will be pointing when a current is generated.

3. Which of the following will pick up more paper clips when an electric current is sent through the wire:
   a) a coil of wire with 20 turns, or a coil of wire with 50 turns?
   b) wire wound around a cardboard core, or wire wound around a steel core?
4. Explain conditions necessary for two electromagnets to attract or repel one another, as do permanent magnets when they are brought near one another.

ANSWERS

Physics To Go

1. Temporary magnets are ferromagnetic material, which have been treated in order to turn on and off with the current. An electromagnet is also considered a temporary magnet, but as will be shown in this activity is much stronger when there is a soft iron core. Permanent magnets are ferromagnetic material (iron, nickel, cobalt, and gadolinium) which retain their magnetic properties even when the current is removed.
2. The right side of the picture will be the north pole (compass needle will be pointing away), and the south pole (the compass needle will be pointing towards the solenoid) will be on the left side of the picture.
3. a) 50 turns

   b) steel core
4. In order for the electromagnets to repel each other, the wire would have to be wound opposite to each other:

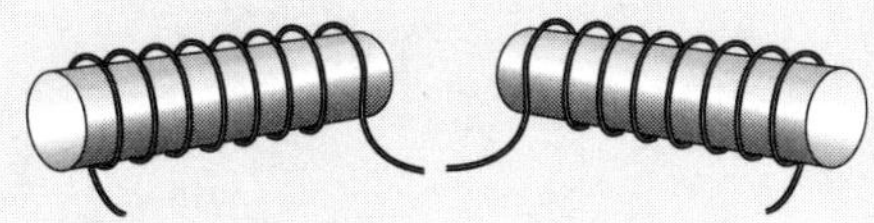

3

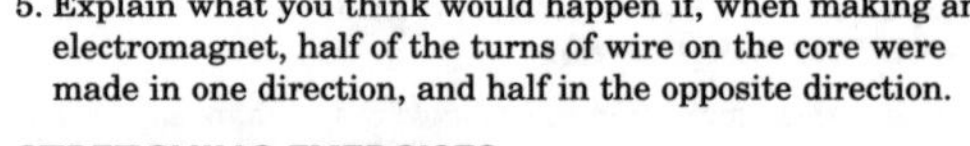

5. Explain what you think would happen if, when making an electromagnet, half of the turns of wire on the core were made in one direction, and half in the opposite direction.

STRETCHING EXERCISES

1. Find out how both permanent magnets and electromagnets are used. Do some library research to learn how electromagnets are used to lift steel in junk yards, make buzzers, or serve as part of electrical switching devices called "relays." For other possibilities, find out how magnetism is used in microphones and speakers within sound systems, or how "super-strong" permanent magnets made possible the small, high-quality, headset speakers for walkman radios and portable tape and CD players. Prepare a brief report on your findings.

2. Do some research to find out about "magnetic levitation." "Maglev" involves using super-conducting electromagnets to levitate, or suspend objects such as subway trains in air, thereby reducing friction and the "bumpiness" of the ride.

   a) What possibilities do "maglev" trains, cars, or other transportation devices have for the future?
   b) What advantages would such devices have?
   c) What problems need to be solved? Prepare a brief report on your research.

INQUIRY INVESTIGATION

Identify as many variables as you can which you think will affect the behavior of an electromagnet, and design an experiment to test the effect of each variable. Identify each variable, and describe what you would do to test its effects. After your teacher approves your procedures, do the experiments. Report your findings.

ANSWERS

Stretching Exercises

1. Student report.

2. a) Students answers will vary. Some students may report that it will reduce the amount of pollution in the atmosphere. Remind the students that the electricity to run the trains must come from some source (usually coal-fired, gas-fired or nuclear power). It might be possible to reduce the number of car and train accidents, the trains may run on time, without worrying about trains having to stop for other trains.

   b) Other advantages might be that cars would all move at the same speed reducing the need for police; reduced need for fossil fuels; reduced noise pollution in cities; etc.

   c) The technology has not moved very quickly, and there are some problems with getting the trains to run consistently. Also, there is a great quantity of energy needed to run the trains.

ACTIVITY THREE
Detect and Induce Currents

Background Information

The physics phenomenon involved in Activity Three is electromagnetic induction.

As discussed for generators in the student text for Chapter Three, Activity Four, which it is suggested you read before proceeding here, an electromagnetic force, or voltage, is produced in a conductor when relative motion between the conductor and a magnetic field happens in a way that causes the conductor to "cut" magnetic flux (or, in other words, cut magnetic field lines) as shown below.

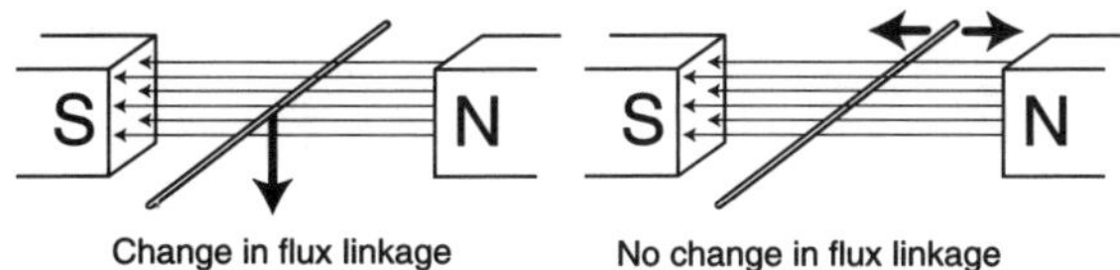

In the above example, thrusting the wire downward causes the field lines in the gap between the magnet poles to be cut by the conductor. This causes electrons in the wire to surge to the far end of the wire, giving that end of the wire an excess negative charge. The near end of the wire then has a deficiency of electrons and is positively charged. The voltage developed across the two ends of the wire is:

$$V = -\Delta F/\Delta t$$

where V is the voltage induced, or caused to arise, between the ends of the wire, and $\Delta F/\Delta t$ is the number of field lines cut by the wire per unit of time. The negative sign indicates that the current which would flow if the wire were to be part of a complete circuit would produce a magnetic field, and a force, which would oppose the original thrusting action which caused the induced current.

The induced voltage, and current if the wire is part of a circuit, happens only while lines are being cut by the conductor, and the amount of induced voltage at any instant depends directly on the rate at which the magnetic field lines are being changed (cut) at that instant. Also, the direction of the induced voltage depends on the direction of the cutting action. If in the above diagram the wire had been thrust upward, the electrons would have moved in the opposite direction. Finally, if a bundle of individual wires were used above instead of a single wire, the effect of induction would be multiplied by the number of wires.

There are many ways to stage situations where a conductor cuts magnetic flux to "induce" or "generate" electricity. One way is to rotate a loop, or coil, of wire in a magnetic field, as in a generator. Another is used by students in this activity: plunging a bar magnet in and out of a solenoid. In both cases, the principle involved is the one described above; only the geometric configuration of the conductors and fields are different.

Active-ating the Physics InfoMall

Our search for "electromagnet" in Activity Two also produced hits useful for this activity, including information on galvanometers. However, you should perform additional searches for "galvanometer*", too.

This activity also provides a great chance to search the calendar cart for information on Hans Christian Oersted. Of course, you should also search the entire InfoMall for information; what were the circumstances of his discovery?

For the Stretching Exercise, you can do a search of the InfoMall, or you can recall that the Textbook Trove's *Household Physics* was useful for much of this *Active Physics* book. Indeed, there is an entire chapter on House Wiring.

Planning for the Activity

Time Requirements

Allow at least one class period (40 - 50 minutes). If time allows, students may wish to change the number of variables in order to see different results (number of windings on the solenoid, on the galvanometer, etc.).

3

Materials needed

For each group:

For making a galvanometer:

- magnetic compass
- coated wire, approx. 1 m length
- sandpaper
- tape
- hand generator
- flashlight bulb and base
- electrical clips

For inducing current and detecting the same:

- coated wire, 2.5 m length
- cardboard tube (toilet tissue roll will do)
- sandpaper
- tape
- bar magnet
- galvanometer (above)
- electrical clips

Teaching Notes

Have students complete What Do You Think? In discussing What Do You Think?, mention that science, contrary to common notion, does not always proceed in deliberate ways. Sometimes accidental (serendipitous) discoveries provide breakthroughs, and Oersted's discovery involves one such occasion in the history of science.

CAUTION: regarding heating of the solenoid and the galvanometer, as in the previous activity.

ACTIVITY THREE: Detect and Induce Currents

Activity Three

Detect and Induce Currents

WHAT DO YOU THINK?

In 1820, the Danish physicist Hans Christian Oersted placed a long, straight, horizontal wire on top of a magnetic compass. Both the compass and the wire were resting on a horizontal surface, and both the length of the wire and the compass needle were oriented north-south. Next, Oersted sent a current through the wire, and happened upon one of the greatest discoveries in physics.

• **What do you think Oersted saw?**

Write your answer to this question in your *Active Physics log*. Be prepared to discuss your ideas with your small group and other members of your class.

FOR YOU TO DO

1. Wrap 10 turns of wire to form a coil that surrounds a magnetic compass. Wrap the wire on a diameter corresponding to the north-south markings of the compass scale, as shown in the diagram. Hold the turns of wire in place with tape, or use the method recommended by your teacher. Use sandpaper to carefully remove the insulation from a short section of the wire ends to allow electrical connection.

2. In step 1, you constructed a galvanometer, a device to detect and measure small currents. Carefully connect a hand generator, a light bulb, and the galvanometer, as shown on page H98 (in a series circuit). Rest the galvanometer so that the compass is horizontal, with the needle balanced, pointing North, and free to rotate. Also, turn the galvanometer, if necessary, so that the compass needle is aligned parallel to the turns of wire which pass over the top of the compass.

ANSWERS

For You To Do

1. Student activity.
2. Student activity.

Activity Overview

The students will build a galvanometer, test to see that it works, then show that moving a magnet through a solenoid, will produce a current. Any moving current will produce a magnetic field, and the magnetic field produced by the generator will cause the compass needle to move (depending on the direction of the current). You may want to remind the students of the left-hand rules to determine in which direction the field is, and in which direction the current is moving.

Student Objectives

Students will:

- explain how a simple galvanometer works.
- induce current using a magnet and coil.
- describe alternating current.
- recognize the relativity of motion.

ANSWERS FOR THE TEACHER ONLY

What Do You Think?

Students' answers will vary. Oersted saw that when there was a current flowing through the wire, the compass needle oriented itself in a particular direction.

3

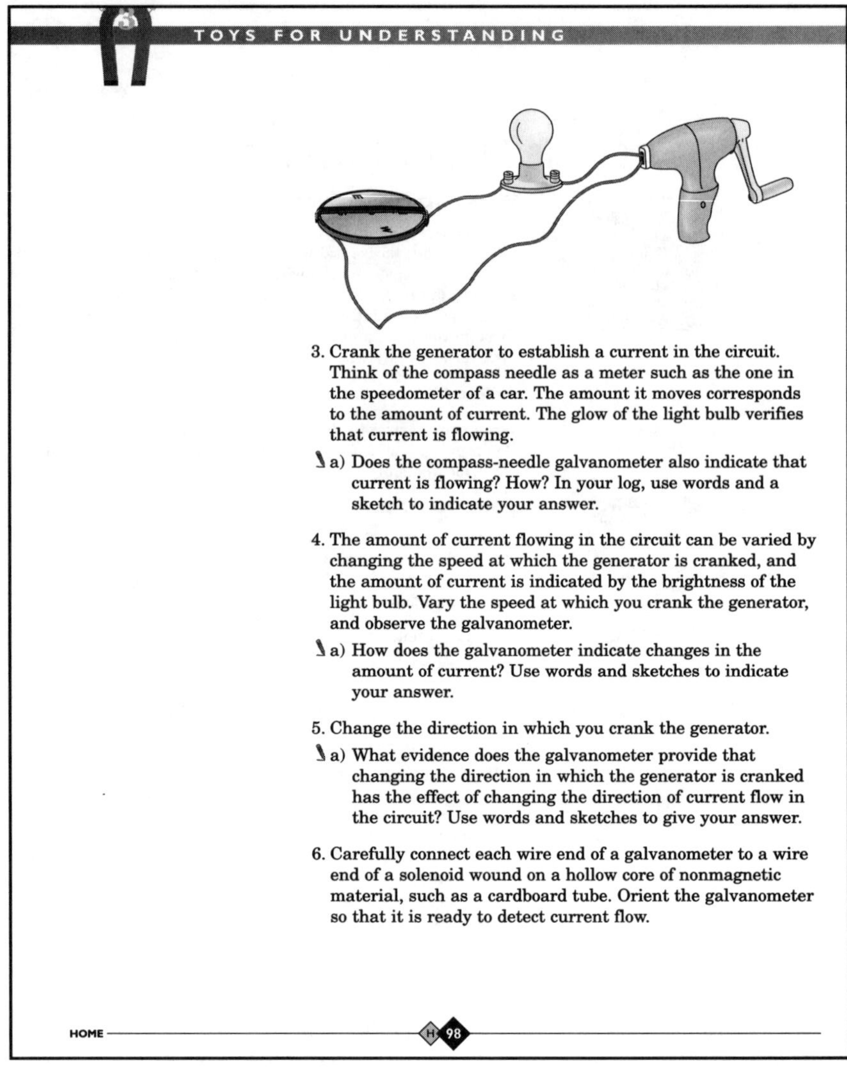

TOYS FOR UNDERSTANDING

3. Crank the generator to establish a current in the circuit. Think of the compass needle as a meter such as the one in the speedometer of a car. The amount it moves corresponds to the amount of current. The glow of the light bulb verifies that current is flowing.

   a) Does the compass-needle galvanometer also indicate that current is flowing? How? In your log, use words and a sketch to indicate your answer.

4. The amount of current flowing in the circuit can be varied by changing the speed at which the generator is cranked, and the amount of current is indicated by the brightness of the light bulb. Vary the speed at which you crank the generator, and observe the galvanometer.

   a) How does the galvanometer indicate changes in the amount of current? Use words and sketches to indicate your answer.

5. Change the direction in which you crank the generator.

   a) What evidence does the galvanometer provide that changing the direction in which the generator is cranked has the effect of changing the direction of current flow in the circuit? Use words and sketches to give your answer.

6. Carefully connect each wire end of a galvanometer to a wire end of a solenoid wound on a hollow core of nonmagnetic material, such as a cardboard tube. Orient the galvanometer so that it is ready to detect current flow.

HOME H 98

ANSWERS

For You To Do *(continued)*

3.a) Due to the magnetic field created by the moving current, the needle of the compass moves. The more it moves, the greater the current.

4.a) The galvanometer indicates changes in the current by deflecting more away from equilibrium, when there is no current flowing.

5.a) The compass needle should be deflected in the other direction.

6. Student activity.

7. Hold a bar magnet in one hand and the solenoid steady in the other hand. Rapidly plunge one end of the bar magnet into the hollow core of the solenoid, and then stop the motion of the magnet, bringing the end of the magnet to rest inside the solenoid. Another person should hold the galvanometer in a steady position so that it will not be disturbed if the solenoid is moved. Observe the galvanometer during the sequence. You may need to practice this a few times.
   a) Write your observations in your log.

8. Remove the magnet from the solenoid with a quick motion, and observe the galvanometer during the action.
   a) Record your observations.
   b) A current is produced! How does the direction of the current caused, or induced, when the end of the magnet is entering the solenoid, compare to the direction of the current when the magnet is leaving the solenoid?
   c) How can you detect the direction of the current in each case?

ANSWERS

For You To Do *(continued)*

7. a) Students should notice a deflection of the needle.

8. a) Again, the students should notice a deflection of the needle, only in the opposite direction.
   b) When going in, the current is one direction and when coming out, the current is going in the other direction.
   c) The direction of the current is observed by the deflection of the compass needle, first in one direction and then in the other.

ANSWERS

For You To Do

(continued)

9. a) Students will see that the current will still be induced, but in the opposite direction of the first case.

   b) As you increase the speed of the movement, the current will be increased, and the compass needle will show a greater deflection.

   c) The magnet must be moving to induce a current.

   d) There will be no difference, as it is the relative movement that causes the induction, not the movement of one or the other.

   e) This will in effect create a greater relative movement, and therefore have the effect of increasing the induced current.

9. Modify and repeat steps 7 and 8 to answer the following questions.
   a) What, if anything, about the created or induced current changes if the opposite end of the bar magnet is plunged in and out of the solenoid?
   b) How does the induced current change if the speed at which the magnet is moved in and out of the solenoid is changed?
   c) What is the amount of induced current when the magnet is not moving (stopped)?
   d) What is the effect on the induced current of holding the magnet stationary and moving the solenoid back and forth over either end of the magnet?
   e) What is the effect of moving both the magnet and the solenoid?

REFLECTING ON THE ACTIVITY AND THE CHALLENGE

In this activity you discovered that you can produce electricity. A current is created or induced when a magnet is moved in and out of a solenoid. The current flows back and forth, changing direction with each reversal of the motion of the magnet. Such a current is called an alternating current, and you may recognize that name as the kind of current that flows in household circuits. It is frequently referred to by its abbreviated form, "AC." It is the type of current that is used to run electric motors in home appliances. Part of your challenge is to explain to the children how a motor operates in terms of basic principles of physics or to show how electricity can be produced from an external energy source. This activity will help you with that part of the challenge.

PHYSICS TO GO

1. An electric motor takes electricity and converts it into movement. The movement can be a fan, a washing machine, or a CD player. The galvanometer may be thought of as a crude electric motor. Discuss that statement, using forms of energy as part of your discussion.

ANSWERS

Physics To Go

1. The electric current creates a magnetic field, which induces a current in a coil of wires. This coil of wire (galvanometer) creates a magnetic field, which causes the needle to move (like poles repel, unlike poles attract). In terms of energy, the magnetic field causes a force in the wire, which moves the electrons (electrical kinetic energy). These moving electrons cause a force to act on the magnet (compass needle), thereby converting electrical energy to the kinetic energy of the needle.

2. Explain how the galvanometer works to detect the amount and direction of an electric current.

3. How could the galvanometer be made more sensitive, so that it could detect very weak currents?

4. An electric generator takes motion and turns it into electricity. The electricity can then be used for many purposes. The solenoid and the bar magnet, as used in this activity could be thought of as a crude electric generator. Explain the truth of that statement, referring to specific forms of energy in your explanation.

5. If the activity were to be repeated so that you would be able to see only the galvanometer and not the solenoid, the magnet, and the person moving the equipment, would you be able to tell from only the response of the galvanometer what was being moved, the magnet or the solenoid or both? Explain your answer.

6. Part of the chapter challenge is to explain how the motor and generator toy works.
   a) Write a paragraph explaining how a motor works.
   b) Write a paragraph explaining how a generator works.

7. In generating electricity in this activity, you moved the magnet or the coil. How can you use each of the following resources to move the magnet?
   a) wind
   b) water
   c) steam

STRETCHING EXERCISE

Find out about the 120 V (volt) AC used in home circuits. If household current alternates, at what rate does it surge back-and-forth? Write down any information about AC that you can find and bring it to class.

ANSWERS

Stretching Exercise

AC (alternating current) is named as such due to the "back and forth" motion of the electrons in the wire. Most household circuits operate on 60 Hz (60 cycles per second). European homes operate on 50 Hz, but with a 240 V circuit. If you try to use an appliance (i.e., hair dryer, shaver, radio, etc.) designed for Europe in North America, you can cause serious damage to the appliance, and possibly to ourselves or the circuits in your home.)

ANSWERS

Physics To Go

(continued)

2. The galvanometer needle is deflected one way with the current moving in one direction. When the current is moving in the opposite direction the galvanometer will be deflected the other way.
3. The greater number of coils around the galvanometer will cause a greater deflection with the same current, so increasing the number of coils, will give a greater deflection for a smaller current.
4. As you move your hand in and out of the solenoid (kinetic energy) electrical energy is produced in the wire of the solenoid.
5. It is only the relative movement of the magnet and the solenoid that creates the electric current. You would not be able to tell which was being moved.
6. a) Answers will vary. Look for the changing electrical current to produce a force on the magnet inside the coils of wire (solenoid) which cause a rotor or axle to turn.
   b) Answers will vary. As you move a magnet through a coil of wire, an electrical current is produced.
7. a) Wind is the kinetic energy required to move the blades of the generator. This will cause the magnet to move through the coils of wire. This, then, generates the electrical current.
   b) The gravitational potential energy or the kinetic energy of moving water will turn the axle of the (turbine) generator, which moves a magnet through the coils of wires. Again, this produces an electrical current.
   c) Using steam drives a turbine which creates the electrical current as the magnet is turned through the coils of the solenoid.

3

Activity Three A: Demonstration

Twin Coil Swings

FOR YOU TO DO

The following is a demonstration to illustrate the change from mechanical energy to electrical energy. This will be the demonstration: (You may ask some students to design this and report this to class as an alternative project. Alternately, you may have this set up as a curiosity as the students enter the classroom. Then ask for volunteers to come up and see what they can do to make one side move, by touching only the other side.)

Demonstrate that the twin coil swings, moving one to cause movement in the other due to induced current. Ask students to identify which is acting as a generator, and which as a motor. Switch to move the opposite coil – reversible?

Ask for, and try, changes in the system that will change the swings from moving the "same way" to "opposite ways." Try moving one of the magnets instead of a swing to start up the system; can you "pump" the swing if you hit the proper rhythm (the natural period of the swings)?

Insert a galvanometer to detect the induced current. What is the "E & M connection?" Expect that students will regard this system as a curiosity and want to know what makes it work. Do not offer a full explanation, but suggest that soon students will have a basis for understanding its principles of operation. If possible, leave the apparatus set up in the classroom so that students can return to it to develop explanations of it as their knowledge increases. For now, use the device to establish the meanings of the generator effect (mechanical to electrical energy) and the motor effect (electrical energy to mechanical energy).

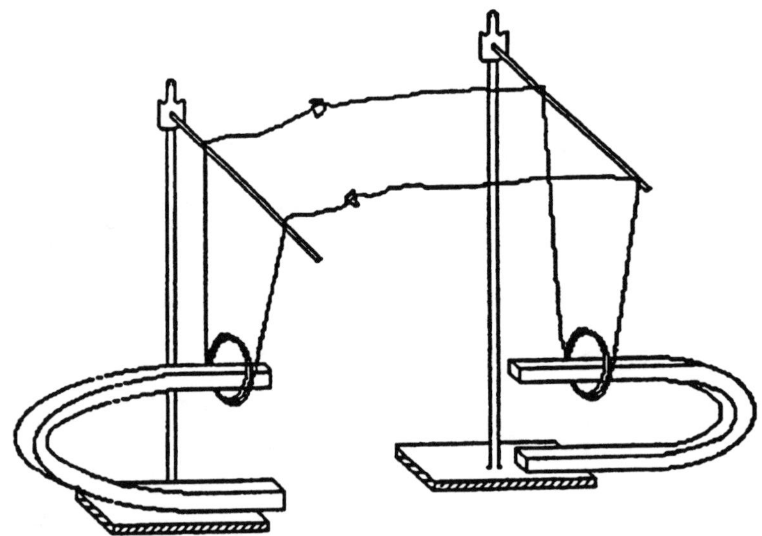

For use with *Home*, Chapter 3, ACTIVITY THREE: Detect and Induce Currents

NOTES

3

ACTIVITY FOUR
AC & DC Currents

Background Information

The principles of electromagnetic induction introduced in Activity Three are applied to AC and DC generators in Activity Four. It is suggested that you read the background information for Activity Three if you have not already done so.

It is also suggested that you read the detailed treatment of AC and DC generators presented in the For You To Read section of Activity Four before conducting the activity with students.

The hertz (Hz) as a unit of frequency. The hertz is introduced in the Stretching Exercise of Activity Four as the unit frequency; here, it is applied to AC electricity. A common misconception about this unit of measurement is shown when a frequency of, for example, 60 Hz is expressed as 60 cycles per second, or 60 vibrations per second, or 60 [fill in the noun] per second. While it is true that terms such as "cycles," "vibrations" or other descriptive nouns may enhance communication, it is essential to recognize that, by definition:

1 hertz = (second)-1 = 1/second

Therefore, the mathematically appropriate way to express frequency in equations is, for example, 60 Hz = 60/s; descriptive words such as "cycles" or "vibrations" are not included because they are not included in the formal definition of the hertz as a unit of measurement. Carrying such descriptive terms in the numerator of expressions of frequency within calculations lead to trouble with dimensional analysis of units because the terms do not cancel; within calculations involving equations it is best to express Hz as reciprocal seconds.

Electric power plants in the USA are required to maintain 60 Hz as the precise frequency of AC voltage distributed on the power grid. The reason for maintaining a dependable frequency is that many devices such as clocks and motors are designed to operate in synchronization with the frequency, or a multiple thereof. It should also be recognized that one complete AC cycle of 1/60 second duration contains two pulses of current, one in each direction. Therefore, the "pulse frequency" of 60 Hz electricity is 120 Hz; sometimes it can be heard being emitted from electrical devices as a "hum" corresponding to a pitch of 120 Hz.

Active-ating the Physics InfoMall

We already did a search earlier for "DC generator" so now we should add to this a search for "AC generator." Again, the results are pleasing. Combine this search with the DC search, and much of this activity is covered. You can also find graphs of the generator outputs in these searches.

For You To Do step 4 begins working with graphs. Graphs are a tool that can be difficult for some students. Search for "difficult*" AND "graph*" in the Same Paragraph. The first hit is "Student difficulties in connecting graphs and physics: Example from kinematics," from the *American Journal of Physics*, vol. 55, issue 6, 1987. The second hit is "Student difficulties with graphical representations of negative values of velocity," from *The Physics Teacher*, vol. 27, issue 4, 1989. While these and many of the other hits are from kinematics, the findings related to graphs can still be enlightening. You should read these.

Planning for the Activity

Time Requirements

Allow about one 40 - 50 minute class period for this activity.

Materials needed

For the class (demonstration):

- AC generator, large demonstration type
- DC generator, large demonstration type
- galvanometer, demonstration type
- light bulb and base to show generator output

Advance Preparation and Setup

It is assumed that limitations on equipment will require that this activity be performed as a teacher demonstration. Large, low voltage, demonstration AC and DC generators are available from science suppliers which have exposed parts, and many are convertible, serving four-ways (AC, DC generators and motors). Such a device, or the equivalent, is needed for this activity.

Be familiar with the progression of For You To Do. The students may or may not be able to fully grasp the concept of a sinusoidal curve. They can better appreciate it when they have seen the dimming of the bulb, and the changing of the galvanometer.

Teaching Notes

Review with the students the result of passing a wire through a permanent magnet. They need to understand that only when the wire is moving perpendicular to the magnetic field lines will a current be produced. Ask them questions such as: What if the wire is moving at an angle? Therefore, only the perpendicular vector portion of the wire will produce the current. Have the students come up with the fact that the magnitude of the current will be less than when passed through the magnetic field lines at 90°. This will help them understand that the current is not simply on and off, but variable.

It may be difficult for all the class to see the galvanometer and the changes, so it is important to have the setup of the apparatus so that all will be able to see. If a physics software simulation program is available, you might allow the students some time to use the software during another class.

Safety issues are the same as they are with any electronic equipment. Do not let the students operate the equipment without proper supervision.

The students may have to be reminded of the Law of Conservation of Energy. Energy cannot be created nor destroyed, only converted from one form to another. Some students may believe that the only energy that has to be added to the system of the generators of power plants is just enough to overcome the effects of friction of the mechanical parts. If this were the case, you would be creating energy from nothing which is impossible. The energy input must be greater than the energy output in order to account for the "loss" of energy due to friction.

Activity Overview

This activity expands on the information presented in Activity Three. In the previous activities, we saw how the movement of a wire in a magnetic field produced a current in that wire. In this Activity, the students will explore step by step, how an AC generator works. It involves the rotation of a coil of wire in a magnetic field to produce a continuous current that can be used for an electrical device.

Student Objectives

Students will:

- describe the induced voltage and current when a coil is rotated in a magnetic field.
- compare AC and DC generators in terms of commutators and outputs.
- sketch sinusoidal output wave forms.

ANSWERS FOR THE TEACHER ONLY

What Do You Think?

Many different answers will come from the students. Look for thoughtful responses. Some answers might include: heat, geothermal, mechanical, nuclear, light, wind, water, gas-fired hydroelectric, etc.

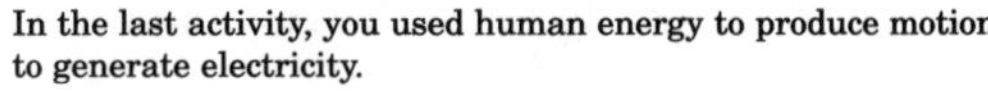

Activity Four

AC & DC

WHAT DO YOU THINK?

In the last activity, you used human energy to produce motion to generate electricity.

- **What other kinds of energy can be used to generate electricity?**

Write your answer to this question in your *Active Physics log*. Be prepared to discuss your ideas with your small group and other members of your class.

FOR YOU TO DO

AC Generator

1. Your teacher will explain and demonstrate a hand-operated, alternating current (AC) generator. During the demonstration, make the observations necessary to gain the information needed to answer these questions:

   a) When the AC generator is used to light a bulb, describe the brightness of the bulb when the generator is cranked slowly, and then rapidly. Write your observations in your log.

   b) When the AC generator is connected to a galvanometer, describe the action of the galvanometer needle when the generator is cranked slowly, and then rapidly.

HOME  H 102

ANSWERS

For You To Do

1. a) The brightness of the bulb appears to increase as the speed is increased.

   b) When the generator is cranked slowly, there is only a small deflection of the galvanometer needle. As the speed increases the needle's deflection increases. The needle also goes back and forth or positive and negative as the generator is cranked.

2. It is easier to understand the creation of a current if you think of a set of invisible threads to signify the magnetic field of the permanent magnets. The very thin threads fill the space and connect the north pole of one magnet with the south pole of the other magnet. If the wire of the generator is imagined to be a very thin, sharp knife, the question you must ask is whether the knife (the wire) can "cut" the threads (the magnetic field lines). If the wire moves in such a way that it can cut the field lines, then a current is generated. If the wire moves in such a way that it does not cut the field lines, then no current is generated.

   a) Look at the diagrams of the magnetic fields shown. In which case, I, II, or III will a current be generated?

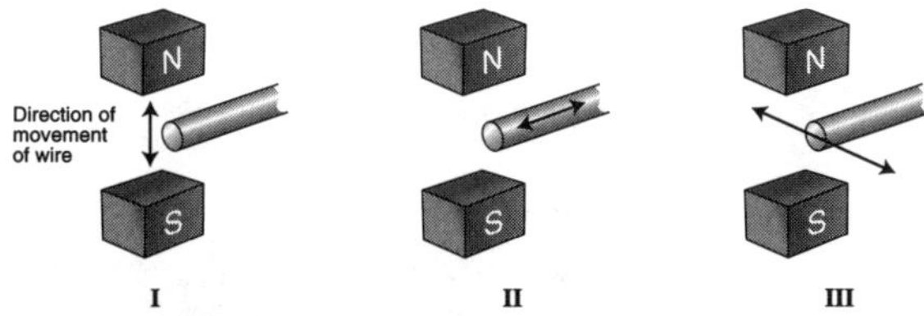

3. The following diagram shows the position of the rotating coil of an AC generator at instants separated by one-fourth of a rotation of the coil. Build a small model of the rectangular coil so that you can move the model to help you understand the drawings. The coil model can be constructed by carefully bending a coat hanger into the shape of the rectangular coil. Rest the coil between two pieces of paper—label the left paper N for the north pole of a magnet; label the right paper S for the south pole of a magnet.

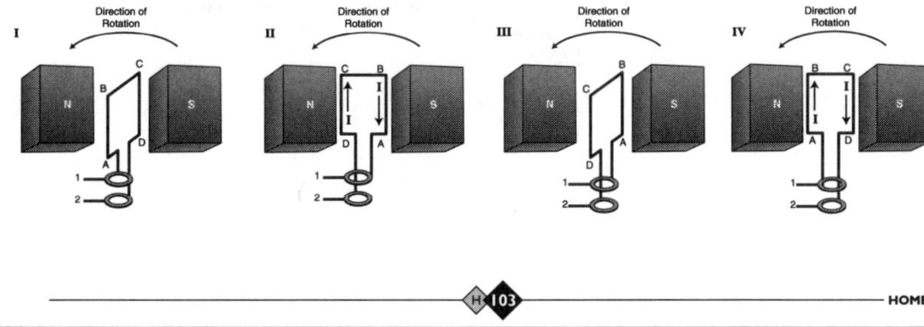

3

ANSWERS

For You To Do *(continued)*

2. a) Case III will generate a current.

3. Student activity.

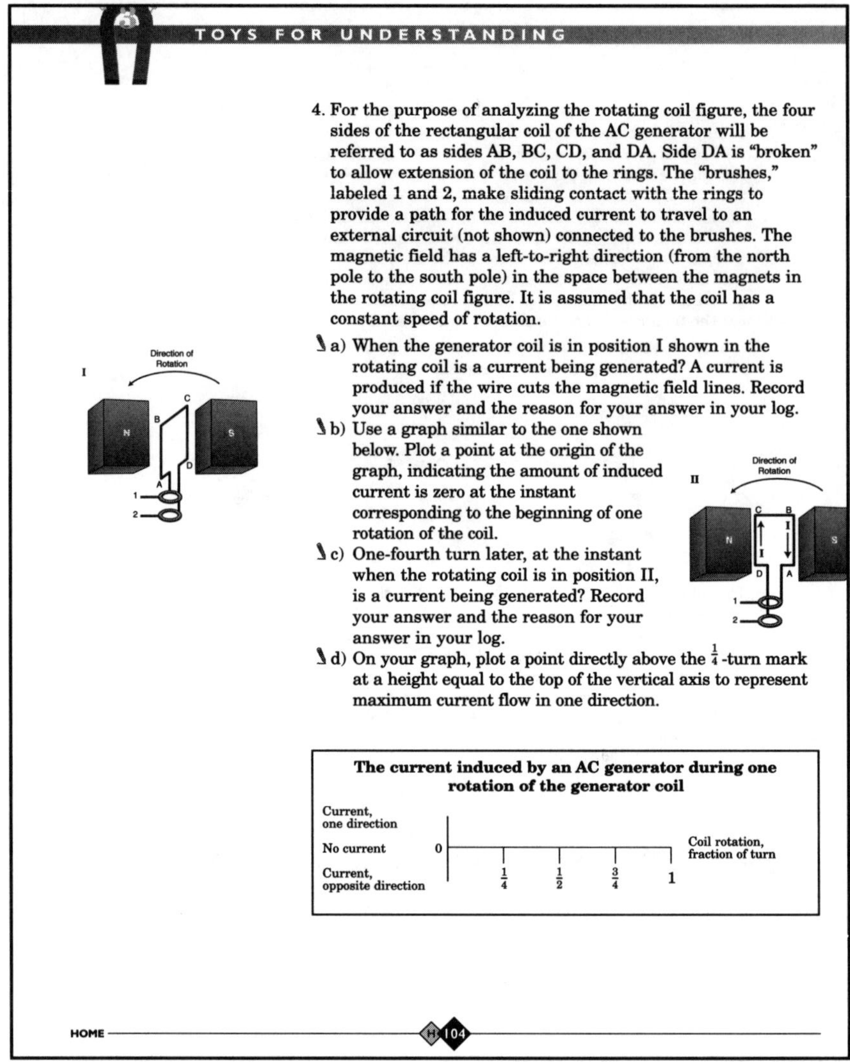

4. For the purpose of analyzing the rotating coil figure, the four sides of the rectangular coil of the AC generator will be referred to as sides AB, BC, CD, and DA. Side DA is "broken" to allow extension of the coil to the rings. The "brushes," labeled 1 and 2, make sliding contact with the rings to provide a path for the induced current to travel to an external circuit (not shown) connected to the brushes. The magnetic field has a left-to-right direction (from the north pole to the south pole) in the space between the magnets in the rotating coil figure. It is assumed that the coil has a constant speed of rotation.

a) When the generator coil is in position I shown in the rotating coil is a current being generated? A current is produced if the wire cuts the magnetic field lines. Record your answer and the reason for your answer in your log.

b) Use a graph similar to the one shown below. Plot a point at the origin of the graph, indicating the amount of induced current is zero at the instant corresponding to the beginning of one rotation of the coil.

c) One-fourth turn later, at the instant when the rotating coil is in position II, is a current being generated? Record your answer and the reason for your answer in your log.

d) On your graph, plot a point directly above the $\frac{1}{4}$-turn mark at a height equal to the top of the vertical axis to represent maximum current flow in one direction.

The current induced by an AC generator during one rotation of the generator coil

ANSWERS

For You To Do *(continued)*

4. a) There is no current as the wire is moving parallel to the magnetic field.

   b) Student activity.

   c) Current is generated and should be at a maximum.

   d) Student activity.

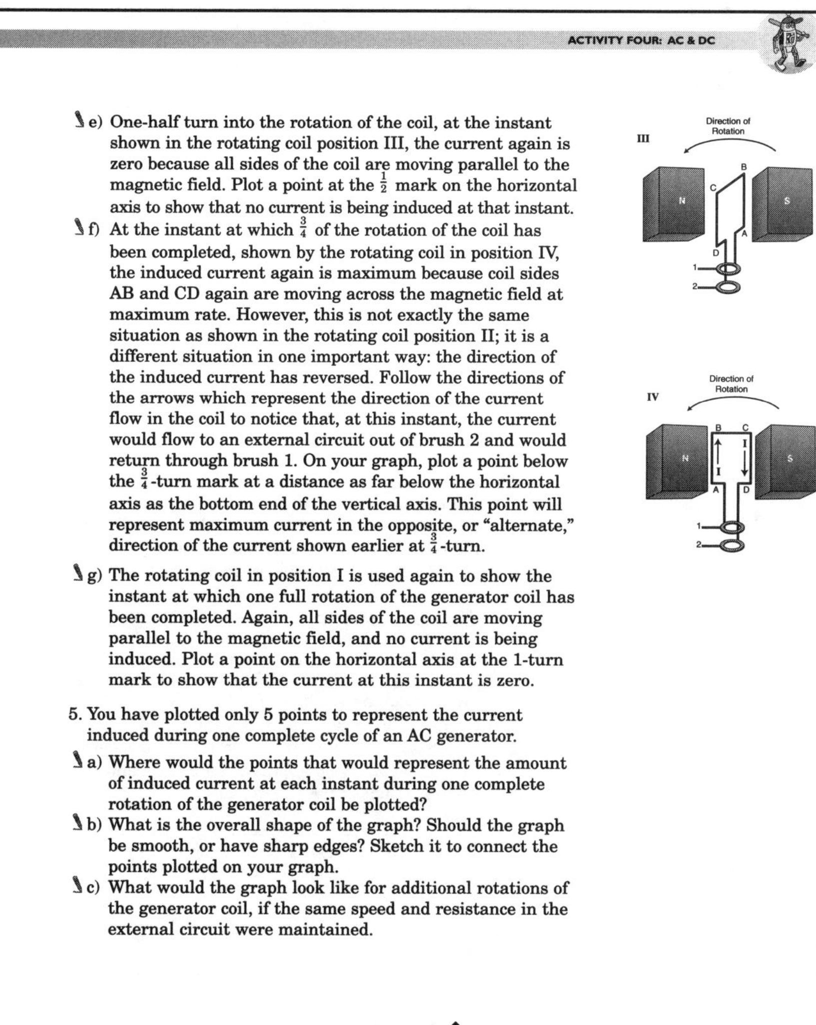

e) One-half turn into the rotation of the coil, at the instant shown in the rotating coil position III, the current again is zero because all sides of the coil are moving parallel to the magnetic field. Plot a point at the $\frac{1}{2}$ mark on the horizontal axis to show that no current is being induced at that instant.

f) At the instant at which $\frac{3}{4}$ of the rotation of the coil has been completed, shown by the rotating coil in position IV, the induced current again is maximum because coil sides AB and CD again are moving across the magnetic field at maximum rate. However, this is not exactly the same situation as shown in the rotating coil position II; it is a different situation in one important way: the direction of the induced current has reversed. Follow the directions of the arrows which represent the direction of the current flow in the coil to notice that, at this instant, the current would flow to an external circuit out of brush 2 and would return through brush 1. On your graph, plot a point below the $\frac{3}{4}$-turn mark at a distance as far below the horizontal axis as the bottom end of the vertical axis. This point will represent maximum current in the opposite, or "alternate," direction of the current shown earlier at $\frac{3}{4}$-turn.

g) The rotating coil in position I is used again to show the instant at which one full rotation of the generator coil has been completed. Again, all sides of the coil are moving parallel to the magnetic field, and no current is being induced. Plot a point on the horizontal axis at the 1-turn mark to show that the current at this instant is zero.

5. You have plotted only 5 points to represent the current induced during one complete cycle of an AC generator.

a) Where would the points that would represent the amount of induced current at each instant during one complete rotation of the generator coil be plotted?

b) What is the overall shape of the graph? Should the graph be smooth, or have sharp edges? Sketch it to connect the points plotted on your graph.

c) What would the graph look like for additional rotations of the generator coil, if the same speed and resistance in the external circuit were maintained.

3

ANSWERS

For You To Do *(continued)*

e) Student activity.

f) Students will note that the current should be flowing in the opposite direction, but at a maximum.

g) Student activity.

5. a) The points should be plotted along a line that would eventually be a sinusoidal curve.

b) Students may have to be shown that the points do in fact represent a smooth curve rather than a straight line of best fit.

c) The graph will have a consistent up and down wave-like motion.

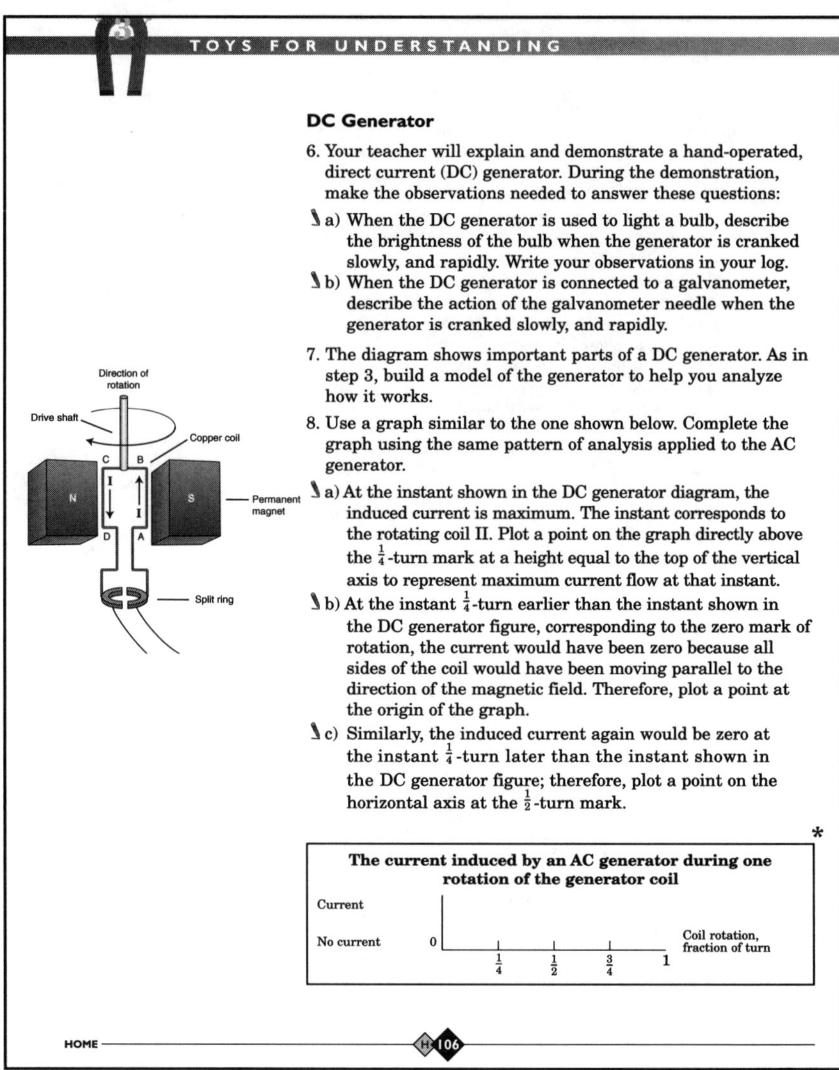

DC Generator

6. Your teacher will explain and demonstrate a hand-operated, direct current (DC) generator. During the demonstration, make the observations needed to answer these questions:
   a) When the DC generator is used to light a bulb, describe the brightness of the bulb when the generator is cranked slowly, and rapidly. Write your observations in your log.
   b) When the DC generator is connected to a galvanometer, describe the action of the galvanometer needle when the generator is cranked slowly, and rapidly.

7. The diagram shows important parts of a DC generator. As in step 3, build a model of the generator to help you analyze how it works.
8. Use a graph similar to the one shown below. Complete the graph using the same pattern of analysis applied to the AC generator.
   a) At the instant shown in the DC generator diagram, the induced current is maximum. The instant corresponds to the rotating coil II. Plot a point on the graph directly above the $\frac{1}{4}$-turn mark at a height equal to the top of the vertical axis to represent maximum current flow at that instant.
   b) At the instant $\frac{1}{4}$-turn earlier than the instant shown in the DC generator figure, corresponding to the zero mark of rotation, the current would have been zero because all sides of the coil would have been moving parallel to the direction of the magnetic field. Therefore, plot a point at the origin of the graph.
   c) Similarly, the induced current again would be zero at the instant $\frac{1}{4}$-turn later than the instant shown in the DC generator figure; therefore, plot a point on the horizontal axis at the $\frac{1}{2}$-turn mark.

*

The current induced by an AC generator during one rotation of the generator coil

* Please note: this diagram is for current induced by a DC generator, not an AC generator.

ANSWERS

For You To Do *(continued)*

6. a) Again, the students should note that the light dims and brightens regularly, with the brightness increasing as the cranking increases.

   b) The galvanometer needle will go from the equilibrium position to one side or the other. It will not go back and forth across the equilibrium as it did for the AC generator. Increasing the speed of the cranking, will increase the amount of the deflection.

7. Student activity.

8. a) Student activity.

   b) Student activity.

   c) Student activity.

9. Notice the arrangement used to transfer current from the generator to the external circuit for the DC generator. It is different from the arrangement used for the AC generator. The DC generator has a "split-ring commutator" for transferring the current to the external circuit. Notice that if the coil shown in the DC generator figure were rotated $\frac{1}{4}$-turn in either direction, the "brush" ends that extend from the coil to make rubbing contact with each half of the split ring would reverse, or switch, the connection to the external circuit. Further, notice that the connection to the external circuit would be reversed at the same instant that the induced current in the coil reverses due to the change in direction in which the sides of the coil move through the magnetic field. The outcome is that while the current induced in the coil alternates, or changes direction each $\frac{1}{2}$-rotation, the current delivered to the external circuit always flows in the same direction. Current that flows always in one direction is called direct current, or DC.
   a) Plot a point on the graph at a point directly above the $\frac{3}{4}$-turn mark at the same height as the point plotted earlier for the $\frac{1}{4}$-turn mark.
   b) As done for the AC generator, find out how to connect the points plotted on this graph to represent the amount of current delivered always in the same direction to the external circuit during the entire cycle.

REFLECTING ON THE ACTIVITY AND THE CHALLENGE

It is time to begin preparing for the chapter challenge. Now that you know how a generator works, you should begin to think about toys that might generate electricity. You should also think about how you could assemble "junk" into a toy generator, or do some research on homemade generators and motors.

ANSWERS

For You To Do *(continued)*

9. a) Student activity.

   b) Again, the students should notice that the points should give a smooth curved line. However, the shape of the graph will differ in that the points will only be on the positive side of equilibrium in the shape of a letter "m." The pattern will appear to be a series of bumps rather than a sinusoidal curve.

3

ANSWERS

Physics To Go

1. a) An electric generator is used to convert mechanical energy (cranking the generator) to electrical energy.

   b) An electric motor is used to convert electrical energy to mechanical energy.

2. Direct current travels in one direction only, whereas alternating current appears to travel back and forth.

AC:

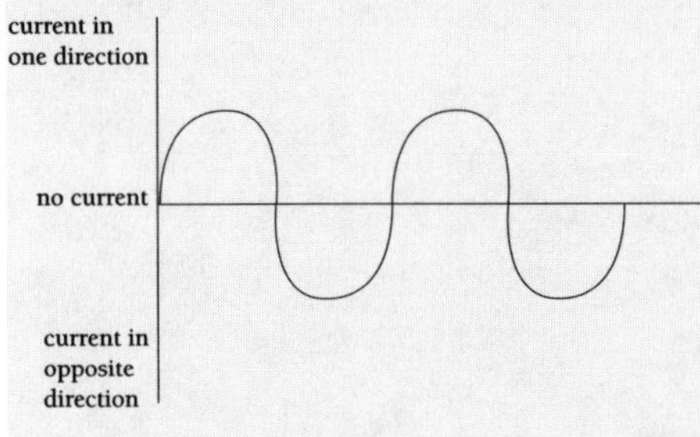

DC:

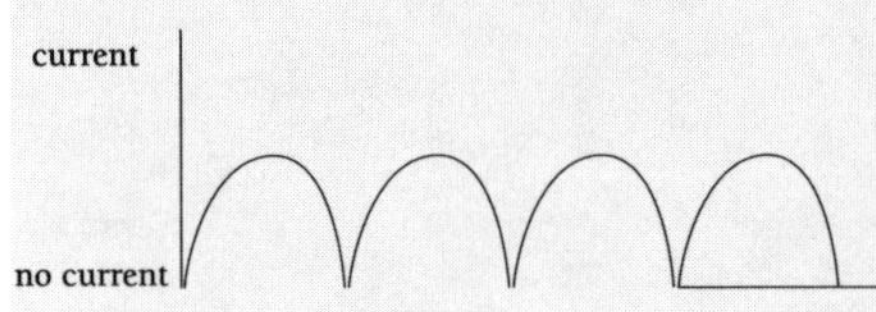

3. A current is produced in a wire only when the wire cuts through the magnetic field lines at a 90° angle. The wire must be moving in order for a current to be produced.

TOYS FOR UNDERSTANDING

PHYSICS TO GO

1. What is the purpose of
   a) an electric generator?
   b) an electric motor?
2. How does a direct current differ from an alternating current? Use graphs to illustrate your answer.
3. In an electric generator, a wire is placed in a magnetic field. Under what conditions is a current generated?

STRETCHING EXERCISES

1. What is the meaning of "Hertz," abbreviated "Hz," often seen as a unit of measurement associated with electricity or stereo sound components such as amplifiers and speakers?
2. What does it mean to say that household electricity has a frequency of 60 Hz?
3. Have you ever heard 60 Hz AC being emitted from a fluorescent light or a transformer?
4. Look at a catalog or visit a store where sound equipment is sold, and check out the "frequency response" of speakers—what does it mean?
5. Hertz was a person, Heinrich Hertz, a 19th-century German physicist. Find out about the unit of measurement named after him, and write a brief report on what you find.

H 108

ANSWERS

Stretching Exercises

1. Hertz (Hz) is the unit of measurement for frequency.
2. In electrical appliances, it is referring to the AC circuit, which in North America is on a 60 Hz frequency. It means that the circuit is changing directions 60 times per second.
3. The sound might be referred to as a low hum. It can be heard by high voltage power lines, as well as in-ground transformers.
4. In speakers the frequency is referring to the frequency of sound. 20 Hz is generally accepted as the lowest sound heard, and depending on the individual, the highest frequency is about 12,000 to 16,000 Hz. In sound Hz is referring to the number of vibrations per second. The greater the number of vibrations, the higher the frequency.
5. Student report.

Activity Four A: Demonstration

Falling Magnet

FOR YOU TO DO

Equipment (teacher demonstration):

- rigid copper pipe, 3/4 inch diameter, 6 foot length (approx.), sold at plumbing supply stores in 10 foot lengths.
- cow magnet (or a cylindrical magnet having a diameter less than the inside diameter of the copper pipe).
- clamps and supports to hold the copper pipe in a vertical orientation with some space between the ends of the pipe and the classroom floor and ceiling.
- stepladder.

As an extension of What Do You Think?, ascend the stepladder and announce that you are going to drop the magnet through the copper pipe. Ask students if a current should be induced in the pipe, reminding them of the effect of relative motion between a magnet and a conductor observed in Activity Three, Part 2. Also ask what effect, if any, there should be on the free fall of the magnet, neglecting any small amount of friction if the magnet hits the wall of the pipe during its fall. Then drop the magnet through the pipe. Students will observe that the fall of the magnet is profoundly retarded.

Ask students why the fall of the magnet was retarded. As a hint, suggest that they think back to using the hand generator under "load" and "no load" conditions – does an induced current "fight back" against the action that causes the induced current [Lenz's Law]? How does the energy output of a generator compare to the energy input? If the magnet was inducing a current in the copper pipe during its fall, how does that explain the retarded fall of the magnet?

AC Generator

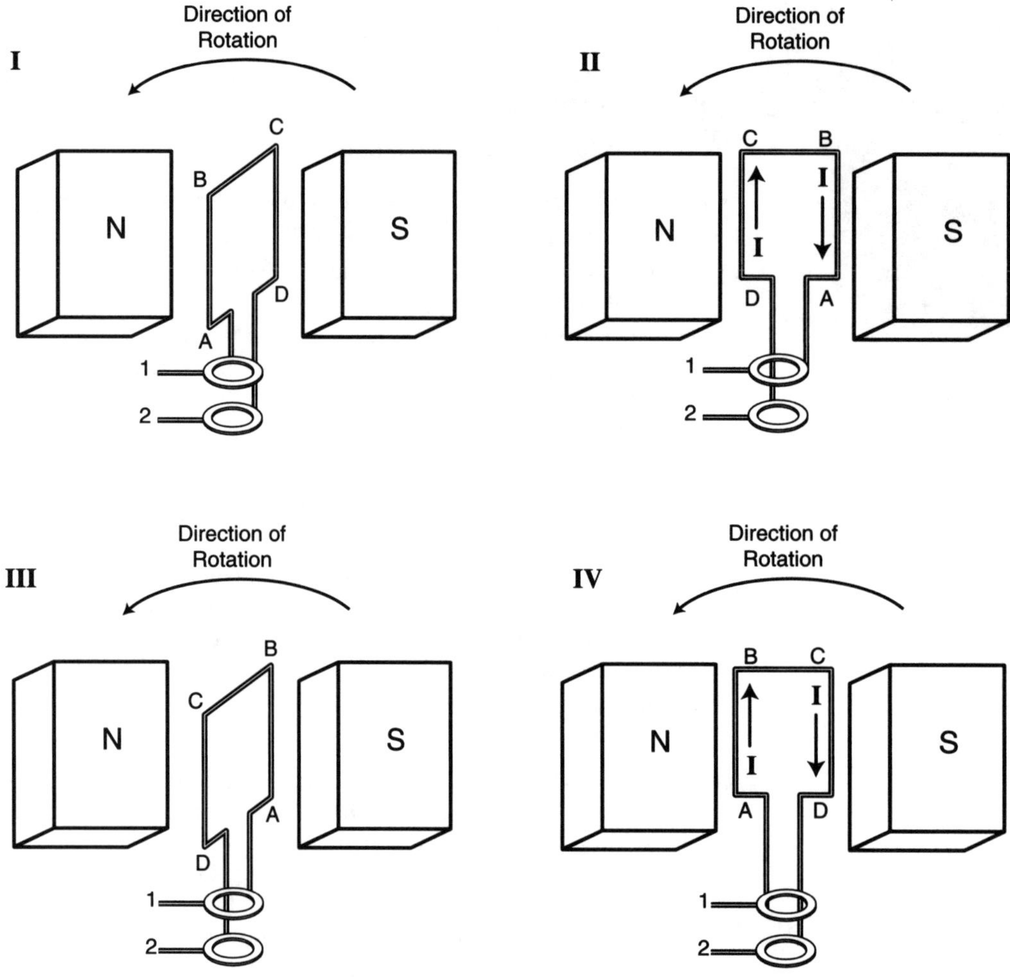

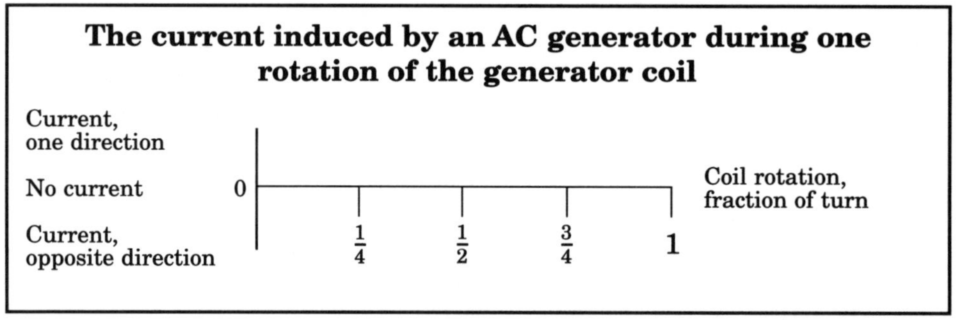

DC Generator

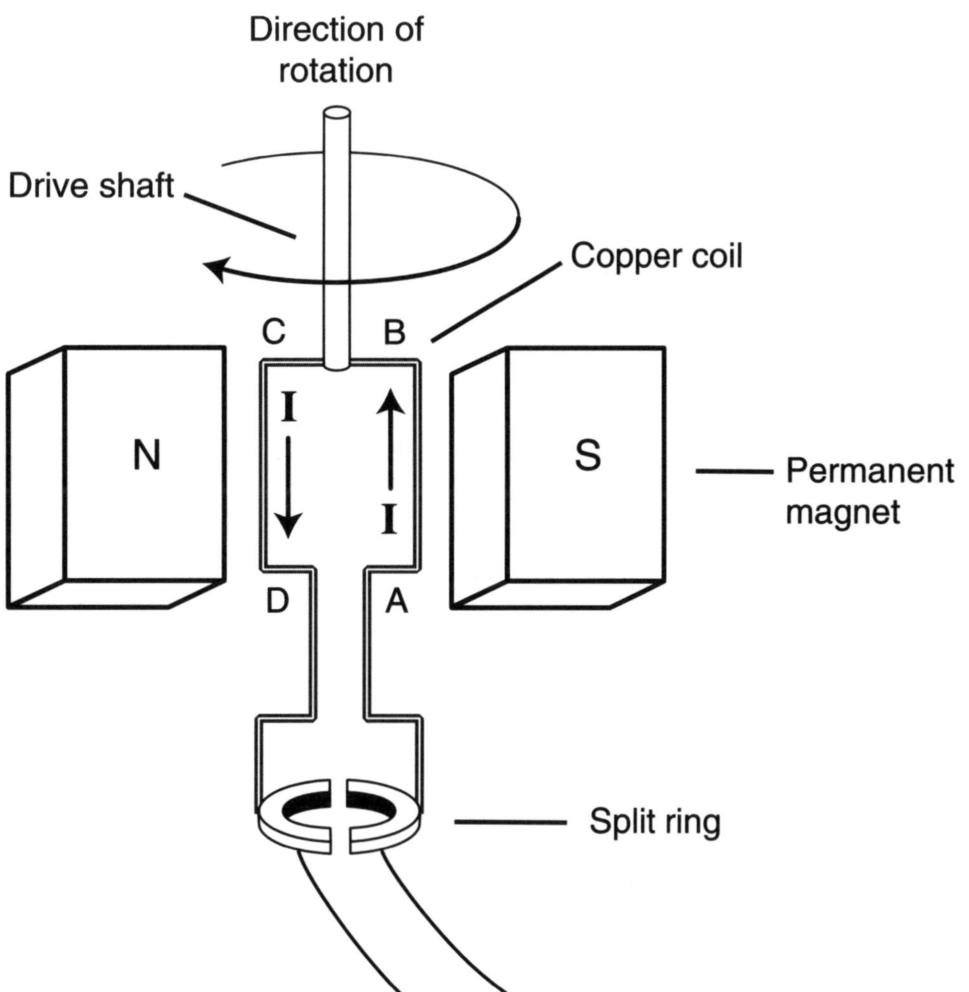

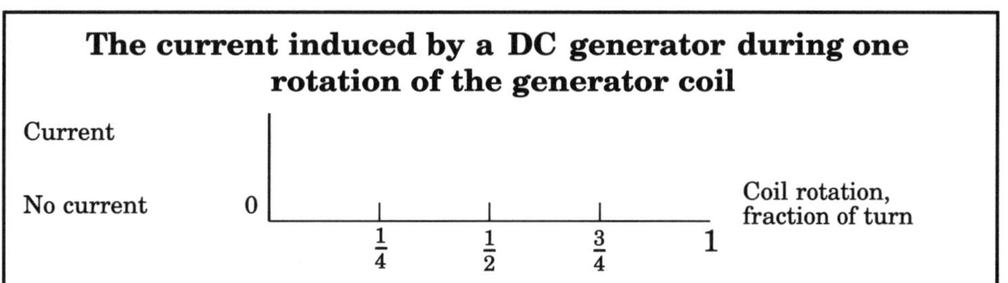

For use with *Home*, Chapter 3, ACTIVITY FOUR: AC & DC Currents

ACTIVITY FIVE
Building an Electric Motor

Background Information

Principles of the electric motor are introduced in Activities Five and Six. The background information presented here will serve for both activities and will be limited to the DC motor.

A DC motor can be thought of as a DC generator "running backwards," and vice versa. Indeed, Gramme's discovery described in the student text for Activity Five shows that this is true in fact as well as principle.

How an electric motor converts electrical energy into mechanical energy is understood in terms of the below illustrations:

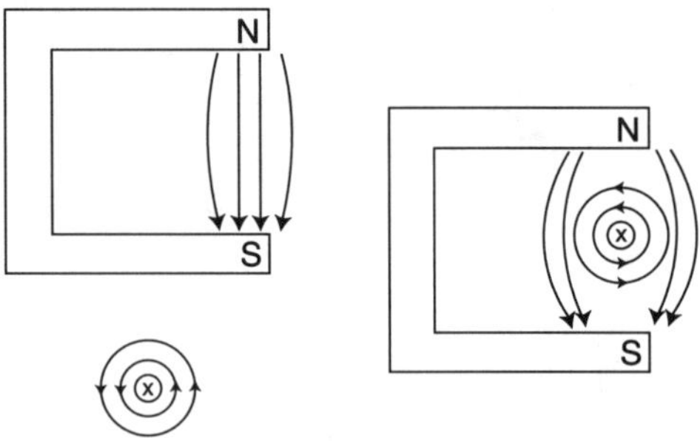

A wire is placed in a magnetic field of strength B created by the poles of permanent magnets as shown in part (a) of the above diagram. When a current, I, is sent through the wire as input from an external source (such as a battery), the wire experiences a force in the direction shown by F in the diagram. The wire tend to move in the direction of the force. This is called the "motor effect."

Part (b) of the above diagram illustrates a model used to explain why the force arises on the wire. In the end view of the wire, the magnetic flux caused by the current forced into the wire encircles the wire. Directly below the wire the magnetic flux caused by the current has the same direction (toward the right) as the flux established by the permanent magnets. Directly above the wire the opposite is true; the fluxes are in opposite directions. Lenz's Law suggests that forces arise to prevent changes in flux, and, in this case, motion of the wire in an upward direction would tend to preserve the uniformity of the flux; the electromagnetic force would move the wire upward in an attempt to move the high density field below the wire to "fill in" the low density field above the wire much in the same way that "nature abhors a vacuum." (It seems an analogous phenomenon exists for magnetic fields).

The amount of force on the wire in the case of the motor effect is:

$$F = BIL$$

where F is the force on the wire in newtons, B is the strength of the magnetic field of the permanent magnets, I is the current in the wire in amperes, and L is the length of wire embedded in the magnetic field.

A convenient "left-hand rule." for predicting the direction of the force on a current-carrying wire embedded in a magnetic field in an orientation which have the direction of the field and the length of the wire mutually perpendicular is shown in the below diagram:

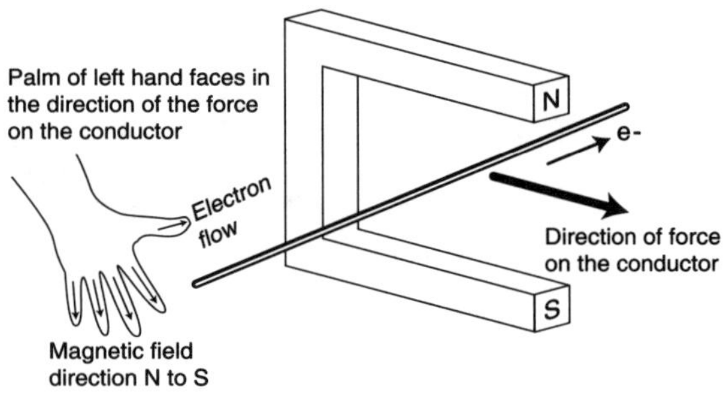

Left-hand motor rule

If the wire did move upward in the above situation, it soon would exit the magnetic field, and the force would disappear. Therefore, electric motors are designed to employ a coil which rotates in a magnetic field. The above described motor effect can be applied to a "thought experiment" in which a current is "fed into" the coil of a DC generator to cause the coil to rotate. It is suggested that you do that thought experiment to satisfy yourself that you understand that motors and generators are basically the same in construction, the only difference being that the kinds of energy input and output are opposite for the two devices.

Active-ating the Physics InfoMall

Ideas for searches include "electric motor" and "Faraday." Most other useful information has already been found!

Planning for the Activity

Time Requirements

Allow at least one 40-minute period. Students may want to explore different arrangements and configurations in order to speed up and slow down the motor, etc.

Materials needed

For each group:

To "replay" the discovery of the electric motor:

- two hand generators
- connecting wires

To build the basic motor:

- coated wire
- sandpaper
- cylindrical form for winding wire (such as a test tube)
- tape
- rubber band
- Styrofoam® cup
- large safety pins (2)
- D-cell
- refrigerator magnet (2)
- hand generator
- electrical clips

Advance Preparation and Setup

Make a demonstration motor for the students to see that it is possible to build it, and show that it does work. Try to build it exactly the same way as it is in the book, and anticipate the different problems that the students might encounter.

Teaching Notes

Take the students back to the diagram of the DC generator in Activity Four, and use the diagram to develop an explanation for what happens when a DC current is fed to the armature through the split ring commutator/brushes. Essentially the motor is running backwards. There may be a need to describe to the students what is happening with regard to the creation of a magnetic field around the wire, which interacts with the magnet of the generator. This creates the force by which the rotor is turned, thus creating the motor effect.

An alert student might observe that the design for the Basic Motor does not include split rings to reverse the current in the coil each 1/2 turn. That is true, and the motor, in principle, should not work. However, the motor does work, but only because lack of symmetry of the coil causes the coil to jump during each rotation, breaking and reestablishing contact to allow the coil to keep rotating. Indeed, students who do a very careful job of shaping the coil may find that their motor will not function, and the solution is to bend the coil a bit to cause some nonsymmetry.

If a student does not bring up the lack of provision for reversing the input current each 1/2 turn, you should bring it up for discussion at the end of the activity - it will be important to deal with it, because students will need to provide a split ring system for the motor/generator which they will design and build for the next activity.

CAUTION: If students will be operating the hand generator, it is important to remind them of the danger of electrical shock, and the safety procedures required.

NOTES

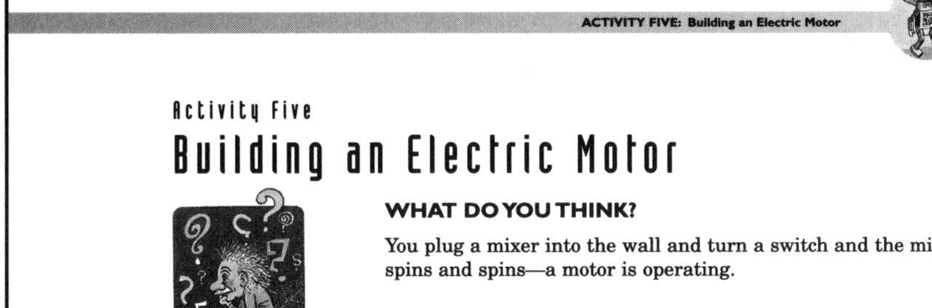

Activity Five

Building an Electric Motor

WHAT DO YOU THINK?

You plug a mixer into the wall and turn a switch and the mixer spins and spins—a motor is operating.

- **How do you think the electricity makes the motor turn?**

Write your answer to this question in your *Active Physics log*. Be prepared to discuss your ideas with your small group and other members of your class.

FOR YOU TO DO

1. Study the diagram on page H110 closely. Carefully assemble the materials, as shown in the diagram, to build a basic electric motor. Follow any additional directions provided by your teacher.

ANSWERS

For You To Do

1. Student activity.

Activity Overview

The students will be building a simple electric motor. The more powerful the magnet, the more dramatic are the results.

Student Objectives

Students will:

- construct, operate, and explain a DC motor.
- appreciate accidental discovery in physics.
- measure and express the efficiency of an energy transfer.

ANSWERS FOR THE TEACHER ONLY

What Do You Think?

Students' answers will vary, but some will note that it has to do with the opposite of the generator effect. Some may even say something similar to what Faraday said, that if electricity can be made from moving a wire through a magnetic field, then why can't movement be created by a moving current in a magnetic field.

ANSWERS

For You To Do

(continued)

2. a) Student data: changing polarity of the battery, more than one magnet, another magnet positioned at different locations around the wire.

3. a) Student observation. The orientation of the magnet needs to be opposite to the orientation of the other magnet in order for there to be magnetic field lines between the two magnets.

4. a) Again, the magnets must create magnetic field lines in order for there to be a motor effect.

5. a) Students' answers will vary. Changing the speed will involve an increase in the force that moves the wire. The force is influenced by the current, the magnetic field strength, and the length of the wire in the magnetic field.

6. a) Student data. They will probably discover that the faster you crank the generator the faster the motor will turn. Some other observations might be that at certain times the motor does not move. At this point, the motor is said to be in a dead zone. This is when the wire is in between the north and south poles so that the armature has an equal force acting on both sides, opposing motion.

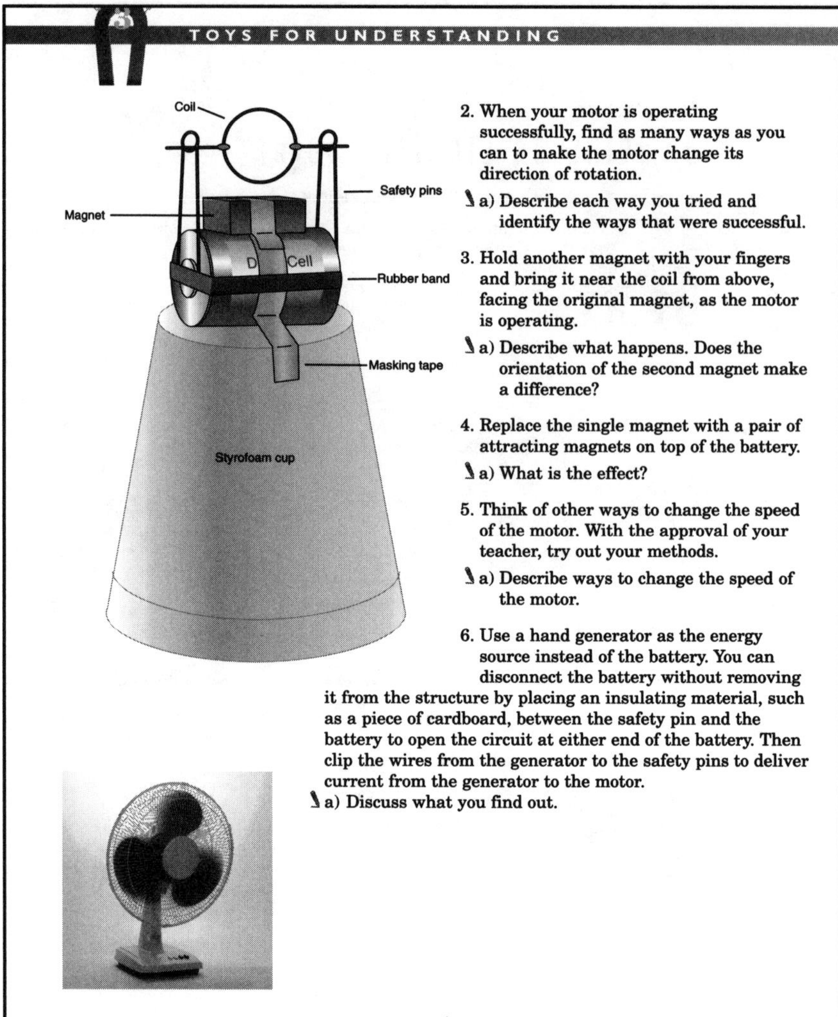

2. When your motor is operating successfully, find as many ways as you can to make the motor change its direction of rotation.
   a) Describe each way you tried and identify the ways that were successful.

3. Hold another magnet with your fingers and bring it near the coil from above, facing the original magnet, as the motor is operating.
   a) Describe what happens. Does the orientation of the second magnet make a difference?

4. Replace the single magnet with a pair of attracting magnets on top of the battery.
   a) What is the effect?

5. Think of other ways to change the speed of the motor. With the approval of your teacher, try out your methods.
   a) Describe ways to change the speed of the motor.

6. Use a hand generator as the energy source instead of the battery. You can disconnect the battery without removing it from the structure by placing an insulating material, such as a piece of cardboard, between the safety pin and the battery to open the circuit at either end of the battery. Then clip the wires from the generator to the safety pins to deliver current from the generator to the motor.
   a) Discuss what you find out.

HOME H 110

FOR YOU TO READ

The history of science is filled with discoveries that have led to leaps of progress in knowledge and applications. This is certainly true of physics and, in particular, electricity and magnetism. These discoveries "favor" the prepared mind. Oersted's discovery in 1820 of the magnetic field surrounding a current-carrying wire already has been mentioned.

Michael Faraday

Similarly, Michael Faraday's discovered electromagnetic induction in 1831. Faraday was seeking a way to induce electricity using currents and magnets; he noticed that a brief induced current happened in one circuit when a nearby circuit was switched on and off. (How would that cause induction? Can you explain it?) Both Oersted and Faraday are credited for taking advantage of the events that happened before their eyes, and pursuing them.

About one-half century after Faraday's discovery of electromagnetic induction, which immediately led to development of the generator, another event occurred. In 1873 a Belgian engineer, Zénobe Gramme, was setting up DC generators to be demonstrated at an exposition (a forerunner of a "worlds fair") in Vienna, Austria. Steam engines were to be used to power the generators, and the electrical output of the generators would be demonstrated. While one DC generator was operating, Gramme connected it to another generator that was not operating. The shaft of the inactive generator began rotation—it was acting as an electric motor! Although Michael Faraday had shown as early as 1821 that rotary motion could be produced using currents and magnets, a "motor effect," nothing useful resulted from it. Gramme's discovery, however, immediately showed that electric motors could be useful. In fact, the electric motor was demonstrated at the very Vienna exposition where Gramme's discovery was made. A fake waterfall was set up to drive a DC generator using a paddle wheel arrangement, and the electrical output of the generator was fed to a "motor" (a generator running "backwards"). The motor was shown to be capable of doing useful work.

ANSWERS

Physics To Go

1. Students' answers will vary. Some advantages: increase the field strength of the magnet in order to increase the output from the motor; maintain a constant magnetic field in order to have more control of the speed. Some disadvantages: reduction in the efficiency of the engine reduction in the energy output; need for cooling of the motor as the current running through the electromagnet will heat up.
2. Student design.
3. Student response. Many of the different kinds of materials might be children's construction toys such as Mechano™, wheels, gears, elastic bands, pulleys, string, bearings, strips of wood, plastic wheels, gears etc., popsicle sticks, toothpicks, straws, etc.
4. An electric motor operates when an electric current is moving through a magnetic field. As a moving current produces a magnetic field around the wire, it either is attracted to or repelled from the magnets in the motor, which forces the wires to move. This turns the armature.
A generator works on a similar principle in that a moving wire is passed through a magnetic field and a current is induced in the wire.

REFLECTING ON THE ACTIVITY AND THE CHALLENGE

Decision time about the challenge is approaching for your group. In this activity you built a very basic, working electric motor. This is an important part of the challenge. However, knowing how to build an electric motor is only part of the challenge. Your toy must be fascinating to children. You must also be able to explain how it works.

PHYSICS TO GO

1. Some electric motors use electromagnets instead of permanent magnets to create the magnetic field in which the coil rotates. In such motors, of course, part of the electrical energy fed to the motor is used to create and maintain the magnetic field. Similarly, electromagnets instead of permanent magnets are used in some generators; part of the electrical energy produced by the generator is used to energize the magnetic field in which the generator coil is caused to turn. What advantages and disadvantages would result from using electromagnets instead of permanent magnets in either a motor or generator?
2. Design three possible toys that use a motor or a generator or both. One of these may be what you will use for your project.
3. The motor/generator you submit for the chapter challenge must be built from inexpensive, common materials. Make a list of possible materials you could use to construct an electric motor.
4. In the grading criteria for the chapter challenge marks are assigned for clearly explaining how and why your motor/generator works in terms of basic principles of physics. Explain how an electric motor or generator operates.

NOTES

ACTIVITY SIX
Building a Motor/ Generator Toy

Background Information

Background information for this activity was provided in the background for Activity Five.

Active-ating the Physics InfoMall

Ideas for searches include "electric motor" and "Faraday." Most other useful information has already been found!

Planning for the Activity

Time Requirements

Allow at least 4 class periods, to collect, design, and build their toys. One class can be used for different groups to try the toys to see if they work and if they are fun. At least one more class will be needed to write instructions on how to build the motor/generator, and how it works in the toy.

Materials needed

For the class:

- a supply of D-cells, magnets, and insulated connecting wire.

For each group:

- "junk" components to be acquired by students.

Advance Preparation and Setup

You will need to decide how you will acquire the items needed for groups who wish to pursue alternate designs.

Teaching Notes

Set a time limit and communicate this to the class. You will have to set aside some time for testing the motor/generators, and for incorporating the motor in a toy. As these will be going to the HFE volunteers, the students will also need some time to prepare the instructions and explain the device to HFE inhabitants.

For assessment, you will need to decide how each group's products will be judged against the assessment criteria. Peer judging can be very effective, as long as the understanding is that they are fair. Have the students arrive at a consensus on exactly how the assessment will be done.

CAUTION: Safety issues must be addressed. Working with electricity, can be dangerous (although the students are working with small voltages and amperages). There are some sharp objects involved, and students should be cautioned.

NOTES

3

NOTES

ACTIVITY SIX: Building a Motor/Generator Toy

Activity Six

Building a Motor/Generator Toy

WHAT DO YOU THINK?

You may have heard the following expression used before: "The difference between men and boys is the size of their toys."

- **What characteristics make an item a toy?**

Write your answer to this question in your *Active Physics log*. Be prepared to discuss your ideas with your small group and other members of your class.

H113 HOME

Activity Overview

This activity is the culmination of Chapter 3 and the unit on *Home*. They will be using their knowledge of motors and generators, to build a toy. This must be a functional toy with the criteria as set out in the assessment on page H117 and should be a fun activity for the students.

Student Objectives

Students will:

- design, construct and operate a motor/generator.

ANSWERS FOR THE TEACHER ONLY

What Do You Think?

Students' answers will vary. Many of the responses will probably include characteristics such as fun, easy to work, durable, inexpensive, not predictable, etc.

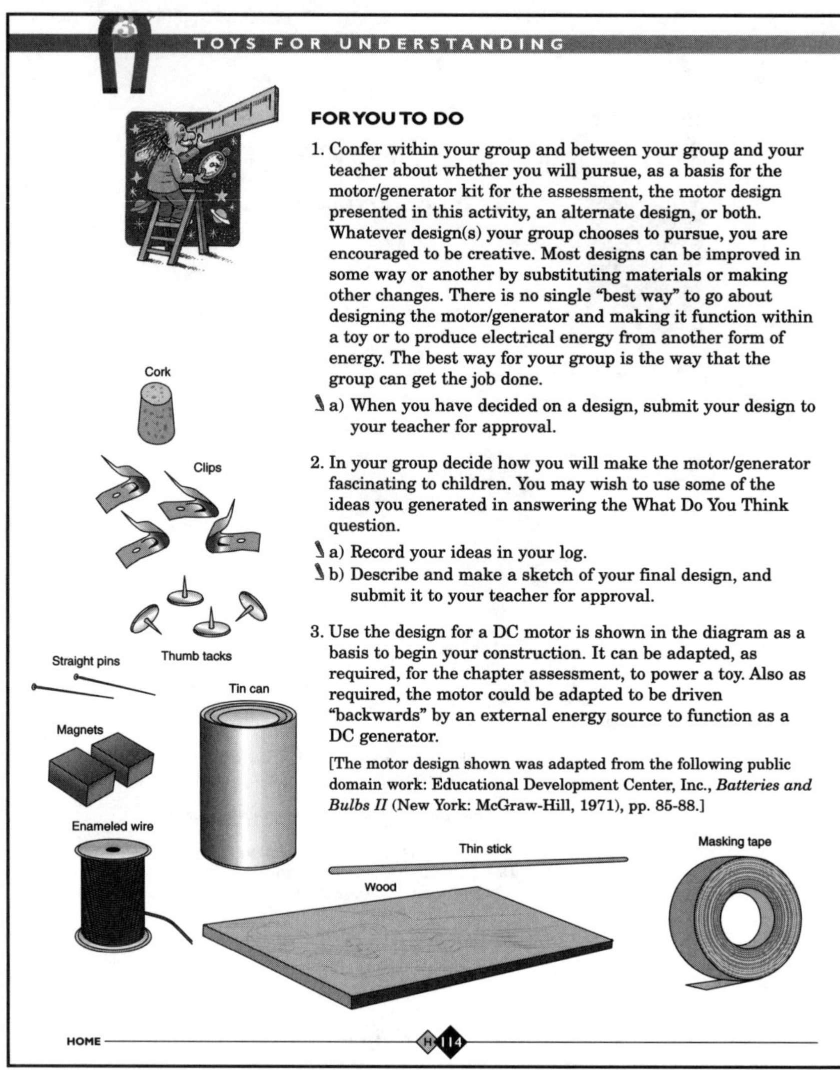
TOYS FOR UNDERSTANDING

FOR YOU TO DO

1. Confer within your group and between your group and your teacher about whether you will pursue, as a basis for the motor/generator kit for the assessment, the motor design presented in this activity, an alternate design, or both. Whatever design(s) your group chooses to pursue, you are encouraged to be creative. Most designs can be improved in some way or another by substituting materials or making other changes. There is no single "best way" to go about designing the motor/generator and making it function within a toy or to produce electrical energy from another form of energy. The best way for your group is the way that the group can get the job done.
   a) When you have decided on a design, submit your design to your teacher for approval.

2. In your group decide how you will make the motor/generator fascinating to children. You may wish to use some of the ideas you generated in answering the What Do You Think question.
   a) Record your ideas in your log.
   b) Describe and make a sketch of your final design, and submit it to your teacher for approval.

3. Use the design for a DC motor is shown in the diagram as a basis to begin your construction. It can be adapted, as required, for the chapter assessment, to power a toy. Also as required, the motor could be adapted to be driven "backwards" by an external energy source to function as a DC generator.

   [The motor design shown was adapted from the following public domain work: Educational Development Center, Inc., *Batteries and Bulbs II* (New York: McGraw-Hill, 1971), pp. 85-88.]

HOME H 114

ANSWERS

For You To Do

1. a) Student design of the project.

2. a) Student responses.

   b) Student design and sketch.

3. Student activity.

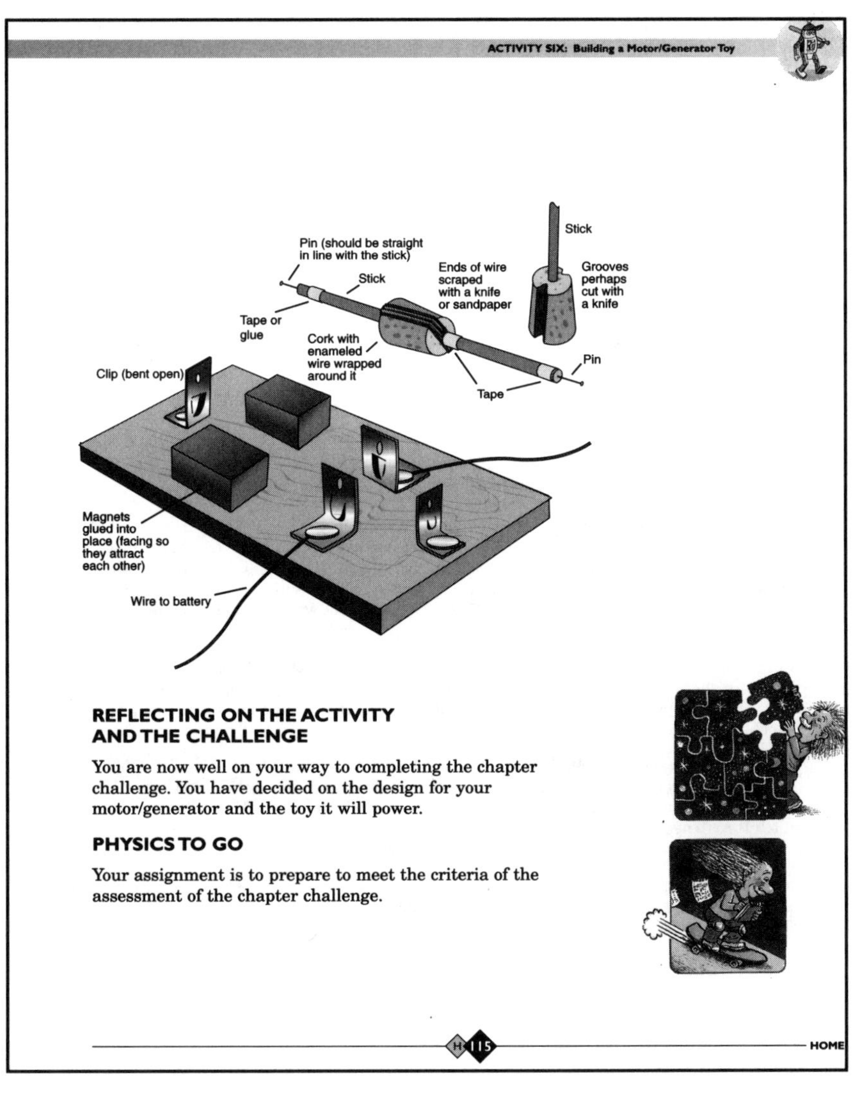

REFLECTING ON THE ACTIVITY AND THE CHALLENGE

You are now well on your way to completing the chapter challenge. You have decided on the design for your motor/generator and the toy it will power.

PHYSICS TO GO

Your assignment is to prepare to meet the criteria of the assessment of the chapter challenge.

H 115 HOME

Answers

Physics To Go

1. Build the motor/generator.

3

TOYS FOR UNDERSTANDING

PHYSICS AT WORK

Uriah Gilmore

HEADED FOR THE STARS

Uriah Gilmore loved to take electric appliances apart when he was growing up. "I couldn't always get them back together," he admits, "but I was so curious I couldn't help myself. I just had to see how they worked." Fortunately, Uriah's parents supported his curiosity.

Uriah and his fellow teammates from Cleveland, Ohio's East Technical High School recently won first place at the National High School Robotics Tournament at Epcot Center in Orlando, Florida for building a robot. "We were counseled along the way by engineers from NASA," he enthusiastically explains. "We called our robot Froggy and painted it green," Uriah continues, "and we used noisemakers so it even sounded like a frog." During the final contest "Froggy" was put in a pit with two other robots and had to place balls of a certain color in a specified area. The robot who got the most balls in won the contest.

"In my sophomore year the school closed and I went to East Technical High School which was the best thing that happened to me." He entered the engineering program and became a member of the engineering team—a team that is more popular than any sports team in his school.

Uriah enters Morehouse College this fall on a NASA scholarship. "But," he states, "it's not enough to be a good student. You also have to be involved with your school and your community." Uriah recently led a march on the Cleveland, Ohio, City Hall to protest a law which threatened to fire certain teachers, including one who inspired Uriah and was responsible for the revitalization of East Technical High School.

"My ultimate goal is to travel in space and explore the galaxy," he states. A shorter term goal is to be as involved in college as he has been in high school.

HOME 

Chapter 3 Assessment

Your task is to prepare a kit of materials and instructions that a toy company will manufacture. Children will use these kits to make a motor or generator, or a combination electric motor/generator. It will serve both as a toy and to illustrate how the electric motors in home appliances work or how electricity can be produced from an energy source such as wind, moving water, a falling weight, or some other external source.

Review and remind yourself of the grading criteria that you and your classmates agreed on at the beginning of the chapter. The following was a suggested set of criteria.

- **(30%) The motor/generator is made from inexpensive, common materials, and the working parts are exposed.**
- **(40%) The instructions for the children clearly explain how to assemble and operate the motor/generator device, and explain how and why it works in terms of basic principles of physics.**
- **(30%) If used as a motor, the device will operate using a maximum of four 1.5 volt batteries (D cells), and will power a toy (such as a car, boat, crane, etc.) that will be fascinating to children.**

OR

- **(30%) If used as a generator, the device will demonstrate the production of electricity from an energy source such as wind, moving water, a falling weight, or some other external source and be fascinating to children.**

Physics You Learned

Motors

Generators

Galvanometers

Magnetic field from a current

Solenoids

Electromagnets

Induced currents

AC and DC generators

Alternative Chapter Assessment

Select the best response for each statement or question.

1. Normally, the magnetism of Earth causes a magnetic compass to point in the direction:

   a) North

   b) South

   c) East

   d) West

2. When a magnetic compass is placed near a wire carring an electric current, the direction in which the compass points is influenced by:

   a) only Earth's magnetism.

   b) only the wire's magnetism.

   c) neither Earth's magnetism nor the wire's magnetism.

   d) both Earth's magnetism and the wire's magnetism.

3. A generator transforms:

   a) electrical energy into mechanical energy.

   b) heat into mechanical energy.

   c) mechanical energy into electrical energy.

   d) mechanical energy into heat.

4. The output energy of a generator:

   a) is much greater than the input energy.

   b) is slightly greater than the input energy.

   c) is equal to the input energy.

   d) is less than the input energy.

5. The shape of the magnetic field caused by an electric current flowing in a straight wire is:

   a) along a straight line.

   b) square.

   c) circular.

   d) impossible to predict.

6. Which factor or factors listed below affects the magnetic strength of a solenoid which is carrying an electric current?

   1.The amount of the current flowing in the solenoid.

   2. The number of turns of wire of the solenoid.

   3. The length along which the turns of wire are wound on the solenoid.

   a) Factor (1) only.

   b) Factor (2) only

   c) Factor (3) only

   d) Factors (1), (2) and (3).

7. If both the current and number of turns of wire per unit of a length of a solenoid are doubled, the magnetic strength of the solenoid should:

   a) remain unchanged.

   b) decrease by a factor of two.

   c) increase by a factor of two.

   d) increase by a factor of four.

8. Which choice of core material for a solenoid will result in the strongest electomagnetic if all other factors remain equal?

   a) wood.

   b) plastic.

   c) aluminum.

   d) iron.

9. If the number of turns of wire on a solenoid is doubled along a constant length of core material, and if the amount of current flowing in the solenoid is reduced to one-half the original amount, the magnetic strength of the electromagnetic will:

   a) remain unchanged.

   b) decrease by a factor of two.

   c) increase by a factor of two.

   d) increase by a factor of four.

10. A galvanometer is meant to be used to:

   a) detect electric currents.

   b) detect magnetic fields.

   c) measure frequency.

   d) measure the efficiency of a generator.

11. The hertz is a unit of:

    a) energy.

    b) voltage.

    c) frequency.

    d) current.

12. Household electricity in the United States is:

    a) DC.

    b) direct.

    c) inverse.

    d) AC.

13. The number of complete cycles per second for household electricity in the United states is:

    a) 12

    b) 60

    c) 120

    d) 240

14. Split rings and brushes are used in a DC motor to:

    a) increase speed.

    b) increase efficiency.

    c) increase magnetic field strength.

    d) reverse current.

15. Using a conductor to cut through a magnetic field can result in:

    a) increased resistance.

    b) induced current.

    c) power loss.

    d) reduction in temperature.

16. When an electric generator is set in motion to produce electricity, the amount of energy needed to keep the generator going is:

    a) only the amount needed to overcome mechanical friction in the generator.

    b) greater than or equal to the energy output of the generator.

    c) impossible to predict.

    d) less than or equal to the energy output of the generator.

17. When an electric motor is set in motion to produce electricity, the amount of energy needed to keep the motor going is:

    a) only the amount needed to overcome mechanical friction in the motor.

    b) greater than or equal to the energy output of the motor.

    c) impossible to predict.

    d) less than or equal to the energy output of the motor.

18. Which of the conditions listed below cause electric current to flow in a coil of wire when a magnet is near the coil of wire?

    1. Only the magnet is moved.

    2. Only the coil of wire is moved.

    3. Both the magnet and the coil of wire are moved.

    a) Condition (1) only.

    b) Condition (2) only.

    c) Condition (3) only.

    d) All of the conditions.

19. If a direct current is fed into the coil of a generator which normally is used to produce DC electricity:

    a) nothing will happen.

    b) electricity will be generated as usual.

    c) the generator will function as an electric motor.

    d) it is not possible to predict what will happen.

20. An AC generator:

    a) always produces AC having a frequency of 60 Hz.

    b) produces direct current.

    c) always produces 120 volt AC.

    d) produces one AC cycle during each turn of the coil.

Alternative Chapter Assessment Answers

1. a
2. d
3. c
4. d
5. c
6. d
7. d
8. d
9. a
10. a
11. c
12. d
13. b
14. d
15. b
16. b
17. b
18. d
19. c
20. d